NEILSON *of Smith*

Eric Stahlberg

1869 W. A. Neilson 1946

President of Smith College 1917-1939

NEILSON OF SMITH

By *MARGARET FARRAND THORP*

FELICITER VITÆ LAMPADA TRADIDIT

New York · OXFORD UNIVERSITY PRESS · 1956

Library of Congress Catalogue Card Number: 56-5767

PRINTED IN THE UNITED STATES OF AMERICA

PREFACE

FEW BOOKS can have had as many collaborators as this one. Everyone who knew William Allan Neilson, who had worked with him for decades or for an afternoon, who had talked with him in daily intimacy or listened to him once in a crowded auditorium, has been eager to share in making the record of a life which seemed to them good, in the highest and happiest sense. I cannot begin to list here all the people who have given me rich and generous assistance. But there are some collaborators whose help was so extensive that I must have the pleasure of thanking them once more:

Mrs. Neilson and her daughters, Mrs. Peter Helburn and Mrs. Caroline Oram; Mr. Neilson's sisters, Miss Elizabeth Neilson and the late Miss Jean Neilson; the Trustees of Smith College, especially the late Mrs. Dwight W. Morrow; Mrs. Ada Comstock Notestein, President Emerita of Radcliffe; Professors Emeriti Sidney B. Fay and F. N. Robinson of Harvard; Professor Emeritus A. D. Sheffield of Wellesley; Professor Emerita Anna A. Cutler of Smith; Dean Emerita Virginia C. Gildersleeve of Barnard; Professor Marjorie Nicolson of Columbia; Miss Annetta Clark, Secretary to President Neilson during the whole of his administration; Mrs. Roy Dickinson Welch; many members of the Smith College Faculty, past and present.

I am grateful also to two institutions—each of them the lengthened shadow of a woman—without which this book could not even have been begun: the *Smith Alumnae Quarterly,* edited during Mr. Neilson's administration by Miss Edith N. Hill, and the Smith College Archives, under the direction of Mrs. Margaret Grierson.

I wish also to thank the Corporation of Harvard University for permission to publish a correspondence between Mr. Neilson and President Eliot, now in the Harvard Archives, and to express my appreciation of the many courtesies extended to me by the Upper Canada College, Smith College, and Princeton University Libraries.

M. F. T.

Princeton
March 1956

CONTENTS

Doune, on the southern border of Perthshire, where Neilson was born in 1869. His father was Master of the Free Church School. This view of the village is from the fourteenth-century castle.

Kinnaber Mills, on the River Esk, near Montrose. The house is at the left; the workmen's boothies at the right. The mills were owned for generations by the Allans, Neilson's mother's family. After his father's death, Neilson spent three years at Kinnaber preparing for the University at Montrose Academy.

The Wee Dominie. Neilson was not quite twelve when his father died. The Doune school gave him employment as a monitor, then, when he was fourteen, as a pupil teacher.

The Edinburgh student. Neilson spent five years at the University of Edinburgh, taking his M.A. in 1891 with Second Class Honors in Philosophy.

Upper Canada College in Toronto, an old and distinguished Government supported school for boys, had just built this "magnificent pile" when Neilson was appointed as an English Master. He served there four years.

The Harvard graduate student. Neilson spent three years at Harvard working chiefly under Child and Kittredge. He took his Ph.D. in 1898.

Elisabeth Muser, daughter of a lawyer in Offenburg, whom Neilson met in Germany in the summer of 1904. They were married in 1906.

When Neilson was a Professor of English at Harvard the dining club was an important Cambridge institution. This one, which he is about to address, was organized by C. W. Thompson, editor of *The Youth's Companion,* seated third from Neilson's right.

College Hall, built in 1875 to house all the activities of Smith College, was in Neilson's time devoted to administration. The Grécourt Gates commemorate the work of the Smith College Relief Unit in the First World War. (*Fred G. Chase*)

Ada L. Comstock was Dean of Smith when Neilson was appointed to the presidency in 1917. They worked together for seven years in a happy and fruitful collaboration which continued even after she became President of Radcliffe. This portrait by Caecelia Beaux was presented to Smith by Dean Comstock's classmates of 1897. (*Peter A. Juley and Son*)

Neilson took great pleasure in "the manipulation of the landscape around the College." He opened many vistas like this of Mt. Tom seen across the waters of Paradise Pond.

Neilson added a large wing to the Library and increased its holdings by 200,000 volumes. After his death, in 1946, the Trustees named it in his honor the William Allan Neilson Library. (*Fred G. Chase*)

By building ten dormitories Neilson made it possible for all of Smith's two thousand students to live on the campus. This view looks from Scales and King on Elm Street across the Great Quadrangle to the Mandell Quadrangle. Each house accommodates sixty girls. (*Fred G. Chase*)

Neilson developed the Smith Department of Music into one of the most distinguished in the country. In 1924 he built Sage Hall for its accommodation. (*D. I. Crossley*)

The President's House, built for the Neilsons in 1920, is a skilful combination of official residence and family home. (*Burditt*)

Members of the Smith Faculty who lectured to the "Alumnae College" in 1934. Their subject was "Germany since 1870." Neilson enthusiastically supported these three-day "colleges" held at commencement time. Top step: J. Seelye Bixler, Kurt Koffka, Karl Putnam, Jere Abbott. Middle step: G. W. Kaufmann, Elisabeth Koffka, Neilson, Everett Kimball, Roy D. Welch, Sidney B. Fay. Bottom step: Walter C. Barnes, William A. Orton, Arthur T. Jones. (*Eric Stahlberg*)

Undergraduates leaving John M. Greene Hall after the daily chapel service at which the President usually spoke. Neilson abolished required chapel attendance but the students instituted what he called "voluntary compulsory chapel." (*Underwood and Underwood*)

Mrs. Laura W. L. Scales, first Warden of Smith College, appointed by Neilson in 1922 (*Bachrach*)

Marjorie Hope Nicolson, Dean of Smith College 1929-40 (*Eric Stahlberg*)

Annetta I. Clark, Secretary to five Presidents of Smith (*White Studio*)

Franklin King, for fifty years Superintendent of Buildings and Grounds (*Eric Stahlberg*)

Charles Hopkinson, painting Neilson in 1930, chose to show him as the administrator sitting at his desk in College Hall. (*Allison Spence*)

"Presiding genius of the President's House" was the phrase Neilson used in conferring on his wife the honorary L.H.D. the Trustees awarded her in 1939. (*Hoffman Studio*)

In 1928 his alma mater, the University of Edinburgh, conferred on Neilson an honorary LL.D. (*White Studio*)

At the time of Neilson's retirement the Head Gardener, W. I. P. Campbell, and the other Scots on his staff presented to the College in Neilson's honor a Scotch elm. (*Stephen N. Lemanis*)

At each commencement season, after the Alumnae Parade on Ivy Day, the returning classes lined the walk between the Library and the Students Building and Neilson "went down the line," greeting the graduates of many decades. (*Eric Stahlberg*)

Neilson and Mrs. Dwight W. Morrow at an alumnae gathering in Chicago in 1937. Mrs. Morrow was President of the Alumnae Association when Neilson took office in 1917, a Trustee of the College from 1920 to 1955, and Acting President the year after Neilson retired.

Paul Cordes

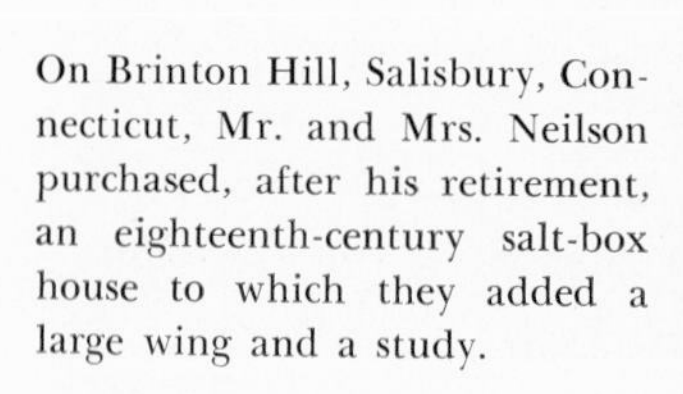

On Brinton Hill, Salisbury, Connecticut, Mr. and Mrs. Neilson purchased, after his retirement, an eighteenth-century salt-box house to which they added a large wing and a study.

NEILSON *of* *Smith*

"A Profession That Has No Equal in the World"

An American college presidency, William Allan Neilson remarked at the time of his retirement as President of Smith College, is "a perfectly impossible position. It never has been adequately filled, here or anywhere else." Neilson was a conscientious philologist and did not use superlatives lightly. When he said impossible he meant precisely that. Professor Basil Gildersleeve of the Johns Hopkins had expressed the same idea twenty years earlier when he suggested that the best way to produce a supply of adequate presidents for our colleges would be to "improve the breed of archangels." *

If anyone had suggested to Neilson that he had archangelic attributes he would have been amused but otherwise unconcerned. The least introspective of men, he would analyze acutely a job, a condition, a colleague, but never himself. What interested him always was a situation, not his own response to it. That is why he declined to write his memoirs and why, since he was an important figure in the educational world through half the twentieth century, a biography becomes necessary.

The elaborately difficult position of college president, which

* Quoted by M. A. De W. Howe, *Classic Shades,* Boston, 1928.

Neilson occupied for twenty-two years, is a uniquely American institution. It is born of the concept that a college or university (I am using the terms interchangeably) should concern itself not simply with the training of a student's mind but with the development of the whole man. And when responsibility for the whole man is accepted a score of problems rise which never trouble the Master or the Rector or the Principal. None of these problems can be solved at a stroke. They must be dealt with piecemeal, in one individual situation after another, day after day.

The first and most fundamental of the college president's problems is a question of emphasis. A college, as Neilson pointed out to his constituency from time to time, must concern itself with the health of the body—yet a college is not a gymnasium; it must be concerned for morals—yet a college is not a church; it must help the student to social adjustment—yet a college is not a welfare agency, nor an employment bureau, nor a psychiatric clinic. From the point of view of the college, all the parts of the whole man are important, but all the other parts are secondary to the mind. It is the student's mind which the college is primarily committed to develop and train. When an institution begins to put too much emphasis on one of the secondary cares, its foundations tremble.

The decisions this problem of emphasis imposes upon a president are often delicate and dangerous. How important is it to win football games? Or to play them at all? Should a new chapel be built before a new library? Should credit towards the degree be given for sculpture or creative writing? Are fraternities desirable? What about television and typewriting and home economics? The chief business of the president of a college devoted to the development of the whole man is to understand the relationship of the parts to the whole and to keep the balance true.

Then, each morning, after he has set the scales for the day, the president must divide his own mind and time and energy among a multitude of legitimate and pressing demands.

A president should be a scholar, teacher, organizer, authority on education, administrator, financier, writer, orator, judge of men, leader, inspirer of youth, publicist, diplomatist, man of the world, moral idealist.*

That is George Vincent's summary, made in the nineteen-twenties when, as President of the Rockefeller Foundation, he had a wide acquaintance among American college presidents. Dean Virginia Gildersleeve of Barnard in her memoirs † adds a few more qualifications.

To be a really adequate head, you should be a perfect paragon in scholarship, in appearance, in public speaking, in tact, social experience and connections, in business and financial ability.

It is desirable also for a president to have some knowledge of architecture, landscape gardening, building, interior decoration, and housekeeping. And there is the function which Neilson called serving as a lightning-rod, for it is the president who must deflect the angry bolts directed against the college from any quarter: the wrath, for instance, of the parent who does not think his daughter should have been failed in geology, or the American Legion Commander who believes that no course in government should mention communism, or the alumna who is distressed because the requirement for daily chapel attendance has been relaxed.

Some archangelic paragons equipped with all these qualities seem to have appeared occasionally in the early days of the Republic, but with the growing complexity of modern life their presence becomes rarer and rarer. There is a handful of men in the last century whom the academic world at large agrees to call great college presidents: Charles W. Eliot of Harvard, Daniel Coit Gilman of the Johns Hopkins, William Rainey Harper of Chicago, James B. Angell of Michigan. In this century there is William Allan Neilson. After these come the controversial figures, hated as well as admired, like Woodrow Wilson of Princeton, M. Carey Thomas of Bryn Mawr, Nicholas Murray Butler of Columbia. And there is a long line of men and women who were certainly good presidents and some of whom, in the eyes at least of their own institutions, were great. Of most of these

* Quoted by M. A. De W. Howe, *Classic Shades,* 1928.
† Virginia C. Gildersleeve, *Many a Good Crusade,* 1954.

presidents who have filled their curious role with distinction there is substantial record, and from these records a striking fact emerges: they were all sharply individual personalities but they had in common a large number of similar characteristics.

Most conspicuous among these is the good presidents' instinctive practice of the three theological virtues, joined with the four cardinal virtues which the middle ages liked to carve at the corners of their rulers' monuments. The good college president exercises daily not only faith, hope, and charity, but prudence (sometimes called economy), temperance, justice (well tempered with mercy), and, most necessary perhaps of all, courage. Patience may not have been instinctive to all the good presidents but all of them learned to practice it, as they were compelled to learn that ability which Eliot once said grimly was fundamental to the exercise of the profession, "the ability to give pain." This occasional necessary sacrifice of the individual to the institution is peculiarly difficult for the good college president, who genuinely loves, and enjoys, his fellow men. It is the only duty of his calling which Neilson sometimes deliberately shirked.

To the moral qualities the successful president should add certain talents and skills. He must, if the balance of the institution is to be kept true, be a scholar, at least most colleges have thought so, for a scholar can best perform the function which all the good presidents agree is the most important part of their work, the selection of the scholar-teachers of the faculty. To enlist the services of good teachers, and to hold them, a president must be able to command their academic respect and must know, at first-hand, in what sort of environment they can do their best work. And only a scholar-teacher, perhaps, will thoroughly understand that the presidential function is less important than the function of the faculty. One is struck, in reading accounts of the good presidents, by their insistence on this point. It is their duty, they say, to create the conditions under which the faculty can work well, to relieve them of as much as possible of the burden of administrative detail, to act as what Neilson liked to call "a hired-man," doing the chores which might otherwise dissipate the scholars' time.

A scholar-president, however, is a paradox. Though he should, when appointed, be a scholar, a president can hardly continue to be one. Opportunities for concentration and consecutive thought are seldom found on administrative desks. The pure scholar, to whom nothing matters in comparison with his work, will not have the necessary administrative versatility; the mediocre scholar will probably make a mediocre president. The compromise would seem to be a good scholar, like Neilson, with the capacity for variety of function, who relinquishes his scholarship with regret, and struggles to salvage bits of it when he can.

Certainly, in addition to learning and wisdom, a president should possess the ability to communicate his ideas swiftly and effectively, not only in individual conversation but from the platform, to large groups of people. Writing well is probably less important than speaking well but it can be an asset. By his writing and speaking, too, the president will influence not only his immediate constituency but the community in which his college stands and, beyond that, the nation at large. The great college presidents have been not only great educators but great Americans.

Beyond these difficult fundamentals there is room for a diversity of gifts and almost any gift or enthusiasm or interest a man has will find space for exercise. As Neilson pointed out, for the profession of college president no professional training is possible. It is preferable to begin with a scholar, but his scholarship may be in almost any field, and any ability or interest he has he can put to use. Among the innumerable things a president might do, he may make choice according to his own idiosyncrasies and inclination. Matters of building and domestic economy he may prefer to delegate; some social and public relations he can safely leave to others; he may even decline to raise funds, though he must be responsible, certainly, for their equitable distribution. Yet it is important that he have in mind the whole plan of his institution, and the larger functions of his office he will delegate at his peril. The current tendency to appoint one "Assistant to the President" after another is sound only if each Assistant's functions are carefully scrutinized.

One final quality shines conspicuously in every presidential biography: the good college president is happy. He may be, he usually is, overworked; he may be acutely conscious of things he has not yet accomplished and probably never will, but he finds his work exhilarating and satisfying. He agrees with Eliot that the American college presidency is "a profession that has no equal in the world."

1

Doune

Again and again, by publishers, by friends, by admiring students, William Allan Neilson was urged to write his autobiography. It never seemed to him an interesting project. But once, working in complete unconsciousness of what he was doing, supposing that he was painting an ideal picture of the American scholar, he sketched the outlines of an excellent self-portrait.

The occasion was the initiation of a series of lectures designed by the Phi Beta Kappa Society, of which he was long a guiding genius, to strengthen the relationship between the humanities and the sciences. The date, 1 January 1936, was very nearly the centenary of the day on which Emerson made to the Harvard chapter of Phi Beta Kappa his address on "The American Scholar," "that high-water mark of the annual tide of such orations." So Neilson termed it, and he suggested to the organizing committee that, in place of a lecture, it would be appropriate for him to read to the Association of American Scientists Emerson's historic address. When the committee demurred and insisted that he compose an oration of his own, he took gentle revenge by making his title "The American Scholar Today" (*American Scholar,* Spring 1936), examining Emerson's tenets from a twentieth-century point of view, and underlining the guidance they offer to the modern scholar. This procedure made it necessary to read—and Neilson's reading of prose or poetry was something those who heard it never forgot—most of the high phrases from the Emersonian oration. From Neilson's point of view he was presenting a Platonic ideal; to his auditors, he seemed to be reading an accurate description of the American Scholar William Allan Neilson.

In this distribution of functions, the scholar is the delegated intellect. In the right state he is *Man Thinking.*

Free should the scholar be,—free and brave.

I do not see how any man can afford, for the sake of his nerves and his nap, to spare any action in which he can partake.

When Professor Neilson of Harvard, at the age of forty-eight, made the decision to exchange a brilliant career as teacher and scholar for the untried duties of a college president, one factor weighted all his discussions of the problem, discussions in his own mind and with his friends: in which capacity, teacher or administrator, could he be of most use to American education? And when, against the advice of most of his Harvard colleagues, he had made his decision, he announced it to one of them in an Emersonian phrase: "You know, Fritz," he said, "I like to function."

Then and always, when asked to address a high school commencement, to serve on a municipal committee in Northampton, to chair a meeting for the defense of Sacco and Vanzetti, to lend his mind and energies to the National Association for the Advancement of Colored People or the Commission to Study the Organization of Peace, William Allan Neilson found it impossible to spare any action in which he might partake.

This same desire to function affected the other fundamental decision of his life, made in 1905, his change of citizenship from Great Britain to the United States. The motive this time he set down, more consciously but still impersonally, in the introduction to *Americans by Adoption,* by Joseph Husband (1920), a little collection of "Brief Biographies of Great Citizens Born in Foreign Lands."

Men want most [Neilson wrote] to count among their fellows for what they are worth. . . The degree of the chance to achieve [this] is the measure of the desirability of a country as a place to live in. . . . we . . . who have come to America of our own accord, have done so because we believed that these United States, above all countries of the world, give men this chance to make the most of themselves.

Neilson took issue with Husband's title, which he thought should have been "Americans by Choice," for

we have chosen her, not she us. . . And we have paid our price. We, and we alone, know what it has cost to leave behind scenes and traditions and affections which clung close to the heart.

The Neilson traditions and affections gathered round three Scottish towns: Edinburgh, Montrose, and the little village of Doune in Perthshire, where he was born on 28 March 1869.

Doune has a few more citizens than the eleven hundred who inhabited it a century ago, but the newcomers live in villas on the periphery and the village itself is almost unchanged. It lies on the southern border of Perthshire, between Glasgow and Edinburgh, eight miles from Stirling. About the village are woods and heather-covered braes rolling away towards blue mountains. There is a mist on the hills in the morning and the dark comes early. The hard dirt road from Stirling runs into the cobbled High Street with its close row of little shops in a curve around the market cross. Of the precise date of the cross no one is quite sure and so weather-worn is the stone creature which sits atop it that only the antiquary would recognize it for a sejeant lion; the local children are firmly convinced that it is a monkey. Near the cross are the draper's and the grocer's, the chemist's, the sweetie shop, and the rabbit wife's. She will skin a rabbit for you any time if you want one for dinner. On the other side of the road is the elegant villa, with statues on its lawn, built by Doune's most prosperous citizen, Alexander Ferguson, known as "Sweetie Sandy" because he invented the candy called "Edinburgh rock."

At the corner of the High Street where the Established Church stands, the road turns left into the Mains, named for the farm to which it runs. A little way along the Mains stands a house which was once the Free Church School, whose master for many years was David Neilson, father of William Allan. The schoolmaster's house stood next to the school; its wall made part of the schoolyard fence.

The Master's house is two and a half stories high, which is large for that part of the country, and is built, like the rest of the village, of the gray local stone, roofed with slate. The rooms are not large but when David Neilson and his family lived there, they were cozy and pleasantly furnished. The sitting room walls were covered with a bright paper and from the window one had a view of the huge dark mass of Ben Ledi, the Mountain of God. From the other side of the house you can see the railroad, which was to the four Neilson children a perpetual excitement, especially on that day each fall when Queen Victoria's train flashed by taking her to her annual holiday at Balmoral. And they remembered throughout their lives the passage of the fairy-story train, all white and gold, which bore Her Majesty on the Golden Jubilee progress.

On the second floor of the house was the parents' bedroom and a guestroom kept always swept and garnished, ready for one of the many visitors, aunts, uncles, cousins, and friends. The children, two boys and two girls, slept in the half-story above.

On either side of the village a little river runs. Uniting finally to flow to the Forth, the Teith and Ardoch swirl and foam over their stony beds but run quietly now and then in shady holes where the lads can swim. Young Will Neilson liked to swim and the earliest memories his own children have of him is swimming with him in the tidal river beside their house in Maine. Swimming was, of course, no sport for girls until long after the Golden Jubilee but Will's sisters, Lizzie and Jean, spent happy afternoons pulling gowans on the banks of the river beside Doune's fourteenth-century castle. Doune Castle has played its part in history and in Scottish literature: *Waverley, The Lady of the Lake,* and the ballad of the Earl of Moray. Today, a fine stout ruin, it is mentioned respectfully by Baedeker. Except for the roof, the castle is quite complete: gateway, courtyard, hall, and high window openings looking out over the water. Out of one of those windows, the village children believe, Mary Queen of Scots jumped one night, slid down the bank, and stepped into a boat which carried her safe away to Stirling. A broad ribbon of earth marks the line of that sixteenth-century slither and the children conscientiously pull out every tuft of grass that tries to grow there so that the legend may never be forgotten.

The caretaker of the castle, who lived in a small house near by, was always an old soldier, usually from India. Sometimes he could be cajoled or bribed into letting the children go inside and then they could see the great hall which was at one time a court of justice for all the country round. When an offender was condemned he was taken straight through the castle gate and hanged just outside on the tall gallows tree. When that old tree became so rotten that it had to be cut down, the wood was made into little boxes and souvenirs which the children eagerly bought and treasured.

There is pre-history in Perthshire, too, which entered into the children's lives. One day the Schoolmaster, walking in the woods of Baru-Murdock, noticed a curious circular depression which did not seem to have been made by nature. It suggested to him one of the underground dwellings attributed to the Picts. He got permission from the owner of the estate to do a little archaeological excavation; he and his sons went back with tools and uncovered by degrees a fine example of a *broich.* The family used to visit it with proprietary delight and a close sense of kinship with the past.

Perth, in the judgment of Sir Walter Scott, is among all the provinces of Scotland "the most varied and the most beautiful." This is in part, he thought, because

> The most interesting district of every country, and that which exhibits the varied beauties of natural scenery in greatest perfection, is that where the mountains sink down upon the champaign, or more level land. The most picturesque, if not the highest, hills are also to be found in the county of Perth. The rivers find their way out of the mountainous regions by the wildest leaps, and through the most romantic passes connecting the Highlands with the Lowlands. (*The Fair Maid of Perth*)

All of this country, and the children walked long miles through it even when they were very small, is full of legend and story. It is the domain of the Earl of Moray, descendant of that bonny

Earl who rode at the ring, and many of its tales have their place in Scottish history. Others, quite as picturesque, live in oral tradition and ballad. It is a country where the present and the past lie close together, where every bush and rock and tree is so drenched with the mist of legend that a romantic turn of mind is as natural to its inhabitants as the diligent industry which hews out a simple living.

David Neilson came to Doune in 1855, called by the Elders of Doune Church to be Master of the Free Church School because of his "calm but firm manner, his kind and winning disposition, and his sterling Christian character."

About his youth we know only a little. He was born in 1826 at Stewarton in Ayrshire. His ancestors had lived in that region for generations, on a farm called "High Bourland," near Kilmarnock. David Neilson's father was probably a weaver; his uncles, farmers. His mother, like Burns's sweetheart, was called Jean Armour. At twenty-five David became a teacher in the Congregational School of St. Ninian's in Stirling and discovered, evidently, that this was his true calling for he entered next year the Free Church Training School in Glasgow. At the end of his year there he received a Schoolmaster's Certificate of the Third Division of the Second Degree of Merit. The great parchment then presented to him—it is handsome and uncracked today—describes the precise degree of merit shown in each of his examination papers "in order that this Certificate may convey accurate impressions as to the nature and extent of his acquirements." These were:

> Religious Knowledge, fair; Reading, good [a skill which his son inherited]; Penmanship, very fair [this skill he taught so thoroughly to his children that William Allan Neilson's handwriting remained beautifully legible through all the destructive influences of American scholarship]; Arithmetic, very fair; original essay on a subject connected with the art of teaching, good; English history, pretty fair; Geography, Popular Astronomy, fair; Geometry, good; Elements of Mechanics, very moderate; Mensuration, Land Surveying, Measuring, good.

The candidate also assayed some subjects which were not required for his Third Division Certificate. In these he was rated:

Vocal Music, moderate [another trait inherited by his son]; Drawing from models, very moderate; Physical Science, failure; Higher Mathematics, fair; Latin, very moderate.

He was subjected also by Her Majesty's Inspector to "a trial of his ability to conduct the instruction of a class in an Elementary School" and "the following report of his skill was made":

David Neilson is personally well qualified for the office of Teacher and secures the attention of a class without undue noise. He exhibits very considerable skill in the art of imparting information.

The first position which these acquirements enabled David Neilson to obtain was a mastership in the Bridegate School in Glasgow where the impression he made was excellent. The recommendations of his superiors, added to those of his teachers at the Training School, obtained for him a year later the appointment at Doune.

His attainments in scholarship are far higher than has been ever called out in his present place, but he can and has accommodated himself to the class he has had to deal with–and possesses in a high degree the teaching art–and while he rules with great kindness still he does so with sufficient firmness to make all know he is master. I feel that if he leave the poor Bridegate sustains a heavy loss, and that he will be a valuable acquisition to the Community that may secure his services as Teacher among them not only for his labours as the Teacher of the week day School but also in the Sabbath Schools, especially in Adult Class and in a Teachers Training class.

It was during the years in Glasgow that David Neilson formed his closest and most important friendship, with William Allan of Kinnaber Mills, Montrose, who, with his brother David, was working among the Glasgow poor. David was superintendent of the Boys' House of Refuge and William worked with him for some time though he chiefly practiced the family trade of milling. The Allans, like the Neilsons, were Free Churchmen, members of that large and liberty-loving body who dissociated themselves in 1842 from the Established Church of Scotland because they declined to accept any civil jurisdiction as higher than the divine. The immediate cause of the dispute was the power of a patron to appoint to a living a pastor opposed by the congregation; the deeper underlying principle was the conviction that no earthly power should attempt to intervene between a man's conscience and his God. The Free Churchmen were liberals and men of courage; belief in the dignity and freedom of the individual marked their social and domestic as well as their religious life.

William Allan was a big, lively, happy man, his energy undiminished by the fact that he had lost an arm in a milling accident. He was not only a good executive but a good talker, eloquent in both political and religious meetings. He and David Neilson liked to read and to discuss their reading and William Allan cherished a desire to write. Except for a brief experience on an Irish newspaper, he never wrote professionally but he was, when he really sat down to it, a lively and engaging correspondent. The half-dozen letters of his which survive are full of individual comment and vivid impressions of the various communities to which his business called him. Transplanted, for instance, to Caledonia in Northern Ireland, he sent home, in December 1855, amused observations on the difference between the Irish and the Scottish peasantry:

How different these small farmers are from the corresponding class in Scotland!—if indeed there be a class that can be called corresponding. Instead of the rustic simplicity and somewhat uncourteous manners and sturdy independence of the one we have here a great deal of wide awakeness and humor—and as much eloquence and as many complimentary phrases as if each Paddy of them had been bred a footman to my lord—a great deal too of the temper we would describe by saying that they are content to take the bite and the buffet with it—with plenty of loud bluster they will be not only submissive, but complimentary under treatment that would make a Scot either fly in the face of his tormentor or turn his back on him in invincible sulkiness.

Six months later he was writing to David Neilson:

My dear Diogenes: It's a great thing to be married and a good thing and a most happy and joyous thing—and the sooner you go and make proof of it, the better for your own comfort and Donald's peace of mind. At the same time you must be content with a very *general* account of its advantages, for it is a subject that comports better with the freedom of a poetical than the precision of a scientific treatment. You speak of the honeymoon—we have now seen two of them out—the last sweetest—and for ought I see, the process of intensification is to go on indefinitely. I find Maggy an unspeakable treasure with all the good qualities I ever expected and two or three more beside.

The wise Diogenes himself made choice of a wife in 1859, William Allan's younger and favorite sister, Mary, whom he had met when she came to Glasgow to keep house for her brothers. It is in a letter of William Allan's to her, written apparently without any foreknowledge of the eventual relationship, that we find the best portraits extant of the parents of William Allan Neilson.

Dated from Caledon, Ireland, 10 September 1856, the letter begins with apologies for not having written. One reason was that "while Mr. Neilson was here it was out of the question for me to attend to anybody else."

We held a great time of it he and I. We generally had a ramble after 6 o'clock for two or three hours and then we would keep it up till 2 or 3 in the morning, intermeddling with all knowledge, discussing all sorts of subjects with frequent episodes of gossip and botheration and abundance of hearty laughing. "As iron sharpeneth iron so doth the countenance of a man his friend." And Neilson, being a pretty hard one, makes a capital sharping stone, so at least I have found it for I have not got my intellectual edges nearly so *set up* for many months past. I never saw him in the same vigor of body nor mind.

Mary had been undergoing a tedious illness and her brother indulges in some rather original and agreeable moralizing on the benefits that one may draw from such "chastening of the Lord," concluding:

But, to be done with my preaching, while I fondly hope, Dear Mary, that a speedy recovery may wait you, I will also hope and wish that while your trouble lasts you may profit by it, that your wise head may grow wiser still and your kind heart still more kindly —and every good thing about you mellowed and ripened into a prosperous maturity. So be it.

And so it was. Mary Allan had a fine balance of head and heart which made her an admirable wife and mother of schoolmasters.

The bans were duly cried and the wedding took place in St. George's Church, Montrose, on 7 September 1859. William Allan, who could not leave his mill in Caledon, wrote, on 30 August:

I am too much of a Scotsman yet to let out, even on paper, much of the feeling with which I greet you as a brother. It is no mere *titular* relationship in this case, for you know that we long ago found each other brethren in spirit.

There is also a charming letter from Mary to David, written just before the wedding and dated "Friday morning." This is, she says, "the last Saturday epistle you will get but I hope we will get something better than letters." And she tries to put an end to the anxiety he evidently felt in the face of the responsibilities he was about to assume:

I am not the least afraid of your not doing your part. You never vexed me with anything but not writing and you know that is nearly at an end. Come you must cheer up and not sit and vex yourself about future difficulties. You know we are promised help when we seek it and we will need to seek *much* and *often*. I dare not sit down as you have done and think of what I have undertaken because I feel I am so unfit in myself for what I have to do that my heart would fail me altogether. I just keep up the bright side as much as possible and will meet difficulties as I am enabled. . . I am just as happy as I can be when I think that I will be always beside you. I am quite sure we will be happy, with God's blessing we will [and she signs herself] Your own Polly.

Polly was quite right; it was a deeply happy marriage. There is a suggestion of its quality, perhaps, in a somewhat sentimental passage from J. M. Barrie which their younger son copied into the commonplace book he kept at the University of Edinburgh:

This family affection, how good and beautiful it is! Men and Maids love, and after many years they may rise to this. It is the grand proof of the goodness of human nature, for it means that the more we see of each other the more we find that is lovable.

David and Mary Neilson had four children: Robert, born in 1860; Elizabeth Valentine (named for Mary's mother), in 1862; Jean Armour (named for David's mother), in 1866; and William Allan (named for the important uncle), on 28 March 1869.

The family life was singularly harmonious. The mutual attachment was deep and enduring but never, it would seem, restricting; each member of the household was free to be an individual and to go his own way. Young Will's disinclination, concerned though he was with matters moral and religious, to commit himself to any specific sect or church, the others understood and accepted unperturbed. Ardent Free Churchmen as they all were, they believed in spiritual independence. All through their lives, though miles and oceans often separated them, the brothers and sisters—Will was the only one who married—remained in constant and affectionate correspondence and visited each other as often as they could. But, despite the underlying affection, the tone of life in the Schoolmaster's household was sober. A good deal of the gray mist from the braes seeped into the stone house and chilled the spirits of its occupants. It was not the ideal atmosphere for a quick and curious small boy. There were many dreary hours when he longed to talk and no one wanted to talk to him; there were innumerable questions he needed to ask which no one felt like answering. Sometimes, when he tried to break through the barriers of adult silence, he was sharply punished. The Schoolmaster, weary from teaching or anxious before an approaching inspection, could be angry and harsh. Will Neilson had a bracing but a somewhat somber childhood.

There was, however, a lively coming and going of relatives. David Neilson had been an only child but the Allan family was large. There were some forty cousins and there was a constant interchange of visits between the different households. Montrose, where Mary Neilson's parents lived, was about two hours from Doune by train and the other families were at distances not much greater. William Allan, then manager of the Tradeston and Clayslap Mills in Glasgow, particularly liked to come down for week-end refreshment.

I believe you will have already heard [runs a letter dated Tuesday night] that I reached home alive. . . Mary must consider the weakness of visitors of delicate stomachs, and be judiciously sparing of her dainties. I am happy that my share of the trouble was not so serious as to detract anything from the pleasure of my sojourn with you. No qualms, nor a reminiscence of it mingles with the recollection of Tellian or Glen Ogle or Blair Drummond. Those and other scenes, beautiful or grand, associated with this holiday will bring with them pleasure unalloyed as

"They flash upon the inward eye
That is the bliss of solitude."

Mary Neilson's happy disposition made her a favorite with all her relatives. She was known in the family as the Peace Maker, so adept was she at smoothing difficulties when they arose among in-laws. Barrie's *Margaret Ogilvy* seemed to William Allan Neilson his mother's prototype. In 1904 he sent the book to his German fiancée to give her an idea of the kind of family life in which he had grown up.

In the summertime the Neilsons usually rented their house —the people of Glasgow liked Doune as a summer resort—and scattered to visit among the relatives. The Schoolmaster, whose wit and gentleness made him a popular guest, was always signed up far in advance of the holidays.

David Neilson was as successful in his professional as in his family life. "As a means of encouragement to deserving Schoolmasters" their Lordships of the Privy Council had provided that Her Majesty's Inspector should "at the visits which he will annually make to the School conducted by the possessor of this Certificate enter at its foot a brief account of the condition of his School." The annotation on the first year's inspection, dated 5 August 1856, states that "the order of the School and the state of instruction do credit to the ability and diligence of the Master," and, though the phrasing changes a trifle from year to year, the tone of approval continues. In 1861 the Certificate was raised to the Third Division of the First Degree of Merit; in 1867, to the Second Division. Once only is there a break in the official satisfaction.

In 1872, under the Scotts Education Act, the Free and Established Church Schools were merged and both taken over by the Government. This meant a new inspector who proved to be a stiff and inhumane person. He would brook no variants from conventional procedure. David Neilson had, for instance, a pupil who stuttered badly but could recite quite well when the Master rested a kindly hand on his shoulder. Such irregularities the new Inspector declined to permit and his report reads in consequence: "There is much room for improvement in the general work of the School." But later annotations are more approving, if a little grudgingly so: the School is in "a very fair state of efficiency," or in "a satisfactory state of progress."

The Schoolmaster's day began at eight when he met his two pupil-teachers in the schoolhouse and gave them an hour of advanced instruction. Then he went back across the yard for his breakfast of porridge, returning to the school at nine-thirty. The morning session began with lessons in the catechism and the Bible. At ten-thirty the Catholic children arrived—Doune had a good sized group of Italians who had been brought over to build the railroad—and some of the older girls of the neighborhood, who worked in the cotton mills at Deanston, a mile and a half away, came in for part of the day's session. There were in all sixty or seventy pupils and the six classes, or "standards," occupied three rooms. In addition to his two pupil-teachers, serving their apprenticeship before going on to the Training College in Glasgow, the Schoolmaster had a female assistant who took care of the younger children and taught singing and sewing. Sometimes, in an academic crisis, one of his sons would be pressed into service. William Allan Neilson remembered standing on a chair to give an arithmetic lesson when he was not tall enough to reach the blackboard, and he retained a vivid recollection of the dark moment when, setting a problem in subtraction, he put the large number below the small.

As a pupil young Will was eager and industrious but often a trial to his father because he so loved to talk that he would try to answer every question the Schoolmaster put to the class. Being quick of mind and tongue he usually managed to get in ahead of the other scholars and had to be constantly admonished to give others their chance, not only admonished but whipped, again and again. These sharp passages had not the smallest effect on the affection between father and son; to the small boy the punishment seemed perfectly just and he accepted it quite impersonally.

At one o'clock the Schoolmaster had an interval for dinner—an hour during the days when school closed at four; half an hour in the wintertime when dark came early and the session must end at half-past three for the safety of the farm children who had long miles to walk home. The noon meal was the principal one for the Neilson household but the Schoolmaster, who was not a little of an artist at his work—phrenological friends always told him he should have been a poet—was usually keyed to such a pitch of excitement by his teaching that his appetite was small, so his wife put aside his bit of meat or chicken and served it to him at the evening meal. The family had tea, with bread and cheese or scones, at five, and supper at eight or even later. By that time the father was rested and relaxed and thoroughly enjoyed the food and his glass of hot toddy. After supper he often read aloud to the children. Scott and Burns were great favorites—his son at Columbia and Harvard was to be known as "Burns" Neilson—but the Schoolmaster was interested also in contemporary writing. The family took in several magazines, *Chambers's Journal, Good Words, Sunday at Home,* and David Neilson was a great admirer of Tennyson. He read each new volume to the family as it appeared. They dearly loved the *Idylls of the King* but his favorite was "Crossing the Bar."

Modern foreign languages were not part of the regular school curriculum but David Neilson learned German from a cousin who had had lessons at a private school and read it to himself with pleasure. He saw to it that his elder daughter had German lessons during the years she spent at the seminary in a neighboring town.

The Schoolmaster not only read aloud well but spoke eloquently in public. He was often pressed into service to supply a pulpit, at home or abroad. On one week-end visit a Baptist host suddenly remembered that he had promised to supply the pulpit on that Sabbath and immediately drafted the Schoolmaster who, though fearful of saying something unorthodox, acquitted himself with credit. David Neilson never wrote down his discourses. Like his son, who was to be the despair of American publicity directors, he required for his best composition the immediate stimulus of an audience. A favorite family story tells of one of his few attempts to get something on paper in advance of a special occasion. When his Glasgow friends arranged a ceremony to celebrate his twenty-five years of teaching, he thought it proper to prepare a formal address. He spent a whole afternoon in his bedroom in the labor of composition while his wife kept the children quiet, and came downstairs at suppertime to show her the results: a sheet of paper at the head of which he had written: "Twenty-five years ago—"

Doune celebrated the Master's quarter-century at the annual Sunday School soirée, held in Volunteer Hall. They presented him with the French clock of malachite and marble—it has a barometer as well as a clockface—which Smith College alumnae were to admire many years later on a mantel in the President's House in Northampton. In addition to the clock the Schoolmaster received a gift of guineas, in an elegantly knitted silk purse. This last it had been impossible to keep as a surprise to his wife who was so skilful a craftswoman that the purse-knitter had to appeal to her for instruction.

The Doune celebration reflected the local appreciation of the Master's Sunday as well as weekday contribution to the community. The Sabbath was for him no day of rest. Morning service at the Free Church lasted from eleven to one and afternoon service began at two, followed by Sunday School in which the Schoolmaster conducted classes. Yet for all the long hours of obligation, the family found the Sabbath a time of refreshment both intellectual and spiritual, as William Allan Neilson in later life recorded. In 1928 he was asked to write an introduction to an edition, published at Cambridge, of *The Psalms of David in Metre* according to the version approved by the Church of Scotland. His lucid historical and critical essay is, like most of his writing about Scotland, a touch less impersonal than his other literary articles.

> The rise and fall of psalm singing [he says] have been a sort of thermometer measuring the rise and fall of Protestant zeal. . . Gen-

eration after generation its rhymes and rhythms, often awkward but endeared by long association, have imprinted themselves on the ear and memory of every Presbyterian Scot.

In conclusion Neilson permitted himself a touch of oblique autobiography:

But to attempt literary criticism of these artless verses is impossible to anyone who learned them before the service of praise was diluted with "human hymns," or the "kist of whistles" was permitted to drown the failure of the quavering voices that strove bravely if pathetically to scale heights beyond their reach. To such a one these verses and the melodies to which they have so long been sung bring back memories and emotions that render impossible an aesthetic judgment. He sees the congregation on a communion Sabbath; he hears, as the elders in their blacks move slowly down the aisle, the stillness broken by the dull tinkle of the leaden tokens as they are dropped into the long-handled boxes passed along the pews. He holds his breath as the minister fences the tables, then reads in tones more solemn than on ordinary Sabbaths the story of the Last Supper, and the bread and wine are shared. He breathes more easily as the congregation raises the postcommunion psalm, and he comes out into the kirkyard still silent and awed. In all the memory of it there is nothing theatrical, nothing cheap. And he recalls that the sole medium for the articulate expression of the feeling of times like these was the "Psalms of David in Metre," and they sufficed.

When he did have leisure one of David Neilson's favorite recreations was sketching, little watercolor landscapes of the Scottish countryside. The children loved to accompany him on sketching expeditions and this is probably the beginning of that interest in painting which made President Neilson so thoroughly enjoy his share in the acquisition of pictures for the Tryon Gallery at Smith.

The children liked to go, too, when their father did surveying for his farmer neighbors. Potato crops were sold by footage so that it was essential to have the fields measured precisely. The more thoughtful farmers would send down a cart on surveying mornings to help transport the heavy chain and some of them expressed their gratitude by gifts of meat or produce, but most took the Master's services for granted. Surveying, as David Neilson's certificate shows, was an art in which a schoolmaster was supposed to be proficient for the benefit of his community.

Some of the farms were so far from the village that the children came down to board during the school week with friends or relatives and when they went home for Saturday and Sunday they often invited the Neilson children to go with them. This was a delight, though the little villagers were often made sick by the rich farm diet. Most of the farmers bred Ayrshire cattle for the stock market and, since transportation was too difficult to make the sale of dairy products profitable, the families feasted daily on rich cream and butter. The Schoolmaster himself did not have land enough to keep a cow but the children could fetch milk for daily use from one of the dairy farms near the village, Easterton, Westerton, Netherton. They had plenty of eggs, for Mrs. Neilson always kept chickens, which roosted in the low coal shed built against the wall of the house.

The house was lighted with gas but there was no running water. There were rain barrels, of course, and the children filled pails in the well below Nancy's house, a fine perpetual spring which served that district of Doune. Nancy's father was Jimmy the Bellman, who rang the curfew every night at nine and acted as crier when there were important announcements to be made.

While the children were young Mrs. Neilson had a maid—they were especially fond of dear Janet—to help her with the work of the house but as Lizzie and Jean grew older they took on their share of cooking and cleaning and sewing and washing. Washing was generally done at home except in the spring when winter blankets were being readied to put away. Then the women carried great vessels down near the well and built fires under them to heat the water. They dried the blankets on the grass and bushes.

Rob and Will helped carry milk and water and they also did the family boots, putting on long work aprons every evening in the kitchen.

It was hard and simple living but a clean and pleasant hardness. Steady, diligent work was so much a matter of course for everyone that all his life long William Allan Neilson took it for granted. His American academic colleagues were continually surprised by the uncomplaining persistence with which he would work through a piece of tiresome administrative or scholarly routine. It never occurred to him to relinquish a task until he had accomplished it, nor did it ever occur to him that a swift and creative mind might decline to be burdened with laborious detail. He went through a day's work in Cambridge or Northampton without question or complaint, as everybody did in Doune.

And thrift, like diligence, became an instinctive virtue, a high and positive virtue, something quite other than the stinginess or niggardliness so often associated with the word. Scottish thrift, own cousin to the thrift of New England, formed part of the deep spiritual kinship between the two great presidents of Smith College. It was New England thrift which made it possible for Laurenus Clark Seelye of Amherst to begin with twelve students and four hundred thousand dollars and create in thirty years the largest woman's college in the United States with an excellent faculty of more than a hundred and a record of never having been in debt. It was Scottish thrift which enabled William Allan Neilson of Doune to carry that institution, always without a deficit, through a war, a boom, and a depression. And Scottish thrift governed, too, the personal habits of the administrator. Dr. Reinhold Niebuhr of Union Theological Seminary tells of attending with President Neilson a government advisory committee meeting in Washington during the 1940's. The session broke up late and the committee members rushed for the New York train. He and Neilson found themselves sitting together when the train pulled out with none of the rest of their fellows in sight. He expressed the opinion that the others must all have missed the train. Neilson said, no; they had caught the train, but they were all in the Pullman. He and Niebuhr, he was sure, were sitting in the day coach for the same reason, and they began to talk to each other about their youthful poverty.

Thrift was also, to the Neilson mind, close cousin to freedom. This he made clear in his book on *Burns, How to Know Him* (1917):

The salient fact in the history of Scotland is the intensity of the prolonged struggle against the political domination of England; and there developed in the individual life of the Scot a corresponding tendency to value personal freedom as the greatest of treasures. The thrift and economy for which the Scottish people are everywhere notable, and which has its vicious excess in parsimony and nearness, is in its more honorable aspects no end in itself but merely a means to independence.

The earliest written reference to William Allan Neilson is on a slightly unthrifty note. It occurs in a letter from his mother to his father, written at some time in the early 1870's when she had taken the two younger children on a visit to cousins. Jeannie and Billy, the letter says, "drink beer and cider like wagoners."

Billy—as he grew older he was called Will—had few of the other qualities of a wagoner; he was never fond of games or good at them; he liked to read; he was gentle and so acutely sensitive that he marked proudly those days in which he did not have a burst of tears. Increasing wisdom and experience brought that sensitiveness under control but it remained as a swift acute sympathy which, all his life long, caused friends, pupils, and bare acquaintances to pour out their troubles to him.

The power of quick response, too, made for wit. Years after he had established a name for himself in America the people of Doune remembered Will Neilson as a "pawky" lad—an expression which he himself defines in his edition of Webster's Dictionary as "possessed of a dry wit." At home he loved to tease his mother and sisters, and he was a great tease all his life, though never an unkind one. The youthful teasing was chiefly a release from tension. The gayety, so characteristic of Neilson in later life, was not a product of Doune. Life there was a somewhat stern and serious matter.

The family stories about Will's childhood are chiefly concerned with an eager curiosity and a search for knowledge. There was the occasion, for instance, when his elder brother asked him a question he could not answer. He retired to the garden and presently called to Rob: "Say yon again; I'm ready for you noo." It is recorded also that he was found one morning breakfastless on the attic floor, a Bible and the Concordance spread out before him. The Sabbath sermon had made reference to "the other

Mary" and he was trying to discover whether Mary Magdalene and Mary the sister of Lazarus were the same person.

He began early to emulate his father as a reader aloud. One of his most patient audiences was composed of two aged maiden ladies, near neighbors in the village, to whose house he used to carry a thick volume of natural history, regaling them most often with the habits of his favorite animals, the hippopotamus and the dinosaur.

The search for knowledge was part of that love and respect for truth which was perhaps Neilson's most fundamental quality, and his care for truth had, like his romanticism and his thrift, its source in the home, the church, the school at Doune. Will Neilson realized first, he once told his wife, the deep importance of truth on a day in school—it may have been in Doune or later in Montrose—when some serious offence had been committed and the master did not know who the guilty pupil was. He told the students that unless that boy confessed he would have to punish the whole class. There was a long agonized silence; then the culprit rose and took his punishment. Young Will, awed and admiring, grasped then the moral and social importance of honesty. Later, as teacher and administrator, lying was the only fault he could not forgive and intellectual honesty became for him the great academic virtue. "His educational policies," ran the Smith College Faculty minute on his retirement, "sprang from his concern for the dignity and intellectual honesty of the individual."

The family life in Doune was sharply broken before Will was twelve years old. In the fall of 1880 David Neilson was stricken with cancer of the liver. He died on November thirteenth. The burden of their grief, in which the whole village shared, was increased for the family by the burden of sudden poverty. The Master's salary had been small but it sufficed for the mother's skilful thrift. Now the salary was gone and there was almost nothing else. The official inventory of David Neilson's personal estate reads:

Cash in the house	£10-10
Household furniture, silver plate and other effects	£30-19

Amount insured to be paid at death of deceased under Policy of Scottish Provident Institution	£200
Sickbed and funeral expenses	£16-1-6
Debts at the death of deceased	£11-9-1

The Allan brothers offered help but Mary Neilson stoutly refused. She could manage. Her elder son, Robert, had been working for some time, chiefly at the family trade of milling. The elder daughter, Lizzie, barely eighteen, found a position as day governess to the children of the local laird. The mother felt that her best recourse was to open a shop. She decided on a stationer's since there was no shop of the kind in Doune, made up a list of articles she thought would sell, and went up to Edinburgh with young Will to purchase them. Mrs. Neilson and her younger daughter, Jean, did most of the work of the shop. Will helped when he could after school. He did not dislike shoptending as his sister did, though he went through a great deal of conscientious worry whenever he was required to cut cardboard for the mounting of photographs; he feared he would cut it crooked and cheat a customer.

In the school Will was given some employment as a monitor and when he was thirteen he became a pupil teacher, teaching Standard IV during the year 1883. For this year's labor he was paid ten pounds. "I earned it," he used to say grimly. After that it was agreed that he must have more advanced schooling and fit himself for the University. The Allans of Kinnaber Mills invited him to live with them and attend the excellent school at Montrose.

Kinnaber was not a wholly strange world, the boy had visited there often, but it was not easy to be so long away from Doune. Montrose is a clean little seaport town at the mouth of the River Esk. It is said to be the place where Greek was first taught in Scotland, an appropriate omen. The Kinnaber Mills were run at that time by Uncle James Allan, who had succeeded his father in the work as his son and grandson were to succeed him. The mills stood three miles outside Montrose in a countryside of which one may gather some idea from Barrie's *Auld Lycht Idyls* and *A Window in Thrums*. The speech in the books is the dialect which the Allans used, somewhat different from the Ayrshire to which Will Neilson had been brought up.

The Kinnaber house was simpler than that at Doune, only one story high—Will slept with his cousin Jim in an unheated attic—and lighted by lamps not gas, but it stood pleasantly among the farm fields, at an angle to the long mill whose wheel was turned by the rapid river. Beyond the mill were the bothies where the workmen, married and unmarried, lived. Kinnaber Mills ground all kinds of grain for men, cattle, and chickens, but chiefly oatmeal. The oats had to be dried before they were ground and a perpetual fire of "seeds," or oat husks, was kept up for the purpose, with an old man in charge. By that warm fire the workmen gathered for talk in the evenings and the small boys sat near to listen. It was from that talk by the oat fire that Will Neilson learned what his generation called the facts of life, a good straightforward method of education it always seemed to him.

How deeply the life of the mill impressed itself on the boy's mind one can guess from the naturalness and clarity of the milling similes that occur now and then in the speech and writing of the man. In 1912, for instance, he said to the New England Association of Teachers of English:

> Teaching composition is like digging a channel for a mill stream: if there is no head of water we are helpless and our labor is vain; but, if the water is there, we can keep it from spreading over a marsh, and can make it flow in a clear and rapid stream straight to the wheel it has to turn.

In a vespers address at Smith College, 1 October 1919:

> Our four years of college are like the damming of a stream which collects power to drive the wheels of life.

To a group of Smith alumnae, 1934, reporting proudly on the community activities in which they were engaged:

> See to it that there is some grist in the mills which you are turning.

Young as he was and kind as the relatives were to him the boy was acutely aware of his obligation for board and lodging and the chance to study. He devoted long segments of his summer holidays to work on the farm and in the mill, helping with the threshing or with the accounts. Uncle James was well versed in business practices and exact in all he did; his training proved of worth to the future administrator.

The immediate household was not large: Uncle James and his wife, a son and daughter, and Grandmother Allan, a lively, merry old lady. Her grandchildren cherished in their memories the picture of her on an afternoon when a wandering fiddler stopped at the house and sat playing in the kitchen. Grandmother, she was nearly ninety then, picked up her skirts and danced on the stone floor while her little dog danced on his hind legs beside her. But she had her serious interests too, of course, and young Will was often drafted to read to her from Spurgeon's sermons, which, despite his interest in theology, he found decidedly dull. When grandmother appeared to be nodding he would try to do a little reading in some book of his own—he always had one in his pocket—but she would wake at once and demand more Spurgeon.

The boy's chief purpose at Kinnaber was his preparation for the University and to that he devoted most of the hours of a long day. The mill was three miles from the town and every morning and evening Will made the journey on foot, a bag of books on his shoulder, his nose in a volume of Greek or Latin. It was those daily miles with the books which gave him the slight stoop which, contrasting oddly with his brisk gait, characterized him all his life. Apropos of this stoop he said once to a Smith College chapel assembly:

> I have been asked by an important committee, whose origin and authority I am unaware of, to announce the beginning of a week of propaganda in favor of correct posture. This College spends a good deal of money and energy telling you how to walk, stand, and sit, and how to get the proper straightness, or curve (I am not sure which it is!) into your backbone. It is evident that after leaving the gymnasium a great many of you slump. I understand that the committee came to me because I am the most awful warning that they could lay their hands on about the results of incorrect posture. This is *not* a joke. I have suffered frequent and acute physical pain as a penalty

for not having been taught how to carry myself. While you, with your more supple spines, can get away with all sorts of attitudes like sitting on your shoulderblades to read, I warn you that you will stiffen into the wrong shape, and you will get lumbago and sciatica and all the evils that affect old age, long before they are due.

The excellence of Will Neilson's rapid mind soon made itself felt at Montrose. Classics were the chief subjects of preparation for the University but it was in Montrose School that the Neilson enthusiasm for English literature first began to glow. Behind every great teacher you will find a good teacher, who has known how to light the flame. Behind William Allan Neilson stands Mr. Campbell of Montrose. We do not even know his first name but we do know that he was both teacher and friend, coming often to Kinnaber as a week-end visitor.

Uncle Peter Lyall was another influence in directing the boy's mind towards literature. He was a grocer, living in Stranraer, who married one of Mary Neilson's older sisters, and had the reputation in the family of being a great bookworm. He lent his nephew books from his library and it was probably he who first directed the boy's attention to the works of Matthew Arnold which, as a university student, Neilson greatly admired.

Another strong influence was a ten-years-older cousin William Allan, son of the uncle for whom Will Neilson was named. William Allan, the younger, was a hunchback with a mind as straight and clear as his body was twisted and a real gift both for teaching and for design. He was a disciple of William Morris and held an excellent position as designer in a carpet factory in Glasgow. Some of his addresses to his fellow workmen are preserved in a little pamphlet published at the time of his early death. The introduction to the pamphlet speaks of the designer's "cabin'd ample spirit" so like his father's in its originality, of his robust commonsense, and his "radiant enthusiasm to be of use."

It would be idle [the account goes on] to speculate on what William Allan might have done had he been endowed with a stronger body: the wonder is that he accomplished so much, fighting almost daily against physical weakness. In addition to his special talents for design and colour, he practised as hobbies various Arts and handicrafts and produced many bits of metal work and wood-carving. That he might interest and instruct the boys and young men of the Factory he himself took lessons in these Arts; and to widen the scope of the Winter Lantern Lectures he became an enthusiastic amateur photographer.

Certainly William Allan stimulated and directed young Will's interest in design and composition, in architecture and painting, though just how far his influence went we can only guess; William Allan Neilson was never interested in analyzing his own mind. He did, though, once say to his wife that he remembered his first conscious impression of beauty: when, as a boy, he noticed one day a pink carnation standing in a vase against a gray shutter.

During his last year at Montrose Will Neilson served as a pupil-teacher, instructing other boys all day long, except from eight to nine in the morning and from four to five in the afternoon when he resumed his own studies. He finished as Dux, the best scholar in the school, losing the perhaps higher honor of the Foote Bursary—it carried a stipend of £60—which went to the best classical and mathematical scholar. Neilson's rival was a crippled boy who gave, of necessity, all his time to study. These scholastic honors, the Academy magazine reported, had seldom been so well contested, and they printed the marks.

	Neilson	Steven
Latin	76	68
Greek	74	88
Mathematics / Arithmetic	140	148
English	88	79
German	76	67
Totals	454	450

The same issue of *The Academical* (July 1886) which reports this contest contains the earliest—at least the earliest we have—of William Allan Neilson's published works. It is concerned, characteristically, with an attempt to right an injustice, and takes the form of a letter to the editor.

Sir,—I am not Athletic, nor do I take any part in the Academy Sports, yet, being an Academy pupil, I take an interest in them. I was therefore much surprised and annoyed to see the strong symptoms of favouritism shown in the Report of the Games in your June issue. I am sure that you, yourself, and all the Academy pupils would be very sorry to see the *Academical* sink into a mere instrument for the venting of private spite; but yet, sir, I am certain that, if a stranger were to see your June number, that would be the opinion he would form of it.

Neilson then details the individual injustices, such as the boy whom the *Academical* censured "cruelly" because, on the line between two age groups, he chose to compete with the younger. He concludes:

I believe that in these remarks I express the opinions of the great majority of my fellow-pupils, as well as of myself. . . It will, in all probability, be said that I also am airing a little private spite, but for that I do not care. It was actuated by no personal motive whatever that I undertook this defence. But I think that, for your own sake, for the sake of your periodical, and of those into whose hands it will soon pass, for the sake of the name and fame of our own old place, and in justice to those who have been so unjustly attacked, you ought to apologise to those whose names have suffered at your hands, and to do all you can to undo the mischief you have done, and make up in some measure for the pain you have caused.

An editorial, printed on the first page of the little magazine, refers to the writer of this letter as activated by "the ripest spitefulness" but makes, fully and handsomely, the apology he demands.

The University of Edinburgh had at the time when Neilson matriculated no entrance examinations or set requirements. Many years later President Neilson of Smith relieved the tension of a heated meeting of the College Entrance Examination Board by remarking that this system still seemed to him highly effective: no Scotsman would think of paying down the guinea registration fee until he was sure that he was equipped to take advantage of the University's instruction.

In addition to the registration fee the Edinburgh scholar paid a guinea for each course he followed and what he could afford for food and lodging in the town. The small sum which he thought would see him through the year William Allan Neilson borrowed from his brother Robert and went up to the University in the fall of 1886.

2

Edinburgh

OVER the gateway to the old quadrangle of the University of Edinburgh rises a lofty dome, surmounted by the figure of a youth bearing a torch. The statue is meant, of course, to recall the ancient Greek relay race in which each runner, as he ended his course, handed to his successor a lighted torch. The motto is, *Quasi cursores vitae lampada tradunt*. Like runners they hand on the torch of life.

President Emeritus Neilson of Smith College, invited in 1942 to make an address at Northwestern on The Function of the University, began with this recollection of the institution where he matriculated in 1886. The statue and its motto made a deep impression upon the young man from Montrose as he passed each day through the gateway under the lofty dome; the torch bearer became his symbol of the teaching function as he was to practice it for fifty years.

> The race itself [the Northwestern address goes on] signifies the element of tradition: the receiving of wisdom from our forerunners, the keeping of it alive, and the passing of it on to posterity. The torch signifies not merely the handing on of the knowledge of the past; but since it is a lighted torch, knowledge illumined by imagination.

Few young scholars have stretched out their hands for that torch with more eagerness than William Allan Neilson, or lighted the wisdom of the past with more imagination.

To the hundreds of men and women who worked with him at Smith it seemed always that President Neilson never had to make a moral decision. He did not appear to go through any intellectual debate as to what, in a given case, was right or merciful or just, but acted always, swiftly and surely, on the side of truth and charity. His colleagues counted so happily on this power that it seldom occurred to them to speculate about its source, yet it was evidently a response founded solidly on intellectual conviction, and such records as we have of Neilson the student, at Edinburgh and later at Harvard, show him at the work of laying those foundations, by question, speculation, and debate, by reading and by talk. Before he could begin to build for himself, he found, he had, like most of his contemporaries, to clear his ground, deciding how much of the vigorous creed in which he had been bred was essential to his own belief. Though difficult, this exercise seemed to him intellectually and morally bracing. He was to pity later the generations who had nothing from which to break away. As he put it in the spring of 1931, addressing a meeting of the American Alumni Council,

> No longer does our youth grow up in an atmosphere of close reasoning of the important problems of life. So free are they to cast off beliefs and adopt others that they do so without apparent cost to themselves. They have no definite starting place and if there is no resistance to their intellectual actions neither is there any of the exhilaration of the feeling that the fight may cost a man's life, the feeling that there are great stakes being played for.

Exhilaration is the precise word for the state of mind of the Edinburgh student. He attacked his problems, serious or minor, with courage, gayety, and wit. There is a legend that during the religious and philosophical discussions which went on till the small hours of the morning in student lodgings, Neilson would pour tea on the head of any member of the company who became too serious.

From the Edinburgh years no letters remain but there is a commonplace book which the young man kept during his university terms in proper Victorian fashion. The passages of poetry and prose which he thought it worth while to transcribe are not the elegant extracts so popular with his contemporaries. There are no paragraphs of purple prose, no poetic descriptions of nature, little of sentiment or romance, sentimental and romantic though we know he was. These selections were chosen not for their felicity of expression but for their content. They present ideas, critical, philosophical, religious, guides to conduct, suggestions of new lines along which to think. Some of them come from books to which the student was undoubtedly introduced in the lecture room but the majority indicate the wide eclectic reading to which he was led by his own curiosity. Here are Carlyle, Arnold, and Emerson, Whitman, Longfellow's *Hyperion,* Shorthouse's *John Inglesant;* here are George Eliot (chiefly *Romola*), Mme. de Staël, Charles Kingsley, Olive Schreiner, Marion Crawford, Rider Haggard, and as many more. On the first page of the notebooks, as superscription, stand, significantly enough, three passages that speak of Truth: Polonius' "To thine own self be true"; Carlyle's Everlasting Yea; and the lines from *Aurora Leigh* beginning

the truth itself,
That's neither man's nor woman's, but just God's.

Typical of the pages that follow, though most of the passages are much longer, are these:

4 April 1888: Be no longer a Chaos, but a World or even a Worldkin. Produce! Produce! Were it but the pitifullest infinitesimal fraction of a Product, produce it, in God's name! 'Tis the utmost thou hast in thee: out with it, then. Up, up!—*Sartor Resartus*

5 May 1888: Nothing shall warp me from the belief that every man is a lover of truth.—Emerson

July 1888: The high stamp of diction and movement goes along with the high poetic truth and seriousness.—Arnold, *The English Poets*

May 1889: She had, in fact, undergone that dissociation of the moral judgment from a special series of religious formulae which is the crucial, the epoch-making fact of our day.—Mrs. Humphry Ward

On the final pages is a list of books * read month by month, and this list, at least the major part of it, records the beginning of Neilson's own library. "I still have books," he told a group of Smith College students forty years later, "that I can identify as having been purchased at the expense of insufficient nourishment." In the record—the first entry is Christmas 1888—we can trace the beginnings of some of Neilson's special interests. We see him reading many of Shakespeare's plays for the first time, starting his study of Chaucer, examining, when they first appeared, the Fabian Essays. It is evident that he shared his father's taste for Tennyson and he read the other important modern poets, Browning, Morris, Rossetti, Swinburne, Kipling. (Asked in the fall of 1936 to read poetry one Sunday afternoon to a group of Smith College freshmen President Neilson chose Kipling because it was just fifty years to a day since he entered the University of Edinburgh and it was on that first Edinburgh day that a fellow student showed him some little gray pamphlets containing the work of "a new poet named Kipling.") Neilson had the usual young man's taste for the novels of George Meredith, whose name appears in the list more frequently than any other. Scott, Carlyle, Stevenson, and Thackeray are here of course and the works of a good many more American writers than one would expect: Hawthorne's *Marble Faun* and *Blithedale Romance,* Holmes's *Autocrat,* essays by Lowell and Emerson, some of Whitman's poems. Neilson tried, too, a little Tolstoy and Ibsen. And he read steadily at history, criticism, and philosophy.

The book which made the deepest impression was John Morley's essay on *Compromise.* A quarter of a century later the President of Smith College wrote to a newspaper editor in Ashland, Wisconsin, who had asked him to contribute to a symposium:

> I am glad to avail myself of your inquiry to bring before your readers a book on "Compromise" by John Morley, which I have found useful almost beyond any other, and which I think is enormously important in helping us to a reasonable attitude towards many of the public and private questions of the day.

What manner of creed these Edinburgh excursions and speculations established one may discover in some of the publica-

* See Appendix.

tions of Neilson's maturity which bear on their surface no sign of autobiography but are actually very personal statements of belief. These are the sermons which, at intervals during twenty-two years, he delivered at Smith College Sunday vespers services. Like most of his addresses they were thought out in advance but never written down. Those that survive were transcribed in shorthand, most of them by a member of his faculty, Ruth Agnew.

These vespers talks caused Neilson more anxiety than any other speaking he did. This was partly because of the mixed audience—students, parents, visiting young men—but there was a deeper reason; he believed that in these vespers sermons he must state not merely general truths but his own profound convictions, must make the kind of confession of faith which was difficult to his Scottish reserve. It was this intimate discourse which, though few of them were directly aware of it, moved his hearers so deeply. And it was this personal element in it which caused Neilson usually himself to undervalue the effectiveness of what he had said. Again and again he reported to his wife that a vespers talk had been unsuccessful, when she was to receive next day strong evidence to the contrary. She made a point of hearing him at vespers as often as she could, though it was his habit to discourage her from listening to any of his addresses, and though she disliked to see him in what she called the "Christian Endeavor coat" he wore on Sundays under his gown.

The emphasis in the vespers, and in many of the shorter morning chapel talks, falls chiefly on truth and on the importance of a sense of proportion, the necessity for making wise choice of occupations to which one is to devote attention and energy. The summarizing phrase for Neilson's students became St. Paul's

> Finally, brethren, whatsoever things are true, whatsoever things are honest, whatsoever things are just, whatsoever things are pure, whatsoever things are lovely, whatsoever things are of good report; if there be any virtue, and if there be any praise, think on these things. (Philippians 4:8)

This is the traditional scripture reading for the Last Chapel of the year at Smith College but, long before he read it from the pulpit of John M. Greene Hall, it had become a fundamental tenet in the Neilson attitude towards life:

When people permit themselves to be absorbed by the trivial, the vulgar, the transient, the second-rate, they are bound sooner or later to fail to find satisfaction. The life made up of the trivial, the vulgar, the transient, the second-rate is bound to meet crises of disillusionment when the world seems no longer worth living in. The only resource that we have is to fall back upon the fresh realization of the elements that do not perish and do not cheat us, that can be counted on for refreshment and invigoration and renewing of hope and faith.

For everyone it is possible to make this change, to get the joy of Easter by turning from the transient and perishable and making up one's mind to concentrate on the values that endure; to stake no part of life on anything which may possibly fail, but to give one's time and energy, one's attention and whole devotion only to the first-rate things, because these are the things that abide. (Vespers, April 1930)

In 1940 Neilson made These Things the text of the only baccalaureate sermon he ever permitted to be transcribed. His baccalaureates were, by his choice, sessions from which not only the press but all visitors were excluded; the President talked in confidence to his senior class.

"If there be any virtue, and if there be any praise, think on these things" is a general injunction to keep your eyes open through life for the fine things in other people and in the world around you, instead of constantly hunting out the meannesses and weaknesses and thinking on them with secret joy. It is easy, when one's eyes are first unveiled to the raw facts of life, to take a kind of unholy glee in discovering the weak things in the best of people and the element of mixture in the best of actions, the mixture of low motives. I am very far from urging you to shut your eyes to anything that seems to you to be a fact. But you will find that there is a great deal of difference in life according to whether you dwell on one set of facts or on another. And not only the happiest life but the life that carries most happiness to the people around is that of the person who is thoroughly alert to the fine things as they occur.

In a vespers address made in 1931 one hears the Edinburgh student thinking. Starting from St. Paul's "Prove all things, hold fast that which is good" he talked about the "moral obligation to be intelligent":

There is the obligation to resist the temptation of intellectual cowardice—the temptation to shirk final conclusions which may be contrary to those of people we love or people we admire or people we fear, or those of the mass of the society about us. Doing one's own thinking is a dangerous, if necessary, occupation. You can never be sure where you are going to come out. You have to give up the idea of a foregone conclusion, be ready to accept the light wherever it leads, and then follow it up with action. The intellectual life, so pursued, is a life of very risky adventure.

To Neilson the college president as to Neilson the Edinburgh student no life seemed finer than that of the scholar-teacher, but he never thought it easy.

The characteristic virtue of our profession is that of intellectual honesty. The scholar is concerned with the search for knowledge, and his honesty depends on the quality of the search that he makes for the facts, on his not stopping until he has exhausted all that are within his reach. He does not begin to draw a conclusion before the facts are before him. He must constantly strive to see them as they are. On top of facts comes reason. Rigorous and courageous thinking makes facts yield up their ultimate significance. What we have to do for the world lies in these two lines: the ascertaining of facts and the drawing of inferences from the facts. It is a very difficult undertaking. Thinking is hard and painful. Facts are hard and stubborn. It needs persistence and it needs courage. (September 1929)

Such ideas as these were crystallized by the reading and by the talk which went on daily in the student lodging houses near the University. Neilson, like the majority of his fellow students, rented a room in a private house—23 Livingstone Place and then 5 Valleyfield Street—whose landlady harbored two or three university men, purchased for them such food as they could afford, cooked, and served it. What they could afford was scanty. "Meal Monday," though no longer observed as it had been in the early years of the century, was still a holiday on the university calendar. On that day—there were once several of them during the year—the student returned to the parental farm and carried back to Edinburgh a sack of oatmeal and potatoes on which, during the ensuing weeks, he chiefly lived. President Neilson, trying to give the carefree American undergraduate some notion of the value the nineteenth-century Scotsman set on education, would speak occasionally of the number of his classmates who died of tuberculosis brought on by cold and an insufficient diet.

He was, by his own account, better off than many. He had a brother generous and successful enough to help him with loans. He had for three years the MacDougal bursary of fifty pounds, and he was able to earn some money by tutoring medical students, who, though they considered themselves the aristocrats of the University, had, nevertheless, to turn frequently for help in languages to the students of the Faculty of Arts.

These three sources of income combined did not furnish funds for more than a meager living. Neilson admitted in later years that he could not bear the taste of liver or of oatmeal; he had eaten so much of them when he was an Edinburgh student. The stomach disorder, finally diagnosed as an ulcer, which harassed him all his life, had its origin in these Edinburgh meals. At that time, too, he began the perpetual cigar smoking so characteristic of him. He was advised by a medical man to try it as a means of soothing his nerves.

But the chief deficiency in Edinburgh student life, he came to feel, was not its hardship but its isolation. The men worked diligently, they took their medals and their prizes, but they failed to ripen as personalities. Speaking in 1936 to the Chicago Smith alumnae on some of the values of campus life, he recalled a group of his contemporaries at Edinburgh who had gone to Oxford for an eight-week term and come back

> completely altered in their attitude towards life, in their sensibilities, in their accent, in their clothes, in their manners, in every part of their external life, and profoundly also in their point of view, through being immersed for even that short time in the intensive life of an English college where they were, so to speak, in a tub of highly concentrated intellectual brine, which pickled them. It got through their skin and did things to them, not because of more brilliant lecturers or harder study, but because of an atmosphere they had breathed and an environment by which they were impressed with

the so-called "Oxford Stamp." At Edinburgh there was no stamp at all.

But the Edinburgh life, though unconcentrated, had its memorable contacts and experiences. The boy from Doune made his first entry into the world of the theater, a performance of *The Mikado* which seemed to him wonderfully glamorous. One day two men walking side by side along the Canongate were pointed out as Liddell and Scott—it had never occurred to the young scholar that those names had any existence off the pages of his Greek lexicon. Another of such "sights of Edinburgh" which Neilson particulary relished, he described several years later in a Canadian periodical, *The Week* (8 March 1895). Professor John Stuart Blackie had retired from active teaching four years before Neilson matriculated but he never ceased to be a part of the University's, as he was of the city's, life:

> A stranger could not be said to have seen the town if he had not met, breasting the long slope of The Mound, or striding along Princes Street or the bridges, that picturesque figure with the grey plaid thrown across the chest, facing the world with the dauntless carriage of a man who stands at the bow of a ship and fronts the breeze. It was worth an effort, too, to get a chance of studying the majestic head, so bravely held up against the years, and the infinite wrinkles of those cheeks that seemed so strangely to run up to the brows and hold the eyes in slits rather than in sockets. Rather like an old Celtic bard he seemed than a modern Professor of Greek.

A Celtic bard, indeed; it was Blackie who, after years of effort, forced into the university curriculum the course in Celtic which was to set Neilson on his philological road. Blackie in retirement lectured rather more than he had as an active professor, and the young men listened.

> It mattered little [Neilson's sketch continues] what you went to hear Blackie lecture on, you were fairly sure to have some of his characteristic philosophy of life thrown at you with a dogmatic brusqueness that recalled Carlyle, except that the frequent "Thou fool" was accompanied by a beaming smile instead of a scowl. The substance was usually much the same. To do what your hand found to do with all your might; never to talk shop—"Greek shop, Latin shop, any shop at all"—except in shop hours; to live as much of your life as

possible in the open air; and to thank God for the sunshine—these and like maxims he returned to again and again, his words of shrewd sense and strong practical wisdom coming forth among torrents of rollicking buffoonery.

There was a meeting with an even greater man. On one never-forgotten day Gladstone got down at the Edinburgh railway station and that ardent Gladstonian William Allan Neilson shook him by the hand. All his life long Neilson was pleased to define himself politically as a Gladstonian liberal. "I represent," he said to a group of historians in 1935, "the liberalism that Right and Left unite today to tell us is dead; and I refuse to be buried!" He went on to speak of the nineteenth century as he had lived in it.

I think the fundamental assumption of the political and social thought and feeling of the nineteenth century was the assumption of the reality of progress. . . . down to the beginning of the Great War there was a general feeling that we were going forward and that we were to continue to go forward towards "one far-off divine event, to which the whole creation moves," in the phrase of the most representative English poet of that period. This was a faith, of course, more than an attitude determined by proven fact—a faith based partly on Christianity, on the belief that what one was working for was the coming of the Kingdom of God on earth; a faith supported by the popular interpretation of Darwinian evolution, which seemed to the man in the street to indicate that the whole creation has always been improving and would always go on improving—to what end, of course, he did not know; "it does not yet appear what we shall be"—but we knew we were going to be better. This faith was supported, further, by the progress of science; the growing mastery over nature, the conquest of disease, the advance of technocracy, all led people to believe in the gradual disappearance of poverty and the establishment of a scheme by which the wealth of the world would be increased and would be shared more equally.

Politically, the English speaking peoples at least, and with them a good part of Western Europe, believed in a political basis of democracy combined with personal liberty, moving internationally towards some kind of federation. Its lines were very vague; but poets talked about it, and political orators were apt to close their perorations with the line—again from Tennyson—about "the Parliament of Man, the Federation of the World."

The world horizon was made clearer for the Edinburgh student by Uncle Burgess. Mr. Burgess had married Mary Neilson's elder sister, Annie, and Will went often to their house in Edinburgh. The young man was fond of his aunt but Uncle Burgess seemed to him pompous and sanctimonious. He could talk at first hand, though, about Egypt and India, for he made frequent trips to Calcutta, first as a missionary teacher and then on business. Better than his talk were his letters, written with a conscientious desire to inform those not so privileged as he.

The student widened his horizons also by listening to preachers of every stripe and color in the city's halls and churches—two, usually, each Sunday. Chief among these was Henry Drummond, curious compound of genuine faith, pseudo-philosophy, and charm, who was just at the beginning of that mission to university men which lasted twenty years and took him round the globe. Though a great admirer of Moody and at one time a co-worker with him, Drummond disliked the system of mass conversion. He preferred what he called an individual "buttonholing of souls" after they had listened to one of the quiet, elegant, and persuasive lectures in which he showed the young men that it was possible to be a Christian without repudiating evolution and other doctrines of modern science and without subscribing to all the tenets of the ancient creeds. They listened with relief and read gladly, as Gladstone did and Lord Aberdeen and thousands more, Drummond's *Natural Law in the Spiritual World* and *The Ascent of Man*.

In an address which Neilson made to some of his fellow students at Harvard on the occasion of Drummond's death in 1897 he spoke of that death as having "the force of a personal bereavement," and described at length the power of Drummond's personality.

> A tall slight figure in a closely buttoned frock-coat; a rather thin face, shaved except for the upper lip; a strikingly large forehead over deep-set eyes that beamed a contagious friendliness; above all, a calm repose of manner that suggested reserve strength. . . He was always restrained, yet without the appearance of self-consciousness. He talked as a man talks of the things he knows, and the things he believes to be of the highest importance. . . "Your lives"—these were the words

that ran through every address; and the direction in which he taught men to look was forward, not back. Not how they were to escape from the past, but what they were to do with the future; not after death, but tomorrow, and after graduation; not fear of punishment, but fear of waste. . . He was the most easily accessible of men, and when he shook your hand and looked into your eyes, you could not choose but confide. You never seemed to have to make a beginning with him, and in meeting him afterwards, he never seemed to have forgotten you. I have never known a tact so perfect, a bearing so winning, a temperament so responsive.

To his university audiences Drummond offered not only faith but works: "holiday missions" to country towns and a University Settlement in the heart of Edinburgh's ugly East End slums. There Neilson, with his close friend E. W. Hobbs, gave lectures and conducted classes, as he was later to do so faithfully for Denison House in Boston and the Davidson Foundation in New York.

There were impressions to be received, too, by a young man sensitive to line and form, from his daily passage under the dome and across the Great Quadrangle. The plan for the new buildings of the University of Edinburgh, drawn by Robert Adam, had been completed after his death, with intelligent modifications, by William Henry Playfair. The University Calendar (1891-2) describes the eastern front, on South Bridge Street, between the Old and New Cities, as a "very fine specimen of monumental architecture, with its monolithic columns twenty-two feet in height." And the ground beneath the architecture was dark with romantic history. The Old Building, which housed the University Library, stood on the site of Kirk o' the Fields, scene of the murder of Darnley.

In other respects besides architecture the University of the 1880's was closer to the eighteenth than the twentieth century. The curriculum was only beginning to relax its mediaeval stiffness, and it had barely dawned upon the authorities that students might have any rights and privileges beyond the payment of fees. The students, however, were beginning to assert themselves; they numbered then some three thousand, of whom about a third were studying under the Faculty of Arts. Just before

Neilson's matriculation, a Students' Representative Council was founded, a University Union organized, and publication begun of a magazine called *The Student*. That Neilson took a lively interest in such activities we know from a letter of recommendation which one of his fellows wrote for him when, after taking his degree, he set out to seek his fortune in Canada. The Gilchrist Scholar for Canada, Walter C. Murray, who was later to become Professor of Philosophy and Political Economy in the University of New Brunswick, added his testimony to the recommendations which Neilson was carrying from his professors. Under date of 14 April 1891, he wrote:

> As a fellow student of Mr. William Allan Neilson I have the greatest pleasure in expressing how highly we all respect him for his candor, honesty and manliness. On every occasion we have found him a perfect gentleman.
>
> His energy and keen interest in all academic and social matters, from the first, made him a leader in all literary and social discussions. The largest of the literary societies has made him an honorary member. He has proved an excellent President of two other Societies. His fellow-students entertain the highest opinions of his literary ability and of the soundness of his judgments.
>
> I feel certain that his ready and clear exposition, his genial manner, his wide sympathies, his high ideals, and his deep interest in all educational questions will make him an ideal teacher.
>
> I know of no student in the University who holds a higher place in the esteem of his fellow-students than Mr. Neilson.

In the classroom Neilson, though not spectacular, was certainly excellent. He impressed his professors with the quality of his mind and of the personality which operated it. The letters of recommendation they wrote for him in 1891, when he took his M.A. with Second Class Honors in Philosophy, are full of enthusiasm. They prophesy accurately his success in the profession he had chosen.

For most of the courses that he followed Neilson paid three guineas. When he entered, the ancient practice was still in vogue —it was discontinued in 1889—of the collection by each professor in person of the fees for his class. The Arts Faculty, in consequence, were frequently referred to by the students as the Forty

Thieves. J. M. Barrie, who preceded Neilson at the University by ten years, tells (*An Edinburgh Eleven,* 1889) how, on the opening day of one session, the whisper went round the quadrangle that Professor Masson was walking home with three hundred one-pound notes in his trousers pockets, how a little group of awed students followed him, and watched in amazement while he stopped and made a six-penny purchase at a secondhand bookstall.

Most of the Arts Faculty bore names of national and international distinction. From the beginning of his term the boy from Montrose sat under eminent scholars, many of whom were admirable teachers as well. In his first year (1886-7) Neilson, by the fiat of the University, devoted his time almost exclusively to Greek and Latin. Professor S. H. Butcher, translator of Homer and expounder of Aristotle, awarded him, in junior Greek, a second class certificate of merit. There had been some opposition, because he was an Irishman, to Butcher's succeeding the famous Blackie, but by the time of Neilson's matriculation he had established warm relations with both his colleagues and his students, towards whom he did not preserve the usual professorial aloofness. His gay vivacity, which could flare into indignation at injustice, public or private, must have commanded Neilson's youthful admiration.

In Professor W. Y. Sellar's junior humanity, which included Virgil, Horace, Cicero, and Latin prose, Neilson took a first class certificate and the sixth prize. Sellar was described by a student who sat under him a few years before Neilson (R. Menzies Fergusson, *My College Days,* 1887) as having "the grave manliness of the Roman." Barrie called him "a Roman senator," who treated his students like a fine gentleman and had their universal respect.

In his second year (1887-8) Neilson took second class certificates of merit in both senior Greek and senior humanity and passed the examination in classical literature required for the M.A. degree. He also had junior mathematics—plane, solid, and modern geometry, and elementary algebra—under Professor George Chrystal. Asked once by a friend at Smith whether he had not been bored by this rather restricted curriculum he replied in surprise, "Bored? I never knew what it was to be bored until I was in middle life."

In mathematics Neilson did not attain any particular distinction, which is not remarkable since in Professor Chrystal's course 20 per cent was considered a good and 30 per cent a phenomenal mark. There was a student conundrum of the day which ran: "Why shall we understand mathematical truths more clearly in a future state? Because now we see them in a c(h)rystal darkly." Barrie says that Chrystal started off the first day with a spurt and that after that most of the class never saw him again. Only the born or the very well-trained mathematicians—and they loved him—could follow his symbolic utterances; the rest sat helpless though impressed.

In this second year, also, began Neilson's interest in philology. The MacDougal bursary, which he had just won, gave preference to the student who followed the course in Celtic Language and Literature and Neilson was too scrupulous not to fulfill a condition to the letter, even though he lacked the preliminary training of most of the students who sat under Professor Donald Mackinnon. He was, however, entering his own country and Professor Mackinnon was delighted with his work.

> Though under the disadvantage of not knowing any of the Celtic Dialects in the vernacular [he wrote in January 1891] Mr. Neilson was able to take honors in the class. He also wrote a paper on the Place-names of Monteith which in addition to a firm grasp of the leading principles of Celtic philology showed a gift of clear exposition and the power of using the English language with ease and grace.

Under Mackinnon Neilson began the reading of the Scottish poets he was to take so much pleasure in introducing to American students.

It was in his second year with Mackinnon that the future editor of Webster's Dictionary made what is probably his first public essay in philology. He wrote a letter to J. M. Barrie suggesting the derivative of a dialect phrase which Barrie had rendered "I sepad." The expression is used several times by the women in Barrie's *A Window in Thrums* (1889), in the sense of I reckon or I wager: "I sepad it had been bocht cheap." "She'll make her own frocks, I sepad." Neilson suggested that the phrase was originally "I'se uphaud." Barrie agreed and in his later books the phrase occurs in that form.

> There is no doubt, I think [he wrote], about your being right on the derivative of I sepad. I am glad you like my book. I cannot but thank you for what you say, for you pay it the highest compliment it could hope for, or indeed desire, and shew at the same time an understanding of its real aims which is naturally gratifying to me.

That letter tells only part of the little story. Actually the philological suggestion was a bit of Scottish reserve drawn over an outburst of emotion. Among the few papers Neilson preserved from Edinburgh days is the anonymous typescript of an article on Barrie written by one of his fellow students and intended obviously for some literary journal, though whether it was printed or where, there is nothing to show. In discussing the *Window in Thrums* the anonymous writer says

> I remember an Edinburgh undergraduate of my time who was moved profoundly by the story of Jamie's going to London and his sorrowful return, and who, thinking of the mother who had been to him what Jess had been to Jamie, and making great resolutions of loyalty to her for the future out of the fulness of his heart, sat down and wrote to Mr. Barrie, and thanked him for his book, and vowed that one man at least would be a better son for having read it. Then an answer came from Barrie of which the youth was half proud and half ashamed, because he was a Scot and had shown his emotion, and in the answer Barrie thanked him for what he had said, and told him he had paid it the highest compliment it could hope for or indeed desire, and had shewn at the same time an understanding of its real aim.

Even when a ripened critical judgment had demoted Barrie in Neilson's literary hierarchy he continued to express for him an admiration which had the quality of a family loyalty.

In his third year Neilson began the study of philosophy in which he was to take his final honors. He sat under the great Berkeleian, A. Campbell Fraser, with whom he was to work again later when he was reading for honors. Fergusson describes Fraser as a "real type of the Scotch philosopher, dreamy occasionally, eloquent always"; filled with the Berkeleian fire he kindled a similar flame in young metaphysicians. And Barrie recalls how Fraser would rise in a daze from his chair, running his hands through his hair, and asking, "Do I exist, strictly so-called? Am I a table?"

In somewhat sharp contrast were Professor P. G. Tait's lectures in natural philosophy, which Neilson followed in order to pass the physics examination for the M.A. Tait's classes had the reputation of being the most orderly in the University because the students were always thoroughly interested, even though the textbook, Thomson and Tait's *Elements of Natural Philosophy,* was popularly known as "The Student's First Glimpse of Hades." Tait liked to have students in his classes who had no previous knowledge of the subject; he said they had less to unlearn.

Impatient because the curriculum offered him nothing in the modern field, Neilson enrolled also that year in a University Extension class in English literature, twelve lectures on "Modern Poetry, 1730-1881," delivered in the Edinburgh Philosophical Institute by H. Bellyse Baildon, Esq., M.A. (Cantab.). There were some seventy men in this class, among whom, Mr. Baildon wrote,

> Mr. Neilson was certainly one of the best and brightest students. His Essays and answers to questions were generally excellent and he showed, besides a clear intelligence and sound taste, an independence of judgment which pleased me much. He was one of *four* who passed the final Examination and obtained Certificates from the Edinburgh University-Lecture-Extension Association, his paper being warmly commended by the Examiners. On the whole I formed a very favorable impression of Mr. Neilson, and I am much mistaken, if he does not add to the qualities above indicated a firmness of character and a geniality of nature which should render him well-fitted for the post of a Teacher of English.

During the summer session of 1889 Neilson made an excursion into another field which was to become of great importance to him. It was in no way required for his degree but he attended the course on Constitutional Law and History offered by Professor J. Kirkpatrick of the University's Faculty of Law.

> [He] acquitted himself [Professor Kirkpatrick wrote] with high distinction both in the Class Examinations and the Essay Competition.

He attended with the utmost regularity and took part with great industry and marked ability in the whole work of the class.

In his fourth winter session Neilson prepared himself to take the M.A. examinations in mental philosophy by supplementing his work in metaphysics with Professor Henry Calderwood's moral philosophy. In this class he became a prizeman. Calderwood, an ordained Presbyterian minister and an anti-Hegelian, liked to show his students how philosophy could be pursued in a devout spirit. His classes were always large, partly because his lectures were patient and lucid, partly, Barrie said, because his subject is one that Scottish students revel in. "Long before they join his class they know that they are moral philosophers; indeed, they are sometimes surer of it before they enrol than afterwards." Once a week Calderwood turned his class into a debating society and argued things out with his students, who delighted in the exercise and usually spent the previous six days in contriving posers for him; but the Professor "never sees that they are posers. What is the use of getting up a question of the most subtle kind, when he answers it right away?"

Calderwood was noted, too, for a personal interest in his students which few of the other professors displayed. He invited everyone in the class to his house for supper, and had the members of his ladies class to meet them. But when the evening was over he saw the ladies into their cabs himself. "It is the only thing," says Barrie, "I ever heard against him."

In this same fourth year Neilson sat under David Masson, who lectured on rhetoric and English literature. In the Introduction to his Lake Classics edition of Milton's Minor Poems, published in 1900, Neilson pays formal tribute:

> The great mine of information on the life and times of Milton is Professor David Masson's magnificent work, *The Life of John Milton,* narrated in connection with the political, ecclesiastical, and literary history of his time, 6 vols., 1881-94. . . To Professor Masson . . . every modern student of Milton owes an immense debt, and I have to add to this general recognition that of the more personal obligation which a student owes to an inspiring teacher.

This is Neilson's only written reference to his connection with the distinguished scholar but of what he learned in Masson's classroom he talked often with academic friends, particularly, perhaps, with Professor Marjorie Nicolson when she was his Dean at Smith College. He told her once that an aphorism of Masson's was one of the most fruitful ideas he acquired in his five years at Edinburgh: "Shakespeare lived in a world of time; Milton, in a universe of space." Though Miss Nicolson has used that idea often in her teaching she has never been able to trace it in Masson's printed work. It is probably one of the phrases that, according to Barrie, he used to wring out of the gas-bracket during a lecture.

> It was when his mind groped for an image that he clutched the bracket. He seemed to tear his good things out of it. Silence overcame the class. Some were fascinated by the man; others trembled for the bracket. It shook, groaned, and yielded. Masson said another of the things that made his lectures literature.

Masson's enthusiasm, whether he spoke of Milton, Chatterton —on whom Barrie thought him best—or on his friend Carlyle, was warm and vivid. "Sometimes he entered the classroom so full of what he had to say that he began before he reached the desk. If he was in the middle of a peroration when the bell rang, even the back-benches forgot to empty."

In Masson's Rhetoric and English Literature Neilson received a first class certificate of merit, honorable mention for merit in the class-examination, and, in conjunction with another student, the fourth prize for English Essay Writing. The prize essay, on "Nationality in Literature," has some interesting concluding paragraphs devoted to "the great new nation" which "proudly hopes that it is to be created of every nation's best."

> Its first generation of litterateurs had virtually nothing characteristically American in their spirit, though they may have had in their subjects; but work has since been produced which is sufficient to prove that there is such a thing as a distinct American nationality. Two forms of the democratic idea have stamped themselves on American thought, and on both of these has Whitman laid hold to elevate and glorify. The first of these is the natural equality of men, and, coming from it, the ideal of the perfection of the individual; the second is that of the people as a great nation moving forward together, brother helping brother, but with no slavish dependence. [And he

quotes from "Pioneers! O Pioneers!"] If America is to solve the problems, so many and so serious, that are gathering round her future, and emerge a strong, robust nationality to take her place among the peoples, she can scarcely have fitter words for the title-page of her literature that is to be.

Though the universities had long been trainers of teachers as well as divines it was not until 1876 that Edinburgh and St. Andrews established chairs, the first in Great Britain, of Paedeutics, or the Theory, History, and Practice of Education. The holder of the chair at Edinburgh was Professor S. S. Laurie, who came to it after a distinguished career as secretary of the Schools Committee of the Church of Scotland and, later, to the Royal Commission on Schools. His course, as described in the University Calendar, covered: science of education; rules of the art or method; moral psychology; rules of the art of moral training and discipline; the organization of a school; state system; school appliances; history of education and of theories; practice in teaching.

In this course, in 1890, William Allan Neilson, quite certain now of his vocation, enrolled and found what he learned so useful to him that he regarded with much less scorn than most of his colleagues in the nineteen-twenties and thirties the expanding Departments of Education in American colleges. In fulfillment of Laurie's practice requirement Neilson presented a certificate covering the year he had taught at Doune. He was one of the twelve members of the paedeutics class who received the Higher Schoolmaster's Diploma.

During this year also Neilson attended a "full course of Elocution," whose instructor, D. A. Moxey, certified that he had proved himself "an excellent Reader, and a good Reciter, in addition to gaining a knowledge of the Art."

In April 1890 Neilson might have taken the usual pass degree but, since he had determined to accompany his family to Canada and seek a schoolmaster's post there, he felt it important that he should take his M.A. with honors. His mother regretted the expense of an additional year but she saw the professional point and acceded. In preparation for his honors examination in philosophy Neilson followed Campbell Fraser's course in metaphysics, in which he received a first class certificate of merit, and Calderwood's Advanced Moral Philosophy, in which he was a third prizeman. The examinations were set in April; three three-hour papers in logic, psychology, and metaphysics; three in moral philosophy. Had the candidate suspected that he was to be a college administrator, he would have heard, in one question in moral philosophy a prophetic note: "State the exact relation between Justice and Mercy, and indicate the grounds on which the merciful disposition is regarded as ethically higher than the strictly just disposition."

At the Commemoration Service held in St. Giles's Cathedral at noon on Friday, 17 April 1891, seventy pass degrees were conferred and fourteen with honors. Among these the M.A. with Second Class Honors in Philosophy was granted to William Allan Neilson.

Nearly forty years later, on 28 June 1928 the University of Edinburgh called this son back and conferred upon him her honorary LL.D. The citation played upon his Harvard dissertation on the *Court of Love* and his present position as ruler of two thousand maidens: "We may fitly associate with our graver Doctors of Laws this learned exponent of a lighter and gayer jurisprudence." And thereafter the President of Smith College illumined academic processions with his "gown of superfine Scarlet Cloth, loose sleeves, the cape and facings down the front covered, and the sleeves lined, with rich silk of the colour proper for the degree [blue]; berretum of black silk velvet."

When Herbert Davis, Smith's next president, was asked to compose the inscription for the books which President Neilson bequeathed to the Smith College Library, he remembered the Edinburgh motto and mingled it happily with a phrase from the Canterbury Tales which Neilson had so gladly taught. The bookplate reads: "From the Library of William Allan Neilson, *Feliciter vitae lampada tradidit.*"

3

Upper Canada College

WHILE William Allan Neilson was essaying the University of Edinburgh his elder brother was also widening his horizons. Robert Neilson had not found in his native land scope enough for his energy and initiative and began, like many of his countrymen then and in earlier times, to think of emigration. New Zealand was the dominion which most fired his imagination but the long voyage was beyond his means. In 1889 some friends of friends invited him to join them in a little town in the province of New Brunswick, Upper Canada, which Scottish immigrants had christened Ayr. He went out alone but with the hope, if the venture proved successful, of bringing over the rest of the family. Robert Neilson's friends, the Goldies, set him to work in their mills and in a short time he had made himself indispensable. He was entrusted first with the care of the machinery, a task which he performed with competence though he had had no previous experience in that kind. Then he began to learn the business in all its branches and details.

In the next year, 1890, Elizabeth, the elder of the two sisters, went out to Canada on a long visit to her brother. She was delighted with the country, with her Scottish-Canadian neighbors, and with the conditions of living, so much easier and more comfortable than those in Doune; she decided that she wanted to live there. She went home to report, though whether their mother could be persuaded to the transplantation the children had no idea. As the mother and her daughters talked by the fire on the first night of Lizzie's return, eagerly exchanging their news, Mrs. Neilson suddenly put her hand on the arm of the low chair in which she always sat and asked, "Do you think I can take this little chair with me to America?" The delighted sisters knew that the emigration was settled.

The idea of transplantation to another section of the Empire was not really startling to any of them.

> I have been accustomed from my youth [said William Allan Neilson in 1935, discussing the sentimental aspects of patriotism] to see the Scot returning from America. He glows with warmth as he approaches his native village and meets his old friends; for three days he has a royal time; but at the end of a week he is already thinking about his return passage to New York.

Will agreed to join the family in their expedition if they would let him have a fifth year at the University so that he might take his M.A. degree with honors. He also managed somehow a brief journey to Paris where he spent his days delightedly roaming the streets and his nights reading Zola by the light of a candle, to save the cost of gas.

In the summer of 1891 the Neilsons made the voyage to America. The little chair stayed in Scotland as a gift to Mrs. Neilson's namesake niece but many of the other household goods and treasures were packed up and carried to Canada.

An undated clipping from a local newspaper, carefully preserved through the years, records the "Departure of the Neilson Family for America":

> Of the numerous removals that have taken place from time to time of families from our neighborhood, none of recent years has been the cause of more general and sincere regret than that which occurred on Monday, when the Neilson family, consisting of Mrs. Neilson, widow of the late David Neilson, teacher, two daughters, and one son, left by the afternoon train *en route* for the United States, there to join the eldest son, Robert, who has for a number of years held a responsible position with a firm of millers and grain dealers in Ontario, relatives of Dr. and Mrs. Andrew, Balkerick Villa. . . Their depar-

ture from Doune Station on Monday afternoon was witnessed by a number of intimate friends, the Rev. G. S. Mackay travelling with them to Glasgow, while handkerchiefs and other available articles were waved in farewell adieus from every spot of vantage so long as the train was in view. The family spent the three following days amongst friends in Glasgow, and sailed for New York yesterday (Friday).

President Neilson of Smith used to relate occasionally an incident of that crossing of the Atlantic. He told it to indicate the kind of naïve young man he was when, at twenty-two, he set out for the new world. He was invited one morning to put a shilling in the ship's pool and handed it over promptly, supposing that he was contributing to a nautical charity. When it chanced that he won the pool on the day's run and he was presented with twenty pounds he was appalled; this was money got by gambling. He gave it at once to the Seaman's Fund—except the original shilling.

All the members of the Neilson family transplanted well, settling contentedly into their new home. Mrs. Neilson presided over the household. Lizzie did some teaching and Jean studied nursing. The two brothers, starting with nothing but their endowment of industry, enthusiasm, and native wit, both rose to distinction in their quite different fields.

Robert Neilson rapidly mastered the business of Canadian milling in all its aspects. Mr. Goldie came to repose so much confidence in him, that, on his death bed, he asked of him a pledge to run the mills till the Goldie sons were old enough to take over. That pledge Robert Neilson gave and kept, at considerable financial sacrifice but much to the advantage of his reputation. When he turned the business over to the Goldie heir, several of the big Canadian milling concerns were bidding for his services and he settled into an excellent position in Montreal. By thrift and wise investment he then accumulated a very comfortable competence which, in the year 1914, he gave away—to Brave Little Belgium. That grateful, and probably astonished, country made him a Chevalier of the Order of Leopold. Robert Neilson began again to save and invest so cannily that when, in 1921 he wanted to retire, he could purchase for himself and his sisters a pleasant farm in Orange, Connecticut. Lily Brook Farm was selected as the ideal location by a characteristic method, as a letter written by William Allan Neilson shows. It is addressed to the Professor of Climatology at Harvard, Robert De Courcy Ward:

> My brother is planning to withdraw from business, largely because he can no longer endure the winter climate of Montreal. He wants to find a place in the country, not too far from Northampton, but far enough south so that the winter will be shorter than he has been accustomed to in Canada, and considerably less severe. He thought there might be some government statistics giving extremes of temperature, rain fall, etc. for states or counties, and I promised to find out if such statistics were accessible.

William Allan Neilson hoped, when he emigrated, that he might find a teaching post in Canada, though he assured his sisters he was quite ready to earn his bread by any sort of work that offered, dishwashing if need be. Not long after his arrival in Ayr he learned, quite by chance—a conversation overheard on a train—that there was an English-mastership vacant at Upper Canada College in Toronto. He made application for the position, a highly presumptuous proceeding he was told by his relatives and his neighbors in Ayr. Upper Canada was an old and elegant preparatory school for boys. Government supported, like the University of Toronto, it dated its founding from 1829 and was proud of the many Members of Parliament, judges, generals, and Q.C.'s it had trained for the Dominion's service; why should it employ an unknown young immigrant? But the good folk of Ayr underestimated the power of an Edinburgh M.A., with honors. Neilson's application was accepted and he began his duties as Second English Master in the fall of 1891.

Upper Canada, having outgrown its original quarters, had just moved to a new site in Deer Park, a suburb of Toronto about a mile from the city limits. There, on a thirty acre tract, the trustees had erected one of those imposing edifices of brick and stone with which the late Victorians liked to express success and progress. "A magnificent pile" the young English master called it in an article on the school which he wrote (March 1893) for the new *Canadian Magazine*.

Like other nineteenth-century "piles" the building had its virtues; it was stoutly constructed, intelligently planned, and commodious within. On the lower floors were classrooms, cheerful and well lighted, a dining hall, and an impressive assembly hall hung with portraits of former principals and great walnut boards inscribed with the names of head boys. On the upper floors lived the "house boys," in single or double rooms furnished, according to the prospectus, in "a substantial home-like manner." The resident masters, of whom Neilson was one, each presided over a "flat" of twenty-five or thirty boys. The College was properly proud of the comfort it provided for its pupils, the care it took of their health, and the absolute modernity of its equipment:

> The whole building throughout is heated by steam. . . The system of lighting is the Edison Incandescent Electric Light. . . The plumbing is of the most modern description, and the drainage is perfect.

The school day began at 9:15 with roll call and prayers. Classes went on, with a half-hour interval for lunch, until 2:30, after which everyone, except those detained for "idleness, misconduct, or badly prepared lessons," devoted themselves to games: cricket, football, hockey, and tennis. There was a swimming bath, too, and a quarter-mile track for bicycling and running.

The curriculum of Upper Canada College was as up-to-date as its physical plant. A student who did not wish to follow the traditional classical course had the option of a commercial course or a scientific course for which there was a well equipped laboratory. The teaching staff for the three hundred boys included three classical masters, three mathematical masters, two modern language masters, two English masters, two commercial masters, a science master, a drawing master, a music director, and a physical instructor who must have been a character for his name was Sergeant Halfpenny. The First English Master was the Principal of the College, George Dickson. W. Allan Neilson, as he signed himself at that time, was appointed as Second English Master becoming First English Master in 1894. According to a report on Upper Canada made in 1893 to the Minister of Education by his official inspector:

Special attention is paid [in the college] to the teaching of the English branches and with very satisfactory results. *The College Times,* an illustrated periodical of twelve pages, edited and managed entirely by the boys themselves is evidence of a degree of supplementary reading on the part of the contributors that is creditable to them.

The mores of Upper Canada were modeled upon those of the English public school. To the young Scotsman, who had never encountered anything of the kind, they were horrifying. The phenomenon of man's inhumanity to man he accepted always reluctantly and those four years of Canadian schoolteaching were the unhappiest of his life. His occasional references to them are tinged with a bitterness which colors no other portion of his memories. In a vespers address delivered to the students at Smith in 1936 he said, apropos of the command to "love mercy":

It is a common delusion among kind-hearted older people that young people are naturally kind. During four of the most painful years of my life I was housemaster in a boys' school, and I know that young people are not naturally kind; and I fear that if I had spent those four years in a girls' school I should have had the same impression.

The following year in another vespers sermon on "Freedom" he said:

I remember at a very early stage in my teaching career being at a boarding school where the new boys were subjected to rather violent physical maltreatment by the elder boys each year. This kind of hazing made me very indignant—I had had no experience of it as a boy—and with all the officiousness of a young master I plunged into it and attempted to stop it. But I found I could not get support even among the victims who had just suffered. Their eyes were turned to the future, and they were already gloating over the prospect of doing the same things to their juniors.

And worse than this. The young master found himself constrained to adopt correspondingly brutal practices; to maintain discipline he was obliged to cane his charges. What would have happened if he had not is amusingly described by one of Neilson's distinguished colleagues in a little essay which he called

"My Memories and Miseries as a Schoolmaster" (*College Days*, 1923).

Stephen B. Leacock joined the faculty of Upper Canada College as Modern Language Master a year before Neilson's appointment. He did not enjoy schoolmastering, but he took its miseries more lightly than Neilson did. He had been an Upper Canada boy himself and "licking" seemed to him inevitable; anyone who attempted to keep order without it merely made himself rediculous. He tells in his essay the tale of a substitute master, a recent university graduate in psychology, who declined the cane offered him by the janitor in the usual routine and announced that he intended to govern his pupils by "moral suasion." Those pupils on the first day

> merely threw paper wads at him and put bent pins on his seat. The next day they put hot beeswax on his clothes and the day after that they brought screw drivers and unscrewed the little round seats of the classroom and rolled them down the stairs. After that day the philosopher did not come back.

Leacock's essay maintains further that the boys he licked enjoyed it.

> Again and again it happens to me that some unknown man, well on in middle life, accosts me with a beaming face and says: "You don't remember me. You licked me at Upper Canada College," and we shake hands with a warmth and heartiness as if I had been his earliest benefactor.

Neilson, though he had a liking for Leacock, refused to subscribe to this easy sadistic philosophy. By the end of his first year he had established so solidly his authority and popularity that he was able to abandon his cane.

An occasional note in Upper Canada's *College Times* indicates that some of the general liking for the English Master grew from his sympathetic interest in the extracurricular activities of his charges.

> 10 April 1894: The names of Mr. Neilson and Mr. Holmes were inadvertently omitted from the list of Camera Club prizegivers. We are very sorry that this mistake occurred, as both have exerted themselves to the utmost on behalf of the Club.

29 June 1893: Mr. Neilson was elected Vice-President of the College Tennis Club. Mr. Neilson donated the prize for the Senior Singles. His classroom was used for the committee meetings.

14 June 1894: Mr. Neilson was elected President of the College Tennis Club. Mr. Neilson again donated the prize for the Senior Singles.

Except for a picture in the *Smith College Weekly* (December 1925) showing President Neilson as an honorary member of the Faculty Soccer Team, this is the only occasion on which the Neilson name was ever connected with any organized sport. Tennis, during the Canadian years, he apparently really enjoyed. His sisters remembered what an impression of elegance his white tennis flannels created when he came home to Ayr for the holidays.

Even more surprising to Neilson's later friends than the tennis references in the *College Times* is a paragraph in the Prospectus which lists W. Allan Neilson among the tenors in the College Choir.

After the disciplinary problem had been solved, Neilson really enjoyed his classroom teaching. Years later he and Dean Marjorie Nicolson of Smith, who had her first pedagogic experience in Michigan high schools, agreed in advising graduate students to try a few years of elementary school teaching before they undertook the conducting of university classes. Neilson had in high measure the essential teaching gift: he could impart his own enthusiasm. He persuaded his pupils to read for the same reason he read himself, because life is so short. No three score years and ten, he told them, can begin to encompass all the experience a man wants but, with books and imagination, you can extend yourself for centuries and leagues. That is why he read so much biography and why he cared so greatly for the Victorian novelists, for Chaucer, and, above all, Shakespeare. To teach Shakespeare, he thought, is the "greatest privilege" and the "greatest joy" in the professional life of a teacher of English. At Upper Canada he encouraged what he found was his pupils' natural desire to discuss Shakespeare's characters as though they were real men and women, insisting at the same time that they give properly scholarly act-scene references for the traits they recognized.

And, though he sympathized with the contemporary fear of using literature as an occasion for preaching, he saw no reason why the degradation of Macbeth or the justification of Brutus were not legitimate subjects of interest for the reader since they had been for the author of the plays. (*Teaching Shakespeare in Schools,* Scott, Foresman and Company, 1906)

Neilson had another reason for reading which he shared with his pupils. We all have at times, he thought, emotions so strong that we feel impelled to give them some sort of expression. Most of us, when we try to express ourselves, find that we can do so only "awkwardly and nosily." The great writers, especially the lyric poets, offer us help and relief, for they can express emotion "adequately and beautifully." To prove this he constantly read poetry aloud to his classes, a method of teaching he practiced all his life with great success.

A testimonial to the lasting results of what went on in his classroom came to Neilson fifty years after he had left Upper Canada, on the occasion of his retirement from the presidency of Smith. The letter is dated 16 June 1939 and is signed by B. K. Sandwell, Managing Editor of the Canadian illustrated weekly *Saturday Night.* Sandwell was Head Boy at Upper Canada in 1893.

> You will receive no letters from an "older student" than myself, who began to sit under you at Upper Canada College in 1891. I acquired my first sense of poetic values under you, and have never forgotten your taking the entire Matric. Shakespeare class to see Mme. Janauschek do Lady Macbeth.

The *College Times* of 9 March 1893 describes further that Shakespearian expedition:

> The honor English boys spent a very pleasant evening at the Grand Opera House last Thursday night. Mr. Neilson was not only kind enough to get the boys off to hear "Macbeth," but treated them to seats. After the performance a very pleasant time was spent at McConkey's talking over the play and doing justice to an oyster supper.

The English Master, while he taught reading and writing, was beginning to express, not himself, that he never tried, but his ideas in print. He contributed from time to time to *The Week,* a journal, on the English plan, of politics and letters, published in Toronto. These literary essays have a kind of stiff carefulness of which Neilson's later work bears no trace. The models, as the Edinburgh commonplace book would lead one to anticipate, were Pater and Stevenson. On the death of the latter in 1894 Neilson wrote for *The Week* (21 December 1894) a critical eulogy.

It is to Mr. Stevenson most of all that we are indebted for the chief impulse which has caused and characterized that revival of the novel of incident and adventure, which has made the complaint no longer possible, that no romance is written in these days. . . *Kidnapped* is not a mere return to Marryatt and Fenimore Cooper, not even to Scott; it is a return to the picturesqueness and dramatic action of these earlier romance writers with the addition of a power of subtle characterization of which they knew little or nothing.

A few months later (22 March 1895) Neilson wrote on the posthumous publication of Pater's *Greek Studies:*

One hardly knows which to admire the more, the lucid certainty of the reasoning, or the art with which the inductive skeleton is hidden. For about the success of his exposition there is no doubt. It is one of the supreme tests of great teaching or preaching that it makes the hearer long to go straightway and teach and preach even such things, and this result is distinctly achieved in these studies.

Successful though he was as a schoolmaster, Neilson was soon convinced that this was not his real vocation. He wanted a wider horizon, he wanted to be a scholar, and he wanted to teach university students. For this it would be necessary to have a doctor's degree and it seemed to him that the place to acquire it was an American university. He had pretty well made up his mind to try the Johns Hopkins when, in 1893, the family decided to visit the World's Columbian Exposition at Chicago. That "World's Fair" was a landmark in Neilson's life to which he always looked back with gratitude; it definitely set the lines of his American career. Whenever during his presidency of Smith there was debate about the College's taking part in any such exhibition he set aside his instinctive economy and urged participation. It was the Chicago World's Fair that sent him to Harvard.

With their eager curiosity about life in all its phases the Neilson family made the Chicago trip a highly successful expedition about which they talked long after, but the high spot for William Allan Neilson was the morning he spent in the educational section of the Fair, talking to college representatives and looking over catalogues. The work on ballads, on Chaucer and Shakespeare that Child and Kittredge were carrying on at Harvard seemed to him precisely what he wanted. With another year of schoolteaching he could accumulate the necessary funds. He made application for admission to the Harvard Graduate School.

Upper Canada College was reluctant to let him go.

> It is with great regret [wrote the Dean of Residence in April 1895] that I see the time of our separation approaching. During the years that we have passed together in this Residence, your strict discharge of duty, pleasant or unpleasant, slight as well as important, has earned my thorough respect. I cannot express here, as I would like, my thanks for the trouble which your punctual, energetic dispatch of business has saved me. For a long time past I have felt absolute security when you were in charge of affairs. The success of your pupils in the University Examinations shews the earnest nature of your teaching in the classroom and the interest that it has awakened. The want of your excellent instruction will be felt there, as we shall miss your faithful services in the house.

4

Harvard Graduate School

NEILSON'S selection of Harvard as his place of graduate study was a strategic professional decision, though not many people could have told him so at the time. In 1895, when he matriculated, the "university idea" was just beginning to be a subject of discussion and experiment in the United States. The kind of advanced scholarly training for which Americans were going to Germany was to be had only at Harvard and the Johns Hopkins.

When the Johns Hopkins was established in 1876 its President, Daniel Coit Gilman, felt that there were enough undergraduate colleges in the United States; what was needed was work on the graduate level, and he began to develop his university with the emphasis there. The Harvard Graduate School, which had been hitherto a rather feeble institution, was spurred to fresh effort, and President Eliot and President Gilman worked in friendly rivalry. In the nineties English studies at Harvard were definitely in the lead, chiefly because of the presence of the distinguished mediaevalists Francis James Child and his brilliant pupil George Lyman Kittredge. These two were training a line of scholars who would shortly carry their principles and methods to colleges all over the United States. To be one of the early Harvard Ph.D.'s was to be in a preferred position, a member of a body whose influence was constantly expanding. The first Harvard Ph.D. in

English had been conferred in 1876 (on Robert Grant). There was no other for twelve years. When Neilson took the degree in 1898 he did so as one of four.

The whole number of students in the Harvard Graduate School at this time was less than three hundred so that Neilson made many friendships among men working in fields quite different from his own. He made them with what seemed to Cambridge extraordinary rapidity. One of his contemporaries, J. S. P. Tatlock, writing of him years later in the *Nation* ("Americans We Like," 4 January 1928), recalls Neilson's saying in the early days of their acquaintance: "Some of the new students from the West complain of the Harvard climate. I don't put up with it. I just go up and talk to people; I don't find them standoffish."

The West and South were well represented in the graduate student body, though the largest group was from New England. There were several representatives of the Canadian universities but Neilson was the only man from Edinburgh or indeed from the British Isles. He was a conspicuous and picturesque figure about the Yard with his long Scotch cape, slouch hat, black beard, and flashing eye. Mephistophelian, some people thought, until they came close enough to see that the flash was amusement, not malice. A better comparison, made more frequently as the years went on, was to the portrait of Chaucer which now hangs in the Houghton Library. There is a striking similarity in the oval shape of the faces and in the little pointed beards, and, in later life, Neilson's expression had that combination of serenity and gayety which make the Chaucer portraits so attractive. In the nineties the serenity was only in process. The photograph taken in 1898 has instead a look of questing eagerness, and that is the quality Neilson's friends were struck by at the time, his interest in the world and curiosity about it, his desire to try every door to knowledge and to truth.

The academic doorkeepers to whom he counted himself most indebted were Child and Kittredge, both of them exacting taskmasters. Neilson began at once to follow the courses which had attracted him in that World's Fair catalogue: Child's English and Scottish popular ballads, his Chaucer, the Shakespeare which he shared with Kittredge, Kittredge's Anglo-Saxon poetry. In addition to these Neilson took a one-hour course on prose writers of the nineteenth century taught by Lewis E. Gates, and Gothic with H. C. G. von Jagemann who had come to Harvard from Leipzig, by way of the University of Indiana. Except for a B in the Gothic, all his grades, in this year and the next, were A's.

The year's work with Child was particularly productive of pleasure and profit. As scholar and as teacher Child had virtues which Neilson admired and was himself to practice, but their association was brief for Child died at the close of the term in June. To *The Week,* for which he had written occasionally in Toronto, Neilson sent an obituary essay, one of the first of those penetrating sketches of character for which he became famous at Smith.

[Child] was a rare instance of a student in whom great and minute learning has not dried up the kindlier juices of his nature. A man to whom sentimentality in every form was abhorrent, he had yet so tender a heart and such a susceptibility to noble emotion that, even after fifty years' familiarity, his eyes would fill with tears over a ballad like "Mary Hamilton," or the beauty of expression in a passage from Chaucer or Shakespeare. . . I have never known a man freer from self-consciousness or affectation of any kind. He never posed, never tried to show himself off in any way, and consequently never disguised himself. No student who came into close personal contact with him failed to fall under his spell. . . His love of thoroughness, his respect for what was genuine, and his scorn of pretense communicated themselves in some degree to all who worked with him.

People who described Professor Child liked to emphasize his roundness—the plump figure, the moon-shaped face, the curly hair. These cherubic qualities, it was agreed, were the outward marks of a kind heart, quick friendliness, and infectious enthusiasm. Henry James thought Child the embodiment of the American spirit. Perhaps it was because he met it first in this agreeable form that the young Scot's appreciation of the American spirit was so rapid and so keen.

After the death of Child, Kittredge became the dominant figure in the department of English. He had graduated from Harvard in 1882 and began his teaching there in 1888. Though he declined to take a Ph.D.—"Who would examine me?"—he had, at the time of Neilson's matriculation, attained professorial rank and would later be chairman of the department and then of the whole division of modern languages. Tall, handsome, brilliant, imperious, he had most of the hardworking scholarly virtues but few of the humane qualities exemplified by Child. Yet, different as their personalities were, Neilson's association with Kittredge was long and close. He wrote his doctoral dissertation under Kittredge's direction, and was indebted to him for an appointment to Bryn Mawr and then a call to Harvard, where they were colleagues for many years. Kittredge seems to have felt for Neilson as much affection as he was capable of feeling for anybody and Neilson had for Kittredge not only admiration and the lively gratitude of a good pupil to a hard master but also a genuine liking. Towards the close of his presidency of Smith, in 1938, Neilson invited Kittredge to give the commencement address at the College, presenting him to the students as much less of a stranger than they might suppose.

> For the last four years a large number of you have been subjected to his influence at second hand. The teaching of English, the study of English language and literature, is the core of a liberal education. And this has come to you through the staff of the English department here, about half of whom had been under the direct training of Professor Kittredge; and his ideals of learning and his rigorous methods have been, I hope, to some degree transmitted to you through his pupils . . . Professor Kittredge has become . . . perhaps the most pervasive academic influence in the colleges of America in our time.

Neilson's work in his second year was devoted mainly to philology: Early English with Gates and F. N. Robinson, his contemporary and life-long friend; Old French with E. S. Sheldon who was then creating the department of romance philology; Celtic with Arthur R. Marsh. He also managed another one hour course, with Gates, on English criticism. In June 1897 Neilson took the Harvard M.A. During his third year he worked at his dissertation, taking his Ph.D. in June 1898.

The subject of his dissertation was suggested by Kittredge, *The Origins and Sources of the "Court of Love."* Begun as an inquiry into that pseudo-Chaucerian poem, the study gradually widened to include the rise and development of some of the leading features of mediaeval love-allegory and this gave Neilson room to present a few original ideas.

The Origins and Sources of the "Court of Love" is an excellent piece of scholarship in the nineteenth-century German tradition, comprehensive, accurate, learned, well organized and set down, a useful addition to knowledge in a fairly restricted field. It established beyond question its writer's competence for scholarly research. Albert S. Cook, for instance, to whom the young Ph.D. sent a copy when it was published (1899) as Number VI in the Harvard Studies in Philology and Literature, wrote: "It seems to me an admirable piece of solid scholarship on a difficult and important subject, and written in a pleasing style." But, successful as the dissertation was, Neilson did not accomplish it with much joy. He could not persuade himself that the months of patient labor he was expending would go far to "reveal literature as a living thing, having a bearing on the life of its readers." That is the statement of purpose which prefaces the Neilson and Thorndike *History of English Literature* and the purpose Neilson had always in mind as he taught. Aside from the training it gave him in the techniques of his profession, his *Court of Love* labor seemed to Neilson comparatively barren. Revolt against the older Germanic scholarship was already stirring in Cambridge and his swift analytic mind moved usually years ahead of any trend in the intellectual world. When one of his able contemporaries abandoned in indignant revolt a similar scholarly project and left Harvard without his degree, Neilson regarded him with admiration and some envy. But, unlike the Canadian schoolboys who looked forward to the hazing of their successors, he emerged from his trial with a sense of compassion towards his future students. He did not share the frequent academic inclination to make succeeding generations suffer the same pains you have undergone.

Living conditions at Harvard, though plain enough, were far less rigorous than they had been at Edinburgh. In his second year Neilson was made a University Scholar (there were twenty of them at the time) with a stipend of $150. In 1897-8 he was one of four Morgan Fellows receiving $500 each. A fellowship of any kind was a distinction for there were always four times too many applicants. Inexpensive rooms were not difficult to come by and the Foxcroft Club, opposite Memorial Hall, provided the graduate student with better nourishment than oatmeal and liver, as well as with a good deal of pleasant companionship. During his first year Neilson had a room at 7 Howland Street in the house of a Scottish family named Tryon with whom he continued a friendly connection for many years. Across the way lived A. D. Sheffield with whom propinquity initiated a life-long friendship. Other distinguished friendships were begun in those days. Many of the young men with whom Neilson talked over the dinner table bore names which have been recorded in academic history: Sidney Bradshaw Fay, for instance, professor of history at Smith and Radcliffe; J. B. Fletcher, chairman of the department of comparative literature at Columbia; Ralph Barton Perry, the philosopher, George H. Chase, the archaeologist, F. N. Robinson, the philologist, all future members of the Harvard faculty.

In graduate student clubs Neilson took a lively part, as he had done at Edinburgh. Some of these, he said later, he joined because he thought they had outlived their usefulness and he wanted to kill them off. One notable one he started himself, the Harvard Religious Union. This group Neilson organized because he felt that the unorthodox among his colleagues were insufficiently provided for. The Cambridge churches presented themselves to be taken or left; the YMCA of the period was a rather stuffy organization with little to offer the man who would not commit himself to a sect yet wanted seriously to test and set his own philosophical foundations. Several members of the Religious Union were agnostics or avowed atheists and discussions were lively. It was Leo Stein, brother of Gertrude, who posed the most awkward questions. During the first year, 1895-6 Neilson conducted the meetings, which were held weekly in the parlors of the First [Parish] Church. Later, the topic was presented by an assigned speaker, sometimes a member of the faculty, most often one of the group, and discussion followed. The list of topics indicates some of the directions in which Neilson was carrying on the intellectual experiments of his Edinburgh days: Personal Influence, Emerson and Self Reliance, Prayer, Tennyson and the Sentiment of Honor, Charles Kingsley's Message to his Time, John Morley and Intellectual Honesty, Browning and Aspiration, Spencer and the Discipline of Consequences, Tolstoi and the Gospel of Non-Resistance, The Ethics of Political Conduct, The Moral Function of the Teacher. Neilson himself spoke, in 1896, on The Place of Aspiration in Religion and The Problem of Conformity; in 1897, on Pleasure and Recollections of Henry Drummond.

The settlement work, begun under Drummond's stimulus in Edinburgh, Neilson continued at Dennison House in Boston where he volunteered to teach literature to a class of working men. The class met on Saturday evenings and Neilson's friends remarked with astonishment that he never missed a session, not even in the week when, on the ensuing Monday, he was to come up for his doctoral examination. His attitude towards the obligation this sort of volunteer work imposes he explained many years later (1932) to a group of Smith College students who were enrolling for the same sort of service, teaching at Northampton's People's Institute:

> If you are paid for a job and do not do it, you are simply dishonest; you are cheating. But if you undertake a thing of this kind voluntarily, so that people trust you to do it, and then do not deliver the goods, you are far worse than a cheat, because you have betrayed a whole set of ideals and gone back on your own integrity in the highest sense.

Since it concerned no one but himself, he was far less faithful to a course he undertook to follow in the Harvard gymnasium. Like most forms of exercise he found it dull and soon ceased to attend.

Neilson tried other doors to knowledge besides those which opened into classrooms. Cambridge in the nineties, like Cambridge today, liked to take her social life with a strong infusion of culture. There were, for instance, the Sunday afternoons of such Brattle Street ladies as Mrs. Ole Bull and Mrs. Crawford Toy, where some distinguished scholar spoke informally and discussion followed with tea and little cakes. A few promising young men, recommended by their professors, might be included among the more important guests. Toy, a Virginian who had fought in the Confederate army, was Hancock Professor of Hebrew. His wife's interests were primarily belletristic and aesthetic. She was a pretty Southerner, all bows and ruffles, very fond of lions. The special ornament of her salon was George Santayana. When Neilson and Sheffield were invited, the latter, going through, by his own account, a very "Paterish period," found the occasions delightful but Neilson, after two sessions, declared himself "satiated with Santayana" and refused to attend again.

Mrs. Bull's Sundays he enjoyed much more. She was the widow of the Norwegian virtuoso whose violin seemed to the unmusical Americans of that generation the most sublime of instruments. Mrs. Bull herself was an American, a black-haired, melancholy beauty who had married the great man when he was sixty and she twenty. She had a passionate interest in music, philosophy, and good causes. In her teakwood paneled drawing room, hung with portraits of the violinist, Josiah Royce talked often on Sunday afternoons, notably on Job. So did William James for whom Neilson had great admiration. Some ten years later he recorded his impression of "William James as Lecturer and Writer," for the issue of the *Harvard Illustrated Magazine* (February 1907) published at the time of James's retirement. The art of the finished lecturer James never attained, Neilson said, and probably never sought.

> Sentences ended in the air, digressions wandered from the main theme, but no one cared. The man thought while he was talking, talked while he was thinking, and what reached the student was hot from the anvil. Thus, whether one could take notes or no, one was always interested, stimulated, exhilarated. Prepared by the splendor of his reputation, impressed by the sincerity of his utterance, and warmed by the spontaneous humanity of his presence, the student felt the hours spent in James's lecture-rooms as possessing a kind of historic significance, not merely for his own life, but for the development of modern thought.

With another type of Cambridge matron, the "modern" woman of the nineties, Neilson made agreeable and stimulating acquaintance. Mrs. Holmes Hinckley, a young widow, had just built, on Berkeley Place, what was famous in those spacious days as "the smallest house in Cambridge," though it provided comfortable room for her, her two little daughters, and, on frequent occasions, her cousin Ada Eliot, who was to become Mrs. A. D. Sheffield. The courtship which preceded that happy union took Sheffield often to 1 Berkeley Place and the fact that another friend, Neil Brooks, a student of German, occupied in summer Professor Kuno Francke's house next door, established the Triumvirate, as she called them, on a footing of pleasant intimacy in the Hinckley household. Mrs. Hinckley was as ready to "prove all things" as Neilson himself. She was, at that early date, a suffragist; she even rode a bicycle, but Cambridge approved of her. They never applied to her that opprobrious epithet "strong-minded"; they said merely, and said even that with admiration, that Mrs. Hinckley was "up-and-coming."

Other feminine friendships there were certainly but only a faint echo of one remains. Driving one day with two of the alumnae to a Smith Club meeting in a Berkshire town, President Neilson slowed the car at the cornor of an elm-shaded street and said: "On that road lived a young lady with whom I was once in love. I went up from Cambridge to see her and her father took me out in his buggy to discover whether my intentions were honorable. They were, but she turned me down." This climax seems to all Smith women so improbable that the tale has never had wide circulation.

5

Bryn Mawr

WHEN Neilson took his Ph.D. in 1898 he was offered a position as Associate in English Literature at Bryn Mawr. He accepted promptly. A call to Bryn Mawr was then a distinction coveted by the young scholar, for, though the College was only thirteen years old, its extraordinary President, M. Carey Thomas, had already established its reputation for scholarship and high seriousness. This had been accomplished in part by admitting candidates only by examination, not, as was usual at that time, by school certificate; in part by setting the enrollment figure at five hundred undergraduate and one hundred graduate students, a proportion unprecedented in the women's colleges; and in part by insisting that all members of the faculty have advanced scholarly training. Miss Thomas herself was known in the profession as a skilful selector of promising young men. She gave their start, to W. E. Hocking, Paul Elmer More, Paul Shorey, and Woodrow Wilson, as well as Neilson, though she did not keep any of them on her faculty long, so difficult was she to work with, autocratic, high-handed, devious in her methods. It was said in the profession that at Bryn Mawr you did not occupy a chair; you sat on your suitcase.

President Thomas' character was a curious compound of high ideals and personal ambition, of intelligence and prejudice, of energy and indirection. For nearly forty years she was a legendary and a controversial figure in the academic world. Neilson was so accustomed to getting on easily with all kinds of people that he did not anticipate any particular difficulty in his relations with his new President though he recalled with amusement in future years that when he announced at his Cambridge lunch club that he was going to Bryn Mawr, Josiah Royce followed him to the door, blueberry pie in hand, to say, "If you can swim there, you can swim anywhere."

The appointment Miss Thomas offered was for two years at an annual salary of $1000. The hours of teaching were to be twelve a week. That part of the contract was in writing. There was also a verbal agreement that if Neilson's work proved satisfactory the appointment would be continued at an increased salary. The courses offered him were interesting and demanding, if a little pretentious for a young college and a young scholar. He was to take over the lectures, formerly given by Miss Thomas and required of all students, on the history of the English language and English literature. This was one of the first "survey" courses given in the United States and was to be copied by most of the colleges in the country. Beginning with the Anglo-Saxon period the course, which ran through two years, came down to the Restoration, endeavoring on the way, to relate English to the contemporary Continental literatures. Neilson was to teach also in his first year a course in eighteenth-century poetry and a graduate seminar in Elizabethan and Jacobean drama; in the following year, a course in Victorian poetry and graduate seminars in Shakespeare and in English and Scottish popular ballads. This last offering, made at his own suggestion, was generally supposed to be a direct challenge to Professor Mamie Gwinn's elegant appreciations of Ruskin and Pater. The young man from Harvard, so student gossip ran, had characterized Miss Gwinn's lectures as "cheap perfume." He was presenting, in opposition, material which was obviously tough and vigorous. This, if true, was bold. Miss Gwinn was a great power, both in the Department of English and in the College. She and Carey Thomas had been childhood friends and had pursued together advanced studies at Heidelberg, though Miss Gwinn had not fought her way through to a degree as Miss Thomas had done. And Miss Gwinn, too, was an eccentric and controversial figure. Tall, dark-eyed, elegant, languid, she either taught in a kind of sibylline trance or wrote elaborate critical comments on the papers of students to whom she never spoke a personal word. The students who were not repelled were fascinated and many of her contemporaries thought her brilliant and subtle, though they admitted that she was devious also and malicious. Certainly many of the excellent educational ideas which Carey Thomas put into action she acquired from Mamie Gwinn.

Miss Gwinn took, not unnaturally, a strong dislike to the new instructor from Harvard and, since she lived with Miss Thomas in the Deanery (Miss Thomas had been dean before she became president) and since they constantly discussed together college affairs, Miss Thomas' opinion was colored by hers. They decided that Dr. Neilson was rude and set this down in part to his Scottish origin. They were both great Anglophiles and his British citizenship had been one factor in favor of Neilson's appointment, but, after all, Edinburgh was not Oxford.

Dr. Neilson had other qualities which troubled President Thomas. The informality, friendliness, and sympathy which, in addition to his excellent teaching, made him very popular with his students, were not in her eyes academic virtues. In recruiting her faculty she had insisted that the majority should be men since, until Bryn Mawr had trained them, there would not be enough women in the country properly equipped for posts at Bryn Mawr. Her trustees objected that she would find herself conducting a matrimonial bureau, and she was, in addition, quite aware that the well-to-do Philadelphia and Baltimore Quakers who permitted their daughters to attend Bryn Mawr College would look with disfavor on marriages with impecunious professors. She felt it imperative, therefore, to keep the relationship between instructors and students, both in the classroom and outside, distant and formal. She wanted her faculty to have the aloofness of the professors under whom she had studied at Heidelberg. It is purported to have been Neilson—legends began early to attach themselves to him—who, walking across the campus on a moonlit night, murmured sadly to a colleague:

Water, water, everywhere,
Nor any drop to drink.

The campus, situated on a high hill (bryn mawr in Welsh), ten miles from Philadelphia, was beginning to grow into a pleasant place but the living arrangements of the faculty were still far from ideal. The bachelor instructors were housed in a rather uncomfortable establishment next door to the Deanery from which, they felt sure, a perpetual surveillance was kept over their comings and goings. They enjoyed, though, one feature of the College's location, its proximity to the masculine Quaker college, Haverford, which was within convenient distance, though the Bryn Mawr trustees had insisted on being far enough away to avoid any danger of becoming a mere annex. Neilson made warm friends in the Haverford faculty.

Among the Bryn Mawr instructors Neilson's particular friend was Charles M. Bakewell (later Professor of Philosophy at California and Yale) who justified the worst suspicions of the trustees by falling in love with one of his students. The handsome Miss Madeline Palmer was President of the Philosophical Club, an organization composed of students and members of the faculty which held evening meetings addressed by distinguished visitors and followed by elegant receptions to which everyone came in formal dress. But even within such an intellectual aura Bryn Mawr disapproved of student-faculty intimacy and the pair had to carry on their courtship during secret evening walks on the campus. Neilson—he and Bakewell were known as "the Twins" —aided and abetted, and love triumphed, discretely: Miss Palmer was married to Dr. Bakewell in the December following her graduation. The young couple managed to obtain an apartment in a house on the campus and there they gave, on Sunday evenings, agreeable little parties to which they invited, all contrary to custom, members of the faculty and some of the bride's undergraduate friends. They even went so far as to serve cheese and beer.

It is not altogether surprising that Miss Thomas hesitated to promote a rude young man who abetted such practices but her method of procedure was characteristically indirect. When the time came for his reappointment she told Neilson that the trustees were disposed to keep him but without the promised advance in salary. They did not feel that he had sufficiently proved his teaching ability. She cited as evidence of inefficiency the fact that a large number of students had chosen his major English course as a free elective and that many were attending as auditors his graduate course in Shakespeare. The inference was that the level of his teaching must be low. She said also, and more importantly, that the trustees were disappointed because Neilson's graduate students had not published any results of research.

Both the criticism and the expectation seemed to Neilson so absurd that he declined the reappointment and, in justice to himself and his successor, asked Miss Thomas to present to the trustees a letter in which he met her points in detail. In regard to the numbers in his courses he remarked that "it is surely possible to be at once interesting and scholarly"; concerning his graduate students he said:

> In no department of this College, nor in any other reputable institution, is it usual or desirable to force students to publish results in the time mentioned. I do not find that such results have ever been obtained by my predecessors or colleagues in the English Department here; and I am not prepared to lower my own ideals of scholarship or to force unripe students to premature production.

Though Miss Thomas agreed to present this letter to the trustees at their next meeting, she did not do so, professing to have lost it. In the meantime Neilson learned from a member of the Board that the trustees had made no criticism whatever of his teaching; the objections were of Miss Thomas' own invention. He wrote at once to Kittredge, telling him that he wanted to leave Bryn Mawr, and Kittredge offered him an instructorship at Harvard.

After that it was possible to treat the situation a little more lightly—Neilson once told his wife that it was at Bryn Mawr that he developed his sense of humor. He even put his sentiments towards Miss Thomas into verses, signed R. K., which he contributed to the little magazine the Bakewell Sunday evening group got out in honor of the birthday of one of their number, Grace

Jones (Mrs. C. F. W. McClure), who was editor of the undergraduate *Fortnightly Philistine*. The birthday issue was titled the *Midnightly Fillastein*. Neilson's poetic outburst was intended, of course, only for the eyes of the small intimate group, and, since their discretion and good manners were far greater than Miss Thomas supposed, its echoes never reverberated beyond the Bakewells' flat. But the young editor was sentimental enough to preserve her birthday album.

I've taught for many men acrost the tank,
An' some of 'em was square and some was not,
The Scotsman, an' the Canuck, an' the Yank
But our Minnie was the toughest of the lot.

I never got a ha'porth's change of 'er;
She squatted on my 'ead and blocked my courses,
She cut my feelings up and tore my fur
And you never yet could tell her what remorse is.

So 'ere's to you, Minnie Carey, in your College in Bryn Mawr,
You're a rather shaky Quaker, but at dodging you're a star.
You give us our new contracts, and if we want 'em signed,
We've got to go and jolly you, whenever you're inclined.

She is all sweet oil and honey when we're hired,
But, before we know, she's got us on the run.
She blames it on the Board when we get fired,
And for reasons she can always take the bun.

She's a daisy, she's a ducky, she's a lamb,
She's a modern Educator with a twist,
She's the only thing that ever brings a Damn
From professors' lips that maidens never kist.

So 'ere's to you, Minnie Carey, at your College in Bryn Mawr,
You're a rather shaky Quaker, but at dodging you're a star;
An' 'ere's to you, Minnie Carey, you are most uncommon smart,
You kind old Christian lady, for you broke a scholar's heart.

As his verse suggests the element in the whole incident which most offended Neilson was Miss Thomas' tendency to "dodge." Dishonesty was one of the few human failings he found it impossible to condone. Years later he would say vigorously when President Thomas came under discussion, "She's a liar; she's a liar." In 1916, when a group of Bryn Mawr alumnae were making a determined effort to break Miss Thomas' autocratic rule, they asked former members of the faculty to put their experiences with the administration on record. Many of them were reluctant to do so but Neilson felt that he owed it to the present faculty to comply. He gave oral testimony to the alumnae committee and also wrote a letter for publication in the *Philadelphia Public Ledger,* 28 March 1916. In this he gave an account of Miss Thomas' procedure in regard to his reappointment and stated that

> I have known a large number of Bryn Mawr instructors, and I believe my experience to be typical. Very few, if any of those I have talked with believe that Miss Thomas is to be trusted to carry out her oral agreements.

Miss Thomas was, of course, much offended by this letter, and still more by Neilson's giving oral testimony to the alumnae committee. When, in 1917 he, too, became a college president and he and Miss Thomas found themselves inevitably attending the same conferences, inaugurations, commencements, and other academic gatherings, she declined to recognize Neilson's existence. He took delight in putting her in positions where she could not ignore him without making the gesture deliberate and conspicuous. Once he even fetched her coat from the cloakroom and helped her on with it.

Yet with all his contempt for her dishonesty Neilson recognized clearly Miss Thomas' excellent qualities and felt always for the College she had built both affection and admiration. It gave him great pleasure to renew his relations when Marion Park, whom he had long admired, became Miss Thomas' successor. Invited to speak at her inauguration in October 1922, Neilson congratulated the College on its choice, emphasizing Miss Park's scholarship, her wide experience, and her personal qualities.

> She has poise, an alert intelligence, a quiet but keen and pervasive humor, and solid integrity. I should find it hard to prescribe a more desirable list of qualities, and the last is the supreme essential.

The official version of that paragraph in the address—which he wrote out later at Miss Park's request—ends there, but those who were present at the ceremony do not forget the consternation of the company when Neilson added: "At last Bryn Mawr has an honest president."

He went on then to congratulate Miss Park on her choice of a college to be president of.

> The honor which she has gained [he said] is a great honor because Bryn Mawr is a distinguished college. Its distinction lies first in the level of scholarship at which it has aimed and which it has so largely maintained from its first administration till now.

On the occasion of Smith's fiftieth anniversary celebration in 1925, Neilson conferred upon President Park the honorary degree of LL.D. Praising her as a "sound scholar and able executive, under whose wise guidance her alma mater promises to add fresh glories to the great and unique traditions established under her illustrious predecessor."

6

Harvard and Columbia

RELIEVED of the curious oppressions of Bryn Mawr, Neilson began his Harvard teaching with gusto. The list of his courses was almost as imposing as it had been in Miss Thomas' catalogue: Chaucer, Bacon, Milton, the Seventeenth Century, sometimes Shakespeare, sometimes Anglo-Saxon—things shifted a little from year to year—and a graduate course in Scottish literature from Barbour to Lyndesay. Often he shared a course with Kittredge or with F. N. Robinson, a contemporary with whom he enjoyed working.

The students liked Neilson at once, both in the classroom and outside it. They elected his courses in agreeably large numbers and they insisted on making him an honorary member of almost every campus organization with any pretension to an interest in letters—Signet, the *Advocate,* the *Lampoon,* the *Monthly,* and others more ephemeral. Of his other relationships in the years between 1901 and 1904 there is no very consecutive record but glimpses are to be had down various illuminating corridors.

On his return to Cambridge Neilson earned his lodging by performing the rather nominal duties of a University proctor in Quincy Hall, which rears its flatiron shape at the corner of Mass. Avenue and Plympton Street. To his oddly shaped room, in the small end of the iron, three young men, all of them at the dawn of distinguished careers, used to mount frequently at midnight, after each of them had put in a hard evening getting up the morrow's lecture. They were Sidney Bradshaw Fay who, in 1929, was to publish the definitive study of *The Origins of the World War,* to teach at Dartmouth and, for many years, at Smith, before returning to Cambridge as the first Radcliffe-Harvard professor; George H. Chase who was to become Hudson Professor of Archaeology and Dean of the Harvard Graduate School; and O. M. W. Sprague who was to be a professor in the Harvard School of Business Administration and one of the few Americans ever appointed a Director of the Bank of England. The four had at these midnight meetings talk which they remembered with pleasure all their lives, most of it on politics and literature. Neilson sat always curled up in his windowseat in the curve of the flatiron, a tumbler of whiskey in hand. Sometimes his visitors could persuade him to read them ballads in his rich Scots and then, Fay has recorded, "It was like being transported into another age. Afterwards we would go back to our rooms immensely refreshed, freed of worries about the morning's lectures, and ready for a sound sleep."

Whether he spent the evening in conversation or working by himself, Neilson in those days kept late hours, usually hurrying across the Yard to breakfast in Memorial Hall just before the doors closed at nine. Chase, who was an early riser, remembered with amusement the morning he met Neilson crossing the Yard at seven-thirty and inquired what was wrong. "I have an exam at eleven," Neilson explained, "and it isn't printed yet." "For Heaven's sake," said Chase, "how do you manage?" "Come on and I'll show you," Neilson answered and they hurried together to the Publications Office. "Good morning, Mr. Wilson," called Neilson, waving his examination paper at the director, a fellow countryman of his, " 'Scots wha hae.' Here's an examination due at ten o'clock. Can ye do it?" The Banockburn battlecry was effective. "Sure, Mr. Neilson," said his fellow countryman heartily, "shew ye proof at eight-thirty." So Neilson ate a leisurely breakfast and the paper was duly delivered to his eleven o'clock class.

Often on a Saturday evening Neilson and Fay took the horse-car across the Charles River Bridge to attend that most Bostonian of institutions a Symphony Concert. Neither of them knew very much about music but they were lucky enough to have the companionship of Daniel Gregory Mason who usually gave them a little lecture beforehand, playing the themes on his piano. After the concert the three adjourned to the Copley Square Hotel, to enjoy a potation composed of three parts beer, two parts Dog's Head ale, and one part Guinness stout. This is the only record of any regular concert attendance on the part of Neilson who used to say that the span of his musical attention was fifteen minutes.

The kind of impression Neilson made at this time on his elders is suggested by a letter from Mrs. Laura E. Richards whom he met in the summer of 1902 during the earliest of his many sojourns in Maine. Neilson was staying with his friend Lawrence J. Henderson (later head of the department of physical chemistry in the Harvard Medical School) and together they went to visit Henderson's classmate Henry Howe Richards who was helping his father with the running of his camp for boys at North Belgrade. The whole Richards family seem to have liked Neilson on sight and a genuine friendship developed. The Richards were delighted to have a real Scot with whom they could discuss R. L. S. and Burns and Sir Walter, and Neilson found particular comfort in talking with the warmly sympathetic Mrs. Richards about his mother who had died in 1899, after long suffering with cancer. On his return to Cambridge he sent Mrs. Richards a little essay of his on "The Preaching Scot" (*Harvard Monthly,* May 1902) in which he had made the point that "the Scot by race and breeding is an inveterate preacher" who cannot express himself in any literary form without working in a sermon. On 30 July 1902 Mrs. Richards wrote

I was very glad indeed to get the Preaching Scot—delightful title! and should have thanked you before for it. I like what you say, and I like your way of saying it; only, I think you might have given us more. . . Don't you want to write another article under the same title, about five times the length of this, and quote somewhat largely from R. L. S. print it in the Atlantic? I wish you would! . . . so, since you are sworn to live your life, and not to wear an easy heart, I lay another burden on your shoulders.—I do hope that you are less tired than when you were here, and that the "venomed sting" is long a thing of the past. . . Please don't work so hard! please remember that the one set of nerves and things has to last the voyage, and that it will be a good long voyage. You will not mind my saying this, first, because every woman is a Scot so far as preaching goes, and secondly, because, as you said, we have really known each other a good while. . . I wish you may have seen Edwin Robinson again, and got hold of him a little. I have read "Captain Craig" five times now, and it is better every time.

Of the acquaintance with E. A. Robinson the only traces are two characteristic notes regretting that he had missed Neilson who called on him twice that fall, once in Boston, once in New York. "I snarled with rage," Robinson wrote, "or something like it, when I found that you had missed me a second time, and then I filled my pipe and went for Dr. Xenophon." Neilson's admiration for Robinson's verse was high; he found in it the quality for which he most cared in literature, an illumination of human nature by poetic insight.

The tendency to overwork which worried Mrs. Richards came in part from Neilson's attempts to supplement by lecturing and reviewing his far from munificent instructor's salary. He wanted to share with his brother Robert, particularly since their mother's death, the care of the sisters who were not always strong enough to carry on their respective professions of teaching and nursing. In the fall of 1903 Miss Lizzie and Miss Jean, as his friends called them, came to Cambridge, where Miss Lizzie kept house for the three at 13 1/2 Hilliard Street while Miss Jean served as a public health nurse.

While he was at Bryn Mawr Neilson had begun to do some reviewing, unsigned, for the *Nation,* and, not long after his return to Harvard, Bliss Perry, who met him in the rooms of a young Southern historian, William Garrett Brown, and was impressed by his talk, enlisted him as a reviewer of scholarly books for the *Atlantic.* Perry was pleased to find that Neilson not only wrote easily and well but could be depended upon to make his reviews the right length and to get them in on time. Neilson wrote long critical articles on such books as Gummere's *The Beginnings of Poetry* and Furness' Variorum edition of Shakespeare's *Twelfth Night.* Perry even entrusted him (December 1902) with Thomas Wentworth Higginson's life of Longfellow, in the American Men of Letters series. The young Scottish reviewer treated Colonel Higginson with proper respect but he did not hesitate to take exception on some points where he knew that he himself was better informed than the biographer.

> Only his [Higginson's] own closeness to his subject explains how he can fail to be aware of the attitude of the younger generation toward the poetry of Longfellow. Whether the reaction is justified is another matter, but reaction there surely is. . . This is easy enough to understand. Longfellow, though rich in allusion, was never precious, never eccentric, never obscure, and those who sniff at him today are apt to be enamored of just those qualities. American poets of the rising generation are in general no more spontaneous, no more free from tradition in phrase and figure than he was, but they are often affected and usually difficult to understand. If this be distinction, Longfellow had none of it.

Nor would Neilson agree with Higginson's statement that Longfellow had a real desire to help in the creation of a native American literature.

> Americanism in the sense in which we apply the word to Bret Harte or Mark Twain, or in which Mr. Kipling defines it in An American, is not to be found in Longfellow, even in germ. He shows no consciousness of its existence, and consequently no effort to express it.

A few months earlier the Scot had risen to a defense of American scholarship, writing as though he thought of himself as an American:

> It is sometimes charged against American scholarship that it does not produce books. Journal articles on special topics, dissertations on the infinitely minute, monographs on remote obscurities,—these we have in abundance, but hardly a book. The larger grasp necessary for handling facts in their more general bearings is said to be lacking; or, if it exists, it is unaccompanied by the courage to state those generalizations which are, after all, the main end of scholarship. This indictment, if it were substantiated, would seem to indicate that our scholars are yet largely in the stage of apprenticeship; but we may at least take comfort in the fact that the fault is one springing from

caution and modesty, and so, if we judge from other manifestations of the national spirit, not likely to be fatal or permanent.

In this article, "Two Books about Poetry" (March 1902), Neilson set in contrast, leaving the inference to the reader, *The Beginnings of Poetry* by Professor Francis B. Gummere of Haverford and *Life in Poetry. Law in Taste* by Professor W. J. Courthope of Oxford. The American book is summarized as "laden with erudition as wide and deep as any German of them all can show, yet revealing a mind alert, many-sided, profound, mastering and not mastered by its learning"; the English volume is "sane and suggestive, a typical outcome of conservative English culture."

Neilson had, as a matter of fact, been thinking for a good many years about Americanism, studying it in the various manifestations in which it occurred in Cambridge and its vicinity. He even took the trouble, by way of research, to attend a Fourth of July celebration in a neighboring country town, where he found himself moved to take issue with the orator of the day whose remarks about the British were influenced more by patriotism than by accuracy. Neilson was fairly certain now that his future lay in the United States but he still felt himself ardently Scottish, as is attested by a printed announcement preserved among the slender stock of Cambridge memorabilia:

The Scotia Club desires the presence of all who may be interested, at its Third Anniversary and Robert Burns Birthday Celebration at Athenaeum Hall, Saturday evening, January 25, 1902, at 8 o'clock. William Allan Neilson, M.A., Ph.D. of Harvard University, will give an address on "Robert Burns" in which he will render several of his best known poems. He will also read "The Last Night," from "A Window in Thrums."

("The Last Night" was the chapter which had caused Neilson, the Edinburgh student, to write his letter to Barrie.)

Like reviewing, teaching at Radcliffe was another standard means of supplementing a Harvard salary but Neilson, differing in this from many of his colleagues, did not do it merely as a remunerative chore; he really believed in the importance of the higher education of women. When he went to Smith in 1917 the *Radcliffe Quarterly* (November 1917) expressed grateful appreciation of the fact that, during his years of teaching at the "Annex," he had never questioned the value of giving women the same intellectual training as men, nor had he asserted it; he took it for granted. That is one reason why he was in demand as a speaker at Radcliffe gatherings even though he sometimes left the alumnae gasping. On one occasion, for instance, he made the sapient remark that Dean Briggs's chief contribution as President of Radcliffe had been to make that college respectable. On another, he drew a contrast between the attitudes of Radcliffe and Harvard students towards their professors.

> In the Yard one lived in a state of war. One collected munitions and conducted campaigns, not against ignorance but against indifference and reluctance. You battered at the minds of Harvard students, who conducted, on the whole, a rather successful defiance. And you came down Garden Street to the Fay House or the Browne and Nichols building into another atmosphere, an atmosphere receptive and responsive and perfectly willing to grow. That is why it was a joy to teach at Radcliffe.

Among the young women who crowded Neilson's Radcliffe lecture room was Helen Keller who entered in the fall of 1899 and took her A.B. degree, *cum laude,* in 1904. She was accompanied by her companion-teacher Anne Sullivan (married in 1905 to Neilson's student and colleague John Macy), who sat beside her tapping the lecturer's words into her palm. One of their fellow students remembers how she used to turn round in her seat to watch Miss Keller's face light up, a moment after the rest of the class had responded to some flash of the Neilson wit. Mrs. Macy's biographer says that Neilson was the only one of Miss Keller's instructors who took the trouble to learn the manual alphabet so that he could communicate with her directly. He told Miss Keller and Miss Sullivan that it was fortunate their minds were so different; it made it possible to tell where one left off and the other began. Always sympathetic with anyone who cared enough for an education to acquire it under difficulties, Neilson admired Miss Keller's extraordinary courage and tenacity but even more the accomplishment of Miss Sullivan which he thought people were inclined to underestimate. Reviewing for the *Atlantic* (June 1903) Helen Keller's *Story of My Life,* he agreed that the superlatives lavished on it have seldom been so well deserved but added that the reviewers "have not always wondered most at the strangest things." Miss Keller's qualities are more moral than intellectual; there is no need to claim for her genius; that was in the teacher. "Nowhere does one read of a process so nearly approaching to the creation of a soul."

It was as another supplement to salary that Neilson began, in a modest way, the editing of Shakespeare which was to become his most important contribution to American scholarship. In July 1901 he signed a contract with Scott, Foresman of Chicago to edit nine Shakespeare plays, three a year, for their Lake Classics, a series of school texts which sold for twenty-five cents apiece. (He had already edited for the series Milton's Minor Poems.) The work required a biographical and critical introduction and fairly copious notes for young readers. That Neilson should be engaged to undertake this was suggested to the firm by L. S. Damon (then at the University of Chicago, later at Brown). The publishers wanted Neilson to agree to edit at least a dozen plays but he felt that that would take too much time from the kind of original research in which he, and Harvard, were primarily interested.

Neilson accomplished his editing with dispatch but the appearance of the little Shakespeares was disappointingly retarded by various publishing delays. Before the work was finished, in 1902, Bliss Perry, who was serving as general editor for Houghton Mifflin's Cambridge Edition of the Poets, asked Neilson to edit for that series *The Complete Dramatic and Poetic Works of William Shakespeare*. This promised to be not only a much more remunerative but a much more scholarly labor since it required the making of a new Shakespeare text, and Neilson was eager to undertake it. As no competition was involved with their school textbooks Scott, Foresman gave their consent and thereafter, though he completed the promised nine Lake plays, Neilson devoted the major portion of his energies to the Cambridge Shakespeare which was published in 1906. The academic world welcomed it as the best one-volume edition of Shakespeare yet produced. "The biographical sketch and the introductions to the separate plays are models of judicious condensation and comprehensiveness," said A. H. Thorndike in *Modern Language Notes* (June 1907). "Nothing of importance in the entire field of Shakespeare research seems to have escaped the editor." A second edition with a few revisions was published in 1908; a third in 1910.

The work on the Cambridge Shakespeare was the beginning of a long and pleasant association with Houghton Mifflin. In the spring of 1904 Neilson suggested to them that he should edit a Types of English Literature series, the plan for which is an example of his propensity to make an original analysis of any subject with which he might be concerned. The chronological method hitherto employed in the study of English literature, he said in his Prefatory Note to the first volume, has certain defects:

> The separation of periods tends to exaggerate the differences between them, and to obscure the essential continuity of literary history. . . The purpose of the series . . . is to attempt the division of the field along vertical instead of horizontal lines.

Neilson interested a number of excellent scholars in his idea and a good series was planned. He himself intended to do the book on Allegory, a subject on which his *Court of Love* thesis had set him working. Five volumes appeared: *The Popular Ballad* by Francis B. Gummere of Haverford; *The Literature of Roguery,* by F. W. Chandler of the University of Cincinnati; *Tragedy,* by A. H. Thorndike of Columbia; *The English Lyric,* by Felix E. Schelling of the University of Pennsylvania; *Saints' Legends,* by Gordon Hall Gerould of Princeton. The writers of these books thought Neilson an ideal editor and scholars generally were commendatory but the books sold slowly and Houghton Mifflin finally decided to abandon the series.

For these and other scholarly projects Neilson found it increasingly difficult to make time. The courses at Radcliffe, added to those at Harvard, made a heavy teaching load and he saw no prospect of fewer hours or a larger salary. There was nothing unusual in his situation. One of President Eliot's serious faults as an administrator was his indifference to the amount of drudgery university routine imposed on the scholars in his faculty. Even Child, Eliot's neighbor and intimate friend, struggled for years under a burden of undergraduate themes, till a call from the Johns Hopkins opened Eliot's eyes to the fact that a distinguished scholar's work on ballad literature was being seriously curtailed by a task which a young instructor could easily perform. It is not surprising, therefore, that Eliot was unaware that Dr. Neilson was not getting on as rapidly as he would like to do with his Shakespeare text.

In the fall of 1903, Neilson's friend George Rice Carpenter, then chairman of the department of English at Columbia, suggested that he accept a professorship there. Neilson had no desire to leave Harvard but it was a kind of principle with him not to ask for an increase in salary—through all his professorial and administrative life he never did. Instead, on 14 December 1903, he wrote to Carpenter:

> The dilemma in which your letter . . . placed me has been made a good deal harder by the kindness of my colleagues here, and I confess that decision has been very difficult. But the opportunities which your proposal offers are too tempting to be overcome, and I shall be obliged if you will communicate to President Butler my willingness to accept the proposal.
>
> I understand that I begin work at Columbia next September as Adjunct Professor at $2500 a year, and that, in the event of my work proving satisfactory, I receive a full Professorship in three years at the latest, at $4000 a year. I should like to have the salary of the higher position clearly understood at the outset and should be glad to have it stated in the official notification of my appointment.

A clause originally included in that last sentence was crossed out in the final copy. It indicates that Neilson had not entirely recovered from his experience at Bryn Mawr. "Because," he had written, " 'the burnt child fears the fire,' and sad experience makes me inclined to a love of explicitness which I trust will not seem discourteous." Carpenter replied:

> I can assure you that you will be welcomed very heartily, and that every effort will be made on the part both of the Department and the University to enable you to lead here the scholar's life of digni-

fied research and the instruction that naturally accompanies it, without burdening you by too many hours of teaching, by too many elementary or trivial subjects of teaching, or by similar disadvantages, of whatever kind.

Neilson's work, it was agreed, would be chiefly with graduate students, he would teach Shakespeare, Chaucer, and mediaeval literature. The whole teaching load would be eight hours a week as opposed to Harvard's twelve.

Not, apparently, till late in the spring did Eliot hear of Neilson's imminent departure. He immediately attempted to stop it by a counter offer for he had a high opinion of the young Scotsman and did not want to lose him. Neilson would have been glad to accept the proffered advance in Harvard rank and salary if President Butler had not declined to release him from the contract already signed. Eliot was disappointed but he refused to accept defeat. He began immediately to make plans two years in the future, so that Neilson set out for Columbia with a recall to Harvard practically in his pocket.

He was by no means sure, though, that he wanted to accept it, and he entered wholeheartedly on his new duties and relationships. He and his sisters established themselves in an agreeable apartment, at 419 West 118th Street, within easy walking distance of the University. They found the city interesting and their new friends and acquaintances cordial and almost too hospitable. Neilson much enjoyed his colleagues, who included Carpenter, Jefferson Fletcher, and Ashley Thorndike with whom he was to work for many years in fruitful collaboration.

The Columbia students were pleasantly enthusiastic about Neilson's classes. One of them, Virginia Gildersleeve, later Dean of Barnard, has recorded that

> His sound and wide knowledge, his imagination, and his vigorous and animated manner made him a really great teacher. His standards were extremely high, and I remember his tearing to pieces the reports made by most of his graduate students of that year in his Shakespeare seminar.

To his regular professional labors at Columbia Neilson added, as he had done in Cambridge, some unpaid teaching of a different type of student. Through his Bryn Mawr friend Bakewell he became interested in the Wage Earners' Institute, established by Thomas Davidson on New York's lower east side. Davidson was a Scot from Aberdeen who emigrated to America as a young man. Though his writing on philosophy and education was respected in academic circles he refused to connect himself with any institution until, towards the end of his life, he became interested in a group of "intelligent breadwinners," who seriously wanted an education. He planned and conducted for them a class in history and sociology which eventually grew into the Wage Earners' Institute, established in connection with the Educational Alliance on Henry Street. There Neilson gave, on alternate Saturdays, a course of lectures on "Types of Character in Literature (mainly Shakespeare)." He also lectured frequently at the summer sessions of the School which were held at Glenmore, Davidson's house in the Adirondacks. When Bakewell edited Davidson's writings on the *Education of Wage-Earners,* Neilson read and advised him on the manuscript and when Davidson's friends wanted to put the School on a permanent basis he served as vice-president of the committee by which the funds were raised. Writing of the School many years later he described it as "a voluntary undertaking carried on with great enthusiasm by both teachers and students and resulting in not only a higher level of culture but in the opening of careers, in some cases of high distinction, to many of the students."

Whether he should decide for Columbia or Harvard it was now quite clear to Neilson that it was the United States which offered him the chance to count among his fellows for what he was worth, the chance to make the most of himself. It was not fair, he thought, to accept America's opportunities without accepting also the responsibilities of an American. He took out papers in the Southern District of New York and in August 1905 became an American citizen.

7

Offenburg

DURING his years as an instructor at Harvard Neilson had become increasingly conscious that his German was not nearly so fluent as his philological studies demanded. By 1904 he was able to arrange a summer in Europe, most of it to be spent in Germany. He went first to join his friend Lawrence Henderson who had been studying during the winter at the University of Strasbourg. Living in the same pension was another Harvardian, Herman M. Adler (later professor of psychiatry in the University of Chicago), and when Neilson expressed his desire to find some family who would be willing to take him in for a few weeks of German conversation, Adler offered to write to his mother's friend Frau Oskar Muser. Her husband was a lawyer in Offenburg, a manufacturing town near Baden, just across the border from Alsace. The letter went off and on a sunny July afternoon a few days later the three young men presented themselves expectantly in the Muser garden.

The Musers' side of the incident was amusingly recorded forty years later by Elisabeth Muser Neilson in a charming memoir, *The House I Knew* (1941).

My mother was a little flustered when Herman [in the book he is called John] asked her help in finding a family who would be willing to take in a friend of his who wanted to learn German. She sat down at once and wrote him that there was no such family in Offenburg; and Lucie [an intimate friend] stood beside her and said

"*Gott,* an American!—we might have taken him if it was not summer—but an American will sit in the bathtub all day long, and that would be inconvenient."

"Well, he is not really an American, he is Scotch," said my mother, pausing in her writing and reconsidering the new possibility, "but I suppose as far as the tub goes it would be the same."

A few days after, my mother opened the door of the livingroom, where I was practicing, and called: "Stop, and come to help with tea. [Herman] has come with his two friends—he still is looking for a place for the Scotchman." Before going down I stepped out on the balcony, for I heard voices in the garden, and wanted to see the Americans before greeting them. They stood in a line with [Herman] just across from the steps, the way people will stand when they come for the first time into a garden, the one in the middle a little stooped, his pockets bulging with what turned out to be a small dictionary in each.

Just as I came out I heard him say, "I feel like a donkey with a pack-basket on each side." "If we have to keep one, I hope we'll keep the one in the middle," I said to myself, looking at the three men like the forester's little boy who when he first inspected three newborn brothers picked the center one to rear. I did keep the one in the middle, for he became my husband; and going down the steps into the garden on that summer afternoon I walked blindly into a life of which I knew nothing.

That passage occurs at the conclusion of *The House I Knew* and is the only direct reference to Neilson, for the book is the record of Elisabeth Muser's life before she met her husband, the record of the growth, from childhood to young womanhood, of an inquiring and perceptive mind. The streets, houses, and people of Offenburg, the close-knit daily life of an affectionate family, are presented as they impinged on that young mind, highly sensitive to form and pattern and color, searching, curious, intensely interested in its own processes, convinced of the importance of feeling deeply. The writer, whose English is precise and subtle, makes shrewd comment on her own and her parents' friends. She indicates her love for music, for flowers, and all growing things. She describes her struggles with the eternal questions, which her father and mother's "gentle agnosticism" left for her unanswered, and her desire "to draw a step closer to our household gods, 'the good, the true, and the beautiful,' charmingly, if somewhat hurriedly, revered by my parents"; she remembers how she felt when she first encountered Nietzsche and Schopenhauer and Kant. She was twenty-five and a cultivated young woman when the meeting in the garden took place.

The Musers received the young men cordially. Nothing was said about the bathtub but Frau Muser suggested that if Dr. Neilson cared to put up for a few weeks at the little Hotel zum Oxen near by they would all try to help him perfect his German. In exchange, he agreed to read some English daily with Fräulein Elisabeth—Li the family called her—who had already had a year at an English boarding school. Neilson was delighted with the plan. Every morning he presented himself in the charming garden on the edge of the Black Forest and there, under the great copper beech tree, he and Fräulein Elisabeth read Creizenach's *Schauspiele der englischen Komödianten* on which Neilson was working in connection with his edition of Shakespeare. Some of the passages in those robust dramas the young man thought that it would be wiser to skip when reading with a lady but Fräulein Elisabeth insisted that they make a scholarly job of every page. After the first few days Neilson was quite regularly invited to stay for lunch with the family. At three-thirty in the afternoon he and Fräulein Elisabeth read Shakespeare together and then, more often than not, he was invited to stay for supper.

Over the Creizenach and the Shakespeare, among the apple trees and the roses, Neilson and Elisabeth Muser fell in love as swiftly and completely as though they had been characters in one of those novels by Scott the young man from Perthshire so much admired. She was eleven years younger than he, slender and lovely with fine features, soft coloring, and golden brown hair. She liked to dress in subtle combinations of pink and blue which emphasized the color of her eyes and the blush rose of her cheeks. She had all the qualities the romantic side of his nature delighted in—"meine romantische Schule" he used to call her—and, in addition, a mind sharp, subtle, witty, which played well against his own. (A Northampton friend, trying to describe the difference between the Neilsons' minds, once said that after you had discussed a situation with President Neilson you saw it much more clearly; when you had discussed it with Mrs. Neilson you felt it much more deeply.)

Before two summer days had gone by Elisabeth was saying to herself, so she confessed years later: "Oh dear, I do not want to go to America! But I must marry this man." She remembered another unspoken thought. She had one morning been showing Neilson a new rose of an exotic kind which her mother had just planted. It stood beside a bush of cabbage roses and she asked him the proper romantic question: which of the two he preferred. Neilson considered a moment carefully and said that he preferred the cabbage rose. "I must try," Elisabeth Muser admonished herself, "to be more like a cabbage rose." In that ambition she never quite succeeded but her friends, all her life long, thought of her surrounded by flowers. One of the factors that determined Neilson's decision to return from Columbia to Harvard was his inability to picture her in New York City; in Cambridge at that time even a young professor could have a garden. When, in 1939, Neilson retired from the presidency of Smith College the members of his faculty sent as a message of farewell to Mrs. Neilson a great bouquet of iris, peonies, and roses with a card which read: "The faculty will always think of you as we have seen you, among flowers—in your garden, in your home."

The rose garden courtship met, in the best romantic tradition, some heavy obstacles, though they were neither violent nor cruel ones. The first was the modesty of the young man himself who felt that he could offer Elisabeth nothing to compare with the comfort and the interest of life in the Muser household. Herr Muser was a successful lawyer and a member of the Landtag of Baden where he represented the Social Democratic party, regarded in those imperial days as a dangerously radical institution. Some of the more conservative citizens of Offenburg declined to have any social relations with the Muser household but the friends who did come were people of lively individuality, interested in the arts and in ideas. The house and garden were full of good music and good talk. Herr Muser sang delightfully to his wife's accompaniment; Elisabeth, too, sang and played with skill, and there were violinists and cellists among the visiting friends. The constant stream of company, political as well as social, was not too taxing a burden for the mother and daughter since they had the assistance of several stout and devoted peasant maids as well as visiting laundresses and seamstresses. There was a woman who came every day to stoke the porcelain stove, a man who pumped the water, and various men to work in the garden. It was a way of life very different from that in Doune.

The second obstacle to romance was the Atlantic Ocean. It is difficult today to realize the vast distance which in 1904 separated Germany from the United States and how strange and crude and even dangerous life in America seemed to the citizen of Offenburg. When the engagement was at last formally announced and Elisabeth Muser sat every afternoon in the salon with her parents receiving congratulatory callers, she was always uncomfortable until "we were past 'the great water'—for 'the great water' was mentioned every time, and I felt it was not water at all, but a rock which would shatter the smile on my parents' faces."

If it had not been for his living in America the Musers would have been delighted to have Neilson marry their daughter. His profession, of course, left nothing to be desired; Harvard they had heard of (it was built, they imagined, of white marble); personally they both became very fond of him, and about Li's sentiments there could be no question. The outcome was inevitable but the hesitations on both sides made for a long delay. After the first weeks' acquaintance, nevertheless, the Musers invited Neilson to join them when they went to spend August by the seaside at Katwyck in Holland. (He went first for a walking trip through the Hartz Mountains with William G. Howard of the German Department at Harvard.) At Katwyck the young couple became to all intents and purposes engaged, though it was agreed that there should be, as yet, nothing announced or formal.

Neilson made a brief visit to Scotland before returning to the United States and taking up his work at Columbia. A steady correspondence went on that winter between New York and Offenburg and in the summer of 1905 Neilson sailed again for Germany. Then the Musers consented to a formal engagement, with the provisos that the marriage should not take place until the summer of 1906 and that Li would promise to come home for a visit every year.

Before he sailed for Germany, Neilson had written his brother Robert of his reason for making the second journey, and on 6 June Robert Neilson wrote from Montreal:

I have already expressed to you the delight and satisfaction you have been to me, Will, and if anything more were needed to fill to the brim my cup of joy in you it was this. To see you happily married would be indeed the height of my desire for you and I am most heartily glad to think that such a consummation seems within reasonable distance. . . I never thought of such a possibility as this in connection with Elisabeth and her German garden and did not pay much attention to what was said about her and consequently don't feel in the least as if I knew her but if she pleases you, Will, I'm sure she will be all right for the rest of us. At least I am prepared to receive her at your valuation.

You ask my blessing, and I give it with all my heart. If it were in my power to grant all the happiness I wish you both perhaps it would not be good for you, but not having the bestowal, illogically I do hope and pray that you may long live to enjoy all the blessings vouchsafed to mortals and among them surely children, for if it is destined that I never have child of my own I shall look forward to the extreme pleasure of some day holding in my arms one of yours. . . God bless you, my dear boy, and believe me ever,

Your affectionate brother, Bob

After the engagement was formally announced the Musers suggested that Neilson's sister Lizzie, who was spending the summer in Scotland, be invited to pay them a visit. He urged her to accept for he thought that the sight of a Scotswoman who had made the Atlantic crossing and survived might have a soothing effect on the worried parents. There was mutual liking between the Musers and Neilson's sister and other visits followed.

During the academic year of 1905-6 Neilson taught again at Columbia, enjoying it so much that he found it difficult to make his final choice between New York and Cambridge.

The chief worry of my life from now [he wrote to Elisabeth Muser in the spring] is to know whether to stay at Columbia or to go back to Harvard. The people here are bringing great pressure of all kinds to bear on me to make me stay and my old chief [Kittredge] wants me to go back to Harvard. I owe my old Master much gratitude and it is hard to refuse him anything. I have always wanted to do something to help to repay all he has taught me; and now I feel base to refuse the opportunity when it comes. But I know that it is seldom possible to pay back obligation direct; one has usually to be content with passing it on.

The domestic argument actually helped to weight the scales. Neilson did not think a great city like New York, so Dean Virginia Gildersleeve remembers his telling students at Barnard, a good place in which to bring up children. She remembers, too, that she and her fellow students thought that Professor Neilson read aloud that winter with peculiar intensity the great love passages in *Romeo and Juliet* and *Antony and Cleopatra.*

In trying to prepare Elisabeth Muser for life in America Neilson used a scholar's device, sending her books which seemed to him to embody a way of thought and expression different from that to which she was accustomed. He chose Milton's *Lycidas* and *Comus,* Stevenson's *Virginibus Puerisque, Alice in Wonderland,* and Emerson's Essays. She liked *Comus* best.

Neilson sailed for Germany again soon after commencement and the wedding took place on 25 June 1906. The honeymoon was spent in the Black Forest, in a house to which Mrs. Neilson had often gone as a child. The kind old peasant maid who looked after them they referred to as the Wicked Uncle because it amused them to think of themselves as the Babes in the Woods. Every morning Neilson worked on his Shakespeare texts while his bride, to improve her English, translated *Wilhelm Meister.* Looking over her work he said always, she remembers, "You can do better than that." After the scholarly labors they took long walks through the forest. Neilson liked to eat black bread and cheese at the little inns and to sample the effervescent local wines, too delicate to bear transportation. In the afternoons and evenings the couple often read aloud to each other: Thackeray's *Esmond* and *The Virginians,* many of Dickens' novels, Shakespeare's Sonnets, and a great deal of romantic poetry. After the Schwarzwald they spent a little time with the Musers in Switzerland, then, in September, sailed from Rotterdam on a Holland-American liner, and went to housekeeping in Cambridge.

The path to the door of their house, 2 Riedesel Avenue, was bordered with English daisies and Neilson's friends promptly christened it Burns Walk. The house had a little garden of its own and a few blocks away was the great garden of the Longfellow house in which they were privileged to stroll. Mrs. Neilson relates that when, as a young housekeeper, she had neglected her dusting, she distracted attention from the fact by filling the house with flowers.

8

Harvard Again

Elisabeth Muser Neilson found life in Cambridge very strange indeed. She had never experienced anything in the least like it. The intellectual seriousness of the society in which she found herself she approved but she thought it an intellectuality singularly lacking in humor and untouched by any gleam of imagination. How to adjust herself to this she did not know, and her nostalgia was increased by an attack of appendicitis which sent her to the hospital for an operation not long after she and her husband landed in Boston. Everyone was sympathetic and very kind and helpful but the hospital experience intensified her sense of being in an alien world.

After she recovered, Neilson urged his bride to accept, at least for the first months, all the invitations that came to her, and she readily complied, realizing that the motive that prompted them was kindness even though the occasions to which they led were sometimes curiously oppressive. Young Mrs. Neilson was disconcerted, for instance, to find herself a member of a morning singing society composed of elderly ladies who sang together, not very well but with great seriousness, what she described to her husband as "rather virginal songs." But what troubled her most were the constant invitations to teas and luncheons attended by ladies only. Why this sharp division between the sexes? She thought it neither reasonable nor pleasant, one of the most curious elements in the American scene. Even at dinner parties, she found, the ladies were expected to retire to the drawing room as soon as the meal was finished. That Victorian custom, which lingered longer, perhaps, in Cambridge than in other parts of the country, was described by Neilson in 1929 when he made it the text of an address urging benefactors to give as generously to the women's as to the men's colleges.

What I am going to recall to those of you whose memories go back to the end of the nineteenth century was the prevailing procedure on a social occasion like a dinner, when the ladies withdrew and the gentlemen remained to talk politics, to talk shop, to talk sport, to talk that other kind of talk which they euphemistically called humor —these and other things from which the ladies were excluded. The ladies were not supposed to know much about politics. They were supposed to be totally ignorant of business and other professional "shop." They were babes in the matter of sport, and the "humor" was not for their ears.

And then, after half an hour or more over the cigars and what were then the liqueurs, some one said, "Gentlemen, shall we join the ladies?" And the ladies were supposed to have occupied themselves in the drawingroom in domestic discussions, in talk over Jack's measles and Jane's cold, and the comparison of symptoms and illnesses, in notes on fashion, in gossip about their neighbors. These trivialities were supposed to be what occupied the minds of women. These were the things from which the men saved themselves.

That was the atmosphere into which they plunged as they came out of the diningroom; and the two sets of conversations, and the separation between them, suggest pretty well what, at least in the days of your fathers, was taken for granted with regard to the minds of women and the minds of men.

The individual who most offended Mrs. Neilson by this attitude towards her sex was Professor George Lyman Kittredge. When her sister-in-law took her to return Mrs. Kittredge's first call the great man stood in the doorway of the drawingroom, vouchsafing an occasional remark but obviously not thinking it worth his while to sit down and enter into conversation with a woman. And when Kittredge came to see her husband, as he frequently did, his manners were no better. Finally Mrs. Neilson, knowing how much her husband admired his colleague and former teacher, determined to win him over. She discovered that Kittredge was a real gourmet and, being skilled in that line, took pains to see that whatever she offered to him in the way of food or drink was of a superior quality. The device worked and Kittredge became in time extremely gracious, making a point whenever they met of engaging Mrs. Neilson in conversation, though always of course on topics like the weather, which he thought were within her range.

Her English, Mrs. Neilson discovered to her pleasure, served her on the whole very well, though sometimes she amused people by referring to her "marriage wows" and she found it difficult to break the European habit of invoking the Deity in minor crises. When, for instance, in reply to a question from Mrs. Barrett Wendell, she answered emphatically, "Good God, no!" she would be firmly instructed that in Cambridge we do not refer to the Deity in that way, an admonition which carried the more weight because, as Mrs. Neilson remarked to her husband, "Mrs. Wendell is not so much a person as an institution." A few days later, at a Faculty Club reception, Mrs. Neilson met President Eliot for the first time. He was cordial and kind, inquiring carefully about her recovery from appendicitis. "It is really," he remarked, "a very simple operation, but for a few days afterwards it hurts like the very devil." "Oh," cried Mrs. Neilson in delight, "I thought that in this country you could not say devil." She felt an immediate liking for the august President, but unfortunately some ladies who had partially overheard the conversation buzzed it about Cambridge that young Mrs. Neilson had reproved President Eliot for his profanity.

Most of her husband's friends Mrs. Neilson found more agreeable than Kittredge. Many of them she thoroughly enjoyed, and there were households in which the talk, both feminine and masculine, was good, though sometimes, it seemed to her, a little self-conscious. The women never quite attained that blend of learning and high spirits which her husband so much enjoyed at his lunch and dining clubs.

The masculine club then, as today, was an important element in Cambridge life. Small, carefully selected groups of friends met regularly to dine and talk, taking off frequently from a paper by one of their number on some phase of his speciality, which might be anything from Celtic verse to paleolithic botany. Some clubs were formed spontaneously by a group of friends, flourished for a while but made no effort to perpetuate themselves; others had a long and distinguished history so that election to them was a kind of public honor. Before his marriage Neilson had belonged to a small group which had no particular name until Mrs. Neilson christened them the "Käsemänner" because their standard refreshment was beer and cheese. After that they referred to themselves as the Cheesemen or the Tyrophagi, for they were all scholars who met primarily to read Greek and Latin together. The Cheesemen included Neilson's colleague F. N. Robinson; E. K. Rand, the Latinist; W. G. Howard, the German scholar; C. B. Gulick, the Greek scholar; and J. D. M. Ford, the romance philologist, to whom Neilson was particularly attached because of his warm heart. He admired, too, Ford's ability to take a critical attitude towards his own Catholicism.

In addition to the Cheesemen, Neilson belonged to two monthly dining clubs. One was founded by C. M. Thompson of *The Youth's Companion;* the other Neilson himself, in conjunction with Thomas N. Carver, the economist, organized in 1909. This club met in rotation at the members' houses and, after an excellent dinner, the host talked or read a paper on some phase of his professional speciality, starting a discussion which went on until a late hour. The discussions had an interesting variety for the membership included John W. Ames, the architect (he and his wife were close friends of the Neilsons); Robert Webster, a Boston lawyer; and, from the Harvard faculty, H. E. Clifford, engineering; Charles H. Grandgent, Italian; Jeremiah Smith and Samuel Williston, law; Joseph L. Goodale, medicine; William Z. Ripley, political economy.

In addition to these personal groups Neilson was a member of two clubs which are part of Cambridge history. In 1903, in his first year as a Harvard instructor, he was elected a literary member of Papyrus, a lively group of practitioners of the arts who liked to call themselves Bohemians and whose monthly dinners were gay with skits and witty verse. In 1920, after he had become

President of Smith, Neilson's Cambridge friends lured him back from time to time by making him a member of the Tavern Club, the most solidly established and respectable of all the convivial institutions. The Tavern Club dates from 1884 when it was organized by a group of young men interested in art, literature, and science. Its first president was William Dean Howells. Its name derived from Dr. Johnson's pronouncement that "there is nothing which has yet been contrived by man by which so much happiness is produced as by a good tavern or inn." Bliss Perry was president of the Tavern Club at the time of Neilson's election; the membership had grown to two hundred; and there was a Boston clubhouse, on Boylston Place, where Neilson made his headquarters when he came down from Northampton.

In the family life which began in Cambridge Neilson took great pleasure, even though, as his daughters used to remark with amusement after they grew up, he had no interest at all in small children. This was, they thought, because he found it difficult to communicate with anyone who could not talk in rational sentences. He had the same trouble with animals. Whenever a new dog was about to be introduced into the household he would try to prevent its entrance, citing all the worries and labors sure to be involved, but, when the dog arrived—for Mrs. Neilson agreed with the children that animals are essential to a home—they noted that after a few days Father was more indulgent and affectionate with the creature than anyone else.

The garden Neilson had imagined for Elisabeth Muser became a reality in 1908 when they moved from Riedesel Avenue to 34 Kirkland Street. The large white clapboard house, of the Greek Revival period, stands on a bank well above the road, at that time little troubled by noisy traffic. In any event family living went on chiefly at the rear of the house where there was space for an ample garden which Neilson worked with great pleasure. Mrs. Neilson's parents wanted to make them a present of the new house, but this Neilson declined, though he was glad to accept a loan which made it possible for them to move in sooner than they might otherwise have done.

All three of the children were born in the Kirkland Street house: Allan on 3 October 1909; Margaret, 30 July 1912; and

Caroline, 5 January 1917. While they were babies Neilson paid comparatively little attention to them but, as they grew older, both son and daughters found their father surprisingly sympathetic and comprehending of their points of view. Allan was a boy full of promise, serious, sensitive, with an alert mind and a strength of character beyond his years. His father was proud when, in his first year away from home, at Milton Academy, he fought through by himself certain difficult situations, not telling his parents about them until they had been resolved. "He consumed his own smoke," Neilson said admiringly to one of his friends. Caroline inherited her father's rapid mind and both she and Allan shared his love of books so that his intimacy with them developed more readily than with the elder daughter, Margaret, who had a real vocation for the land. "Is it my fault," she asked her mother, "if a calf seems to me more important than Shakespeare?" This point of view troubled her father, but when he became convinced that it was genuine he lent her generous aid in preparing herself for her calling. She herself admired her father even when they seemed very far apart and, after she had children of her own, she set down on paper a sensitive and understanding account of their developing relationship.

Earliest Memories: Awe, respect, prevailing emotions at that time; feared his impatience. Earliest memories—Maine—swimming (on his back), digging clams, row boat rowing to island. Watching him doing carpentry in basement of barn in Maine, picking vegetables in the garden. Seemed to me to be surrounded by an atmosphere of books, papers, tobacco smoke and fierce concentration.

Early Northampton Days: *Xmas*—walking round and round the candlelit tree with a pair of bellows ready to blow out any twigs that might catch fire. Occasionally joining in the singing with great pleasure and off key.

Scene with Sir Walter 2nd. Sir Walter snapped at Caroline. Father became very angry and whipped the dog. I had never seen him use physical violence before. It frightened me and at the same time I remember taking it as a proof of his love for us children that the snapping of a dog would be the cause of such violent emotion on his part.

During my grade school years I never remember his criticizing me for my low marks but he showed great concern for my lack of interest in acquiring knowledge. For him to learn was a privilege. His disapproval of my attitude towards school created a gap between us. In spite of his very diverse interests he could not reconcile himself to my preoccupation with animals and strenuous outdoor activities.

Later Northampton Days: When did he start reading aloud to the family? I seem to remember this as starting in my early 'teens. At any rate it caused a very profound change in my relationship with him. We had an interest in common. Great variety in his choice of reading matter—anything from Chaucer to Hyman Kaplan.

1929: Just before leaving for my year abroad—a very vivid interview in the study. About the difficulties of growing up in one's own family. How hard it is for a family to follow and accept the change from child to adult while one is in daily contact with them. After a year of absence it would be much easier for the family to accept me as a more grown up person. My return from Europe would be a very opportune time for me to turn over a new leaf. I should make the most of the opportunity. I was quite overcome by such sympathy for and understanding of my personal difficulties.

Caroline, the younger daughter, cherished as indicative of this understanding of their developing minds her father's response one evening when she interrupted an official dinner party in Northampton by wailing from the staircase, "Father, I haven't had enough asparagus." The President left his guests and went out into the hall to answer her gravely, "No, Caroline, no one ever has enough asparagus"—a remark she found at the time both wise and comforting, and which still seemed so after she grew up.

The family dinners were often noisy, for all three children, like their parents, were fluent of speech and each of them enjoyed dominating the table. Neilson often resorted to conducting the conversation like an orchestra leader, pointing now to Margaret, now to Caroline, now to Allan as he thought it appropriate for one or the other to take up the theme. One of the favorite dinnertable topics was the comparative excellence of European and American customs and manners. In these discussions Allan usually sided with his mother, the girls hotly defended the United States, and Neilson attempted to maintain a judicial neutrality. Wearied by the noise of their battles, he often referred to the children as the Feenians, but this seemed to them simply a good joke. Actually their voices were well modulated for Mrs. Neilson, with her sensitive musical ear, checked them constantly when they rose too loud. Both parents carefully corrected mispronunciations.

In the year after the move to Kirkland Street the Neilsons, following the example of President Eliot and many of the Harvard faculty, acquired a summer place in Maine. In Edgecomb, not far from Newcastle, they purchased for $3500 a ten acre tract on the shore of the Sheepscot River, with a house of ample size which needed only a few alterations to make it very comfortable for simple summer living. The tidal river runs cold but not too cold for swimming, the one sport Neilson really enjoyed. He swam well, though he never used anything but the breast stroke he had learned as a boy in the rivers near Doune. The Edgecomb land included a copse of birch and hemlock, a hayfield which a neighboring farmer paid ten dollars for mowing, promising to stop short at the end where the blueberries grew, a stretch of river shore where clams could be dug at low tide, and a vegetable garden which Neilson worked with energy. Various Cambridge friends—they particularly enjoyed the Ripleys—lived near enough to make a pleasantly informal social life possible, and the quiet, the coolness, the bracing salt air were ideal, Neilson found, for scholarly labor. His study was a tent set up at some distance from the house and protected by an imaginary line which no child was permitted to cross. It was true Maine country, bleak and beautiful. "God did not finish this place," said little Caroline, but it was a landscape they all grew to love and almost every summer was spent at Edgecomb until the shortage of servants during the years of the First World War made housekeeping difficult and the demands of the Smith presidency cut Neilson's summer holidays shorter and shorter. Reluctantly they sold the place in 1926.

With his departmental colleagues at Harvard Neilson's personal relations were pleasant but professionally he differed with some of them sharply and, since he could not refuse an action in defense of principle, he was frequently obliged to contend with one or another in the long and disputatious meetings of the department of English. Bliss Perry applied to the Harvard of that day Ascham's phrase, the "Cockpit of Learning," and the fiercest bouts seem to have been waged on the English side of the pit. Some of the survivors recall an occasion when Kittredge, flushed with combat, strode across the room to look at the thermometer, and F. N. Robinson remembers that Perry, leaving his first department meeting, turned to him to ask, "Is it customary at these gatherings to carry firearms?"

Perry does not record that question in his memoir *And Gladly Teach,* but he does describe his surprise at the pre-empting by certain professors of large sections of the academic terrain. A division of knowledge in which it seemed that half a dozen experts might work with profit, was considered so much the property of one man that no other teacher dared to set foot upon it. This vested right to scholarly territory Neilson was obliged to attack when, on his return from Columbia, he wanted to offer a seminar in Shakespeare. Kittredge, one of whose interests was Shakespeare, approved, but George Pierce Baker protested that Neilson would be trespassing on his preserve, the drama. The matter was discussed in Cambridge while Neilson was still in New York and some fairly heated correspondence ensued.

BAKER TO NEILSON 10 March 1906

I have been somewhat disturbed recently to hear, but indirectly, of a proposed Shakespeare seminar next year. I can perfectly understand your offering it since I hear it has been decidedly successful at Columbia, but I wonder if you have considered—apparently Kittredge has not—the bearing of it on my own work?

Kittredge wrote at the same time that Baker's attitude was "queer and indefensible" but that his animus was not against Neilson but against him, Kittredge, who had, Baker thought, suggested the Shakespeare seminary. He offered to deal roundly with Baker if Neilson would leave the matter to him, but Neilson preferred to handle the situation himself and Kittredge agreed:

I am sure you can be trusted to write to Baker with the proper mixture of common sense, friendly tact, and perspicuous *decision!* So go ahead. I think our "plays" will not get tangled.

NEILSON TO BAKER 16 March 1906

. . . As you supposed, I wished to give the Shakespeare Seminar because my work of the last four years has equipped me to do this better than anything else. I meant it to alternate with my Scots course, and put the Shakespeare for the first year because I am full of the stuff just now. But it does not greatly matter which I begin with; and if it seems best to leave the matter over till I come, the Scots can be substituted.

I am sorry you feel the proposal an encroachment upon your rights. . . There seems, however, to be a principle involved which I should like to have the Department pass upon as soon as may be. I recognize heartily your accomplishment in the Dramatic field; and the prospect of cooperating with you, both in my own work and in the training of students, was one of the pleasant prospects in returning to Cambridge. I am strongly opposed to regarding candidates for the Ph.D. as the special or exclusive products of any one member of the staff. The best results can be got only by giving the student the advantage of the scholarship and advice of all the men interested in his subject. If this can be done best by additional courses, then I see no valid objection to such courses.

The theory involved in your objection would exclude the possibility of any graduate course by another instructor from the earliest period of the drama down to our own time. I cannot believe that you contemplate this, both in view of the history of Harvard courses in Shakespeare and the Drama, and in view of the size of the Department, which does not admit of monopolies on such a large scale.

The Seminary I proposed was meant for a limited number of men, preferably such as had taken Eng. 2 and 14 [Baker's courses], and would in no sense duplicate the work of those courses. But from what you say with regard to these, I gather that the details of my plan do not affect your position. On a purely personal matter I should be eager to oblige you; but as this involves an important element of Department policy, I think it better to let my suggestion stand, that the Department may decide on it at once. Cordially yours,

The Catalogue for 1906-7 lists: "Shakespeare—Study of Special Topics, Monday, Wednesday, Friday at 9, Professor Neilson."

Those letters were preserved, apparently, because Neilson forgot about the discussion as soon as the point was settled, but they are so enlightening as to the manner in which the affairs of the department were conducted that one wishes Perry's discretion had not prevented him from furnishing us with other examples of the same kind. *And Gladly Teach* does, though, comment instructively on the complete lack of co-ordination in the departmental course offerings, and goes so far as to record that one of Perry's colleagues admitted to him that "We *have* no real department and never have had."

The great point of dissension was the relative importance of literature and linguistics. The older Germanic scholarship was just beginning to be questioned by the younger academicians. Was philology the only way to learning? Might not literary criticism also be a discipline? The older men laughed. Criticism is dangerously close to "appreciation" and dilettantism. The ability to practice it is no test of a man's merit. The mind which prefers that road is obviously too soft and lazy for the academic profession.

The foremost proponent of this point of view and the dominant figure in the department, whether or not he happened to be serving as chairman, was George Lyman Kittredge. His learning, his brilliance, his arrogance, all worked to the support of linguistics and philology. That there might be other roads to truth he would not admit, and Neilson, much against his will, felt obliged to take issue with him. He did not like to oppose Kittredge, for whom he felt both respect and gratitude, but the kind of scholarship he stood for seemed to Neilson a means not an end. Literature for Neilson was the great illuminator of life, the provider of experience, and literature was, he thought, in the Harvard of that day, insufficiently respected. Henry James, looking at Cambridge at the same moment, said that literature there was moribund:

> We see the great University sit and look very hard, at blue horizons of possibility, across the high table-land of her future; but the light of literary desire is not perceptibly in her eye (nothing is more striking than the recent drop in her of any outward sign of literary curiosity). (*The American Scene*)

James, of course, was only an observer. Those who were looking to Harvard for literary guidance were much more bitter. On 14 May 1906 Stuart Sherman sent a letter to the *Nation* which provoked from both camps a storm of intemperate utterance.

Sherman had taken a Harvard Ph.D. in 1906 and gone to teach at the University of Illinois, so he spoke of what he knew. His letter described the fate of the young men of literary tastes and aspirations who make their way to the great Eastern universities supposing that there they will come in contact with professors who are men of letters.

> They are much surprised. They are bidden to provide themselves with an adding machine to count the occurrence of "fish" and "flesh" in the poetry of the fourteenth and fifteenth centuries; they are asked to hearken to the vowels and consonants singing together through the Dark Ages; they are invited to embrace inspiring relics of the Gothic gospels. . .

Their teachers wish them to be "scholarly," by which they mean

> true to the bare literal fact, objectively presented, unrelieved by humor or feeling, embanked and barricaded with notes . . . every mouse must be accompanied by the mountain that brought it forth.

Those Gothic gospels were the great bone of contention among the requirements for the Harvard Ph.D. No one could pretend that Gothic opened the door to any literature worth reading but its defenders stood for it stoutly. There were strong contenders on the other side. Even Robinson was ready to let Gothic go, though he held out for Anglo-Saxon and Old French. Neilson, characteristically, suggested a compromise. He wanted Robinson to offer, as a substitute for Gothic, a course in English historical grammar. The argument was hot, but Gothic stayed. Kittredge was not only a powerful personality but an astute academic politician.

Neilson's interest in the "modern" period—1640-1900—resulted in his taking charge of most of the men who were writing doctoral dissertations in this field, a roster which soon topped the dissertations in Anglo-Saxon and Middle English. His supervision was in demand, too, because he had the reputation of taking a personal interest in anyone who worked under him and of being very generous with his time.

In the undergraduate program Neilson shared with Robinson and Kittredge the work in Middle English, Chaucer, and Shakespeare, taught a course in the romantic poets, and gave the half-year courses in Bacon and Milton which had formerly been taught by Child. He often gave the course in Shakespeare during the summer session. His attitude towards the average Harvard undergraduate one may deduce from a passage in a lecture he delivered in 1938 to the Association for Adult Education. He was speaking of the difficulty of learning to read well and said that what first drew his attention to this problem was his experience when

Autumn after autumn I used to attempt to teach a group of Harvard undergraduates to read the works of Bacon. I gave the course at eleven o'clock in the forenoon on Monday, Wednesday, and Friday—a time when the athlete is up and is not engaged in football practice. Consequently, I had the honor of leading through the works of Bacon a large number of well-born, well-fed, well-developed specimens of American manhood, some of whom now adorn the Halls of Congress.

Bacon is perhaps the leanest of the great English writers in the sense that his prose is pure muscle—no fat, no extra words. . . Here was material fit to test whether men could actually follow pure thought. Bacon has a trick of style, by which he will open an essay by writing, "It was a wise saying of so-and-so and worthy of our consideration." In the next sentence he will proceed to tell you what the saying was.

Time after time, day after day, year after year, I called on the gentleman at the end of the third bench and would say, "What does Bacon mean by 'it'—'it was a wise saying'?"

He would look at the sentence and say, "I don't know."

I would say, "Would you kindly read the second sentence aloud?"

He would read the second sentence, flush slightly, and provide the answer. Three times a week, on it went. That simple little device threw them off the track. So accustomed were they to intellectual feeding, spoonful by spoonful, that they had no power of suspending their intellectual attention until they got what came after.

Expressions of enthusiasm for Neilson's teaching are many and warm. One of the most detailed and interesting was set down by Howard R. Patch who was his student at Harvard and later his colleague at Smith. Patch followed almost all of Neilson's courses, both undergraduate and graduate. Of the course in the Romantic Poets he says:

I learned what it may mean to play with ideas under the rules of strict intellectual honesty and discipline. Mr. Neilson made us aware of what delight there may be in a really detached approach to the consideration of an idea for its own sake. His mind was rigorous and searching and at the same time showed a flexibility that was almost —it seemed to the beginner—irresponsibility. He had the power to reveal the fun (among other things) of the intellectual life.

In his course on Middle Scottish Literature he showed us what was in his blood. Surely few people could read Scottish poetry as he did. Here we found a combination of the scholarly approach (never for a moment relaxed) with a sense of literary values and artistic importance. He was willing to let himself go in showing his delight in some poem. On the other hand in his seminar on Shakespeare it was the scholar who was uppermost. He taught us the right methods in editing the text and in the investigation of the period.

I shall never forget my amazement at how detailed his comments on my long papers and the chapters of my thesis were. He would exert himself to see the student's point of view and would help us to find expression for even those ideas that he himself found antipathetic.

To Neilson's ability to teach poetry—Scottish or English—by reading it aloud there is a continuing testimony from the men and women who sat in his classes. You always felt, one of them said, as though he had written the poem himself and so knew exactly how it was meant to be timed and phrased.

> Milton, thou shouldst be living at this hour,
> Neilson is reading thee,

ran the caption under a cartoon portrait in the *Lampoon*. It is on record, too, that he could read the whole first sentence of *Paradise Lost* on one breath.

While he was at Columbia Neilson had been favorably impressed by the relationship between that University and its woman's college. Barnard was treated as a co-ordinate unit, not, like Radcliffe, as an annex where Harvard professors, prompted by altruism or a desire for money, might, if they choose, repeat their courses. At Columbia a man could be appointed, as Neilson was, to teach at both Columbia and Barnard. To promote at Harvard the joint-professorship idea, Neilson declined, during the first year of his return to Cambridge, to teach at Radcliffe at all.

But, as he told a gathering of Radcliffe alumnae twenty years later (1929),

> Nobody noticed it. I needed the money and, being by nature a realist and a compromiser, I decided that it was futile to make this determination in the dark, and that I had better go on teaching at Radcliffe College and keep talking about the other way. Again nobody noticed. I went on for ten more years and then I went away, and then Miss Comstock did it. And now the system of joint appointment is beginning [with Sidney Fay from Smith].

The scholarly reputation which Neilson had established by his editing of the Cambridge Shakespeare he steadily increased and extended. He was one of the few Americans invited to contribute to the *Cambridge History of English Literature,* published in this country by Macmillan. He wrote the chapters on the Elizabethan dramatists Ford and Shirley (vol. vii, 1911). In the same year he edited for the Cambridge Poets Series *The Chief Elizabethan Dramatists.* In 1916, for the same series, he edited, in collaboration with his colleague K. G. T. Webster, *The Chief British Poets of the Fourteenth and Fifteenth Centuries.* The adjective "British" replaces here the usual "English" of the series because, as the Preface states, Neilson was projecting a little of the national propaganda about which he felt a missionary zeal.

> A notable feature of the collection is the prominence given to the Scottish poets of the period . . . in the matter of poetic quality none of Chaucer's English disciples is the equal of Henryson or Dunbar. The latter, it is true, is often mentioned if seldom read; but it is doubtful whether there is in the whole of English literature a case of neglected genius so remarkable as that of Henryson. This book will justify itself if it does no more than make accessible and call attention to poetry of so much interest and distinction.

With Ashley Thorndike, his contemporary at the Harvard Graduate School and his colleague at Columbia, Neilson began, in 1911, to edit for Macmillan the Tudor Shakespeare, each play in an inexpensive single volume designed for school and college classes. The texts were those Neilson had prepared for the Cambridge Shakespeare. For editors of the individual volumes they enlisted such distinguished scholars as Raymond Alden, Carleton Brown, Hardin Craig, J. W. Cunliffe, R. M. Lovett, F. M. Paddleford, T. M. Parrott, Louise Pound.

Two years later, 1913, the collaborators published a handbook, *Facts about Shakespeare,* which was warmly welcomed by the academic world. Later they wrote together a school *History of English Literature* (1920). Collaboration with Thorndike Neilson found exceedingly pleasant. They were both hard workers, each ready to take more than his share in any task, and they were scholars of the same stripe. Writing of Thorndike in the *Dictionary of American Biography,* Neilson described him as combining "a profound respect for facts with a lively interest in their significance," and as retaining "a sense of the emotional values of the literary documents with which he dealt."

Neilson's several publishers speak more kindly of him than publishers often do of academic authors. They found him not only agreeable to deal with but very dependable about deadlines and word-lengths and quality. He worked rapidly but so conscientiously that there is only one record of a job he tried to turn off too fast, the volume on *Burns, How to Know Him* which he prepared for Bobbs-Merrill in 1917. Bliss Perry has recorded that the first draft was "so hastily and sketchily put together that the editor of the series begged me, as a friend of Neilson, to tell him frankly that the Burns must be re-written in parts, which it was!"

Neilson's most extended piece of writing during these years was *Essentials of Poetry,* the chapters of which were read as Lowell Lectures in the spring of 1911 and aroused much discussion in the Boston community. An invitation to deliver a series of Lowell Lectures conferred upon the lecturer both an ample fee and a pleasant prestige. The appointments in 1911 were made by A. Lawrence Lowell, not as President of Harvard but as sole trustee of that curious "corporation sole" the Lowell Institute. (The only other "corporation sole" in Massachusetts is the Roman Catholic Archbishop of Boston.) The Institute, founded in 1840 by the will of John Lowell, opens its lectures to the public without charge.

Essentials of Poetry was published by Houghton Mifflin in 1912. (It is dedicated, with a lack of originality indicative of emotional reserve, "To my most severe critic.") The brief Preface states that the point of view maintained was reached in the course of discussions with a Harvard class in English literature, discussions partially motivated it would seem by a desire to defend romanticism against the current attacks of Irving Babbitt.

> In some of the most vigorous critical writing of the day [the Preface runs] there appears a tendency to charge this phase of art [the Romantic] with the whole burden of modern artistic sins, and it has seemed to me that in this attack there was evident a serious lack of discrimination among the various elements roughly grouped under the term. In attempting to separate these elements and to decide which of them could be regarded as really Romantic in any coherent sense of the word, I found it necessary to come to an understanding also with respect to such terms as Classic, Realistic, and Sentimental; and the conclusion of the investigation yielded the view of the constituents of poetry which this volume presents. I am not without hope that some contribution has been made towards that freeing of terminology from ambiguity which is so necessary for the further progress of literary criticism.

This modest purpose was, many of Neilson's audience thought, abundantly realized, though the simple schematism of the analysis is not highly regarded by modern critics. He tried, during his discussion, to be strictly impersonal but he could not entirely suppress his pleasure when an objective examination seemed to give the advantage to romantic verse.

> It appears, then, that though intensity is necessary to all types of poetry . . . it is nevertheless peculiarly related to the imagination . . . affording an explanation of the fact, often denied by the critics, but recognized by the general sense of the public, that in romantic verse more constantly than in any other kind are we likely to find burning the true poetic fire.

And, in conclusion:

> I cannot feel it is so unfortunate as some have found it that the dominant element in the poetry which most powerfully appeals to our generation is that of imagination.

Babbitt's response to this challenge was to review *Essentials of Poetry* before the Modern Language Conference—the monthly gathering of graduate students and professors. The scene is recalled with pleasure by those who were present, Neilson sitting in the front row listening gaily to Babbitt's diatribes, waiting for his chance to retaliate. And then, when the general discussion began, the combat, as someone put it, of rapier against bludgeon.

Essentials of Poetry sold well and steadily; in 1939 Houghton Mifflin brought out a second edition.

Besides the books there were, of course, articles and reviews, though Neilson's connection with the *Nation,* for which he had been reviewing since the Bryn Mawr days, was roughly broken in 1907. In a review of H. H. Furness' Variorum edition of *Antony and Cleopatra* (17 October 1907) Neilson took sharp exception to the elderly scholar's growing tendency to give disproportionate space to his own conclusions and comments. "This tendency has now reached such proportions that the new volume contains more of Dr. Furness than of any other one critic." Neilson remarked also that Furness is "allowing himself to relax," citing as one example an outburst in the Preface against the study of Shakespeare's sources while elsewhere in the book the editor points out the high value of just such study.

In response, apparently, to outcries from Furness' Philadelphia friends and other admirers, the *Nation,* without consulting Neilson, expressed in their issue of 28 November, deep regret at having done "injustice to Dr. Furness's monumental work." Although Neilson's review was, as usual, unsigned, this struck him as an unbearable restriction on freedom of expression and he declined to write further for the *Nation.* A few months later, Bliss Perry invited him to say in the *Atlantic* (March 1908), over his signature, exactly what he thought of Furness and his Variorum editing. Neilson's expression was moderate, as always, but his stricture was sharp: The "almost official standing" of these volumes makes it necessary to weigh with care the personal judgments Dr. Furness appends to almost every note. "The critic's laurels are not always to be awarded to the scholar." Furness says, for instance, that Antony's love for Cleopatra "was not of the senses, for . . . Cleopatra was not beautiful; she had no physical allurements."

Another phase of the teaching profession to which Neilson rendered important service was adult education. His most extensive contribution was the assistant editorship of President Eliot's famous Five-Foot Shelf, a story amusingly told by Eliot's biographer, William James's son Henry.

In 1909 Eliot, in the course of an address to a group of working men, expressed the opinion that a five-foot shelf would hold books enough to afford a good substitute for a liberal education to anyone who would read them with devotion, even if he could spare no more than fifteen minutes a day. Shortly after this, when his forthcoming retirement from the presidency of Harvard was announced, Eliot was approached by Norman Hapgood and William Patten of the publishing house of P. F. Collier and Son, who reminded him of his dictum and asked him to assume the editorship of such a library as he had had in mind. They fired his imagination with the prospect of putting good books into thousands of American homes, promised him an assistant in the work, and persuaded him to accept. As his first choice of an associate editor Eliot named Professor Neilson, whose imagination was also excited by the project. The work offered him besides a substantial addition to income; Collier paid him the equivalent of fifty dollars a week during his year and a half of editorial labor.

A few weeks after the contract was signed, Eliot, in an address delivered in Atlanta, announced that he was about to make a selection of books for a five-foot shelf which could serve as the foundation of a liberal education. Public curiosity was immediately aroused. The idea of such a selection was then quite novel. The other "Libraries" on the market were anthologies of excerpts from great works, while Eliot insisted that his volumes contain the great works entire and unabridged. Collier suggested the title Harvard Classics and Eliot obtained from the Harvard Corporation permission to use that name but the Corporation made no public announcement of this fact and a large section of the academic community was enraged at the appearance of the University's name in a commercial venture. Neilson had to bear the brunt of vituperative attacks made in a heated faculty meeting. Many of his colleagues, though, approved the scheme thoroughly and lent learned collaboration in fields where Eliot and Neilson were not at home.

Other attacks on the Shelf were made by the newspapers. Criticism of Eliot's selections and inclusions became a kind of national game where the sport was heightened by the fact that no one knew just what Eliot's selections were. He had made his dictum in general terms with only a few specific books in mind. In February he and Neilson began the labor of making the fine general phrase concrete in fifty volumes.

The method of work Neilson devised was to lay out huge sheets of paper with the centuries listed in the left hand column and, in other columns, categories such as literary forms, countries, events, discoveries. In this way the problems to be settled presented themselves clearly: What is to be used to explain the Renaissance? How shall folklore be dealt with, the drama, religious thought? Eliot's idea, as he said in his Introduction to the Harvard Classics, was not to present the hundred best books or a compendium of literary masterpieces but to offer to the "careful and persistent reader" a view of "man observing, recording, inventing, and imagining."

Some of the choices in the fifty volumes would have been made by anyone; others reflect interestingly the personal tastes of Eliot and Neilson. One volume, for instance, is devoted to the Essays of Emerson. The complete poems of Milton are included and the complete poems of Burns, because, as Eliot explained in his Introduction,

> The works of these two very unlike poets contain social, religious, and governmental teachings of vital concern for modern democracies. Milton was the great poet of civil and religious liberty, Puritanism, and the English Commonwealth, and Burns was the great poet of democracy. The two together cover the fundamental principles of free government, education, and democratic social structure, and will serve as guides to much good reading on those subjects provided in the collection.

The problem of what to do about lyric poetry was solved by Eliot's admiration for Palgrave's *Golden Treasury;* the editors printed the whole of that collection, interspersing it with other poems of Neilson's choosing.

On all the titles selected Eliot consulted and passed final judgment though he did not read all the books through. Neilson selected the texts to be used, wrote the footnotes and the introductions. He was appalled to find that Collier expected him to deliver copy at the rate of three or four volumes a month, but he learned not to be too much disturbed by their incessant demands. He worked, nevertheless, at surprising speed and his ability to utilize odd minutes was a source of wonder to his scholarly colleagues. He did not seem to need any warming up. If he found, for instance, that he had come home twenty minutes early for lunch, he could sit down at his desk and turn off a competent paragraph or two on Emerson or Plato or Bacon.

Most of the collaboration between Eliot and Neilson was verbal and unrecorded but the letters written when Eliot was, from time to time, away from Cambridge throw some light on the way they discussed and worked together.

ELIOT TO NEILSON

6 March 1909

Your suggestion of enough Walton's Lives to fill up the volume containing Pilgrim's Progress seems to me a good one; but I am not sure that Locke's short book on the Conduct of the Understanding would not be better, assuming that the quantity of Locke's Understanding would be about right. The question would turn in my mind, on the comparative interest of the Walton and the Locke for the American reader. If they are in haste, for that volume, settle that question of interest yourself.

29 August 1909

I agree that we should continue to avoid translated lyrical poetry. To cut out of the Elizabethan dramas the obscenity which was intended to be amusing would be a large piece of work for you, and it is a kind of work that provokes criticism—particularly when the fundamentally nasty situations cannot be cut out of the plays.

7 September 1909

If you take the smut out of the obscene passages in the Elizabethan drama, will they not be left flat and unintelligible. The supposed fun was in the obscenity. Voltaire says "we don't laugh in reading a translation." Will anybody be able to laugh at any part of an expurgated Elizabethan drama?

On 9 July 1910 Eliot wrote:

I heartily congratulate you on having furnished the last piece of copy for the Harvard Classics. Although it has been sometimes a disagreeably pressing or urgent job and has taken longer than you expected, I think it must have been on the whole an interesting one, and fairly profitable to you as a man of letters.

The success of the Harvard Classics was far beyond anything even the publisher had imagined. The sets sold rapidly and they continued to sell. At the time of Eliot's death, in 1926, 350,000 sets had been sold. Twenty years later the number had reached 500,000, and there was no indication that it would not continue to rise. The Collier firm valued Neilson so highly as a collaborator that they continued all through his life to draw on him in one capacity or another. The year after the Harvard Classics appeared Collier issued a set of selections from it, graded for youthful readers from twelve to eighteen and known as the Junior Classics. Neilson had no hand in the choice of these but he wrote for each volume a short introduction which he described as "of a somewhat pedagogic nature." In 1914 he edited a volume of Lectures on the Harvard Classics by a distinguished roster of two score Harvard professors which included such names as Frederick Jackson Turner, Ralph Barton Perry, J. D. M. Ford, Roscoe Pound, and Kuno Francke. Neilson himself wrote the lectures on What the Middle Ages Read, The Elizabethan Drama, and The Elizabethan Adventurers.

Two years later, 1916, Eliot's reluctant omission of novels from the Five-Foot Shelf was repaired by the Harvard Shelf of Fiction, twenty volumes which he and Neilson selected and edited, dividing the labor as they had with the original Classics. A letter written by Eliot in Asticou, Maine to Neilson in Edgecomb, Maine, is an interesting commentary on contemporary taste.

12 July 1916

I reluctantly give up Pater on the ground that he is not a writer of fiction.

If you agree, we will include Pride and Prejudice, and we will exclude the Brontës and the Vicar of Wakefield.

If Tom Jones and The Sentimental Journey will really go into two volumes, we will include those two in our definitive list.

Silas Lapham and The Portrait of a Lady do not seem to me possible. Are they in the same class with the novels we have determined on? [The James novel was included.]

How much space will Turgeniev's Fathers and Sons, and Dostoievsky's Crime and Punishment fill? Did Tolstoi write any short stories? . . .

I agree that the present taste of young readers must not affect our selection. They constantly violate Emerson's rule—"do not read a book until it is at least one year old"; and they want to be "thrilled" or "excited" in a superficial and transient way. . .

Neilson prefaced each volume with a biographical note on the author and a selection of critical comment. *Guy Mannering,* for instance, is introduced by quotations from Carlyle, Richard Holt Hutton, Bagehot, and Ruskin.

While work on the Five-Foot Shelf was in progress, Neilson had his first experience of the American far West. He taught during the summer of 1909 at the University of California, invited at the suggestion of C. M. Gayley, late of Harvard, in the hope that he might be persuaded to accept a permanent appointment. He found the experience very pleasant, as a letter to his wife indicates.

Faculty Club, Berkeley
15 July 1909

. . . Let me tell you about my day. I get up at eight and have breakfast in the Club Dining Room. Then at nine I go to my room and prepare lectures till ten. I lecture from ten to twelve and then see students and come back here for luncheon. Then I loaf a bit till two, when I usually go to the library and work for Collier till it closes at five. Then I go for a walk till dinner time, which is early here. About every second night I am out for dinner, and that takes the evening. The other evenings I work again, though sometimes I ~~waste~~! spend a good deal of time talking with the other men. The talk is usually good.

One of the friendships Neilson made in the Faculty Club dining room was with a Harvardian whom he had not known before, Professor Samuel Williston of the Law School, who was also teaching at Berkeley that summer. Neither of them had classes between Friday noon and Monday morning so they spent most of the week ends together on exploring expeditions planned and organized, with great ingenuity Williston thought, by Neilson. They went to Monterey and Santa Cruz, to Mt. Tamalpias, where they saw a sunrise as well as the redwood trees, and to the Yosemite where they spent a night on Glacier Point and rode the winding trail down the mile high cliff.

But, though he enjoyed both the country and the people, Neilson never seriously considered settling permanently in the West. Gayley was not the only one of his friends who thought that he would adapt easily to a Western or Middle Western atmosphere and would enjoy its liveliness and challenge, but here, as in the matter of co-education, Neilson never freed himself from the provincial Harvard prejudices. One could not live happily, he was sure, beyond the Appalachians. There were not enough books; Europe was too far away; life was not intellectually rich; the emphasis was all on material progress and gain. He added another objection which really carried weight with him: Western voices are ugly to listen to. Even after, as President of Smith, he had traveled widely about the country and made agreeable visits again and again to such cities as Cleveland, Chicago, St. Paul, Neilson the Scot remained a rooted New Englander. He could write, for instance, to a colleague considering a call to the Pacific coast:

> The place is young and out of reach of libraries. . . You would find it difficult to keep in touch with the academic game in the East and you would be in a country which is foreign in a much more decided sense than Ontario is.

To the end of his life Neilson was a thoroughgoing Harvardian, in the sense that it was to Cambridge he turned instinctively whenever he wanted academic aid or counsel. When, at Smith, he felt the need for expert advice, in art, science, music, he called first upon his former Harvard colleagues, and his appointments had, many of the Smith faculty felt, a heavy Harvard preponderance. He was aware, to be sure, unlike some dwellers in Cambridge, that Harvard is not the whole of the academic universe, but it always seemed to him its hub.

9

The Sorbonne

WHEN Neilson was asked to accept appointment as the Harvard exchange professor at the Sorbonne for the year 1914-15 he agreed with alacrity. Those dates held then no tragic overtones and both he and his wife were delighted by the prospect of a winter in Paris. The children, Allan, five, and Margaret, two, were a little young perhaps to derive much educational benefit from the experience but at least they were old enough to make the journey.

The Harvard-Sorbonne exchange was instituted in 1904 by James Hazen Hyde who had been interested since his undergraduate days in Franco-American amity. Appointment was considered by both faculties as a distinction and an opportunity. Neilson's predecessors had included such names as Barrett Wendell, who inaugurated the exchange, George Santayana, Archibald Coolidge, George Pierce Baker, and William Morris Davis. Neilson was to take the place for the year of Professor Henri Lichtenberger who would proceed to Harvard. The English faculty at the Sorbonne received with pleasure the news of Neilson's appointment, and his schedule was arranged in an agreeable correspondence with Professor Emile Legouis whose acquaintance the Neilsons had enjoyed during his exchange year in Cambridge.

That they might have a long summer with Mrs. Neilson's parents, the Neilsons sailed for Europe soon after commencement. Miss Lizzie Neilson, who had been in Scotland, joined them, and in August, when war was declared, they were all together in the Musers' home in Offenburg. Offenburg lies close to the border of Alsace, that many times disputed province which the Germans captured once more in the first days of their westward drive. With the German declaration of war on France, 2 August, the town began to fill with troops, while hundreds more passed daily through the railway station, a junction on the road to the Alsatian capital, Strasbourg. As an American citizen of British origin married to a German wife Neilson found himself in a curious, and quite possibly dangerous position. With the danger he seems to have been unconcerned but he was greatly interested by his opportunities for observation. Aware that these were unusual he began to set down notes of what he heard and saw, the only time in his life when he kept anything approaching a diary.

All the entries are characteristically objective. They record what the writer observed, not what he thought or felt. It was in Mrs. Neilson's memory that the personal emotions of the time were inscribed. She was in constant fear for her husband who never dreamed of taking the simplest precautions. He and his sister continued to speak English together not only in the house but on the street although the town was full of strangers and anti-British feeling ran high. Moreover Neilson, fascinated by the spectacle of the mobilization and all its elaborate and efficient organization, often spent hours watching the railroad, making notes of the number of cars with troops and guns that went through to the front. Could a German guard be expected to understand that this was historical scholarship, not espionage? Mrs. Neilson went to the Mayor and got him to sign a statement that he knew William Allan Neilson personally; that he was an American citizen and the son-in-law of Herr Oskar Muser. This paper her husband agreed to carry constantly in his pocket, a precaution which relieved her mind a little.

Troops were soon quartered in the Muser house and grounds. Supplies had to be got for them and straw for bedding. Neilson helped his father-in-law as he would have with any household labor, but when news came in of the first German victories and

Herr Muser began to set out flags his son-in-law said gravely, "You will excuse me, Vaterle, if I do not help you with this," and the older man replied, "I quite understand." Their personal relations remained unchanged.

Neilson's war notes were begun on 16 August and continued until 5 September when, as he wrote, "the general success of the German advance seems now so clearly established that it is not worth while to record here what everybody will soon know." The notes summarize the war news as it reached Offenburg, with occasional speculation on the probability of exaggerations, but they are concerned chiefly with the German state of mind.

16 August

. . . The news of the opening of the war was received in this district without enthusiasm. The people at large, from whom the rank and file of the army are drawn, seemed serious and at first even depressed. The soldiers themselves accepted the situation stoically. One heard almost no grumbling against the government; and the persistent press campaign to prove that Germany was forced into war, that her enemies were all guilty of bad faith, and that the war was necessary to the existence of the Fatherland, seemed to have done its work. One feels that any one openly questioning the uprightness of the German policy would be in serious danger.

I saw personally something of three men during the week of mobilization. J. B. was a Reserve officer in charge of the Bahnhof Commands in Offenburg. After three days he seemed to be on the verge of nervous prostration. He could not sleep, and all other considerations seemed banished by his overwhelming sense of the responsibility on his shoulders. A. S. was in the 170 Regiment here as an Einjähriger. He is a University-bred man of cultivated mind and a good musician. He had absolutely no illusions and no enthusiasm; and seemed to regard himself as forced to go and probably lose his life in a quite unnecessary struggle. A. M. is an engineer who has never served. He had plenty of patriotism and faith in the German success, but saw himself sentimentally and tragically leaving his bride and unborn child. His intellectual view of the situation was completely blurred by emotion. Peasants I spoke to took the orders to march fatalistically or lightly. I never saw a trace of the instinct to resist the orders of the government in thought or word or deed.

As the mobilization proceeded, the mood of the people and the army became more martial, and spirits rose. Of the warlike demonstrations reported from other cities I have seen nothing here so far. The soldiers are cheered as their trains pass through to the front, but one feels the town profoundly anxious, if not depressed. . .

The only instance of defective organization I have noted was in the quartering of the soldiers in the town, and that was due to the local municipal authorities, not to the military. Even this was soon put right. Practically every family has some. This last week we had at one time as many as eleven men and three officers. The latter eat outside —I presume at the Casino in the barracks or at hotels; the men are fed here, simply but substantially. Some are grateful, some discontented. It is a great nuisance to everybody, and a great burden to many.

18 August

. . . The women of the town are very busy, putting up preserves, knitting socks, making bandages, etc. At the station large groups of girls supply the passing soldiers with bread and coffee. . .

A few days ago I walked out to the country church at Weingarten near Fessenbach [an error for Zell] with L. and as we were leaving it two little children, a girl about eight and a boy about five, came in and knelt down—presumably to pray for a soldier father. Hardly anything I have seen was as touching as these two mites in the quiet empty church.

The townspeople remain singularly undemonstrative. I cannot even say whether they are confident or anxious. They certainly take the burdens of the war so far with great apparent patience and courage.

20 August

. . . More factories are closing in O. this week, and preparations are being made to feed poor children in private houses. But as yet, a small town like this shows little evidence of the economic disturbance, save that the shops, other than those of provision merchants, do little or no business. Herr M's law business is almost at a standstill.

The spy-fever has gone by, and now the authorities are trying to restrain over-zealous sentries from shooting at automobiles and arresting harmless veiled ladies. Many painful and several tragic results of over-suspicion have occurred. I have seen only one flier since the war began—a French one flying very high. . .

22 August

Last night came the news of a great victory south of Metz on the frontiers of Lothringen. This morning it is reported that the French had over eight army corps, that over 10,000 prisoners and 50 guns were taken, and that the Germans are still pursuing. The town had just begun to show signs of jubilation, flags were hung out and the bells were ringing, when the first trainload of wounded pulled in. As the stream of bandaged men in furniture wagons, automobiles, and on foot poured past to the hospitals, a hush settled down over the people, and the signs of rejoicing abated. The brutal cost of war is so apparent at every step that there is little chance for enthusiasm to let itself go. . .

Li, who spent yesterday at the cooking school, where they are putting up preserved fruit for the hospitals, is sent today to the Station, where they are preparing to receive large numbers of wounded. Everywhere about the town one sees the women, down to little girls of nine, knitting socks for the soldiers in the field. Plans are being made to feed the children of poor families whose fathers are at the war. Never was a nation so organized for a single purpose.

I listened today to the talk of some of the wounded standing about the hospital surrounded by groups of eager questioners. One told of the boldness of the French fliers and the futility of the attempts to shoot them. He had seen 32 shots aimed at one, without a hit.

23 August. Sunday

The Landsturm is now reporting each morning, the Bezirk being divided into groups of villages, and one group reporting each morning. One sees many of these middleaged peasants in costume! No contrast could be greater than these men in costume and in uniform. . .

Some days ago the Ober Stabsartz quartered here told us of two mares, commandeered for his column, that came with a notice tied to their heads that they must be milked daily, as they had just foaled. This seemed to touch him rather more than the necessity of refusing one of his men permission to visit a dying wife. . .

24 August

. . . Herr E. and his wife spent yesterday with us, and I talked the politics of the war with him.

The wounded I spoke with yesterday are eager to get back to the line, and the men of Reg. 172 (Essen) are grumbling at the tedium of waiting here when they want to go to the front.

26 August

Yesterday I went off into the Schwarzwald for the day, walking to the Brandeck Lindle, down to Dürbach, and back to Offenburg. On the Brandeck I found five soldiers—part of a patrol kept up apparently all along the western ridge of the Forest. They did not seem to know what they were looking for, and it is hard to see why any enemies should wander so far into the woods. The villages were stript of the younger men, of course, and the old men and the women were busy with the oemdgrass [*emdgras,* second crop of hay]. The inns were doing no business. In Dürbach were two families from Strassburg. Even on the Brandeck, the patrol told me, they had been hearing cannon. . .

American public opinion seems to be anti-German, but whether this will continue when the German point of view is presented is doubtful. At home, here, the German press seems to me to be overstating its case, but there is no trace of opposition in the country visible.

5 September

On Sept. 1, we all came up to the Brandeck, hoping to spend the month here. . . All day yesterday we heard cannon, and the rumbling goes on this morning—presumably the siege of Belfort, about 75 miles away. With the new German 40 cent: guns, the fortress seems to have no chance.

Communication with Paris, where Neilson had intended to present himself in September, was, of course, for a long time impossible. In October he made a journey to Geneva, hoping that letters might reach him there. He took lodgings and waited for a month before a letter came through from the Sorbonne. The Directeur wrote that Neilson was on no condition to present himself before January; by that time, it was hoped, the necessary reorganization would be completed and it would be known whether there were enough women students to make the offering of courses worth while. The continued enforced waiting, his mind and emotions more and more wrought upon daily by the progress of the war, seemed very difficult to bear. In an attempt to fix his attention for at least part of the day on something else, he decided to take up residence during the week in Freiburg where he could follow some courses at the University and work on his lectures for the Sorbonne. From there, Gartenstrasse 11, he wrote on 16 November to his sister Jean in Montreal:

At present I am working away on "The Faerie Queene" here; but it is hard to get absorbed in things so remote when what is going on around is so distracting. Yesterday, when I was at Offenburg over

Sunday, Mutterle, Lizzie, Li, Allan and I took a long walk in the woods back of Offenburg, and we were hardly away from houses before the infernal booming reached us—apparently from the central Vosges, though there is little doing there just now. But they seem to think it necessary to keep wasting powder all along the line. —Allan is a great walker. He was on his pins for three or four hours and did not seem tired when he reached home. He was much excited about going to an inn, where we had afternoon coffee. He develops steadily, though he has no interest or intelligence for letters or figures. But his German is quite wonderful. Perhaps Lizzie told you of his correcting Grandmother for her peasant speech. The little maiden [Margaret] is now beginning to talk very fast. She has new words each week I go back, and is very bright and pretty. . . The children are a godsend in the house, as they help to keep us all from the ever-present subject.

Tell Bob he can send the letter he wrote, if he sends it to Mr. Ames, or anyone on that side to mail. Your last was still in German, but of course you know now that that is unnecessary any longer.

I have been seeing something of the family of the English Church Minister here—an Aberdonian called Mackintosh. . . Apart from the Mackintoshes I speak with no one but waiters from Monday till Saturday—which is a trifle monotonous. But I get some work done.

In October President Lowell learned that Professor Neilson had not yet presented himself at Paris. A violent Anglophile himself, Lowell leaped to the conclusion that it was pro-German sympathy which was keeping Neilson in Offenburg. He tried to bring pressure on him to go to Paris, by asking other members of the faculty to write, by sending a cable, long delayed because of misdirection, and finally by a letter which offended Neilson deeply. He resented the unwarranted assumption about his political sympathies and even more the suggestion that he would permit any consideration, political or otherwise, to interfere with his discharge of a duty. He wrote:

My dear President Lowell,

Your letter of Dec. 10 has just reached me, and I confess that it disturbs me very much. It conveys the impression that you consider that I have done less than my duty in the matter of fulfilling my obligation as exchange Professor. I do not think this is a just judgment, nor do I think it necessary to plead any extenuating circumstances. But here are the facts.

I have done my best to keep you informed of my movements and my address. This is the fifth letter I have written you, though it would appear that several have not reached you. My Offenburg address, which was in the hands of the Chairman of my department, has all along been valid, even after letters addressed to my bankers in England were held up. Your cablegram of Oct. 12 reached London Oct. 28, and was delayed until near the end of Nov. because it arrived addressed to Neitzon. My bankers as a last experiment to find the addressee sent it to me.

It was not that MM. Coulet and Legouis "hardly wanted to ask" me to come as you put it. They distinctly told me not to come in November—in any case, they said, it would be necessary to wait until January, "en tout cas il faudrait attendre au moins jusqu'en Janvier prochain." I do not see how I could have thrust myself upon them in the face of these instructions.

I myself took the initiative further in writing to M. Legouis as soon as I found he was in Paris, saying that I was very anxious to come if he could find anything for me to do, even with a handful of students. He waited till a decision was arrived at about holding examinations for the women students, and immediately on hearing from him I set out.

I got here only about three weeks after the others had begun, and I purpose to stay two months after my appointment from Harvard expires. I shall then have taught considerably longer than any of my predecessors on the present foundation.

In view of all these facts, I find it difficult not to resent the reproval implied in your letter.

I have already written you from Paris the details of the opening of my courses.

It was this correspondence which was chiefly responsible for the tension between Lowell and Neilson of which Cambridge was almost as well aware, though it did not know the cause, as it had been of the friendship between Neilson and President Eliot. The strain was finally relieved in 1917 by Lowell's cordial letter written when Neilson decided to accept the presidency of Smith.

Late in November 1914 Legouis wrote that, as the University had finally decided to hold in 1915 competitive examinations for young women, and as "our Department is the Kingdom of 'Feminie,'" the work Neilson had prepared for them would be of great use, the more so as two colleagues of mine out of five have joined the army. Consequently we shall be happy and thankful for your assistance in our Department when you come, and as early as you can do it without putting yourself to any inconvenience, whether in December or January.

Neilson managed to reach Paris early in December. A lively account of his months there is contained in some letters to his sister Jean.

21 bis rue d'Alésia, Paris
15 December 1914

Dearest Jean,

I have waited to write again till I should have had my first lecture. It came off this morning in an amphitheatre in the Sorbonne, and went, I think, quite well. At least my colleagues seemed well pleased, and the audience was attentive and responsive. As all the ablebodied students are at the war, I had mostly women, but I was backed on the platform by an imposing row of men: Croiset, professor of Greek, Doyen of the Faculty of Letters, who introduced me; Poincaré, brother of the President and director of Higher Instruction, Legouis, titular professor of English, Liard, Recteur of the Academy of Paris, and Coulet, who seems to be universal secretary of University affairs.

Most of these men I have had to call on officially and in all the cases except Legouis, have to talk French to them. My French is improving rapidly, and I am taking daily lessons with Mme. Foulet, in whose house I am boarding. Her husband, whom I knew in California, is in the trenches by St. Dié, and there is no one in her pension but her and her boy of fourteen and me. I have two rooms, and am very well off. As at Geneva I have the advantage of talking French at meals, so that I get a lot of practice.

I have dined with Legouis and his family—wife, son and daughter of about seventeen or so. The elder son is south of Verdun. We spoke French all evening, as Madame does not understand English. I enjoyed the evening very much, as also a lunch with Cazamian * and his wife, one of the younger members of the Eng. Dept. He had me thus early, because he expects to be called to the colors any day. One hardly comes across a family without members at the front.

Today I called on the new American ambassador [William G. Sharp], decent and commonplace. I hope no serious business arises

* Professor Louis Cazamian. He and Professor Emile Legouis published together in 1924 the widely used *Histoire de la Littérature Anglaise.*

for him to do, I cannot say I think much of Mr. Bryan's choice. At the Embassy I found two of my old Harvard boys.

Everybody here is very eager to hear about my impressions from Germany. Here as there, there is complete assurance of ultimate victory, and no notion of stopping short of it. The French are very un-French now—that is, quiet and calm, and willing to wait and persist. The mood seems to me less feverish than in Germany. Both nations, of course, get only censored dispatches, and both exaggerate greatly the favorable side of their own situation. I see no complete victory in sight for either. I don't think a hostile army will reach any European capital—unless it is Vienna.

The great event since I came here has been the battle at the Falklands. The Germans feel that pretty badly, but console themselves by supposing that the enemy was eight to one. They have, of course, absolutely no evidence for this. If Whistler were alive, he would have to withdraw his book on The Decay of Lying.

Everything seems to be going smoothly in Offenburg, by a letter I had from Li this morning. I was very sorry to leave them all—but I confess the atmosphere here suits me better, after months of discretion and neutrality.

I went to the Comédie Française on Sunday afternoon. Six actors and twelve actresses gave patriotic recitations, and then we had Corneille's *Cid.* I had just read the play and could follow the action, but few of the lines. The house was full and enthusiastic. The play to me is ridiculously conventional, but the French relish the rhetorical speeches, and they can recite.

Through the day, Paris seems quite normal; but after dark, with the few lights, it is sometimes hard to find your way. All the omnibuses are at the war, but the trollies run, and the underground till 10 P.M. After Legouis' dinner, however, I had to walk home about three miles. I have now got my bearings pretty well and can avail myself of the seven or eight subway routes; but the surface cars, except the nearest route, are still a mystery to me.

Altogether, the prospect of an interesting Winter is better than I dared to hope; and I will save something out of the wreck of my year.

I have written three or four of the folks in Britain. I do not know if I will see them, as Li is so strongly opposed to my crossing the channel.

I hope you have given up worrying about us. Tell Bob to send on his long letter, even if it is not up to date.

French cigars are dear and rotten: likewise matches. But wine is good and cheap and so is food.

Much love to both of you, Will

Paris, 27 December 1914

. . . I did not reply [to your Xmas cable] because it is no small matter to send telegrams abroad from here. You have to go from the P. O. to a police commissioner, translate and explain your message to him, and then return to the P. O., and my French is still so feeble that I avoid when possible conversations with official persons, who are apt to be very suspicious of foreigners. . . My letters from Li take from three to six days; mine to her about eight, as the French Government holds up foreign correspondence for five days in place of censoring it. . . Everybody seems to be well at Offenburg, and the photos will have shown you how well the children get along.

My courses are now moving along regularly, and I am getting a good deal of work done on my Allegory, though of course I cannot use the Sorbonne Library as easily as the Harvard one. It is very cold there, as half the heating apparatus of the Sorbonne had been sent to Longevy for repairs, and the Germans are still there. So only a few rooms are heated, and the Library not at all.

I have dined with two or three of my colleagues, and ate my Christmas Dinner at the house of M. Bozon, manager of the Credit Lyonnaise, father of Mme. Baldensperger,* with whom she is staying, her husband being at the front . . . I have been again at the Comédie—to see Racine's *Andromaque,* which I followed a little better than the *Cid* . . . My days are usually not very exciting. In the forenoon I work in my room, or go to lecture and then to the Library. After lunch I have a French lesson with Mme. Foulet, and after the three o'clock dispatch from headquarters has time to get printed, I go into town, get a paper and read it while I take coffee at a café. Then I come home or make calls; have dinner at 7:30, and read through the evening. Sundays I usually go to the theatre in the afternoon. I speak French (of a sort) at meals here and usually when I go out. . .

24 January 1915

Certainly the mails between Canada and France are in poor shape. I have still no word that you have received anything from me from Paris but my first postal. I hope you are hearing from Offenburg regularly. I have no difficulty in getting answers from Cambridge.

* Fernand Baldensperger had been an exchange professor at Harvard.

My life here moves on quietly on the same lines. I am somewhat disappointed that my ear for French improves so slowly. I went to a lecture today and got nothing out of it; but it must be said that the man spoke in a difficult way, dropping his voice so that much of it I did not even hear.

Last Sunday I lunched again at Madame Baldensperger's father's, and met among others, a M. Guiffray who bought for the Boston Museum for several years. This week he leaves for America again to arrange the French pictures at San Francisco. This morning I went to see the Belgian part of the exhibit. It was strongest in laces, about which I understand nothing; but I saw some fine tapestries.

I see a good deal of Mrs. [R. Lathrop] Shields, who is very hospitable, though the Art Students' Club House is a hospital; and I meet some people there. Otherwise my social engagements have been confined to Cazamian and Legouis of my department and a cup of tea at the office of the Brooklyn Eagle, which is run here by a Harvard man. I have got the American Embassy, which has charge of the German interests, to write to Walter Muser [cousin of Mrs. Neilson] to find if he wants money or clothes. He is in a camp on the Isle d'Yeu, off the coast of Vendée. I gather from the men at the Embassy, who are continually visiting the prison camps, that the German prisoners are pretty well treated. It is astonishing how their spying mania persists. One of them had enclosed a photo of himself in a letter home, and the French authorities getting suspicious soaked it off the mount and found a lot of valuable military information written on the card: number of trains and troops passing through the town, and so on. The information was correct, but how he got it, shut up in a camp, they cannot guess. This kind of thing naturally leads to a reduction of freedom of correspondence. . .

Things seem to go on at Offenburg as before I left. . . Margaret is a constant entertainment. I gather that they have fewer soldiers in the house. They have earned a rest for a while. . . We have no snow here, but almost all the fields of battle are white. . . I don't know whether the snow will be a great improvement on the mud. The fighting conditions have been awful since New Year's.

I hope you and Bob are in good shape, and that his drilling does not take too much out of him.

8 February 1915

I have Bob's of the 24th, so communications are pretty good now. May they continue . . . I have just had a letter . . . telling me that

Sir Walter died in December from the wound he had in the thigh since last spring . . . Poor old dog, he has given us much pleasure, and was the humanest beast I ever knew . . .

I have had two events since I wrote Bob. On Saturday I formed one of the jury at the defense of the thesis by a lady, aet thirty-seven, candidate for the degree of Doctor-ès-Lettres in English. Six or seven of us sat on the platform while the victim faced us on a little platform by herself. Behind her the amphitheatre was crowded with about two hundred of the female public. It had been announced in the newspapers. The main thesis was a big critical work on Jane Austen that had been sent us a week or two before in printed form. The attacks were very detailed and sometimes severe, but she stood her ground like a man. I tackled her for about twenty minutes, and I guess I was more nervous than she was. She got her degree with very honorable mention. Her job was really excellent—better than any of the English criticisms of Miss Austen.

On Sunday I went to Boulogne-sur-Seine, just outside Paris, to a luncheon at the Club "Autour du Monde" of which I have been made a free member for six months. The nucleus of the Club consists of the men and women who have been round the world on the Kahn scholarship. Mr. [Otto] Kahn, who was there, founded the Club and gave the very attractive house, which is adjoining his wonderful gardens—Italian, Japanese, and Chinese, with real habitable Japanese and Chinese houses and pagodas. Of course, at this season, it was nothing to what it must be in summer, but lots of the trees were evergreen, and the primroses were blooming.

It was a Belgian lunch—with perhaps sixty people, some of them quite distinguished, like M. Boutroux, the philosopher and member of the Academie Française. This was the first of the Immortal forty I have met. He and his wife were very friendly and he gave me his address, which means I have to call on him. We had some good talk. There was a member of the Government there who seemed to me far from discreet.

There is little new from the front this week. The chief talk has been the submarine affair, which I guess will not amount to a great deal and will hurt Germany still more with the neuters.

My last news from Offenburg was on Feb. 2, but I expect a letter tomorrow. Don't take too much stock in this economy of flour in Germany talk. Thank Bob for the clippings.

25 March 1915

This will be my last letter from Paris, as I leave for Geneva on the night of the 28th. . . I have had "Posts" but no letters from you for about ten days.

Last week my chief event was my French lecture. Well, the amphitheatre was full—that is, I suppose, three or four hundred people. I was introduced by the Doyen, Croiset, who said pretty things about my teaching, and then I held forth for about an hour. At first I simply poured with perspiration; but as the audience got warm, I got cool, and during the last half hour I rather enjoyed myself. Certainly French is a great language for public speaking—if one can only speak it. I can only claim, however, to have been intelligible, and the audience was more than kind. As the lecture is already in type, I needn't tell you about it, but will send it you when it is published. Liard, the Vice-Recteur, made the concluding speech and presented me with the medal of the University of Paris as a souvenir of the exceptional circumstances of my visit. I am not likely to forget them!

I finished my courses on Tuesday and Wednesday of this week, on very good terms with my students. I am sending you an article on my work in one of the Educational Journals.

I dined on Saturday night with an American who lives here, Henry Church,* married to a Munich girl. They live more elegantly than anybody I have had to do with here, and he writes French poetry and has gout. I don't quite know what they think God made them for, but their dinner was excellent. Mrs. Church is Bavarian of the before-the-war-type—that is, she hates Prussia, seems only moderately interested in the German Empire, and stands for Bavaria. Also she dresses like a Parisian before the war.

I went home with Legouis to dinner after the lecture, and Cazamian came too. He has gone to be a hospital orderly this week, and Legouis is left alone in the department. If the family had been here, I should gladly have stayed another semester and helped him through.

I have been out to tea twice—once at Lansons (professor of French lit.) and today at Boutroux's. The latter is the grand old man in philosophy here, member of the Academy, etc. He is extremely kind and simple. I met another Academician at his house, Delbos, and two or three professors whom he had asked to meet me. Nearly all could speak English, but wouldn't; but I have got to a point where this matters less.

* An expatriate American, a patron of art and letters, editor of *Mesures*.

Mme. Oster gave me a pleasant lunch on Monday, with Professors Abel Lefranc and Bemont of the Collège de France. Mme. O. is of Lorraine and Mme. Bemont of Alsace and the talk was largely of the lost provinces that they are all so sure of winning back. I wish I was half as sure. . . The old lady is a splendid type of French intellectual dowager.

On Sunday I lunched at the "Autour du Monde." The gardens had lots of primroses, squills, and crocuses, and a good deal of fruit blossom, almonds and the like, was out. I go again next Sunday to an American lunch for the Ambassador, Lichtenberger, and me. I lunched with Lichtenberger, this year's French exchange man at Harvard, on Friday. . . I have got all my passports, laisser-passers, permits de séjour, etc. fixed up, and my ticket bought, so that after a few calls and some packing I am ready to start after four of the most interesting months of my life.

I forgot to speak about the Zeppelins. I didn't go out to look for them, but saw the search lights and counted the cannon shots. Nobody was killed, and Paris seems to have rather enjoyed the excitement. There have been two alarms this week but neither time did they really arrive. Don't worry.

Among the events the letters do not chronicle was a luncheon, at which the Legouis were present, given for Neilson in February by the founder of the exchange professorship, James Hazen Hyde. There is a note to be added, too, to the tale of Neilson's lecture delivered in French. The subject was "Les Universités et l'Etat," and it was suggested to Neilson at the last moment that it would be more convenient for his audience if he pronounced the names of the American institutions to which he referred as the French are accustomed to pronounce them. He found the difficulty of uttering in complete seriousness statements about 'Arvárd or Shi-ca-gó enormously increased by the evident amusement of a Harvard colleague, Professor Roger Merriman, who had arrived unexpectedly and planted himself in the front row.

The lecture itself was on so serious a topic that there was no room for laughter or even for a touch of wit. Neilson dealt with the relationship between educational institutions and the government, in America, England, France, and Germany, inquiring into the possibilities, under each national system, of undesirable government regulation of the teacher and of what is taught. His conclusion was that in Germany alone the university operates not as a free association of thinking men but as a special corps under the orders of the GHQ. This divergence from the other nations is the product not of differences in the systems of control but of a difference in the fundamental nature of the governments involved: the minister in France, England, and America is elected by popular vote; in Germany he is an irresponsible autocrat.

The lecture, published in the *Revue Internationale de l'Enseignment* (vol. 69, p. 115), is written in grammatical French but the phrases have an English ring. Neilson composed it in English and the French friend who helped him with the translation stayed close to the original sentence structure.

The elegant and formal sentiments which had accompanied the presentation of the University's medal, described in Neilson's letter to his sister, were made concrete a little later in a personal letter from Professor Legouis, written in response to Neilson's thanks for his winter's experience.

25 April 1915

Why do you express thanks to us when we owe you so many more for visiting us under such untoward circumstances? Of our students' gratitude I need not speak for you must have felt it. They are not likely ever to forget your lectures. Their only regret is that your appointment could not be made permanent. Personally I wish the opportunities I had for chatting with you had been more numerous. It seems preposterous, now you are gone, that I should have let so many precious hours fly away unemployed. There was a tonic succession of consent and dissent on the main points at issue which made your conversation invigorating to me, and preferable to the level unanimity of all personal talks in our parts.

We are happy to hear that after such a long separation you found Mrs. Neilson and your children in good health. Do not forget to tell her that we trust better days will come when husband and wife need no longer be parted whatever land they are bound to.

I rejoice to hear that the little plant of friendship sown in Cambridge soil has not suffered from being transplanted here and only grown more vigorous in spite of the blasts of a dreary winter.

The Neilsons made their way home through Holland. Herr Muser traveled with them to the border in case there should be any trouble but there was none except for an interminable wait.

The inspector, finding in Neilson's luggage a great sheaf of papers, his lectures and notes on Allegory, carried them off to his office to examine, while the Neilsons, sitting on an uncomfortable bench, tried to calculate what their chances were of making the boat if the officials insisted on digesting the whole book. The Dutch liner on which they at last embarked steamed slowly through the Channel, preceded by a minesweeper. Again and again her course was altered while a mine was exploded in frightening proximity to her decks. Neilson sat all the while quietly reading. He was by no means unaware of the danger but danger, like illness, is something about which one does not talk.

The America to which Neilson returned was trying to be neutral but neutrality for him was an impossibility. Invited in June 1916 to make the Phi Beta Kappa address at Columbia he took for his title *Inter Arma Veritas* and said to the young men before him:

> I am no advocate of mental neutrality. I should be ashamed to appear before an audience such as this, and urge the rising generation of American scholars to abstain from a judgment on the most momentous issue in the history of the modern world. You must not only watch this war; you must study its causes and conduct, and you must make up your minds. You must not bring upon your heads the judgment delivered to the angel of the church of Laodicea, "because thou art neither cold nor hot, I will spue thee out of my mouth." The quest of truth in the midst of war which I am here to urge upon you has nothing in common with indifference or that intellectual indolence which takes a false pride in coming to no conclusion.

When, a year later, America entered the war, Mrs. Neilson found herself in a position in Cambridge curiously like that her husband had occupied in 1914 in Offenburg. The Cantabrigians, most of them, were as strongly Anglophile as President Lowell so that even during the years of neutrality they had looked askance at the Germans in their midst. Now that those Germans were officially enemies it seemed justifiable to treat them cruelly. There are unlovely tales of old friends cut in the street, of distinguished scholars insulted by their colleagues. Such treatment

Mrs. Neilson escaped chiefly because she went out very little during the spring and summer of 1917. Her third child, Caroline, born in January, was a good excuse for avoiding society. She took, also, the advice of her friends and never went to any large reception or general gathering unless her hostess had made a special point of urging her to come. And, in the fall, came the move to Northampton.

Neilson made his own position clear not long after his arrival in an address on the formation of public opinion in Germany, which he delivered to an audience of Northampton citizens. He described the duping of the German people by careful and insistent propaganda which made skilful use of education, politics, and the press. He assured his listeners that the Germans' belief in their cause, intensified by the suffering they had endured for it, was so strong that it could be shaken only by the destruction of the weapon with which they were attempting to prove themselves right. But he begged them to believe that the strength of Germany's resistance is proof that there is substance in her people, that she is a nation worthy of respect whose people have been blinded and fooled, and he urged them to learn from the German example to avoid the terrible consequences of hate.

Mrs. Neilson explained her own attitude to the Smith faculty when they sent her a great bouquet of flowers to say that they were anticipating her coming to Northampton. In sending her thanks she wrote that she wanted them to know that her love for her country was very deep but absolutely silent. She further indicated her state of mind by taking pains, soon after her arrival, to entertain the members of the department of French. The Smith faculty appreciated her position and treated her with unblemished courtesy and kindness. It was only the occasional visiting lecturer whose diatribes against Germany, uttered on the platform and sometimes even in the President's House, she had painfully to endure. One of the most vituperative was Sir Johnston Forbes-Robertson who stayed with the Neilsons when he played at the Academy of Music. After his departure Mrs. Neilson was obliged to send him a scarf he had left behind and she took the occasion to write a plea for her country.

I feel troubled that when we had the pleasure of your visit I let an occasion pass to speak a humble and yet courageous word for my country which, before my marriage, was Germany. I gathered from the little that was said about the war the other night that Germany is to you what she is to the world: an odious symbol, a bringer of unspeakable terror, the home of a people who destroy the results of the labor of generations.

I have always been quite silent during the war when my native country was mentioned. I am still so if a soldier or a man of business talks. But it is different with the artist who cares for things which hardly exist for the others, and yet are the most precious possessions of mankind. And there is a Germany who treasures these possessions and looks for help to the men who are by profession and temperament their natural guardians. Perhaps you know it, and then you may smile—I hope indulgently—at my efforts to remind you of that other Germany which stands reverent before beauty—as you do, which is gentle to lovely things—as you are. I only plead for that Germany and beg you to grant her shelter in your thoughts.

10

Harvard or Smith?

PROFESSOR NEILSON of Harvard enjoyed his work and his way of life. His adopted country had given him what he had hoped to find: the chance to count among his fellows for what he was worth, but one of his friends who had known him from graduate school days, Sidney Fay, had a conviction that he might count for even more, that he had a variety of talents beyond those on which he was drawing. Anyone who had watched Eliot's transformation of Harvard knew what power for good in American education a really first-class college president could wield, and Fay thought that Neilson's potentialities, though so different, were as great as Eliot's.

In June 1916, when President Marion Burton's departure for the University of Minnesota left Smith College without a president, Fay, recently become a member of the Smith faculty, thought of Neilson as the ideal man for the place, but the trustees had not asked for faculty advice and, as a newcomer, Fay felt hesitant about proferring it. A year went by without the appearance of any satisfactory candidate and at the end of the term, in June 1917, Fay made bold to take his suggestion that Neilson would make a good president to Dean Ada Comstock who was in charge of the College during the interregnum. (The whole Smith community was so strongly opposed to the idea of a woman as chief administrator that the trustees had not even given her the title of Acting President.) Miss Comstock was much interested in Fay's suggestion and approved his plan of inviting Neilson to make him a personal visit over the commencement week end when members of the Board of Trustees would be in Northampton. The project seemed too large and unexpected to be broached on the telephone so Fay went down to Cambridge hoping to bring his candidate back with him.

He reached 34 Kirkland Street at noon of a broiling June day and found Mrs. Neilson waiting lunch for her husband who was delivering the commencement address at Radcliffe. She was somewhat appalled at the prospect Fay presented but when Neilson returned from his sweltering but successful oratory they discussed the matter over the luncheon table and Neilson's imagination was fired by the idea of what, in a college presidency, he might accomplish for American education. His interest had always been not only in scholarship but in the whole educational process and, like Fay, he had watched at close range President Eliot transforming Harvard from a small New England college into a university of national importance.

Of Smith Neilson knew nothing except at second-hand but most of what he knew was good. Here was a field, he thought, in which he might effectively work. Had the college been coeducational or had it been situated far from the Atlantic seaboard he would probably not have considered the proposition further, but Northampton was in Massachusetts and the education of women, though he believed that it should be done apart from the opposite sex, seemed to him quite as important as the education of men. Perhaps today it was even more important, since it was obvious that women would soon be voting citizens. He had taught for fifteen years at Radcliffe not only to augment the family income but because he genuinely believed that the students at the "Annex" were as much worth educating as those at the University.

Smith, Neilson knew, was the largest woman's college in the country, two thousand students drawn from every state in the Union; the standards were high; the faculty, good, though it included only a few names of national distinction. Fay could add to this his admiration for the first president of the College, Clark Seelye, who as a young man of thirty-seven had laid the broad outlines of the institution with such prescience that it had moved smoothly into the twentieth century. From Smith's opening in 1876 he had insisted on entrance requirements and a course of study as rigorous as those in the best colleges for men and, in advance of his day, had included in the curriculum art and music taught not as female accomplishments but as scholarly disciplines. He had managed with such skillful thrift the $400,000 bequeathed by Sophia Smith for the founding of the college that the institution had never had a deficit. Seelye's successor, the energetic young Marion Burton, had in his seven years of office, increased the endowment by a million dollars and reset the college's nineteenth-century machinery to modern speeds. Both of these presidents were men who cared about education but neither of them was a scholar and, to the delight of the faculty, the trustees were convinced that what the College now needed was a scholar at its head. The faculty Fay had found on the whole right-minded and congenial. The proportion of men to women was far higher than in most female institutions, about one to three. Neilson had few acquaintances among them for Smith had never drawn heavily on the Harvard Graduate School, in part perhaps because of the skepticism concerning female education which President Eliot had voiced when he spoke at President Seelye's inauguration. There were, of course, some well entrenched lady professors who might resent innovations but anyone who wanted to improve the quality of the instruction was likely to find cordial co-operation. Neilson listened to all this, asked many questions, and finally agreed to go to Northampton, meet the trustees, and look over the ground. He and Fay took the afternoon train.

During the week end Neilson met and talked informally with several of the trustees, particularly with the members of the committee on the selection of a president: John C. Clark, Treasurer of the College, Marguerite Wells of the class of 1885, and Thomas Lamont of the firm of J. P. Morgan. They were all impressed by Neilson's personality, by his genuine concern for the education of women, and by the quality of his academic ideas. Only Lamont had a point of hesitation.

> I, as a business man [he wrote to Mrs. Dwight Morrow thirty years later] had some misgivings about his administrative ability, and so took the next train to Cambridge to see ex-President Eliot. . . I asked him flatly the question as to his capacity for administration. President Eliot's reply, you remember, was: "Neilson has a certain Scotch canniness that enables him to cope with any administrative situation. You will find if you get him that he can conduct Smith College as it has never been handled before." . . . That was enough of an endorsement for me.

The trustee committee asked Professor Neilson to permit them to present his name to the full Board as candidate for the presidency of Smith College.

Neilson at first declined. He hesitated chiefly because he had found the trustees much concerned with a grandiose scheme for the future of the College devised by President Burton shortly before he left for the University of Minnesota. This was a project to buy a large tract of land from the Massachusetts State Hospital, whose property adjoins that of the College, and to expand Smith into a great woman's university with medical, law, and other professional schools. To Neilson, who did not equate progress with size, this did not seem an academically desirable development. Moreover it would require the raising of a large sum of money, an enterprise which Burton undertook with pleasure and success but for which Neilson did not feel himself competent. In any case, it was teaching which interested him, not money raising.

The trustees declined to accept his refusal. They agreed to lay the woman's university project on the table and not to take it off until he wished to do so. (It is still on the table.) They went farther. Assuring Neilson that they were quite sincere in their desire to have a scholar in the presidency of the College, they promised to relieve him of the whole business of money raising for the institution.

With this new presentation of the position Neilson began to consider it again, weighing all the factors, professional, personal, and domestic, and consulting friends whose opinions he valued.

Kittredge, Robinson, Palmer, and Bliss Perry were the four with whom he discussed the problem in most detail. Perry, whose advice he had asked by letter, replied from Greensboro, Vermont:

> As far as I can look at the Smith matter dispassionately—for your going would dishearten me and pretty nearly ruin the department—it seems to me that it is not *your* job. You have made one career [Neilson was then forty-eight], at great toil and with great success. This would be thrown over, and you would have to give your days and nights to administrative work,—for which of course you have capacity, but so have plenty of other men. . . I don't see that the change would add anything to your reputation with the public. . . Nor do I think it would increase your personal happiness and contentment. . . In short, Neilson, I *can't see it.*

To George Herbert Palmer's advice on this occasion Neilson referred in the tribute he paid to Palmer at the Wellesley Semi-centennial in 1925.

> Twice in my life I have resorted to Professor Palmer for advice and he has allowed himself to be treated as an adviser ought to allow himself to be treated and seldom does. On one occasion I asked whether I should stay on at Harvard or whether I should go. He said, "Go. You will do better if you go." So I stayed. At a later time I asked him if I should go away from Harvard to Smith and he said, "No, stay." So I went. On both occasions he took it like a man. He was, I think, more easily reconciled to my disregard of his advice than a physician. He understands the function of an adviser is to stimulate thought in the advisee, not to dictate. So long as he stimulates thought we know that he has fulfilled his function.

Kittredge and Robinson "honestly felt," as Robinson recorded later, that with his special gifts Neilson could have as wide an influence in a university professorship as in any college presidency.

But Will said, "I can't be guided by you and Kittredge. There's too much of an element of personal friendship in your advice. I am glad you want me to stay but I'm going to talk to the Old Man."

Fortunately for posterity when Professor Neilson called upon President Emeritus Eliot he found that he had just left Cambridge for Maine. The consultation had to take place by correspondence, and we have in consequence, in the Harvard Archives, a clear record of the basis on which the Neilson decision was made, together with an admirable picture of the relationship between the two men.

Neilson to Eliot

Newcastle, Maine, 6 August 1917

My dear Mr. Eliot,

I made a vain attempt to see you the day you left Cambridge, and since then I have hesitated to trouble your vacation. But a letter tonight from Mrs. W. H. Baldwin contains an allusion which leads me to infer that you have already been troubled about my affairs, so now I want your advice.

The committee of the Trustees of Smith College are putting considerable pressure upon me to allow my name to go before the whole board as a possible President. I have been to Northampton for a short visit, and after some consideration I withdrew. This decision was arrived at largely because the group I saw seemed to be eager about acquiring a large tract of land, and I felt neither inclination nor ability for the raising of a large sum of money.

Later, I was informed that I had been misled and that in deciding to seek a scholar for the position they had meant to relieve him of the whole business of raising money. I had this confirmed by Mr. T. W. Lamont, whom I saw last Wednesday. The matter is now again open, though I am in no way committed to candidacy.

I have talked with some of my colleagues, notably Kittredge and Palmer, and have written to Bliss Perry, and all are strongly opposed to my going. But I feel that they view the matter pretty exclusively from the point of view of the Department of English (which can easily fill my position) and of my personal ease. There is clearly a larger educational question involved, and it seems that the point for me to decide is where on the whole I can accomplish most. I realize that it is balancing a risk of failure against an assurance of whatever degree of success I have already had at Harvard, and this makes me feel that the odds in favor of Smith ought to be quite decided before I take the risk. Perry thinks that the agreement about not raising money could not be lived up to, and as he had once to decide the same question and looked into the situation at Smith, I give his opinion a good deal of weight.

I write at this length that you may see as precisely as possible the nature of my problem. You know the job and you know me and my present work. I want your opinion, not as an officer of Harvard, but as a person interested in American education. There are matters, domestic and other, which may finally be decisive; but the issue I have stated seems to me the first one to be clear on, and if you can find time to give me a word of guidance on this I shall be very grateful.

Very sincerely yours,

ELIOT TO NEILSON

Asticou, Maine, 8 August

. . . I have known for some weeks that the presidency of Smith was open to you and indeed I was asked to express my opinion of your qualifications for that place. I testified that you were a first rate candidate for the presidency, but that I did not think you would accept it. My reasons for believing that you would not accept it were, first, that teaching language and literature and authorship were more congenial employment for you than educational administration, and secondly, that your present position and prospects promised greater serviceableness for American education and scholarship than the presidency of Smith. Naturally, I did not say all this to the persons interested in Smith who wrote to me about you; but these seemed to me clear considerations in favor of your remaining at Harvard.

If you go to Smith you will surely be involved immediately in the controversy which is going on there in the Board of Trustees and Alumnae concerning the future of the institution. One party wants to raise a great sum of money, buy a large tract of land on the opposite side of the river, and develop Smith in the direction of graduate study. The other party, which is at this moment in a majority, I believe, or at any rate in a strong minority, is opposed to any such expansion. President Burton seemed to me to be a strong advocate of both material and scholarly expansion.

It is difficult for me to give advice which is not colored by my zeal for Harvard; and in this case I feel no doubt that it is in the interest of Harvard University that you remain a professor therein. Nevertheless, I incline to think that if I were capable of looking solely to the interests of American education, I should advise you to stay where you are. . .

NEILSON TO ELIOT

Newcastle, Maine, 9 August

Many thanks for your prompt reply to my request for your view of the Smith matter.

I am not at all sure that I should find College administration less congenial than my present work; but as my experience of anything approaching a College presidency is almost nil, I have little basis for a judgment. Yet I am much interested in the education of women, and believe it to be a matter whose importance is going to increase in the immediate future, and I am confident that I should be keenly interested in the problems involved.

I am given to understand that, with my acceptance, the controversy about buying the State Hospital grounds and the development of graduate studies would be laid aside, unless I care to raise it again. In fact, between the first and second approach of the Trustees to me, they met and decided to give up this, if by so doing they could induce me to accept. I had told them at once that I should not be interested in a position where I was expected to raise money. If I should decide to consider the matter further, I will take pains to make certain on this point. I have an opportunity to do this through seeing T. W. Lamont, who is a Trustee and is at present in this neighborhood.

There remains your general opinion that I can be of more service to American education where I am than at Smith. This opinion has very great weight with me and may finally decide me to withdraw. At present, however, I confess I do not see grounds for it, unless I am unlikely to succeed at Smith, for to do at Smith what needs to be done there seems to me much more important than what I do now. I say this after very generous estimates from Briggs and Kittredge as to my value to the department. Mr. Lowell, I imagine, would be glad to save my salary; but this does not weigh with me, since under this regime one serves Harvard, not the President. . .

ELIOT TO NEILSON

Asticou, Maine, 11 August

In choosing between untried work at Smith and your present work at Harvard and Radcliffe, I hope you will give due weight to the risk you run at 48 years of age in abandoning work you know you can do well for work of a new sort under conditions which in all probability you cannot fully apprehend now or subsequently control. Furthermore, I trust that you will give no weight at all to your somewhat uncomfortable relations to President Lowell, or your lack of personal attachment to him. All full professors in Harvard serve the University and not the President; and on the whole, the service of Harvard University is the best service in the country for a scholar and teacher.

Let me report to you a bit of my own experience. When I went to Harvard University as its President in 1869, I fully expected to be able to keep up my acquaintance with Chemistry, and indeed to carry on certain chemical investigations in which I had lately been interested; but before I had been three months in office, I came to the conclusion that I could not possibly read enough Chemistry to keep up with the progress of the science, much less do any work in a laboratory. I think you would have the same experience if you went to Smith College as its President. You would find yourself compelled to abandon your present studies and your literary occupations. Doubtless you could deliver a few lectures to the Senior Class on English Literature, but that would be about all you could do in your present line of work.

Smith College is a young and very imperfect institution, and the education of women is in an unformed state in this country; so that you would have to give all your time and thought to the affairs of the College. That is, you would have to become an educational administrator.

I remain of the opinion that you can be of more service to American education where you are than at Smith; but I admit that I have had but little opportunity to form an estimate of your capacity in administrative work.

The relative importance of educating Harvard men and Smith women was a question which the Smith trustees were constrained to leave to Neilson's own judgment. His other points of hesitation they met with cordiality and promptness, as they had met the question of fund raising. One of these points was domestic. Fay had described Northampton to the Neilsons as a pleasant community to live in, a Connecticut Valley town of some twenty thousand inhabitants, most of them workers in the near-by paper and textile mills. The College was an important element in the civic economy but pretty much of a social entity. Northampton's streets were wide and elm-shaded; the architecture, both collegiate and domestic, was ugly but comfortable; the air was invigorating, and the climate would not seem rigorous to anyone accustomed to a Cambridge winter. But it was midsummer when the Neilsons visited Northampton and they saw both the town and the surrounding country at their worst. The day, to begin with, was much too hot; the Valley's trees and meadows spread parched and brown; the hills were hidden by a haze of heat; the whole place looked lifeless and thoroughly uninteresting. The

Ruskinian-Gothic President's House on Elm Street had been for the Seelyes a pleasant country residence; now trolley-cars clanged past its door and campus walks crossed the meadow where the presidential cow once grazed. Compared to her lovely Kirkland Street garden it seemed to Mrs. Neilson a dreary place in which to bring up children. She could not imagine, either, how the parlor, where it had once been possible to offer supper to the entire senior class, could be adapted to the kind of entertaining which should be done by the president of a college of two thousand. The trustees saw her point at once for they had been thinking along the same lines for some time. Buttressed by a personal pledge from Lamont they agreed to build in the immediate future, on a more peaceful site, a new President's House which should combine the functions of private family living and large scale entertaining.

Neilson was troubled also because, though the College was, by the terms of its foundation, nonsectarian, both its previous presidents had been ordained Congregational clergymen. He himself was not a member of any religious body and his beliefs were not entirely orthodox. He would wish certainly to address the students on moral and religious topics but he did not feel competent to conduct services as his predecessors had done, particularly services involving the offering of extempore prayer. The trustees, who had talked with him sufficiently to understand that this hesitation implied no lack of interest in the spiritual life of the college, agreed at once to any stipulation in this matter he chose to set.

The final decision, in which Mrs. Neilson played an important part, was made during the summer while the Neilsons were at Edgecomb in Maine, and on 14 September Neilson wrote to Eliot:

> It is with real surprise that I find myself writing you that I have decided not to follow your advice. I had not supposed that in a matter of the importance of this affair I should have failed to be guided by your opinion, especially when nearly all my colleagues whom I have consulted agreed with you. I hope to make my decision appear reasonable to you, and to find that you are disposed to give me further advice, in spite of my obstinacy this time.

One thing I may say—I believe I have acted without being influenced by my relations to University Hall; and now Mr. Lowell has written me in the most friendly fashion. So I leave Cambridge with only pleasant relations behind me—but with very many regrets.

On 17 September Eliot replied:

I must confess to being surprised at your decision to go to Smith College as President; but I dare say you will make your decision seem reasonable to me. At any rate, I shall always be glad to give you as well as I can any advice you may ask from me.

The lamentations from Harvard, and indeed from many other parts of the academic world, almost drowned the delight at Smith. Morris Cohen, Professor of Philosophy at the College of the City of New York, voiced a common opinion when he wrote of his "regret that one more productive scholar should be sacrificed to the administrative Moloch."

It is the devil and all your leaving Harvard [said K. G. T. Webster]: it just puts into mourning the Department and all your committees and clubs; the Department in fact is demagnetized, and the division, for graduate students, is irreparably maimed.

But a few other Harvardians were as prescient as Fay.

I know no one [wrote J. D. M. Ford, Professor of Romance Languages] of whom I can say with as absolute conviction as I can say it of you that he is thoroughly well constituted to be a college president. . . You must view with eminent satisfaction the step that you are now taking, and it is certainly a joy to your friends to behold a real scholar of great and solid achievement assuming the chief administrative post in a leading academic institution.

And Neilson's close friend Alfred Sheffield wrote:

The news of your call to Smith has come to me with a good deal of a pang, convinced though I am that your decision is the wise as well as the courageous one. I shall miss you immensely, and the family ties too: for 34 Kirkland had come to mean a spot where—whether I appeared often or seldom—the roots had struck so deep that they could be taken for granted.

The comments that we begin to hear on your change will, I think, continue to be in the same strain: viz., that it is evidence of powers as yet untapped, and of a fine readiness to break away from a life that could have become very comfortable as well as honorable, for the sake of making your ideals operative in the life of a whole college. What I look forward to is your initiating a new type of college president, one that really appreciates the contagious power of productive scholarship in a teacher's influence, and that keeps a watchful eye on all the symptoms of intellectual tone in the student body. I believe that good men will find themselves drawn to Smith largely for the advantage of teaching under you.

Although the Smith trustees had agreed to let Neilson wait until February if necessary before taking up his office, both Lowell and the Department of English agreed that he should be allowed to leave Harvard at once. "First Chapel," the opening exercise of the Smith year, was scheduled for 20 September and Neilson arranged to present himself in Northampton a few days in advance. The shifting of living quarters was never a matter of any moment to him but the transplanting of the family was another matter. The new baby, Caroline, was only eight months old; Mrs. Neilson was having one of her recurrent bouts of arthritis; and she had not merely to move herself and the children but ten years' accumulation of household goods. It was agreed that the family should not take up residence until the Christmas vacation; Neilson would in the meantime camp out in the President's house and take his meals at Rahar's tavern. This proved, quite without premeditation, an admirable method of establishing easy, informal relations with a group of bachelor members of the faculty who regularly ate there. Ladies seldom went to Rahar's in those days because the agreeable Irish proprietor served beer.

The new President reached Northampton incognito, late in the evening, a few days before the opening of College. The town was overflowing with the parents of entering freshmen, but the proprietor of the old Draper Hotel on Main Street received him cordially and installed him in one of his own family rooms. Neilson took a short walk before going to bed to orient himself in his new home.

Northampton began for him, as it does for most arrivals, at the long platform of the Boston and Maine Railroad which spans the foot of Main Street. That broad thoroughfare ascends, with a curve or two, for half a mile to the college campus, whose prow divides Main Street into Elm and West. There are few trees left on Main Street now but it has the fine breadth proper to a New England town and it has the requisite number of churches: the First Church (which means of course the First Congregational), the Edwards Church (commemorating the pastorate of the great Jonathan), a Unitarian church, a big Catholic church near the campus. Opposite the Edwards Church stands the Academy of Music, then vacillating between municipal theater and the movies. The character of the Main Street shops is obviously influenced by the presence of two thousand young women. There are two good bookstores, several spacious dispensaries of ice cream, many dress shops, and a very elegant florist's.

College Hall, oldest of the Smith buildings, stands at the entrance to what Neilson once called "the campus proper (if it isn't too suggestive to refer to Paradise Pond as the campus improper)." College Hall is a pleasant specimen of the collegiate Gothic of the 1870's. By virtue of a well-proportioned tower, weather-darkened red brick, plenty of ivy, and the patina that comes from serving as a sentimental symbol, it has acquired an agreeable individuality. It houses chiefly administrative offices, the "Assembly Room" having been replaced in 1910 by spacious John M. Greene Hall, named for the young clergyman who advised Sophia Smith to leave her fortune for the founding of a female college. Near College Hall stands Dewey House, a dignified Greek Revival mansion, built in 1827. It was purchased from Judge Dewey with part of the college land and made into the first dormitory. It is still in active service. None of the other buildings, recitation halls or dormitories, have any pretensions to aesthetic grace. What virtues they have are strictly practical, for President Seelye's qualities did not include a taste in architecture superior to that of his day. Building was done as the College grew, without any particular plan, producing what Neilson once described as "a certain confused picturesqueness." He enjoyed also calling the attention of the alumnae to "how well we have succeeded in hiding our architecture" by skilful planting of elms and apple trees, of azalea, ivy, and rhododendron. To the north of the campus lies the little lake which Jenny Lind, on her honeymoon, christened Paradise Pond. The College uses its waters for boating, its grassy banks and the woods beyond for what, in 1917, were called "bacon bats."

On 20 September the new President wrote his wife:

I have got over the first two days without catastrophe and with a steadily improving digestion—which I am sure you will regard as a good sign. . .

As I wrote you, I had a busy day in Cambridge on Tuesday, and got here hungry at 9 P.M., had supper and a walk and went to bed incognito, except for the hotel keeper, who gave up one of his family rooms to me, since every place was full of freshmen's parents. I had fortunately telegraphed from Boston in the morning. In Cambridge I had got a colossal mail which kept me busy for hours. I suppose since I left you I have had over a hundred letters of congratulation, and they still come. . .

On Friday afternoon I went to a faculty reception for parents and relatives and was pleasant to all the Mrs. Joneses from Little Rock, Arkansas. I dined with Gardiner [chairman of the Department of Philosophy] at his inn, and then went to Faculty meeting. After routine business, I made a short speech on my general attitude, which seems to have been well received. Then I met all the faculty and returned to Gardiner's room for some whiskey and a smoke after a somewhat exhausting evening. I did not smoke from 9 A.M. till 7 P.M., having lunched with ex-President Seelye.

This morning I was presented to the College at Morning Chapel by Seelye. It was his eightieth birthday, which enabled me to switch my speech quickly off myself and on to him, and I came off pretty well, it seems. It rather took my breath away—the huge hall, packed with over 2300 people. Then Seelye and I walked from the Hall to my office and the girls were lined up all the way—it seemed a mile, and sang to or at us. Later I had to go out on the steps to make another speech. I felt like a damned prima donna.

So far there is nothing but friendliness and cordiality. Doubtless I shall soon see where the difficulties are to be, but the good will is evident.

At eleven I gave fatherly advice to the Freshmen, and I spent the afternoon going over the College property with the professor of botany, Genong, who also superintends the trees, etc. on the grounds. [Much as he enjoyed Neilson's interest in the shrubs and trees Genong was disturbed because the new President, as they talked, puffed steadily at a cigar. Finally he told him that there was an unwritten law that no one smoked on the campus. Neilson replied pleasantly that he was being obliged to learn so many new written laws that he would not attempt to keep the unwritten ones.]

Seelye's attitude is perfect, and he is a most likeable old boy. His wife is a frail bit of old china. Miss Jordan [chairman of the Department of English] is going to be all right: at present, anyhow, she is ready to eat out of my hand. I think she is a good sport.

Between times I receive people in my office and read letters. The Chapel matter is being arranged all right.

So far the prospects are better than I had dared to hope. Hurry up and get well, and get into the game.

I am eager to see you and Liz and tell you lots of things. The letters are in some cases very funny.

We shall come through all right, dear.

11

The President and the Faculty

"Good scholars," said Neilson in his inaugural address (1918) at Smith College, "can usually be found by searching; great teachers are the gift of heaven. All we can do is to cherish those we have and hope for more." He did not use the verb "cherish" lightly. Every day, for twenty-two years, with care, with ingenuity, Neilson cherished his scholar-teachers, building at Smith a faculty whose quality and *esprit de corps* were a constant wonder to his fellow presidents. This labor he thought the most interesting and the most important part of his administrative function, and the most difficult.

When Sidney Fay first broached to him the possibility of becoming a college president, Neilson said that he felt few doubts about his ability to handle the academic part of the job. He had his experience at Columbia and Bryn Mawr as well as Harvard and a wide acquaintance with promising young men and women in many parts of the academic world; he thought that he would have no difficulty in recruiting and steering a good faculty; but about the administrative side, budget making, investments, bricks and mortar, he felt very dubious; these were practical matters in which he had little experience and he was uncertain of his ability to handle them. A dozen years later, when President Neilson had raised faculty salaries, landscaped the campus, built six new dormitories, a music building, and a gymnasium, Fay recalled this statement and Neilson confessed, a little ruefully, that the situation had proved precisely the reverse of his anticipation. He had found it relatively easy to deal with finance, building, and administrative detail; the hard thing had been to get and hold as good a faculty as he wanted.

This was, of course, not so much an admission of lack of capability as a statement of his awareness of the great problem which presents itself to all college presidents. He phrased it in June 1932, in an article for *Scribner's:*

> There are not nearly enough first-rate teachers to go round. The art of teaching is a difficult one, requiring solid learning, imagination, the power of arousing curiosity, the faculty of clear exposition, industry, patience, enthusiasm either for a subject or for the young, and a sympathetic personality. Such qualities are highly marketable, and many departments of life compete for them.

This competition in the open market Neilson met with both spiritual and material weapons. His faculty knew that they could count in any situation on administrative integrity and courage; they felt, as they phrased it in a resolution passed on the occasion of his tenth anniversary, the "eagerness" with which he welcomed suggestions looking towards increased vitality of teaching; and they were pretty certain that for almost any problem, academic, economic, personal, the President could invent a swift, ingenious solution.

He was resourceful, for instance, in devising means of increasing faculty stipends without the expenditure of money. Smith's salaries equaled those of the other women's colleges but, like them, she operated on a budget which would have seemed to her masculine compeers entirely impossible. Amherst, for example, just across the Connecticut River, with half as many students as Smith had an endowment four times as large. It was all too easy for the men's colleges and the state universities to offer a teacher more than Smith could ever pay him.

One of Neilson's substitutes for salary was time, which, he knew, the good scholar values beyond money. He kept committee and administrative work down; he kept the teaching load light: nine hours usually for a full professor, not more than twelve for anyone. In addition to this the Smith schedule set classes on consecutive instead of alternate days so that if a professor chose he might do all his teaching at one end or the other of the week, preserving a stretch of free time for his own research and writing, or even—Neilson was quite ready to permit this—giving a course or two at some institution in Boston or New York. Then, too, a Registrar and other administrative officers who were encouraged to be humane rather than bureaucratic, catered as far as possible to such individual faculty whims as a dislike of early classes or a preference for free Saturdays. Anyone in the upper teaching brackets could expect to arrange his time pretty much as he liked.

He could employ his time as he liked, too. If, instead of scholarly articles, professors wanted to write criticism, like Newton Arvin, or poetry, like Grace Hazard Conklin, they were encouraged to do so. Young instructors asking advice about the necessity of proceeding to the Ph.D. were told that if they wanted to move from Smith they would probably find it essential but if they remained in Northampton and proved their worth in other ways it might be dispensed with. Yet, despite his broad definition of the term, Neilson believed strongly in research.

> The antithesis between teaching and research [he said in 1927] which is reflected today in many educational journals and on many platforms is a false antithesis. So far from having an institution make up its mind whether it will teach or seek new truth, I do not think that it can teach effectively unless a large part of its faculty is interested in new truth and is participating in the search for it.
>
> It is my opinion that effectiveness of teaching, which I believe is our first interest here at Smith, is dependent upon the intellectual activity of the teacher. I do not believe that you will find a college teacher accomplishing the best results who is not interested in the progress in his or her particular field and is not following the research at the frontier. Nor do I believe that it is possible to follow research at the frontier without an impulse to take part in the pioneer work there, to experiment and find out for oneself.

Another practical device for increasing the comfort of a faculty, Neilson realized, is pleasant and inexpensive housing. It had long been the practice to have in each college house a "resident faculty," a woman who had no responsibility except what she cared to take in the way of friendliness to the undergraduates. Neilson made these positions, which offered lodging and board at very low rates, still more attractive by seeing to it that the faculty suites in the dormitories he built were agreeable and commodious. He also began the practice, when the college needed additional land for dormitories or for protection, of buying, and frequently moving, houses which could be offered at low rentals as additional inducement to men he was trying to attract or keep.

Sometimes Smith managed to enlist a good man by offering a position to his wife as well. Neilson saw no objection to a husband and wife teaching in the same or different departments, though this occasionally produced amusingly inconvenient situations. Late one spring, for instance, he wrote to the head of another institution asking that a young instructor, under contract there, be released to take a position at Smith.

> I should hesitate to make any request of this kind were there not very special circumstances. Mr. W. is to be married this summer to a member of the faculty here and there are obvious economic as well as sentimental reasons why they should wish to be in the same place.

And, two weeks later:

> Many thanks for your considerateness in the matter of Mr. W. You have the satisfaction of having smoothed the course of true love.

Both previous Smith presidents had believed in having a large proportion of men on their faculties and this practice Neilson increased. His faculty was approximately half men and half women. Some of the women teachers, especially those of an older vintage, were unalterably convinced that the men were favored in salary and promotion, and there were occasional alumnae flurries on this point which Neilson answered squarely:

> Every salary is an individual bargain. In making these no distinction is observed between women and men and the fact that there are more men at the top is due to two things;—first, that there are more men of superior ability and equipment in the profession, and second, that such men are in more demand than the women and con-

sequently, through receiving calls, have often more rapid promotion. At the same time we attempt to prevent the women from suffering from their smaller chance of getting calls, and increases of salary since I came have been overwhelmingly more numerous for women than for men. We are now approaching the point where in my judgment women of the faculty get as nearly their deserts as the men do. (Letter to the Boston Smith Club, 1 February 1921)

Occasionally Neilson was constrained to defend the men of the faculty when he thought *they* were being discriminated against. Early in the twenties an informal faculty tea hour originated in one of the college buildings and Neilson, who liked to attend from time to time, found that the well-mannered gentlemen of the faculty frequently went hungry because there were so many ladies whom they felt obliged to serve before they filled their own cups. He saved the situation by affixing to the wall a neatly printed placard: "No civilities to women, no incivilities to men."

Another bond by which Neilson held his faculty he forged without premeditation. When anyone remarked that his professors were devoted to him he brushed the idea aside as a pleasant exaggeration. His interest in people was genuine and spontaneous, quite without ulterior motive. He really wanted to know how a new course or a new baby, a book or a piece of research was progressing. If he could lend advice or assistance he proffered it swiftly. An associate professor who went to tell him of her approaching marriage, and ask whether she might continue her teaching, recalls with affection the way in which he gave a quick glance at her record which lay on his desk and said, "It seems to have been some time since we made any acknowledgement of our appreciation of your services. I think your marriage would be an appropriate moment for an increase in salary." Scrupulously economical as he was about most expenditures, he would agree readily to the purchase of a costly book or piece of apparatus needed to facilitate some original research. Occasionally his spontaneous interest was too keen and he had later to reassure an alarmed department that his expressed pleasure in the special work being done by some young member did not necessarily mean that he wanted her to offer a full course in the subject.

Neilson was generous not only with funds but with his time. If anyone wanted to talk with him about affairs professional or personal he was ready to listen, and his ability to analyze a situation swiftly and accurately was highly illuminating. He would give his opinion but never imposed it and insisted always that the individual make his own decision. In professional matters he could draw on a wide range of knowledge of institutions and of people and was frank to indiscretion in expressing his estimate of what it would be like to teach at this or that university or to work under a certain professor as a department head. His faculty were aware that they imposed on him but they continued to do so, bringing to his office an astonishing range of problems and dilemmas. In professional questions Neilson would separate, often with amusement, his opinions as administrator and as friend:

> Speaking as President [he wrote, for instance, in September 1924], I should have to say that a resignation at this date would be very awkward for us. Speaking as a friend, I should advise getting as specific a proposition as possible to lay before the Administration, in order to extract the maximum benefit.

The professional problems were only a fraction of those laid on the desk in College Hall. "What!" a young instructor's wife was heard to say to a new colleague apropos of a matter of garbage disposal. "You didn't? I always run straight to President Neilson when anything goes wrong." And that was common practice. The devout young man who was wondering whether he would not be serving God better in the ministry consulted Neilson, and received an assignment to an interesting piece of committee work which more than absorbed his surplus energies. The devoted daughter who asked whether she should give up teaching and go home to care for her aged mother had her problem settled by a year's leave of absence. The spinster professor who went to tell the President that she was going to adopt a baby found herself walking out of his office a Class Dean with four hundred daughters.

And there were even less conventional situations. A classical scholar of international reputation recalls an incident which bulked large in her first year of teaching. She had come to Smith fresh from graduate school where she had been so seriously and thoroughly immersed in the obtaining of her Ph.D. that she had given no thought at all to matters other than academic. During her first semester at Smith she was so absorbed in the new delights of teaching that she scarcely took time to look about her but one spring day she began to sense the color and gayety of Northampton. The trees were just coming into leaf, the daffodils were blossoming, every undergraduate looked fresh and pretty in a bright skirt and sweater; she, in her ancient tweeds, she suddenly realized, was the "only ink spot on the campus." Obviously some new clothes were a necessity if she was to continue to make an impression on the bright young persons who sat before her, but the means? The only method which occurred to her was an advance on her salary, and, in a surge of courage, she asked for an appointment with the President. She was a shy young woman anyway and as she was ushered through the office door the absurdity of the situation came to her and she longed to retreat but it was too late. She sat down beside the administrative desk and blurted out her story. Neilson listened pleasantly, looked her carefully up and down, and agreed that there was certainly need for alteration. A salary advance, he said, was not a usual practice but he would be glad to make her a personal loan. "I should think," looking her over again, "you might want as much as two hundred dollars?" That, she gasped, would be wonderful and she began to express her gratitude. There was no need for that, he assured her, this was a business transaction; she would pay him back, with interest, at her convenience. The matter would be quite confidential between them. He would send her the check just as soon as his secretary was out of sight and he could get at his personal check book. In a few days the ink spot had vanished from the campus and the teaching of Latin prose had materially improved.

Not all the personal problems were so pleasant. He had not supposed, Neilson once said sadly, that when he went to Smith he would find himself conducting a bureau of marital counseling but his advice in difficult domestic relationships was in constant demand. In these situations Neilson absolutely declined to sit in judgment; he would lend what help he could to either party but he would not take sides.

These methods, conscious and unconscious, of maintaining a staff did not, of course, all go into effect at once, nor were the attitudes of mind that initiated them immediately apparent. Some less agreeable administrative manners presented themselves first and some personal ones, too, although most of the faculty were immediately delighted with Neilson as a colleague. Some of them, though, found him critical and sharp-tongued, and, as the students did in his first years, not infrequently imagined that he was mocking them. As they learned to know him better and as he learned to temper his wit, most of the faculty resentment turned to affection and enthusiasm, though there were a few intransigents who continued for twenty years to oppose and disapprove and some others whose New England manner concealed from the President the fact that they had come around. Part of the individual dislike was engendered by an impression that, if they had not had tenure, Neilson would have been glad to separate certain persons from the Smith faculty. He had found there what he occasionally referred to as "a wad of associate professors" who did not have the advanced scholarly experience he wanted in his teachers and whose enthusiasm for their calling had withered with the years. But the most serious source of discontent was undoubtedly Neilson's manner of conducting faculty meetings.

President Seelye, and President Burton followed suit, had been accustomed to interpret the role of presiding officer as that of an impartial chairman who proposed a question, permitted the faculty to discuss it as long as they pleased, listened objectively, and then put the matter to a vote. Neilson took a vigorous part in the debate, presenting his views so forcefully and convincingly that the younger men and women, who were inclined to admire him enthusiastically, often accepted his opinion without thinking about the subject further. And Neilson, who made his own decisions swiftly, frequently grew impatient with the academic predilection for prolonged discussion of minor points and brought a controversy to a vote before some laggards felt that they had had their say. This procedure was not really so much the result of temperament as of experience. Eliot had conducted Harvard faculty meetings in this manner and so had Lowell. It simply did not occur to Neilson that this might not be the universal American method.

Neilson had also to contend with the fact that he was not President Burton. Among Burton's administrative gifts was an ability to express convincingly to his associates his admiration for the work they were doing. Neilson seldom put his approval into words, partly through Scottish reticence but chiefly because he so deeply believed that work well done was its own reward. Praise seemed to him superfluous, if not impertinent. Many of his colleagues, especially those of the feminine sex, missed the outspoken Burton encouragement. Burton also was accustomed to take the advice of certain older members of the faculty whose judgment did not always seem to Neilson sound, and they naturally resented their diminished power. Often it was less diminished than they thought. Neilson might oppose them flatly in some of their attempts to direct college policy but he had a keen eye for their real value and a delighted appreciation of the individual idiosyncrasies which, particularly perhaps in New England, add so much color to academic life. Again and again, on the occasion of the resignation or the death of an elder member of the faculty, he painted for the undergraduates a discriminating and appreciative portrait of a teacher who had effectively influenced and shaped Smith College even though she might, on occasion, have inconvenienced its third president. Neilson's skill in detecting latent virtues was so great that one member of his faculty announced to her friends during that lowest point of the academic year, the weeks before spring vacation, that she had decided to let herself be run over as she crossed Elm Street—a very easy thing to do—and then listen to what the President said about her in chapel next morning.

Many of the subjects of Neilson's academic portraits were surprised at what he said of them but they could hardly be displeased.

Of Associate Professor Louisa Cheever, for instance, of the department of English, on her retirement in 1934:

To many college generations Miss Cheever has stood as the embodiment of certain virtues and graces which have been none too conspicuous in the generations that she has latterly taught. I know that the older generations will remember her for these, and I trust the younger generations, as they get further away from College, will see them in the proper perspective, and will see a greater need than they have always shown for their imitation.

Of Professor Julia Caverno, chairman of the department of Greek, at her retirement (1931):

Miss Caverno has always been the candid friend. This is a phrase which the cynical might interpret as dubious praise—but the extraordinary thing has been that she has always been candid without malice, and always not only with beneficent intention—a dangerous thing really, if it is only intention—but with real beneficence. No member of the faculty did more to guide my faltering footsteps when I was new here. No member added so much to the gayety and wisdom of faculty councils as Miss Caverno. It would be a happy thing if the trustees could invent some position like "Commentator at large," and confer it on her!

Of Professor Anna Cutler, chairman of the department of philosophy, at a luncheon given in her honor at the time of her retirement (1929):

Miss Cutler is outstanding in being one of a small group of people who are always able to think first in terms of the College rather than in terms of their specialties. No one who has not been connected with a college faculty knows how rare this quality is. . . I feel I must touch on Miss Cutler's prevailing vice, which is discretion. I say this with regret, because Miss Cutler could have meant so much more to me—had she been less discreet! You had to get to know her very well before you found there were ways around her discretion. I might almost say that she is leaving us just as I was able to find my way around her discretion by a hidden path.

The most complete of Neilson's portraits was that of Professor Emeritus Mary Augusta Jordan of the department of English who died on 14 April 1941. Neilson, then President Emeritus, happened to be in Northampton at the time and President

Davis asked him to describe to the undergraduates "Jordie" whom they had never seen but knew as a Smith tradition.

When I came here twenty-four years ago [Neilson told them], I think I can say, without making any unpleasant comparison or slighting anyone, that the most vivid personality on this campus was Miss Jordan. She had been here in the department of English since 1884. She came when the College was only nine years old. And she had been the dominant figure in the department of English in spite of the fact that there were several other women in that department of very striking personality. She was the person on the faculty whom her colleagues listened to and waited for with a particular kind of interest.

She was a little woman, with tiny hands and feet, and bright birdlike eyes; and she darted about the campus interested in everybody and everybody's business and taking a hand in most of the things that occurred here. . . she was a trifle eccentric; and I don't think she resisted the temptation to be eccentric. She was a piquant and interesting personality—piquant and interesting to herself as well as to other people.

She taught English writing and English literature. Her courses were events. . . They were courses in Miss Jordan rather than in Pope or Dryden. . . The class exercises were occupied with a running comment on things in general, on human nature and events. She had a great curiosity about human nature, not just in general but in individuals; and she believed that she could be of use to individuals. She was of use to a great many . . . she stimulated people to write, and most of the distinguished authors who have come out of this college have been products of Miss Jordan's teaching. . .

Her influence . . . was a sound, clarifying influence—against sentimentality, against self-deception, and in favor of straight thinking. Yet in my experience her own thinking could not be described as straight. I never could follow her thinking. It zigzagged; it went like lightning now in this direction and now in that, with great rapidity and great suddenness. You never knew what was coming next. It was the quality of the incalculable that made Miss Jordan such an entertaining figure on the campus, and made the College such an interesting place to live in while she was here. . .

With Professor Harry Norman Gardiner, a transplanted Englishman, chairman of the department of philosophy, Neilson early formed a warm friendship which ripened for ten years, unimpaired by Gardiner's tendency to rise in faculty meetings saying sternly to the Chair, "Sir, I take issue with you!" When Gardiner died in December 1927, Neilson spoke at the memorial service held in his honor in John M. Greene Hall.

One of the most characteristic things in Mr. Gardiner as I saw and knew him was the combination of quietness with intensity. I think everyone knows what I mean by his quietness. He lived, apparently, a placid life, interesting himself in many of the current affairs of this community, of the country, and of the world, and yet kept his repose, but it was a repose which was in no sense dependent upon a sluggishness of nature. There was fire in his inside.

He cared intensely and could express himself intensely. Mr. Gardiner was capable, I rejoice to say, of losing his temper, of being really angry, of speaking to a colleague in the height of that feeling, but it was a temper directed against what he believed to be error. Those who did not know him, and who might be victims of the outburst, would not know what to make of it when they met him the next day and found him supremely unconscious of having had a personal encounter, for it had not been a personal encounter at all.

He was a great lover of good form. He cared enormously about form in life. He carried good taste into all his activities, professional, social, academic. . . No one in our community spoke so beautifully as Mr. Gardiner. So long as he was with us and could talk to us there was something to point to when one wanted students to understand what the English language is. . .

Mr. Gardiner was a great friend. He had a genius for friendship. . .

[Then, reading from a letter of Gardiner's to a former colleague], "the contribution to the world of a life of beauty of spirit . . . is worth more than the contribution of a good book, unless it is a very good book indeed, and to write that one needs to be gifted."

There is Mr. Gardiner's philosophy of life. There is the explanation and defense of the paucity of his printed documents—the contribution to the world of a life of beauty of spirit. . .

The holograph notes for this character sketch, which survive, indicate how Neilson planned beforehand the content and structure of his speeches, leaving the stimulus of the moment to supply the garment of words.

Quiet yet intense
Temper—not against persons
Love of good form
conduct and manners
English style
Hand writing
Speech
Genius for friendship
England, Amherst
Gallantry
His ripeness and end

Analyses such as these Neilson could have made of almost any member of his faculty. He knew them all, from the moment of their appointment, and before. The recruiting of the teaching staff he considered one of the most important parts of his function. And he believed that it was his function. He consulted, in making an appointment, with the department concerned but most of the correspondence, the personal interview on which he insisted, and the final decision were his.

In this recruiting of teachers and in holding them, duties which often involved sharp competition with other administrators, Neilson was always scrupulously candid, laying all his cards on the table. Asked, for example, to suggest a candidate for the presidency of a college of good standing, he recommended warmly one of his class deans:

> I am making this recommendation partly because since you ask my advice I give you the best I have, and partly because Miss Benedict [Professor Suzan Benedict of the department of mathematics] deserves further opportunity than she has here. At the same time, I will say candidly that I will not advise her to go, since I should find it very difficult to fill her place here and the interests of Smith seem to me to demand that I do my best to keep her here. But it by no means follows that she will take my advice or that my efforts will be successful. [They were.]

In another case he wrote:

> I think it is entirely proper for you to write for information, and of course also to invite any member of the faculty here to come to

you. I warn you, however, that I shall do my best to hold Mr. Welch here.

And he went on to describe Professor Roy Welch of the department of music as an uncommonly good lecturer and a very delightful member of the community.

And again:

> Sidney Fay is generally and justly regarded as about the best man on the faculty here, both as a scholar and as a teacher. He is very wise so that we always want him on committees. You can get him only over my dead body.

In making appointments Neilson was correspondingly frank:

> My intention was to offer you an appointment as assistant professor at $2,000 [this was in 1921]. Of course, I should be glad to get you at this price, but I should also be glad of the opportunity to consider a higher salary in case you are given more favorable opportunities elsewhere.

In the tangled administrative situations that sometimes arise from calls to another institution made late in the year Neilson never stood on his rights. He proceeded, he said, on the principle that "a man has only one life and the College is more or less immortal so that I always feel that the individual's career should come first."

When a man did decide to leave Smith for what looked like a greener field Neilson was generously friendly in his comprehension of the factors which had weighted the choice. To a sociologist, for instance, going to a large state university in the Middle West, he wrote:

> I cannot pretend not to understand the ground for your decision. In your subject the mere fact that you are in a large urban community gives great advantage over our situation here and I can see the opportunities in every direction which appeal to you. . . I wish you all kinds of success in your new surroundings.

To an historian, whom he had tried to keep by every kind of pressure, he said finally, "I don't blame you. Under similar circumstances I should have decided just as you have." But he felt free to tease these delinquents in public about their bad judgment.

Mr. Curti is going [1937] to Columbia University. Mr. Becker to the University of Wisconsin, and Mr. Grant * to Williams. I think all these gentlemen are laboring under the delusion that somehow it is more dignified, or more worth while, or more important, or more something to teach men than to teach women. It shows again that we have not yet completed our work in the education of our faculty. I know that they will repent it. I look forward to their change of mind with a certain amount of satisfaction. I am torn between my good will towards them and my desire to make them realize their failure to see their privileges here. It is not only a matter of sex: they think that they are going to be more important because they are going to teach graduate students. Now I have great respect for our graduate students in this College and anything I may say will not reflect upon them and their quality. I have had long experience in the teaching of graduate students. I do not think they are as much worth while as undergraduates. These professors believe that because they are going to a great university and going to teach graduate students, they are going to be in a more advantageous situation for the pursuit of their own researches—another illusion. The graduate students will take all their ideas, all their time, all their energy; their own productive work will slow up. To these gentlemen and to their wives, I extend sympathy, but to the institutions that have acquired them, I extend congratulations.

Often the departing scholar went looking longingly back over his shoulder. Smith under Neilson was, one of them said, "an academic Eden such as we shall never see again."

All these teachers whose departure Neilson mourned had in common the quality which he thought most essential to the profession, "enthusiasm either for their subject or for the young." *Accidia* was for him the unpardonable academic sin. Its eradication from the profession was, he thought, the great unsolved problem of education. He devoted much thought to remedies for what he called the "soggy middle" of the faculty, teachers who should never have entered the profession at all and those who, beginning well, had eventually ceased to grow.

* Professors Merle Curti, history; Howard Becker, government; Elliott Grant, French.

> A man or woman who has reached middle age in a profession in which normal promotion has indicated proficiency, and in which life tenure is guaranteed, will in many cases be tempted to relax unless other forces, internal or external, stimulate to continued development. The necessary repetition called for by each succeeding student generation makes for the digging of ruts from which after a time escape is difficult.

In those terms Neilson described the situation in an article he wrote for the *Survey Graphic* (October 1939) near the close of his administrative term. Much as he admired the work of the American Association of University Professors in exposing and correcting cases of unjust dismissal, he thought it incumbent on them to help the presidents also with the larger and more difficult problem of disposing of the unfit. (He never quite forgave the AAUP for removing him from membership when he changed from a professor to a president. He insisted that they would attain all their objectives more rapidly if they worked with the administrators instead of excluding them from their councils.)

> Security of tenure [the *Survey* article runs] for the able and efficient teacher, as long as he remains able and efficient, is wholly desirable. But to assure it to all teachers after a certain length of service and without any condition except abstinence from theft, adultery, or murder, is not in the best interests of education. The greatest problem of the educational administrator, greater even than that of the finding of good teachers, is the problem of getting rid of dead wood.

With individual cases of dead wood Neilson often ingeniously dealt. Sometimes for a man who had lost the teaching spark he would invent an executive position which could be filled by mere industry and good will. Sometimes he put into practice a method he advocated in an address to the Modern Language Association in 1924:

> I am inclined to think that early retirement on a pension would in many cases be a better economy than to continue to pay full salaries to men who kill the interest of students and discredit their subjects.

At a meeting of the Associated Harvard Clubs in 1940 he suggested that each college president should be provided with a fund for this purpose.

That, I admit, is not a very statesmanlike proposal, but it is a practical one, and personally I feel that in the few cases where I have been able by good fortune to put it into practice I think I have done more for the institution which I was connected with than I ever have done in a positive way by the selection of the right people. The removal of obstacles of that kind in the case of department after department has led to revivification, revitalizing of the department, and has been worth a great deal more than it cost.

That the success of a teacher is not an entirely one-sided affair Neilson was perfectly aware. He took pains from time to time to impress upon the undergraduates a sense of their responsibility for the effectiveness of the educational process.

The faculty has a great many interesting and learned people on it. I want you to take this statement of mine on faith for the moment and regard it as a challenge to your instincts for discovery—regarding yourselves as having these one, two, three, or four years in which to see how much you can make out of that faculty, the active role having passed from them to you. They are willing to deliver to you what they have got in the way of erudition and ideas and stimulus. But it is for you to get it out of the faculty, just as you do out of the books in the library. . . If you leave here not knowing the riches that might have been yours, the criticism is against you. We will cooperate, we will be more than passive, but the burden of activity is on you.

There was a corollary to this matter of academic zeal: the devoted teacher, usually a woman and a New Englander, who was inclined to work not below but above her strength, to take on burdens not really required or to hurry a convalescence so that she would not be neglecting her classes. Neilson, with his own inclination to finish a job at any cost, became adroit in cajoling the too zealous into caution.

I am very sorry to know that your arm is giving you so much opportunity for the cultivation of patience. . . I suggest your sending on to a member of the department lists of reading for those classes that can be so employed and let the others have a cut. I am sure they get their money's worth out of your course in any case and we need not have it on our conscience that they have two or three days free.

The high value Neilson placed on enthusiasm caused him to be accused now and then of having faculty "favorites," people who were sure to get anything they asked for from the administration, and the accusation had its truth. Neilson liked to further the activity of anyone who was really doing a job. A departmental chairman with eagerness and energy could sometimes push his subject to a place of disproportionate importance in the curriculum, but there was in general lively appreciation for the devices by which the President encouraged faculty zeal.

One of these was the promotion of graduate study which, he knew, was an excellent incentive to better undergraduate teaching. He did not think that Smith was equipped, either in library facilities or in faculty, to offer work for the Ph.D. but she could give an M.A. which would have real value and distinction. During his administration the number of graduate students increased from twenty-five to nearly one hundred, and Smith was giving more masters' degrees than any other woman's college.

Neilson's theory was that many young women with A.B.'s from the smaller colleges were totally lost during the first year of graduate work in a large, impersonal university, such as Columbia. Smith, where attention was paid to them as individuals, could teach them—to their advantage and the universities'—the methods of graduate study.

Another device for keeping the faculty active was the encouragement of publication. Neilson knew from personal experience that seeing your work in print is an instant incentive to doing more work. He increased the subsidies for the series of *Smith College Studies in History* and in the *Classics,* which had been started under President Burton, and added to them *Smith College Studies in Modern Languages,* and a series on the economic history of the Connecticut Valley. When the College celebrated (1925) the anniversary of its founding, nine books by members of the faculty were issued as Fiftieth Anniversary Publications.

Occasionally Neilson regretted this stimulation of scholarship. Commenting (Last Chapel 1933) on the departure to Harvard of Professor Julius Seelye Bixler of the department of philosophy, he said:

Mr. Bixler has been one of the very best of our teachers. During these last years he has brought a further but partly dangerous distinction to the College by his own publications. One is supposed to encourage publication, especially distinguished publications by the faculty, but I am not quite sure it would not be better to penalize it, and hide our light under a bushel, and not let envious brother colleges know what we have got.

The appreciation of Bixler included another professional quality on which Neilson put great stress:

He has been one of the members of our community who seemed to me to matter even more because of their stimulus to their colleagues than through their direct teaching.

Experience in the Cambridge lunch and dinner clubs had led Neilson to put a high value on the vivifying effects of good talk. He realized that Smith's collegiate size and Northampton's isolated situation worked to turn the faculty in on themselves so that the personality of a prospective member was more important than it might be in a large university. Again and again in letters to academic friends asking for information about a candidate, the questions on scholarship and teaching ability are followed with, "I should like your judgment on him as a member of our community."

The academic sin which, next to *accidia,* most troubled Neilson was departmentalism. He felt, however, that it was not incurable. As a matter of fact he had once practiced departmentalism himself, as he confessed to the Alumnae Council in 1920.

Getting the faculty to think educationally instead of in terms of departments . . . is the hardest thing you can ever try to induce a faculty to do. Lest I seem superior—if you had not asked me to come to Smith College I should never have thought educationally, although I had been a teacher all my days. I had some ideas about the teaching of my subject and a bundle of prejudices about other subjects, and that is the normal condition of the college professor. Yet I think it is possible to draw a faculty out of their departments and get their ideas directed towards educational progress. You thought they did that in committees on curricula and so on. They do not. The committee on curriculum in the ordinary college is an organization for bartering and making compromises. They do not think educationally.

They simply say, "We will vote for your subject, if you will vote for having our subject compulsory."

One of the strongest of the bonds by which Neilson attached his faculty was the uncompromising stand he took in defense of academic freedom. This was a position which seemed to him inevitable.

Neither twenty-one years ago nor now [he said at the time of his retirement] is there any discussion in this student body or in this faculty or among the trustees or the alumnae of the question of academic freedom of speech. This has been from the foundation of the College taken for granted. It is taken for granted now. It has never been seriously assailed. We see no prospect that it will ever be. Of course we stand for freedom of speech and we find no one to dispute it with us.

That statement, though quite literally true, minimizes the courage and pertinacity with which the President, particularly during the witch-hunting twenties, warded off attacks by individuals outside the College, by parents, by alumnae even. There was in the United States between the Wars a widespread fear of "radicalism" or "bolshevism," a vague specter supposed to be engaged in undermining not only the national government but the sanctity of the American home. Pacifism was dangerous, too, the first step towards communism. Professors who discussed Russia in their classrooms, or labor problems, or the new social mores were immediately suspect. Their accusers seldom troubled to inquire in what terms the discussion was couched. Even worse, because more conspicuous, was the professor who made public addresses on subjects of current controversy, or wrote letters to the papers, or signed petitions.

Many members of the alert and lively faculty which Neilson recruited and encouraged were full of interest in the important issues of the twenties and thirties and ready to take action in support of their beliefs. Conservative colleagues who did not agree with them frequently found their points of view stimulating, and in any case were not frightened, but timid citizens outside the campus gates trembled for the minds and morals of the young women exposed to dangerous doctrine within. Neilson was obliged to spend many hours in stating again and again, in letters, in conversations, on the platform, the point of view of the College in this matter: Smith is trying to teach her students not what to think but how to think.

> We realise [he said, summing up the whole matter towards the close of his administration] our responsibility for turning out students who are well aware of the problems of their epoch, and we think it is our duty to teach them how to find out the facts concerning social order, to make them keep as long as possible an open mind about what should be done about these facts, to teach them as far as we can to reason rigorously and accurately about these facts, and to present in the College itself all sides of debated questions.
>
> That is done not by choosing members of the faculty who are so lukewarm that they have no opinions—good teaching could never come from people who did not care—but rather by attempting to create a balanced faculty, and to have in each of the important subjects representatives of each important point of view, these members of the faculty regarding it as their business not to act as propagandists of their particular faiths, but to explain sympathetically their points of view, and, as far as human nature makes it possible, to give a critical attitude towards those points of view. Obviously, that is never going to be done by any one person in a perfectly impartial way; and the College attempts by having different points of view represented by different teachers to produce the balance one cannot expect in the individual.

A good many extremists, in the course of his administration, required Neilson to come to their defense. The classic case, which attracted national attention, was his refusal to dismiss Professor Harry Elmer Barnes.

Barnes was a sociologist who believed in teaching by shock. He was a professor at Clark University at the time in the 1920's when a large group of alumni, students, and faculty were working for the removal of President W. W. Atwood who, in addition to other actions his constituency disapproved of, had seriously hampered freedom of thought and discussion on the campus. Active in the faculty group were Barnes and Professor Frank Hankins, chairman of the department of sociology. Neilson, who had been concerned for some time to strengthen the teaching of sociology at Smith, found it not difficult to persuade them to transfer to Smith, Hankins in 1922, Barnes the following year. The stimulus to social thinking at Smith was even greater than he had anticipated. Some of Hankins' ideas disturbed the Smith constituency [see pp. 286-7]; nearly all of Barnes's did.

Barnes was an energetic and industrious worker, capable of producing books in rapid succession and at the same time a flow of articles and speeches so that his name was constantly before the public. His command of facts was remarkable and he knew how to present ideas in a striking manner but some scholars questioned the quality of his judgments and many of his audiences were disturbed by the violence and often vulgarity of his expression. Much of this was deliberate; he wanted to shake people out of their prejudices, to force them to pay attention to new theories and new ideas. Many Smith students found his classes stimulating; others were distressed. Their parents, the alumnae, and the public read him with the same diversity of sentiment. The distressed were, of course, the more vocal, and letters calling for Barnes's dismissal began to pour into Neilson's office. Barnes, the letters said, was immoral, irreligious, pro-German, and on each count unfitted to be a teacher of youth.

The charge that Barnes taught immorality was founded on his studies in criminality, the field in which, in the opinion of many of his colleagues, he did his most effective work. He was one of the early publicists of the idea that the criminal is not wholly responsible for his actions—and what, in that case, asked the letters, becomes of individual morality? The charges of irreligion came from statements made in class and quoted by startled students, or made in public lectures and reported, frequently out of context, by delighted headline writers. The pro-German alarm rose in 1921, when Barnes published (1926) one of the earliest books on war guilt, *The Genesis of the World War*. His point of view, that the responsibility for the war was not Germany's alone, was similar to that taken by the Smith College historian Sidney Bradshaw Fay in his definitive *Origins of the World War* (1928), but Barnes's way of stating the case was much less scholarly than Fay's, and much more horrifying to the not yet disillusioned public. The summer of 1926 Barnes spent in Europe where he was of course enthusiastically received at many German universities.

Neilson frequently disagreed with Barnes's pronouncements, as he did not hesitate to make plain to him; he often disliked the language in which an idea he did agree with was couched, but he did not think either his own taste or the public clamor a reason for restricting the professorial right to freedom of speech. And Barnes, as Neilson patiently explained in letter after letter, was only one member of the Smith College faculty. Points of view diametrically opposed to his were well represented. Smith students sat not only under radicals and free thinkers but under Catholics and Methodists, reactionary Republicans, and cloistered scholars who seldom looked beyond their study walls.

> Whether the teacher is discussing chemical elements or social elements, the government of New York or the government of Athens in the days of Pericles, his object should be to seek and to teach the truth and nothing but the truth. It is his business to present the facts in the clearest, whitest light of which he is capable. There may be times when his conscience bids him give his students his opinion upon an issue. It is then his obvious duty to discriminate sharply between the facts and his private opinion about them. The teacher who does that does all that any governing board has the right to demand of him. It is his right and his privilege to put his heart into his teaching; otherwise he becomes the automatic recorder of facts too unimportant to excite in him or his students either thought or feeling. The only security for education or for society is the security that comes from the power of independent thought.

Nevertheless Neilson was greatly relieved when, in the spring of 1930, the Scripps-Howard newspaper syndicate offered Barnes a position as a columnist writing on public affairs. Neilson advised him strongly to accept the offer which would give him far more scope than he could find in an academic post, and was openly delighted when Barnes took his advice. Yet, through all the months of weary correspondence, he had never lost sight of Barnes's real qualities and attainments. When he announced the resignation at the Last Chapel exercises in June 1930 he said:

> Professor Harry Elmer Barnes, who has been so conspicuous a figure for six or seven years, has decided to engage in other fields of

activity. Mr. Barnes's treatment of his interests has not always commanded the admiration of our constituency. But I wish to say that he has stimulated a large body of students to think for themselves and has displayed and employed in his work the largest range of information of any scholar that I have ever known.

Neilson's expenditure of time and strength in Barnes's defense had not been wasted effort. The widespread publicity that attended the case made clear to the country at large that Smith College not only preached academic freedom but practiced it under the most trying circumstances.

Yet some members of the Smith faculty felt that the President wearied at times in well doing. In 1928, while Barnes was still a member of the faculty, Neilson failed to reappoint an excellent teacher in the department of English because he was a forthright and outspoken "radical." Granville Hicks was not dismissed but he was, in the academic phrase, "let go" when his three-year appointment ended. To the questions of his colleagues Neilson responded that he thought there was a saturation point in the number of radicals a college faculty could absorb.

To the super-patriots the whole situation at Smith was intensified by Neilson's own liberalism. His name was on the DAR Blacklist, in Elizabeth Dilling's *The Red Network* ("I am proud," he said, "to be included"), and in a dozen similar publications. He urged the United States to join the League of Nations; he advocated recognition of Soviet Russia; he worked for the National Association for the Advancement of Colored People; he lent support to Loyalist Spain. This was clear indication to some minds that the young women at Smith were being poisoned daily with red propaganda. In addition to a steady bombardment of letters Neilson was subjected to a good many attacks in print.

One of the earliest, 1921, was contained in a series of articles in a popular woman's magazine, *The Delineator*. The headpiece showed a little flock of lambs being instructed by a wolf in mortarboard and sheep's clothing. The signature was Calvin Coolidge, which gave special force to the accusations against Smith with whose operation Governor Coolidge, a citizen of Northampton, was supposed to have first-hand acquaintance. Coolidge stressed the point that the spread of radical propaganda is essentially a woman's problem for "to make a home is to be a capitalist." The account of radical teaching and thinking in the women's colleges was vague and couched in carefully guarded language.

> Coolidge's article seems to me so feeble as to be not worth a serious reply [wrote Neilson in answer to a letter from Professor Manley Hudson of the Harvard Law School]. It is clear that the data about the individual colleges which has been collected for him turned out to be much less sensational than had been expected so that he found himself with an anticlimax.

A few years later (December 1923) the *Southern Churchman,* an organ of the Episcopal Church published in Richmond, Virginia, launched a series of direct attacks on Smith College which used about Neilson language so violent that it might well have been construed as libel. He was accused of "misusing the property and betraying the trust of a dead woman," Sophia Smith of course, whose legacy to the College the *Churchman* said had been thirty-five million dollars; Neilson, Scottish born, was said to be sneering at American patriotism; and he, in company with Professors Barnes and Hankins, was turning Smith College into "a nest of atheism"; finally, it was noted with alarm, the President of this women's college had published a book called [sic] *Origins and Sources of Courts of Love.* Connecticut Valley Episcopal clergymen and alumnae members of the Church stepped to Neilson's defense, but he decided to let the matter drop when it became clear that the editor of the *Churchman* was "an unbalanced person with whom it is unwise to enter into controversy."

The material for this attack came, it transpired, from an alumna of the class of 1910, whose husband was connected with the Navy and who was obsessed with the idea that the College must be cured of its supposed pacifism. She was particularly angry because Neilson had declined to answer a detailed questionnaire about his political and religious beliefs. He had written her, 6 March 1920:

> It is not difficult to conjecture from the nature of the questions that the organizations to whom the answers were to be submitted

belong to a type which has given us a good deal of trouble through fragmentary and inaccurate quotations from utterances attributed to members of the College. Under these circumstances I do not think it wise to send you replies to the questions.

The alumna, being a lady of energy, continued her dissemination of rumor and falsehood though with no very tangible results beyond the burden of explanatory letterwriting imposed upon the President and the trustees. She must be credited, too, with the most magnificently lurid phrase ever applied to Neilson, for she furnished some of the material for *Sinister Shadows* (1929), a pseudo-novel by E. M. Hadley. In its pages Neilson, that destroyer of innocents, appears as the protagonist of a chapter entitled "The Shade of Herod Stalks at Dusk."

Most of the people who disapproved of Neilson's liberalism made their attacks in print or in writing but on one occasion they met him face to face, in 1936 when he opposed the Massachusetts Teachers' Oath bill. In 1935 the idea was beginning to spread that our youth might be protected from subversive doctrine by requiring all their teachers to take an oath of fealty to Federal and State constitutions. Massachusetts was in the forefront of the movement. Twelve presidents of Massachusetts colleges made protest to the Legislatures when a Teachers' Oath bill was proposed but they did not succeed in stopping its passage. The whole Smith College faculty took the oath in due order but were unanimous in their opposition to this discrimination against their profession and joined the other institutions of the state in working for repeal. When a legislative hearing was set in the Boston State House for 5 March 1936 Neilson agreed to be one of the speakers.

More than a thousand people attended the hearing, administrators, professors, and students from schools and colleges in all parts of the state, representatives of the Teachers' Union, and of the A. F. of L. The addresses which attracted most attention were those by President Conant of Harvard and President Neilson of Smith, both of whom, as soon as they finished, were vigorously cross-examined by the legislators. Those gentlemen, according to the *New York Times,* were very much surprised to learn that Harvard professors are free to determine the truth as they see it and to teach it without interference.

Neilson, who concluded the hearing, emphasized particularly the futility of the bill which had produced a result quite opposite from its intentions.

> I understand that the chief purpose of the teachers' oath law was to increase respect for the constitution and the law. It has accomplished neither. Its effect has been to reduce respect for the constitution and the law, for the almost unanimous belief of the faculty and students of Smith College, if they are any criterion, is that the law is perfectly silly.
>
> The effect of its passage has been to reduce respect for the powers of the General Court since its members are so naïve as to suppose that people who are engaged in treachery will cease their treachery because of an oath. I read that oath to the students of Smith. I put as much solemnity into that reading as I could muster. I emphasized the provisions which say that although a teacher must take an oath to the constitution, he still has the rights guaranteed under the constitution. And that reading evoked laughter. I ask that the law be repealed since it has not accomplished its objective.

The legislators who questioned Neilson passed quite openly from hand to hand a little pamphlet entitled *Who's Who Among American Radicals.* Most of the questions were put by Representative Frederick McDermot of Medford.

"Are you," he asked Neilson, "connected with any foreign university?"

"I received a degree from the University of Edinburgh."

"No, no. Isn't it a fact that you are connected with the University of Moscow?" Shouts of laughter from the audience while McDermot tried another tack. "Didn't you participate in the defense of two murderers who were defended by communists?" Neilson explained patiently that the Sacco-Vanzetti meeting at which he had presided in 1927 was not called by communists and that it had merely exercised the right of petition.

"Are you a member," McDermot went on, "of the Professional Patriots, a communist organization?"

"I am not," said Neilson wearily. "If you want to know whether I am a communist, I am not." But McDermot consulted his handbook again: "Are you a member of the American Society for Cultural Relations with Russia?"

Neilson said that he had been a member and explained that the Society was formed, during a period when Russia was not recognized by the United States, to facilitate the interchange of information and opinion between members of the scientific and scholastic world.

"Who financed it?" McDermot demanded.

"I financed it," said Neilson, "as much as I could and my friends financed it. We never had enough money and we never got any from the Soviet Union."

The session adjourned amid applause, but the bill was not repealed.

Even stronger, perhaps, than his defense of academic freedom was a subtler bond by which Neilson attached his faculty: the sense he gave them that they were not simply employees hired to do a particular job but component parts of an institution building by a common effort. One simple device by which he encouraged this feeling was the substitution of elected departmental chairmen for the previous system of permanent department heads appointed by the president.

> It not infrequently happens [he wrote to an administrator who had asked him about the system] that the head of a department is old and has ceased to be progressive, with the result that ideas from younger members have no chance of reaching the administration or of being tried out. By the chairmanship system, the position, at least in the larger departments, rotates and any member of the department can bring up matters for discussion and get plans tried, if he gets the majority. It has seemed to me that these results have been obtained here. On the other hand, the permanent head relieves the president of the college to a much greater extent than the chairman, since he assumes more responsibility and decides many things by himself. In spite of the extra work involved, I prefer the more democratic system, and think that it enables the college to avail itself to a much greater extent of the ideas of the whole staff, and it develops initiative.

Certainly any member of Neilson's faculty who thought that he had an idea for the improvement of the College's functioning felt that the President would listen to it with attention and interest. Perhaps there were administrative obstacles which the originator had not foreseen; or there might simply not be funds, but, whatever the outcome, you always felt, as one young instructor put it, that "the President was on your side." One departmental chairman, for instance, remembers with pleasure the way in which Neilson declined a request which seemed to her very important. "I hate," he said, "to refuse *you* anything," and she still recalls with pride the inflection on that *you* though she had entirely forgotten what was denied to her.

Professor Mary Ellen Chase in *A Goodly Fellowship* (1939, dedicated to President Neilson) relates another incident of this kind. After she had been a short time at Smith she went to the President's office to ask if she might be freed for one year from the teaching of freshman English. She made the request, she said, not because she disliked teaching freshmen or even reading their themes but because, if she was even passably decent to them, they overwhelmed her with invitations to tea and dinner which left her no time for anything else. When she had finished Neilson said:

> "Now I could let you off from teaching, I suppose, or from reading your themes, but I really couldn't let you off from tea and dinner. Perhaps you don't know it yet, but to go to tea and dinner with freshmen happens to be the most important thing you're doing around this place. So run along and do it. Remember that a teacher who isn't asked to tea and dinner probably isn't worth her salt, and don't come asking again to be let off from what is your most important job to this college." *

It was incidents like this which built up that *esprit de corps* so often commented upon by other administrators observing the Smith campus, and it was incidents like this which the faculty had in mind when they passed a minute on Neilson's retirement.

> By example he fortified in all who worked with him—trustees, faculty, staff, and students alike—a faith in the common cause. Intol-

* Quoted with the kind permission of Miss Chase and the Macmillan Company.

erant only of arrogance and hostile only to deceit, he was ever more ready to believe than to doubt, to help than to judge; and encouraging all in the best they had to give, he so vigorously defended academic freedom in its broadest interpretation that under his presidency Smith College rose to take her place among the foremost leaders of truly liberal thought in the country.

12

The President and the Curriculum

DURING his twenty-two years at Smith Neilson made, so he insisted, only one original contribution to "the theory of my profession as college president." That was the idea of establishing in an undergraduate college a chair of pure research to be held by a series of visiting professors. Other educational innovations, like Special Honors, the Junior Year Abroad, the Pre-vocational Majors, were simply variants, he said, on schemes with which other institutions were also experimenting. For Neilson did not believe in preconceived educational programs, like those of Meiklejohn and Hutchins, programs elaborated in the void and then imposed upon an existing institution. He agreed with Eliot that the best procedure for an administrator is to take his college as he finds it, study it carefully, and develop it along indigenous lines, not fostering innovations for their own sake but because they have a special relation to the given conditions. He took issue with Hutchins also on his lack of interest in anything except the intellectual development of the student. A liberal arts college, Neilson thought, should be concerned with "the training of personalities."

We are trying to teach our students to discover new values in life, as many kinds as possible; to get a hierarchy of values and to proportion their time and efforts according to that hierarchy. And these values are of a much greater variety than the intellectual virtues as classified by Saint Thomas Aquinas, though they include these virtues. . . We are concerned with the moral obligation to be healthy. . . We are concerned also with the emotional and aesthetic life, with the developing of insight and sensibility to beauty through the study of art, music, literature, the drama. We are concerned with spiritual values. . . We are concerned with social values, since the life of the college, as has so often been said, is a microcosm of our national life. (Address to the Chicago Smith Club, 1936)

The majority of the Smith faculty shared Neilson's point of view; they believed in the training of the whole personality and they did their educational experimenting gently.

We try our little mild experiments from time to time [Neilson told the Alumnae Council in 1936], we maneuver to get an opportunity for experiment, but there is always a great inertia, founded, I think, on the most persistent tendency prevailing in the educational world, namely the tendency to assume that the education "which produced *me*" must have been the right kind of education. That is almost the fundamental axiom unconsciously or consciously entertained by most people engaged in teaching.

The mild experimenting, was, however, perpetual. The faculty engaged constantly in what Neilson called "the major sport" of curriculum revision, and this he approved because

Whether the new curriculum is better or worse than the old it is always operated with most zest during its early years; and anything that induces a staff to go at their work with more curiosity and zeal is worth while.

This did not prevent him from teasing his colleagues about their proclivity for change.

We go round and round, perhaps in circles, but we try to think that they are spirals.

It was healthy, Neilson believed too, for the students to concern themselves with the program under which they worked; suggestions from the undergraduate curriculum committee were listened to with attention.

In addition to the continuous spiral tinkering there were two major curriculum revisions during Neilson's administration. The first, made under Dean Frances Bernard, came into operation with the class of 1931. It simplified the whole curricular structure, releasing freshmen and sophomores from a too rigid prescription of studies, and giving them opportunity to read in fields like philosophy, once thought beyond their power. It provided also for increased specialization by upperclassmen in their major subjects. The second revision, made in 1936 under Dean Marjorie Nicolson, freed the student working for General Honors from one course requirement in her junior and another in her senior year, substituting reading under direction, the writing of a long paper, and the passing of a comprehensive examination.

This was in line with Neilson's contention that the American college ought to devote to its brilliant students at least as much attention as it lavished on the weak. He had begun to work in that direction in 1921 when he introduced the Special Honors plan, a project on which he labored with particular energy and pleasure. Special Honors was designed to correct also another weakness in the American educational system, the tendency to "superficiality and fragmentariness," as Neilson put it in an article in the *New Republic,* 25 October, Part II, 1922.

> The student aiming at many things fails to get much of any of them; and may, and often does, leave college without having learned how to master one.

The A.B., he felt, is too often "a certificate of what a student has known rather than of what he is or can do."

The Smith Special Honors plan, one of the earliest in the country, was widely studied and copied. It differed from the English tutorial system chiefly in allowing during the first two years of college rather wide experiment in many fields. In the last two years, the student, entirely relieved from the usual class routine, chose "a certain field of learning for intensive cultivation." Six subdivisions of this field were worked, two in each semester, under the guidance of specialists who met the student in personal conference, suggested reading she might do, proposed problems, and criticized the work done. Papers written weekly or fortnightly gave practice in accurate presentation and in the use of methods of reasoning appropriate to the subject. During her last term the

Special Honors student wrote a thesis and prepared herself for a comprehensive examination.

The objection raised by other administrators that individual instruction of this kind is very expensive, Neilson met with the bland response that Smith had not found it so.

> Most, if not all, members of the faculty [he wrote to an inquiring college president] who have acted as special instructors find so much satisfaction in the opportunity this scheme affords that they are willing to give an hour or two a week to it.

He pointed out also that it had been possible to discontinue some small advanced courses which were previously offered for the benefits of the Honors type of student, and that the intention was never to extend the plan to more than 10 per cent of each class. Actually the proportion never rose so high, for many eligible students did not feel ready for the close concentration demanded and preferred to work towards a degree with General Honors. Yet almost without exception those who enrolled in the Special Honors program were full of enthusiasm. What the academic world thought of the plan is suggested by a letter of Neilson's written in 1933.

> At London our special honors students rank with the honors graduates of London and go on to their doctorate there under very favorable conditions. We have the same arrangement with Cambridge. In the case of Oxford, the arrangements have been made for one student at a time.

The Junior Year Abroad was another device for the better education of the better student. The idea that one of an undergraduate's four college years might profitably be spent in a foreign country was a product of the expanding internationalism in American thinking after World War I. The University of Delaware began in 1923 the supervision in Paris of a small group of students, both men and women, drawn from a number of different colleges. When the French Department at Smith became interested in the scheme as a means of giving their pupils real mastery of the language, Neilson appointed Professor Hélène Cattanès, to study the possibilities for Smith and draw up a detailed plan. The scheme she devised and which went into operation in 1925, met the fundamental problems involved so effectively that only minor variations needed to be made from year to year, and when Junior Years in Spain and Italy were initiated, they worked on the same outline.

The French Juniors—the group numbered usually about thirty—spent September and October in Grenoble whose University had set up some excellent courses for foreigners in phonetics, grammar, and composition. In November, when courses began at the Sorbonne, they transferred to Paris and enrolled in the University's *Cours de la Civilization Française*. This set of courses, conducted by professors of the University of Paris especially for foreigners, included lectures on French literature, history, geography, philosophy, art, and *"la vie française."* There, in competition with two hundred students from all parts of the world, the Smith girls made year after year an enviable record. The relation of the Sorbonne courses to those in Northampton was carefully worked out with the Smith faculty so that each junior received the necessary credits towards her A.B., in philosophy, art, or whatever, as well as in French.

One of the most effective elements of the scheme was the housing of the Smith girls, singly or in pairs, with French families, where they were expected, Neilson made it clear to them, not to live like Americans in Paris but to conform to their hostess's ideas of decorum and learn what it is to be a *jeune fille*. Each year he made a point of talking to the group before they sailed, explaining what the opportunity offered and urging them not to make the mistake of confusing plumbing with civilization.

Part of the success of the project was due to the careful coaching of the students by the directors of the group—members of the Smith Department of French serving in rotation—in the French method of study. The Smith juniors were not demoralized, consequently, like many young Americans abroad, by the unusual degree of freedom permitted them in the planning and accomplishment of their work and they learned that in a French university, a paper or an answer to an examination question is expected to be not just a summary of facts, however accurate, but an elaborate and original essay, well composed and elegantly expressed.

Another factor in the successful operation of the Junior Year

Abroad was Neilson's enthusiastic personal interest in all its details. During the first experimental year he made a trip to Paris where he discussed the project at length with the French professors who were teaching Smith students and had a private personal interview with each girl, learning just what she did and did not like about her experience. Frequently, in succeeding years, he made winter trips to Europe to check on the working of the plan. But, as always in matters of academic progress, Neilson credited the Junior Year in France to the faculty rather than the administration. When, in 1935, the French Government decorated him with the Cross of the Legion of Honor and the French consul at Boston came down to perform the ceremony, Neilson arranged to have it in his office in College Hall in the presence of the members of the department of French and accepted the honor "as the representative of the French teachers of the College who have earned what has come to me."

A Junior Year in Spain was organized in 1931, a Junior Year in Italy in 1932. Neilson later explored the possibility of a Junior Year in Munich but the political situation made that project impracticable. As a consolation a German House was established in Northampton with a member of the German faculty in residence and all conversation carried on in German. This proved so successful that a French House was opened when the Junior Year in France was interrupted by the war. In 1937 the Junior Year in Spain was transferred to Mexico.

The financing of these years abroad was a good example of the Neilson thrift. The cost to the students was precisely what they would have paid in Northampton for board and tuition, plus only their steamer fare and any traveling they cared to do during the holidays.

> Their tuition [Neilson told the alumnae in October 1931] costs us less than it does here and what we save enables us to pay for direction, and for the other overhead expenses, so that after six years of experience of this, we can say that we have sent something like 220 girls for the junior year to Europe and it has not cost Smith College one dollar.

The Junior Year Abroad gave impetus, of course, to language study at home and the various departments flourished. In the late twenties, for instance, Smith had more students studying Italian and more teachers teaching it than any other college or university in the United States.

Facility in the use of the language, which Neilson thought important for the comprehension of a contemporary culture, did not seem to him essential to the study of ancient civilizations. Ease in the use of Greek and Latin, he said, takes far longer to acquire than a practicable knowledge of French or German, and, moreover, we have, through good translations, access to a large body of classical literature. This point of view, to which he came years before most educators, Neilson stated at some length in his inaugural address, to the sharp distress of the Smith professors of Latin and Greek.

> The foundation of the revolt against the classics is a widespread indignation at being cheated. Hundreds of thousands of students have spent the major part of their studying time for years upon two languages with the implicit understanding that they would finally have access to two great civilizations through reading the records in the original tongues. They paid the price in time and energy and at the end they did not get what they paid for. [He admitted that for the professional scholar] the mastering of the tongues is essential to thoroughness and self-respect [but insisted that] within the select group of the college-trained this is the necessary equipment of a still more select group; and do not let us pretend that a man cannot be cultivated without an accomplishment that most cultivated men will confess they do not possess.

Neilson then drew a parallel with the other knowledge generally considered essential to any broad scheme of cultural education, Hebrew literature and civilization.

> But the teachers of this subject have never forbidden us to read the Bible or study the history of the Israelites until we had mastered their language. The barrier which has shut off generations of students from a knowledge of classical civilization has been the classical teacher's infatuation for the subjunctive.

The Smith classicists who heard this were not only saddened but shocked. Translation in 1918 was a word one did not mention in respectable academic society. The use of a trot was held a heinous undergraduate sin. That this criminal practice was blithely advocated by a scholar bred in the British academic tradition made the barbed statement doubly wounding. If they had not liked the President so much personally the Smith professors of classics would have found it difficult to go on teaching.

They laugh about that attitude today. Neilson did not force reform upon them; he merely pointed out the path and, eventually, they took it for themselves. Twenty years later the Smith College catalogue was offering: "Greek 28, Survey of Greek Literature in English Translation," and "Latin 15b, Masterpieces of Latin Literature in Translation." But even then the battle was not won and cries of distress went up around the country when Neilson published in *Harper's* (March 1943) an article on the "Future of the Humanities." He started from the premise that "Education in the liberal arts for men is out for the duration."

To most of our college and university faculties this decision comes as a heavy blow. But in one respect at least it offers them a great opportunity. The enforced suspension of much of the instruction they have been giving in the liberal arts will break so many of the threads of academic habit and custom that it will be possible to reconsider the whole liberal arts program and, if this seems best, to alter it as would be well-nigh impossible in normal times. . . What is needed is a severe scrutiny by the humanists themselves of the adequacy of their procedures and interests to the task of giving the student the deepest possible insight into human nature.

Neilson suggested particularly a reconsideration of the questions: How valuable is linguistic study in itself as a discipline, and to what extent can the results of that study be obtained through translations?

The translations of the Greek and Latin classics [he answered] can give us the main content of facts and ideas in these writings, imaginative, historical, philosophical. Even in literature they can give us the structural symmetry, the characterization, and much of the atmosphere, in epic and drama. They cannot give us with any fullness their verbal felicity or their beauty of sound.

For the fortunate few who can master the original languages, he insisted, and for the research scholars, "there must always be generous provision, lest the springs should dry up."

> But our concern in planning the salvaging of the humanities is for the nine-tenths who do not belong to this élite, but for whom we covet as great a share as possible in the heritage of the past.

Further than this Neilson did not want to see the established colleges go. He was, however, pretty well convinced that some minds quite worth educating are incapable of dealing with either Latin or mathematics. He made no attempt to account for the phenomenon but it was one reason for his generous encouragement of new colleges like Sarah Lawrence and Bennington which might, he thought, experiment to advantage with entrance requirements and courses of study outside the traditional pattern.

> One reason why art schools and conservatories do not fill the need of the rejected candidates is that . . . they do not supply a sufficiently broad cultural background. But there is no reason why music or fine art should not be given in a new college such a central position as a subject like the classics enjoys in the traditional institution, and be enriched and supported by history, literature, aesthetics, philosophy, psychology, and physical science. . . Or again, considering the tendency of women to occupy themselves with social betterment, the social sciences might in another case be made central, and appropriate subjects grouped round them. ("Overcrowding in Women's Colleges," *The Nation,* 13 May 1925)

About the junior college movement Neilson felt more skepticism. When a plan was being considered for the establishment of a number of junior colleges in northern New England he wrote to the principal of a Vermont academy about

> the difficulty . . . of finding adequate staff of the calibre of college teachers. I am painfully familiar with the scarcity of the supply, and it would be unwise to embark on a scheme like that proposed here on the assumption that an indefinite number could be obtained by simply going into the market. . . Unless the junior college can afford to add staff whose scholarship will enable them to conduct their classes as college classes, it is an illusion to suppose that the students are getting the first two years of college training.

Observing the changing scene in science with the same open mind he had turned on the classics, Neilson was among the early advocates of descriptive science courses for the "nine-tenths who do not belong to the élite," the students who will never spend more than a term or two on astronomy, say, or chemistry. The Smith scientists were delighted and surprised by his comprehension of the new point of view. He was thoroughly interested in their ideas as to what might be done to familiarize the undergraduate who has no scientific bent with the scientific way of thinking and with the fundamental concepts of physics or zoology. Quite possibly his attitude here was colored by that autobiographical element about which he liked to joke—"the education which produced *me* must have been the right kind of education." Tait's course in natural philosophy which Neilson had followed at Edinburgh had included no laboratory practice yet had given him a point of view which he found illuminating and highly useful.

Always pleased at any loosening of departmental barriers Neilson was glad to facilitate another of the scientists' schemes: co-operative pre-vocational courses. His President's Report for 1923-4 announces:

> A new departure in the organization of the curriculum which may prove to be the beginning of an important development is the establishment of Pre-vocational Majors. These have already been planned for students intending to prepare themselves later for the practice of medicine and of public health, and others are in preparation.

The new departure guided the student in her selection of courses beginning with her freshman year so that when she took her A.B. she was ready for immediate entrance to a medical school. The revolutionary element in the scheme was the breaching of hitherto inviolable walls; a student was no longer required to be a physics or chemistry or biology major, simply a premedical major. The pre-vocational major in landscape architecture, established in 1929, crossed the lines between botany and art, and in 1930 a dramatic arts major brought art and literature into co-operation.

The research projects in which his science faculties engaged Neilson made no pretense of understanding in detail but he had a shrewd sense of the qualities of each individual scientist and, when he felt confidence in a man or woman, was very ready to supply apparatus, even expensive apparatus, which seemed to the experimenter essential. If it could be demonstrated that the new equipment would be of use also to the graduate students Neilson was all the more ready to find the funds, for he was proud of the number of younger scholars in the science departments who were stimulated by the example of their professors to undertake individual investigation, as he was proud of the fact that Smith was the only woman's college to have a chapter of Sigma Xi.

In the improvement of the teaching of his own subject, English, Neilson was somewhat less successful than he was with the languages and the sciences, though he was well aware that some reform was needed. Seelye, too, had been a Professor of English, at Amherst, before he became President of Smith, and, during the first years of the College, all the English teaching was in his hands. Principles of literary criticism he taught chiefly from the Bible, for he thought the King James version the greatest monument of English prose. He believed too, that English composition should be taught by all members of the faculty in all courses, "an ideal," as Neilson said in his History,* "towards which many college administrators have wistfully gazed." When the growth of the College obliged Seelye to devote more and more of his time to administration, teachers were appointed in English literature, rhetoric, and speech, a division which made for endless confusion and jealousy. Literature and rhetoric eventually came together but the situation was further complicated by Neilson's introduction of the teaching of the drama; was it English or Spoken English? The fact that appointments by both Seelye and Neilson to all these departments included some brilliant men and women with very marked personalities tended, while it produced much stimulating teaching, to a further disintegration of the curriculum. Courses were introduced not because the department needed strengthening in a particular area but because some instructor wanted to teach his pet enthusiasm. The English curriculum was not planned but simply grew by individual accretions, confusion increasing with the years.

* See p. 343.

This confusion Neilson made no attempt to dispel even when he saw that the department itself had no intention of attempting a reform. The fact that he was the ranking scholar in an English faculty of thirty caused some of the older members to regard him with suspicion, fearful that he might attempt to exert more influence than that commanded by his individual vote. He did exert such influence, though not by his own desire; most of the younger members of the faculty were pretty sure that the President was always right. This delicate balance in which the whole situation rested prevented Neilson from working vigorously for change as he would have done in any other field. He contented himself with the encouragement of certain phases of English teaching which seemed to him to have been underemphasized. In 1921 the poet Grace Hazard Conklin, who had taught literature for many years at Smith, offered a course in "Versification," and one of Neilson's early appointments was Samuel A. Eliot, Jr., grandson of President Eliot, who gave courses not only in dramatic literature but in playwriting and play production. Neilson's chief reason for encouraging play production was his hope that it might work some improvement in undergraduate speech. He was constantly distressed by the harsh tones and careless enunciation he heard on the campus and, in his chapel talks, tried to make the students realize the importance of listening to their own voices. His conviction that good speech is an essential attribute of the educated person led him to increase the department of Spoken English to what seemed to many of his faculty a disproportionate size.

President Seelye had not thought of creative writing or play production as subjects to be taught in college but he did, from the beginning, emphasize "aesthetic culture." Music and art he insisted in including in the Smith curriculum. "Surely," he said, "the intelligent study of one of Beethoven's sonatas or Michael Angelo's statues may be as profitable to some minds as the dissection of a fish or a flower!" * And he made it quite clear that music and painting were to be taught not as elegant female accomplishments but as academic subjects on a par with the other

* Harriet Seelye Rhees, *Laurenus Clark Seelye,* 1929.

disciplines. "Ultimately," wrote Neilson in his History, "this promise was abundantly fulfilled, but the early years were marred by a good deal of groping and some false starts," such as the attempt at affiliated schools. Finally good departments were organized in which credit was given for "practical" as well as theoretical work.

The department of music began to flourish before the turn of the century and did not make much change in its methods through the years. Neilson found it in 1918 a good deal less modern than the rest of the College. Some attempt to raise the standard of scholarship had been made during President Burton's regime by two young appointees of his, Roy Dickinson Welch and Arthur Locke. Change, however, was difficult to effect under the chairmanship of Henry Dyke Sleeper who had been the leading figure in the department since 1903. A man of much personal charm he had instilled in generations of Smith students a real love of music if not a very profound knowledge of it. When Neilson made the change from appointed to elected departmental chairmanships there occurred in the music department what he referred to as a "minor revolution" and the younger members came into power. The time seemed ripe for change and in 1922 Neilson asked Professor Archibald T. Davison of Harvard to make a survey of the Smith department of music, offering suggestions for changes in courses, methods of teaching, and personnel. Some members of the music faculty were delighted by Davison's suggestions. Others, whose training and methods of teaching had been criticized, cried injustice. Neilson, nevertheless, following the main lines of Davison's report, effected a fairly drastic reorganization. Some retirements (and pensions) were anticipated, promotions and new appointments were made, courses were rearranged and reorganized. Neilson acted in these matters with generosity and with tact. Only a little bitterness remained. The department began again to function in advance of its time and, under the imaginative direction of Welch, offered admirable training to those who looked forward to musical careers while at the same time opening doors to knowledge and enjoyment to hundreds of amateurs. Music became an element of increasing importance in the life of Smith College.

One of the recommendations in the Davison report the Smith music faculty declined to accept. Harvard believed that university music teaching should not concern itself with performance and Davison recommended that Smith do away with credit for "practical music." This the Smith department felt would be retrogression. Much, they thought, could be learned in the thoughtful performance of music if a student had sufficient skill, and sufficient to them meant high. Their point of view seemed to Neilson sound, and he had additional reasons for encouraging the teaching of "practical music." Many young women, he thought, who had a real vocation for music and intended to make it their career, would be far better and more intelligent musicians if they had the benefit of four years of liberal studies, but, if a college required them to give up for so long a period the daily practice of their technique, they would feel themselves obliged to choose instead the narrower education of a conservatory. He thought, too, that

> the presence on the faculty of a considerable number of teachers who were also skilled performers of instrumental and vocal music made it possible to offer the students, and incidentally the whole local community, generous opportunities for the hearing of a great range of musical literature in historical recitals. (History)

A particularly happy instance of this benefit was the Department's revival of operas by Monteverdi and Handel, works seldom produced in Europe and never before in America. Under the inspiration and direction of Professor Werner Josten, Monteverdi's *Coronation of Poppaea* was staged in celebration of the opening, in the spring of 1926, of the new music building, Sage Hall. The performance—for one role only was it necessary to import a singer—attracted national attention and commendation. It was followed in succeeding years by Handel's *Julius Caesar,* a double bill of Monteverdi's *Combat of Tancred and Clorinda* and Handel's *Xerxes,* Monteverdi's *Orfeo,* and Handel's *Apollo and Daphne.*

Neilson was quite aware that his appreciation of the importance of music in education derived in large measure from his wife's knowledge and love of the art. He was delighted when, at the time of his retirement, the department of music made her an honorary member, "hoping that thus your spirit will continue to dwell among us and your standard of music continue to guide us."

The history of the teaching of art at Smith was, Neilson found, very similar to that of the teaching of music. It began with a fine pioneering idea, ran into material difficulties, tried the unsuccessful experiment of an affiliated school, and finally worked out a fairly satisfactory program combining theory and practice. But, as in the department of English, courses had been added to suit individual teachers rather than in accord with any comprehensive plan; there were omissions and overlappings. It seemed to Neilson, when he took office, that only objective external criticism could straighten out the situation. Encouraged by the success of the music department survey, he asked Professor Arthur Pope of Harvard to make a similar study of the department of art. A less complex and delicate job, it was accomplished with efficiency and dispatch and the department began to grow in size and effectiveness. Like the musicians, the teachers of art believed in the academic value of creative work and, to Neilson's pleasure, combined it with history and criticism.

The department of art had in one respect a great advantage over all others in the College: it commanded two funds of generous proportions presented to it for the purchase of laboratory materials, that is for paintings and sculpture. In a circular issued in 1877 President Seelye stated that "An Art Gallery has already been furnished with casts of noted statues and several hundred autotype copies illustrating the different schools of painting." To these he added happily from time to time but the funds at his disposal were small until Winthrop Hillyer, a quiet Northampton citizen who lived so frugally that no one supposed he had money for benefactions, made a gift, which provided a small gallery, and later a bequest for the increase of the college art collection. The second and more substantial endowment came from Dwight W. Tryon, the painter, who for more than twenty-five years was director of the Hillyer Gallery and critic of student work. On his retirement in 1923 he made the College a gift of $100,000 for the erection of the Tryon Gallery, and bequeathed the major part of his estate as an endowment for the department. The collection in the Tryon Gallery, though small, was so carefully chosen that it soon attracted national attention and many of its pictures—Courbet's *Toilette de la Mariée,* for instance, Degas' *Fille de Jepthé,* the early Corots—were in constant demand for loan exhibitions all over the country. In the building of this collection Neilson took an active part, consulting on each purchase with the Director of the Museum and with the art expert whom he made it a point to have on the board of trustees. For Neilson, as for Seelye, picture buying was one of the most enjoyable functions of his office. Partly, one feels sure, because by the terms of the Hillyer and Tryon bequests the funds could be spent only for paintings and sculpture. The Calvinist consciences—the New England and the Scotch—were thus relieved of the burden of decision between utility and beauty. Duty required them to spend the money as they wanted to spend it.

The riskiest gamble he took in the whole course of his administration was, Neilson said, the establishment of the Smith College Training School of Psychiatric Social Work, "a phrase which terrified my constituency until they learned how to spell it." A war measure, put into rapid operation in the summer of 1918, the School not only accomplished its immediate purpose but, under a slightly simplified title, became a permanent and valuable part of the College.

Before the end of the war the United States Army realized that even more difficult than the problem of rehabilitating the wounded soldier would be the readjustment of the "shell shocked" soldier. Army hospitals began to look for workers who could help the doctors in their psychiatric treatments, taking case histories and serving in the social readjustment of the mental patients when they were discharged from the hospitals. Seventy students were admitted to the Smith School. All of them had A.B. degrees or the equivalent, many of them were social workers with experience. They were taught first the elementary principles of psychiatry, normal psychology, sociology, and social case work. Then the summer session of concentrated study was followed by a winter of practical case work under the supervision of social agencies in Boston, New York, and, eventually, thirty cities. After that the students returned to Northampton for a second summer session of theory, in the course of which each wrote a thesis on material she had collected during her winter experience, and became eligible for the Smith M.Sc.

The demand for social workers with the psychiatric point of view was spreading rapidly during the twenties and there were few sources of supply. A graduate of the Smith School found that she could take her choice of positions. Under the efficient direction of Professor Everett Kimball of the department of government the School so flourished that in 1936 it was obliged to limit its enrollment to 250.

Neilson had first become interested in psychiatry and mental hygiene through Herman Adler, the Harvard friend who, as a medical student at Strasbourg, had introduced him to Elisabeth Muser. That interest was expanded by discussions, during the organization of the Smith School, with some of the foremost workers in the field, such men as Dr. Frankwood E. Williams, of the Office of the Surgeon General, Dr. E. E. Southard, of the Boston State Hospital, Dr. William Houston, Director of the Massachusetts State Hospital. As he talked with these experts Neilson began to imagine the role that psychiatric counseling might play in the solution of undergraduate problems. In 1919 he appointed a psychiatrist to the office of the College physician. Some patient sentences in his History of the College describe how long he had to wait for this admirable idea to take root in the Smith community.

> As early as 1919 a psychiatrist was added to the staff. Our constituency, however, was apparently not yet ripe, and the appointment lapsed after one year. Six years later attitudes had changed enough so that when Dr. Douglas Thom was made Consultant in Mental Hygiene he received such cooperation from the medical and administrative staffs as enabled him to make a valuable contribution to the health of the College. Dr. Thom came to the College only two days a month, and on his retirement in 1932 Dr. Uno H. Helgesson came into residence as Associate Physician, later on half time.

Several part time arrangements followed and finally, in 1944, Neilson's successor, Herbert Davis, appointed as College Physician

Dr. Marion Booth '21, a fully qualified psychiatrist. Thus at last the aim of the administration was attained in the complete acceptance of Mental Hygiene as part of the regular responsibility of the health service of the College.

But the Smith community, deliberate as it was, moved far more rapidly than the rest of the country in accepting psychiatry as a natural and present help in trouble. The Mental Hygiene Association, seeking to educate the American public, asked for Neilson's assistance and the cause seemed to him so important that he gave it a generous share of his time, speaking, writing, serving on advisory boards and committees.

The School for Social Work commanded Neilson's interest also because it made use of the college plant during a time when it usually stood idle. He was always troubled by the unthrifty waste of grounds and buildings between June and September and was ready to forward any scheme for summer work which might be presented by the faculty or the alumnae. Various experiments were tried, the longest lived operated by the department of music.

Since he was troubled, too, by those "yawning three months in summer so tremendously wasted in our American life," Neilson gave generous encouragement to a scheme developed by the energetic chairman of the department of geology, Howard Meyerhoff. In the summer of 1931 he began, in the Black Hills of South Dakota, a series of field courses which not only offered undergraduate students excellent scientific experience but also, year after year, turned up rich geologic finds on which both graduate students and faculty worked with profit.

The success of the Smith College School for Social Work encouraged the College to the adoption of another professional school. In 1932 the trustees voted to admit as an affiliated graduate school the Cambridge School of Architecture and Landscape Architecture. Begun in 1915 by a small group of women determined to have professional education in these fields, the School was training fifty or sixty students annually and had established an excellent reputation. To the college graduates who completed its courses, Smith granted her M.A., the first Master's degrees in

Architecture and Landscape Architecture ever conferred by a woman's college.

Apart from their tardy acceptance of mental hygiene, Neilson had high respect for the department of hygiene and physical education whose admirable organization and performance during the greater part of his administration he credited to Dr. Florence Gilman. In 1923 he conferred on her an honorary D.Sc., praising her as

> the wise physician who for fourteen years has directed the measures taken for the health of the students at Smith College, and by her judgment, skill, and devotion to an arduous task has steered them through pestilence and panic and trained them in the laws of wholesome living.

The members of the department who taught physical education were constantly delighted by Neilson's understanding of what they were trying to do. This, from a man who took no pleasure in games or exercise of any kind, seemed to them remarkable. He saw the necessity for expanded playing fields and provided them; he appreciated the introduction of various forms of exercise beyond the traditional field hockey and basketball; he approved, in 1937, the introduction of graduate training for teachers of physical education. He was disturbed, too, when he found that the department was insisting that the members of class teams in any sport must have a fairly high academic standing. The scholastically lazy young woman, he thought, was probably in particular need of outdoor exercise. Deprived of it, she was likely to spend her time in bridge and indoor loafing. He discussed the matter with the chairman of the department, Professor Dorothy Ainsworth, and the academic requirement was quietly dropped.

Like most members of liberal arts colleges in the twenties Neilson was appalled by the blight that Columbia's Teachers College and its offspring were spreading over America's public schools. He observed with distress the number of good students in his senior class each year who declined to go into school teaching because the approach to it seemed so devious and futile. The way to learn to teach, he said, is to teach, increasing at the same time your command of history, or whatever your subject may be; very little can be gained by taking courses in methods of teaching history in the third grade, and in the fourth grade, and in the fifth. But Neilson was less defeatist about the situation than most of his colleagues; he remembered the stimulus and help he had found in Laurie's paedeutics at Edinburgh and saw no reason why training with the same quality could not be given at Smith College. He set about the revitalizing of Smith's not very lively department of education. After one abortive experiment, he found, in 1925, the collaborator he wanted in Seth Wakeman, whom he called from Cornell to the chairmanship of the department of education. As the years went on more and more Smith students who were interested in school teaching found that they could prepare themselves for it without diluting the quality of their liberal arts degree.

Wakeman believed that the fundamental basis of a department of education should be the study of children's development and behavior. His own special field was educational psychology, so Neilson, with one of his characteristic rapid moves, transferred the courses in educational psychology from the department of psychology to the department of education. The action seemed to him so obviously desirable that he did not take time to discuss it at length with the professors of psychology and a resentment was engendered which it required many years to smooth.

Wakeman believed also, and Neilson concurred, that laboratory schools in which the student might observe children and practice teaching them were essential to a good department of education. The Smith College Nursery School and the Smith College Day School (elementary) were opened in the fall of 1926, serving a dual purpose since they offered a good progressive education to the faculty children. Graduate work in education was subsequently developed and in 1939 Smith, first of the women's colleges to do so, conferred the degree of Master of Education. The work was designed to permit the student to devote a large measure of her time to the field—history, English, science, or whatever—in which she wished to teach, while acquiring at the same time technical credits which would satisfy a Board of Education in almost any state. To Neilson, who believed that the training of good teachers was a service the college owed to the community, this was a source of genuine pleasure. Shortly before his retirement he said to Wakeman that nothing in the course of his administration had given him more satisfaction than the development of the department of education.

Belief in the importance of educating women which had influenced Neilson's decision to come to Smith grew firmer year by year. Asked by *Collier's* (3 October 1925) to answer the question "Do Women Learn Faster than Men?" he replied in the affirmative, though with certain reservations.

> On the whole, women are better students than men because they are more docile and industrious. Through long habit and tradition the female mind gives obedience readily to authoritative tuition. Indeed, this instinctive readiness to accept authority is, sometimes, a handicap to women students, for in the classroom they may be as curious, they are certainly as alert, but they are not as disputatious as men.
>
> The woman student is normally more attentive than the man. While women have their share of silly topics for gossip and distraction, my experience at both Harvard University and Smith College impressed me with the fact that the diversion of men's minds at the undergraduate age affects their studiousness the more. . .
>
> It is true that women students are less inclined to deal with abstract instruction than men; they prefer the concrete, personal, dramatized method. And in a subject like economics it is a general rule that the men excel. But in other subjects, especially the purely cultural subjects, it will be found that young women will usually lead young men.

As women made further invasion of the professions, Neilson thought, men would be stimulated to greater effort to meet their competition and the balance between the sexes in the classroom might be restored. "For the moment, women have the advantage."

He went even beyond this. Writing in 1926 to the president of a women's college which was undertaking a campaign for funds he said:

> I believe that the capacity of the American woman for cultural development is so great that in the long run women's colleges may

contribute more to the *quality* of American life than the men's colleges.

That woman's education should take account of her most usual profession, homemaking, Neilson believed but he never succeeded in doing anything very constructive about it. In 1924 he appointed a faculty committee to plan an inter-departmental major in home economics. It should be possible, he thought, to combine courses in chemistry, biology, economics, sociology, and art which would prove a stimulus to the future homemaker and provide her with theoretical background for her profession. He opened a discussion of this idea at a faculty-alumnae roundtable held at commencement time, but the major never materialized. The Smith faculty always withdrew in alarm when anything even faintly savoring of vocationalism approached the curriculum.

A little later, in 1927, Neilson received hopefully under the Smith aegis an experiment known as the Institute for the Co-ordination of Women's Interests. Conceived and directed by an alumna, Mrs. Ethel Puffer Howes of the class of 1891, and financed for a period of years by the Laura Spelman Rockefeller Foundation, the Institute grappled with the then emerging problem of the housewife who wants to carry on professional or business activity outside her home. A co-operative nursery was set up, a cooked-food service organized, studies were made of home assistance projects in the United States and abroad, and some interesting publications were issued, but the curriculum remained inviolate though much hot and healthy discussion was engendered among Smith alumnae, co-ordinated and unco-ordinated.

The "single contribution to the theory of my profession as a college president" took shape in 1927 when the trustees wanted to make a gift to the College in honor of the tenth anniversary of Neilson's incumbency. Keeping the idea quite secret from him, a small committee of trustees and faculty, under the presidency of George McCallum, collected a fund which would finance for five years the William Allan Neilson Chair of Research and found that it would be possible to call as the first incumbent Kurt Koffka of Giessen, the Gestalt psychologist. Consulted about the appointment, Neilson was very happy at the prospect of having Koffka on the campus but quite incredulous when told that funds for the Chair were in sight. It never occurred to him that it was to bear his name.

The anniversary gift was announced at the chapel exercises by McCallum, who presented it as a token of the trustees' "admiration, affection, and esteem" for their President. Neilson expressed his satisfaction in the form the gift had taken:

> So far as I know there is no purely undergraduate college in America which has a chair devoted entirely to research. No college I know of has had the courage, the resources, the insight to do what this group of friends have done for Smith. . . Nothing could have given me more appropriate pleasure—hardly anything I think a deeper pleasure—than this gift. It is a recognition not only of momentary value, not only of reflective value on the past, but of future value, and it is in the future that I shall hope to deserve it.

In the fall Neilson introduced Koffka to the College as "the first installment of my immortality."

> In an astonishingly short time [says the President's Report for 1927-28] it became apparent that this new departure was likely to surpass the hopes of its initiators in its effect upon the College. Dr. Koffka's personality and the interest his researches [on the theory of learning] are evoking are proving a very remarkable stimulus to the intellectual interests of our community.

The successive holders of the chair, most of them on one year appointments, whom Neilson had the pleasure of knowing, during his administration and when he was President Emeritus, continued that intellectual stimulus in a rich variety of ways. They were G. Antonio Borgese, comparative literature; Sir Herbert J. C. Grierson, English; Alfred Einstein, music; George Edward Moore, philosophy; Karl Kelchner Darrow, physics; Carl L. Becker, history; Albert F. Blakeslee, botany; Edgar Wind, art.

The trustees' intention to put the Neilson Chair immediately on a permanent basis was thwarted by the depression but, even before that cloud had lifted, Mrs. Dwight Morrow agreed to head a committee to complete the endowment in time for Neilson's twentieth anniversary in 1937. This proved an easier task than anyone had anticipated, so many of Neilson's friends, in and outside of Smith College, wanted to have a share in the gift. The donors included, as Mrs. Morrow put it, making the presentation at commencement time in 1935:

> The trustees and former trustees; the alumnae, every class from 1879 to 1935; the faculty; the undergraduates; the fathers and mothers who have sent their girls to Smith College (in many cases because of you, Sir) . . . Also, the great educational world outside of Smith College is represented. We are rather proud of our ten college presidents. We have the heads of the organizations and institutions that President Neilson has served. We have principalities and powers.

So eager were these givers, she went on, that the money had been raised two years too soon, but, believing that a thrifty Scot would not like to have a present "put away in the bureau drawer for two years," they were presenting it to Neilson on his eighteenth, instead of his twentieth, anniversary.

Neilson expressed his gratitude, and his surprise. He had not supposed the trustees could possibly bring the thing off. Then he stated in detail the fundamental purpose of the Chair of Research.

> In a college, and especially in a college somewhat remote from a large city, as this is, one has to pay attention not merely to the ordinary requirements that an academic person makes in talking about an appointment—standards of personality, of scholarship, of teaching power, and the like—but also to the capacity a member of his staff might have for stimulating the intellectual interests of the community, for being among his fellows one of the people who makes conversation worth while, and who helps merely by the quality of his mind and personality to keep up the spiritual level of the academic community. We have a number of persons on our faculty here who are quite good in scholarship and quite good as teachers, but whose supreme value is in what they do for the general level of living in Smith College and in Northampton.
>
> It seemed to me that the appointment of a person from abroad or from outside the College to a chair like this would, if the chair were endowed, insure us a constant succession of persons who would stimulate us in this way—would give us new ideas, help us to look critically at what we are doing, contribute his personal quality to the life that we have here. I never expected or hoped to have a position made on such a magnificent scale; and I am profoundly grateful to

all who have made it possible to associate my name with an institution which will remain here long after I am gone, and will, I am sure, continue to contribute stimulus to the life of the community and to make more effective the purposes which you all wish to see fulfilled.

The Neilson Chair, as this account makes clear, was one more, and perhaps the most conspicuous illustration, of the Neilson theory of administration. He had once imagined an ideal campus arranged in concentric circles but he made no attempt to adapt Smith's sprawling grounds to any such design. He contented himself with removing excrescences and widening outlooks and vistas. In the same way he dealt with the curriculum, banking up its strong points, pruning where he could, introducing no exotics, however beautiful, but only schemes and ideas which could strike deep roots into the New England soil. The originality so often remarked in Neilson's educational ideas lay primarily in his quick comprehension of what was and what was not indigenous to Smith College.

13

The President as Administrator

As President Eliot had predicted to Thomas Lamont, Neilson proved able "to cope with any administrative situation," but he did this by reason of certain special qualities of his own, not by the conventional virtues of the high-powered executive, in most of which he was rather strikingly deficient.

He had, for one thing, little skill in delegating work. This was not because he wanted absolute authority nor because he thought that he could do things better than other people. It was simply the habit, formed in Doune and nourished by Carlyle, of doing with his might whatever work came under his hand. That his time was too valuable to be expended on quotidian matters did not occur to him. His secretaries found that if a routine letter to the Registrar or the Board of Admissions got onto his desk by mistake he would dictate a carefully considered reply. Sometimes a newly appointed executive would wait patiently for days for the President to tell her what to do. Eventually, if she was a good appointment, she began to observe that the administrative staff, the chairmen of trustee and faculty committees had, most of them, created their jobs by snatching pieces of work away when the President was not looking, doing them swiftly, and bringing to him for comment the finished product. He was agreeably appreciative of relief but it never occurred to him to ask for it. This made working for him an exhilarating experience in independent action, and, besides, one knew that he would always take the responsibility for a task performed and back a subordinate stoutly against the world.

Another trait which the conventional executive would not regard as a virtue but which proved in Neilson's case to be one, was indiscretion. Neilson had what was to his colleagues a heartening way of saying in a private conversation on college matters exactly what he thought about an academic situation, accompanied frequently by sharp comments on the individuals involved which, if carelessly repeated, would have brought whole hornets' nests down about his ears—but they never were carelessly repeated. The man or woman to whom he had spoken freely, as a friend, respected Neilson's frankness as a mark of confidence. There was a general self-flattering conviction among his faculty that the President was discreetly indiscreet, that he talked thus freely to *you* because he knew that *you* were a person he could trust. This was probably a correct impression, for Neilson did not speak carelessly in a committee or a group and he once wrote, when consulted as to whether a certain professor would make a good headmistress, that he did not think she would because

> She rejoices in the complete freedom that she has here to express herself about persons and things, and I suspect that it would be very hard for her to accommodate herself to the kind of discretion necessary in the head of an educational institution.

At variance, too, with the conventional executive pattern was Neilson's optimistic opinion of human beings. He almost always thought them better than they were, or better at least than they seemed to the majority of their colleagues. This came partly from his readiness to give a good worker free rein, partly from his ability to disregard adjunctive inconveniences—a hasty temper, perhaps, or a lack of respect for the rights of others—if the man in question had some special talent which could be put to work for the College. Occasionally, of course, this optimism led Neilson into serious mistakes in judgment: he sometimes took the mediocre for the good; he was reluctant to believe in real depravity. But brilliance he always recognized and delighted in. "Never stand in the way of genius," he said once when making, against departmental disapproval, a special grant for the work of an unco-operative but gifted scholar. Quite as much as genius, though, he admired the unspectacular virtues: loyalty, industry, patience; the quiet, inconspicuous service rendered to the College by devoted individuals he recognized and liked to bring to light.

This interest in the individual had its dangers. "Our difficulty is going to be that he will not always see the wood for the trees," predicted a wise elder member of the faculty not long after Neilson's arrival, and it was a just fear. The man or woman in trouble he wanted so much to help that he would, for instance, make a job for them on the basis of their need rather than the College's, to the consternation sometimes of their immediate colleagues. Yet, as we have seen, it was this personal interest of the President in his faculty which formed one of the strongest ties attaching them to Smith.

Related to his concern for the individual, and again unconventional in the executive, was Neilson's slightly suspicious attitude towards administrative machinery. The twentieth-century conviction that all problems can be solved by systems, statistics, and questionnaires seemed to him fraught with danger. Of a proposed investigation of "the aims and methods of the liberal college" he wrote in April 1923:

> I am trying very hard to get time to attend to my own job and understand the problems which Professor Q. enumerates as they bear on the institution where I am employed. I have to spend a good deal of time on committees and questionnaires which frequently seem to me quite fruitless. I am, therefore, reluctant to have any part in increasing the number of these distractions, although I am well aware of the advantages to be gained from comparing notes with people engaged with similar problems, but I feel we are all becoming victims of the investigation habit.

And one of the few sharp comments in his History of Smith College was occasioned by the inclination of his predecessor in the presidency to rely too heavily on machinery:

The innovations [Mr. Burton] introduced he regarded with an ebullient optimism, not unaccompanied by a certain amount of wishful thinking. Not all proved as effective as he hoped and thought. The business methods he applied to the administration were beneficial and permanent; in his educational methods he perhaps at times tended to put too much reliance on mechanisms for results that in the long run depend on personality.

Yet Neilson felt genuine gratitude to Burton for the efficient functioning of many sections of the College:

He found a College that had grown gradually from very small beginnings, without the apparatus of administration which is necessary for knowing what you are doing in the conduct of what is from one point of view a large business, and he introduced into the administrative offices methods of modern business in the keeping of records and the like. . . He was here only seven years, but he did an extraordinary amount to move the College from one basis to another, and the College will always be grateful to him for what he did. I myself question whether I could have found the burdens which I found here tolerable at all had it not been for what Mr. Burton had done with the special kind of equipment which he had and to which I could not lay any claim. (Announcement to the College of Burton's death, 18 February 1925)

Much of the modern apparatus for obtaining efficiency and dispatch seemed to Neilson both futile and extravagent. He seldom used the long-distance telephone; he always preferred a letter to a telegram; and when he was obliged to telegraph he made his message severely brief. Dean Nicolson tells of an occasion when he was abroad and she, in charge of the College, had to consult him on an important decision. His reply was so terse—he was counting the words—that she was quite unable to discover what he meant.

To the automobile Neilson did eventually adapt himself, purchasing a car in 1931 and learning to manage it well enough except for the fact that he drove always at whirlwind speed. He could no more loiter on the highway than he could when he was packing a suitcase or solving a problem. Mrs. Neilson let him take the wheel only when there was a perfectly straight and empty stretch of road before them. When appointments outside

Northampton could be kept more conveniently by motor than by train the President put himself in the hands of Dean Nicolson, his secretary, or one of his friends in the Alumnae Office. The kind of car he owned concerned him not at all, except that, preferably, it should be second-hand.

He had the same attitude towards all official trappings. He flatly refused to have his College Hall office redecorated, though he saw the point at once when one of his colleagues asked for better lighting or a more adequate desk. Comfort and convenience, he thought, were good, so was beauty, but it must be sought always with strict limitations against luxury or show. Neilson liked to tease his fellow administrators when he thought they had permitted architects or trustees to surround them with ostentation. Dean Nicolson tells of attending with him a conference at Wellesley just after the completion of a new Administration Building where one passed, as Neilson phrased it, through a series of offices "into the presence." When, at the close of the conference, President Pendleton expressed concern that the President and Dean of Smith were returning to Northampton by a way-train which had no parlor car, Neilson assured her that they were doing this by choice. "We must make the descent to Avernus somehow, and the day coach will help us to get used to living at Smith again."

Academic regalia, too, was a matter of indifference to Neilson. When the Class of 1921, who entered Smith in the same year he did, wanted to make him a present on the occasion of their first reunion, Annetta Clark, his secretary, wrote that

> He needs and wants a silk gown. His present gown is serge [it dated from his early days at Harvard] and is, of course, very inappropriate for the dignity of his position. I have been trying to make him buy a new one, but this is one of the things in which I have thus far been unable to force obedience. It seems to me that it would be very appropriate for his classmates to present him with this.

Touched by the affection of his "classmates" the President wore the silk gown with pleasure until, in 1928, his honorary doctorate from Edinburgh imposed the purchase of the gown of "superfine scarlet cloth" and "rich blue silk" with which he brightened academic processions during the rest of his administration. That Edinburgh gown Neilson really enjoyed wearing, partly, his wife said, because he had paid so much for it.

The trustees encountered the same sort of indifference to the trappings of office when they wanted to have a portrait of the President painted for the College just before his retirement. The principle involved Neilson was bound to recognize for he had welcomed warmly a portrait of President Seelye, and had urged the gift by her classmates of a portrait of Dean Comstock, but all the advice he would give the trustees on the choice of an artist to immortalize him was "thrift in a matter of small importance." When the painter, Alexander James (son of William) was finally chosen, Neilson found the sittings a genuine pleasure for James liked to talk with his sitter as he worked and Neilson thought their conversations some of the best he had ever enjoyed. The finished picture, which now hangs at the head of the stairs in the Neilson Library, was admired as a piece of painting and a fine use of the dramatic colors of the Edinburgh gown but there was much controversy among faculty and alumnae as to its success as a likeness. Neilson himself said that he was "content to have future generations of Smith College think I look like that," but his opinion in this instance carried small weight. He spent so little time on self-analysis that he probably would not have recognized a picture of himself if he had met it in a strange college. He certainly did not realize, as the portrait's critics did, that the artist had been faced with the almost insuperable difficulty of stabilizing light. Part of the pleasure of talking to Neilson was in watching the swift and delicate shifts of expression which changed with each idea or phrase he uttered. One felt always a sense, never of hurry, but of exhilarating speed. Mrs. Morrow, in her *Atlantic* essay, comments on the way in which people who try to describe Neilson's personality or his teaching use constantly symbols of light: "lambent," "incandescent," "luminous." Photographs, merely through their instantaneousness, come nearer to catching this quality than painting. The most satisfactory likeness among the portraits was painted posthumously by John Folinsbee, working from photographs. The painter of another portrait, Charles Hopkinson, working in 1929, confined himself to picturing Neilson the executive. The pose is characteristic. The President, wearing a grey suit and soft green tie, sits at his office desk, alert but leaning back a little in his chair, a cigar poised in his left hand; he is looking directly at the spectator and his expression suggests that he is saying to himself, as one member of the faculty put it: "Now can I get this man for three thousand or must I make it thirty-five hundred?"

The painter was quite right in making Neilson the executive look as though he were enjoying himself, not as though he were harried or worked to death. The President admitted to his wife occasionally that he felt rushed but none of the people who talked to him in the chair beside his desk ever thought so. He seemed to be enjoying—and he was—the conversation that was going on, to be in no hurry to finish it. Many a young instructor, leaving the President's office, noted with amused delight the distinguished company who were being kept waiting until *his* business was thoroughly finished. Actually Neilson did find the pressure of scheduled appointments tiresome. One of the things he enjoyed about a holiday was the absence of set engagements. If Mrs. Neilson even casually suggested that he might return from a morning expedition early enough for them to take a walk before lunch, he would remind her entreatingly, "No times, no times."

Travel, whether by boat or train—he rarely flew—was one of the things that refreshed him most. What he sat on or slept on was to him a matter of complete indifference. Only when he was traveling with his wife did he take any care about accommodations because, she said, he knew that she was more agreeable when she was comfortable.

On transcontinental train trips or on a steamer Neilson occasionally played solitaire, though he thought card games of any sort dull and profitless. He was always made melancholy by the amount of bridge playing he saw when he walked through a campus dormitory. Chiefly he utilized the comparatively uninterrupted hours of travel to do some of the reading for which he could never make time enough at home, but, since his cigar was a necessity, he had frequent recourse to the smoking compartment where he liked to talk with anyone he met. The often repeated story of his smoking car chat with a drummer is so characteristic that many of the people who knew him best believed it to be authentic. As he was getting off the train, the story runs, the drummer, who had enjoyed their conversation, asked, "By the way, what's your line? Mine's skirts," and the President of Smith responded promptly, "So is mine." Actually, Neilson stated a little wearily on one of the occasions when a chairman used the story in introducing him, that story was told of his predecessor, and would undoubtedly be told of his successor, unless, as seemed not improbable, his students had ceased to wear skirts.*

The only drawback to travel, really, was the ubiquitous Smith alumna who, according to Neilson's daughters, was always starting up suddenly in unexpected places and rushing to greet father, and gush over him. The family used to consider vacationing in places like Labrador or the Belgian Congo to which the species alumna might not yet have penetrated.

A good deal of the traveling was done, of course, in the interests of those ubiquitous alumnae whom Neilson, despite his family, really enjoyed meeting. Her graduates live, Smith likes to boast, in every state in the Union and Neilson believed it important to report to them as frequently as possible on the condition of the College. An efficient Alumnae Office planned and regulated these appearances, trying not to work the President too hard, though that was difficult; he always wanted to be away from Northampton as short a time as possible and local Smith Clubs always wanted to have him talk not only to them but to schools and other organizations in the vicinity. They knew the kind of impression he could make, even in ten minutes. The Smith Clubs in Boston and New York thought it impossible to hold their annual luncheons without him; smaller clubs, not too far from Northampton, felt that they might put in a request every few years; and almost every year the President visited some section of the West. Some of the schedules were grueling. Neilson in his retiring address to the alumnae recalled one of their number

* The president who helped a girl climb into a dormitory window after hours was not Neilson but Henry Noble MacCracken of Vassar. See his *The Hickory Limb*, 1950.

"who made me deliver eight speeches between eight o'clock in the morning and eight o'clock at night."

There were business journeys, too, across the Atlantic, visits to the students spending their junior year in Paris, Florence, or Madrid. The European days on land were often crowded to exhaustion but Neilson was a good sailor and found the ocean voyage restful. When the trustees began to insist that if he was going to spend the summer in Northampton supervising building operations he must take a spring vacation, he and Mrs. Neilson often went for a few weeks to Bermuda or the West Indies. In the summer of 1924 he earned a Raymond and Whitcomb North Cape cruise for his family by lecturing to their fellow tourists on Scandinavian history and literature.

In the fall of 1927 he and Mrs. Neilson spent a semester of sabbatical leave in France and Italy. On 26 November Neilson wrote from Sicily to his sister Jean:

> We have been here for three days now, and agree that all you said of Taormina is true. We are not, of course, seeing it to advantage, for the Sirocco is blowing, Etna is invisible, and the sky has been overcast ever since we came. But the town is extraordinarily full of interest, and even in this weather so picturesque that it is a constant delight. . . Capri delighted us and is one of the places I should like to go to loaf in a long time.

In 1933 the condition of the President's health, diagnosed as ulcer, became so serious that the trustees insisted on his taking a three months' vacation. On 25 February he and Mrs. Neilson sailed for Europe, planning to divide their time between Spain and Italy. On 20 March Neilson wrote to his brother from Ronda:

> I find it hard to learn much about the Spanish situation, but it seems to be, though precarious, about as promising as anything on the Continent. The German situation is beyond words, and Li is much disturbed. It reads like a return—not to 1914, but to the Middle Ages.
>
> In spite of the outside world time is passing here very pleasantly. I have ideal conditions for my cure, and I feel extremely well and have no discomfort. . . Life is comparatively little modernized here. There are at least fifty donkeys to every motor car. I have heard one gramophone. There is one movie theater, but the bullring is more

conspicuous. I haven't been able to find out what the town produces beyond donkey harness and saddle blankets. One sees few priests and the churches seem seldom open. There are not nearly so many churches to the population as in Mexico. The children and old women beg for pennies incessantly and never seem to get any. I have seen one youth under the influence of liquor in nearly three weeks. I have seen one man ill use a beast—and that was because it stumbled and caused him to fall ignominiously from its back. Mostly one sees great kindness to children and animals—apart from the bull-ring.

After a month in Italy the Neilsons spent some weeks with the Musers in Offenburg and returned to Northampton in time for Commencement.

With his daughters Neilson had two summers of English travel, the first in 1932 with Margaret, just turned twenty; the second, with both girls, in 1935. All the children had more European experience than most Americans of their years for, in addition to visits to the grandparents in Offenburg, the girls had spent a year in Munich and a summer in France, but the British Isles were a new experience. On 26 July 1932 Neilson wrote to his brother from London:

> It is hopeless to begin to tell you what we have been seeing, for that would mean a guidebook. The important thing is that Margaret is keenly interested and very appreciative and very much in love with England. . . I am getting to know more about England than I ever knew before—I mean geographically.

They went up the east coast to Edinburgh, from which they made trips to Melrose, Dryburgh, and Abbotsford—"all new to me," Neilson wrote to his sister Jean—and then on visits to Montrose and Doune.

In the summer of 1935 a post card sent from Cambridge to the Roy Welches announced that "A model father with two model daughters is touring England in perfect weather."

Neilson as a traveler was interested not only in architecture and scenery but in trying to get impressions of the life and the character of the people in the country he was visiting. The proper time for that, he told the undergraduates, reporting in 1929 on a trip to Mexico, is from one to three weeks; "any time longer begins to destroy your assurance." The Neilsons had flown to Mexico in November for a visit to Ambassador and Mrs. Morrow. Elizabeth, the eldest Morrow daughter who graduated from Smith in 1925, was their principal guide and told her mother what a pleasure it was to go about with people who always admired the right things; Mexico is so flamboyant that it is easy to be distracted to the trivial. This trip was one of the rare occasions on which Neilson flew instead of traveling by train and the student *Weekly* sternly reminded him, parodying the college rules on motoring and plane travel, that he seemed to have overlooked an important regulation: "The President must not travel in airplanes without the consent of the entire student body."

Neilson thought that Mexico had an extraordinary variety of "perfectly gorgeous beauty, comparable without exaggeration to the beauty of southern Italy and Sicily," but he was even more delighted by the country's rich history and pre-history. "The thrill that one gets out of it is not inferior to that of one's first trip to Europe."

Excursions such as these supplied the refreshment which kept Neilson the administrator working for twenty-two years not only with energy but with pleasure. An even stronger reason for his enjoyment of his job was the kind of working-partners Smith College provided him. Among faculty, trustees, alumnae, student government officers he found each year many women who thought about Smith College in the same terms that he did. Important among this company were two Smith graduates whom he found at work in College Hall when he arrived: Annetta I. Clark, Secretary to the President, and Ada L. Comstock, Dean of the College.

The role of Secretary to the President, as interpreted by Miss Clark through four administrations, was something quite unique in academic annals, a continuous demonstration of the superiority of personality to machinery. She never assumed authority or asserted power behind the throne, but subtly supplemented each President, extending his energy, his range, and vision. And she did this with great success for four utterly different individuals, over a period of thirty-six years. "Woe to the president who has to carry on without her!" wrote Neilson in his History of Smith College.

Annetta Clark was one of those Northampton girls to whom, since its opening, Smith College has offered free tuition. Her family had lived in the town for several generations. Her grandfather started the first horsecar line and her father was its superintendent. Annetta went through the Northampton High School and graduated from Smith with the class of 1904. Instead of settling down, as her family expected, to a domestic life at home, she learned shorthand and typing, taught them in a New Jersey high school, and then took a job in the Smith College Registrar's office. In 1909-10, President Seelye's last year in office, his secretary was obliged to leave and, looking for someone who was familiar with both the College and the community, he enlisted Annetta Clark, a "fateful appointment," Neilson called it. When President Seelye retired, Miss Clark wanted to go back to the Registrar's office but President Burton asked her to help him get started and, after she had worked for him a little while, declined to let her go. That acquaintance with the College and the community which President Seelye had looked for when he appointed her had been greatly increased during her work for him, for he soon found, as all Miss Clark's friends and colleagues did, that she was completely discreet in the use she made of her wide knowledge. President Burton worked her hard—there were many hours of overtime—but he was so pleasant about expressing his appreciation that she never tired and she developed a great liking and admiration for him. She was distressed when he left for Minnesota and had no intention of carrying on the heavy burden of her position under any other president, but, with her usual kindness, agreed to stay long enough to help Neilson get settled. He recognized her qualities at once—President Burton, he once said, did not understand "the real greatness of Annetta"—and she began to feel the exhilarating sense of partnership he gave to all his co-workers. Their collaboration lasted for twenty-two years.

Annetta Clark had in her head not only a fund of administrative history and practice but a treasury of personal secrets larger even than that of Neilson himself. People who were a little in awe of the President would pour their troubles into her motherly ear or weep on her broad kind shoulder. One of her friends illuminated a line from the *Aeneid* and hung it on her office wall: *Sunt lacrimae rerum.* But even more people made excuses to look in at her open door, as they went up and down the College Hall stairs, to tell or hear the latest piece of campus gossip. Annetta knew most things before they happened and she was a superb raconteur. Both men and women, from laboratory assistants to professors emeriti, enjoyed her company; she seldom managed to eat her lunch alone.

Miss Clark was usually the first person any new member of the faculty met. In search of a house, a cleaning woman, or a kitten he would be told to "Ask Annetta," and "Ask Annetta" became the standard faculty answer to any unclassified problem. She was, too, an important adjunct to the Neilson household, beloved by the children and lending a hand often in domestic crises. At the twenty-fifth reunion of her class, in 1929, the College made Annetta Clark an honorary Master of Arts. Neilson in conferring the degree cited her as

> Keeper of the secrets of the Board of Trustees and of the three presidents of Smith College, the repository of all knowledge of its past and of its present, confidante of student, teacher, and alumna, wise in counsel and indefatigable in kindness, whose sympathy, tolerance, and saving humor render her adequate in all emergencies, our only indispensable.

In Dean Ada Louise Comstock, appointed by his predecessor, President Burton, Neilson found an ideal working partner. With an integrity like his own and a care as great for education and for the individual, she could yet approach a problem with an objectivity which was impossible to his quick instinctive sympathy. "The Roman" he called her when, from time to time, she pointed out to him a person whom he ought to distrust or disapprove. Her thinking had a quality of absolute justice which he knew he could never emulate and which he deeply admired because it was a justice tempered with kindness and with humor. "Her mind, as I have conceived it," he said after they had worked together for six years, "is the mind of an admirable judge. In a different world Miss Comstock would have sat on the Supreme Bench of the United States."

Ada Comstock, a native of Minnesota, had graduated from Smith in 1897, studied at Columbia and the Sorbonne, taught English at the University of Minnesota and served there as Dean of Women until Burton, himself a Minnesotan, called her to Smith in 1912. The College had had previously a masculine Dean of the Faculty, Professor Henry M. Tyler. Miss Comstock took over his admirably performed duties and added to them the care of the social welfare of the students which, with the increasing size of the College, had become a problem too complex to be dealt with by teachers and heads of houses without the aid of a centralizing power. "It is doubtful if any action of President Burton's," wrote Neilson in his History, "was of greater benefit to the College than the appointment of Dean Comstock."

Under the Comstock-Neilson partnership the office of Dean of Smith underwent a reorganization, becoming something a little different from the deanship in other institutions. In 1922 the responsibility for the social life of the students was transferred to a newly appointed Warden and the Dean was able to devote herself entirely to academic duties. These included the chairmanship of the Administrative Board, responsible for standards of undergraduate study; of the Committee on the Course of Study, which considered and recommended to the faculty changes in curriculum and course offerings; and of the Committee on Graduate Study, a position of increasing importance under the Neilson regime. The Dean did not, as in many institutions, have responsibility for faculty promotions or for appointments—those Neilson, consulting with the departmental chairmen, made directly—but she was called on for a variety of functions of a vice-presidential nature. She spoke often to the students on academic and campus matters; took, with full responsibility, the place of the President when he was absent from the campus; and daily gave him assistance in the never ended business of smoothing relationships with alumnae, parents, and the general public. "An ideal position," Miss Comstock called the deanship of Smith, for a woman whose interest is in education.

Dean Comstock, unfortunately, could not be hidden under a bushel. Other institutions began to make advances to her. Most dangerous was President Burton's attempt to lure her and Doctor Florence Gilman, who was performing valuable work as head of the Department of Physical Education, to the University of Michigan, where he had proceeded from Minnesota. The temptation, in salary and in opportunity, was great but Neilson and the trustees fought back vigorously and the Neilson-Comstock partnership was saved, for the time being. It was partly in celebration of this continuance that Neilson enthusiastically encouraged the class of 1897 when it occurred to them to present as their twenty-fifth reunion gift a portrait of their distinguished classmate. Trained in New England thrift, Miss Comstock's classmates hesitated to proffer to their Alma Mater anything not definitely practical and so wrote to consult Neilson. He advised them to "take advantage of the very special opportunity of doing something distinctive next June."

It is your twenty-fifth anniversary and Miss Comstock's tenth as Dean. We have no portrait of a woman in the College except that of Sophia Smith herself and we ought certainly to have a portrait of our first Dean in her prime. Greedy as I am for money for the College, my vote, even as an administrator, would be for the portrait, and for it next June. As for her consent, I think we could bully her into that.

A little later he was writing:

If I were a member of the class, I would much rather double my subscription and get Miss Beaux than give half as much for a cheaper article.

The class of '97 agreed with Neilson and a fine example of the work of Cecaelia Beaux, which is at the same time an excellent likeness of Smith's first Dean, now hangs in the dining room of Comstock House. The College marked the Dean's tenth anniversary by an honorary L.H.D. which the President conferred upon her as "the member of the College most loved at home, most honored abroad."

As celebrations of Dean Comstock's remaining at Smith the portrait and the degree were not altogether successful. Within a year she received another call, this time so important that it could not be denied; she was invited to become President of Radcliffe. She made her choice by asking the same question Neilson had asked when he was called from Harvard to Smith: in which capacity could she be of greatest service to American education? The justice of her decision Neilson was obliged to admit but he could not take it calmly. He did not like the idea of administering Smith without her. The combination of devotion and gayety with which both of them approached their work had engendered a genuine friendship which made their academic partnership singularly happy and fruitful.

Speaking at President Comstock's inauguration, 20 October 1923, Neilson made it clear that the women's colleges would be keeping a sharp eye on the future relationship of the two parts of Harvard University.

I have never [he said] been in the position of a father giving away a daughter in marriage. That is due to the accident of my own life. But I think that I can today, in imagination, conceive pretty well the feelings of such a person. The working out of my figure is interfered with by the difficulty of conceiving Radcliffe College as a bridegroom. Even colleges for men are usually referred to as "she"; how much more colleges for women!

And yet I insist on the essential validity of the figure. I am giving away Miss Comstock to Radcliffe College and I have very much the kind of feeling that I suppose a father has in these circumstances, a feeling of profound affection and solicitude for the young woman, a feeling of suspicion with regard to the young man.

I know that the young man in this case will provide food and shelter and a kindly attitude, but in this assemblage, and before so many friends of women's colleges, I may say with assurance that the day has gone by when all that is expected of the young husband is to provide for his young wife. The woman of today demands, above all, scope, and opportunity to develop her personality as an individual; a chance to make the most of her powers, to count for what she is worth in the community, and not merely to be a caretaker at home and the mistress of domestic felicities.

In the application of this figure to our present situation, I wish to say to the young man, Radcliffe College, that we are handing over—we of Smith—our daughter to you on the understanding not only that you will care for her and be kind to her and appreciate the ornament that she will be to your household, but that you will give her scope.

I might pursue this figure a little farther. Our daughter is entering your family somewhat in the position of the young woman who marries into a family of old tradition and great dignity and importance and self-importance. The bridegroom has a big brother, the head of the house, and most of us are familiar with the painful position of the young bride who comes into a family with such overshadowing personages standing about the drawing-room.

What she has to do, as a rule, is to teach the big brother his place, and to make it clear that she has not married him; that she has married his little brother, who must now no longer be regarded as a little brother, who has set up an establishment of his own, and who must have his chance, and whose wife must have her chance.

[Neilson turned then to Miss Comstock.] I bring from the alumnae, the students, the faculty of Smith, the College you have loved and served, and which has loved you, their especial greetings and good wishes, and the assurance that they will follow your career with sympathy and affection. And if you find this household into which you have been taken intolerable, you can always come home.

Smith promptly made Miss Comstock a trustee so that the College might continue to draw on her wisdom. The President's frequent letters of consultation began often, in gentle reproach, "Dear Dean."

The filling of Dean Comstock's place was a difficult task. For a year the President carried the double administrative burden, finding it far too heavy and obliged, in consequence, to decline many outside calls upon his energies which he would have liked to accept. Finally, in February 1924 he was able to announce the appointment to the deanship of Mrs. Frances Fenton Bernard, Educational Secretary of the American Association of University Women. Neilson told the news to the College in chapel on a particularly wet and icy morning when only a handful of people were present and when a distraught publicity director asked why she had not been forewarned to gather the photographs and data for which the newspapers were clamoring, he explained simply that he had not intended to say anything about the appointment until the next week, but the morning was such a vilely disagreeable one that he thought the people who had taken the trouble to come out to chapel ought to get some reward.

Mrs. Bernard's deanship lasted only until 1928 when she resigned to marry Professor Edwin A. Park of Yale, but she left her impress on the College in the new curriculum, the construction of which she supervised, and in the Neilson Chair of Research, in the establishing of which she was an active worker. In announcing her resignation in his annual report to the trustees Neilson said that he would miss "the stimulus of her fresh and untrammelled mind, her frank and friendly criticism, her eagerness to heighten the intellectual quality of the college life." In bidding her, for the College, a public farewell, he laid emphasis on the success with which she had transferred her loyalty from Vassar to Smith, illuminating as he did so his own interpretation of loyalty.

One might easily get into a tangle about the transfer of loyalties. I could give you a long discourse about that. I have had to transfer my loyalty from country to country and from institution to institution, but I assure you that there is a very good kind of loyalty that is quite portable.

Loyalty is an attitude, an attitude which is determined by the relation between what one is getting out of things for one's self and what one is getting out of things for the sake of one's object or the institution or the organization. I know that I have the whole College with me when I say that Mrs. Park has thoroughly and completely survived any evil effects of her early training, and has in no way been hampered in her effectiveness for this College.

In April 1929 Neilson reported that the search for a successor to Dean Bernard had been long, painful, and difficult. "Providence does not seem to have provided many people with the particular assembly of qualities that would fit them to be dean of Smith College. The required qualities of mind, personality, and experience are such that I doubt whether there exists more than one person at a time. I think now we have found her." And he announced the appointment of Professor Marjorie Hope Nicolson who, since 1926, had been a member of the department of English.

A graduate of the University of Michigan in 1914, a scholar of distinction—her special field was the seventeenth century—a brilliant and exacting teacher, Miss Nicolson had also a grasp of general educational principles which made her opinion of value in matters of policy and curriculum, and a fluency of effective platform speech which gave her great influence with the undergraduates. Unwilling to curtail sharply either her teaching or her scholarly writing, she accepted at first only the position of Acting Dean, but soon found, for she had energy as well as talent, that she could carry administrative duties without too severely diminishing her professorial effectiveness.

Dean Nicolson served Smith with distinction until 1940 when she resigned to become the first woman professor in the Graduate School of Columbia University. In the same year she was elected to the national presidency of Phi Beta Kappa, the first woman to hold that office. Neilson, then President Emeritus of Smith and a Phi Beta Kappa Senator, wrote in the *Key Reporter* (Autumn 1940):

> Her appointment at Columbia along with her election as the head of Phi Beta Kappa must be a matter of extreme satisfaction to those who have waited impatiently for that equality of opportunity to which we pay lip-service. It is not too much to say that the recognition implied in these appointments is a milestone in academic and democratic progress, and that through them Marjorie Nicolson becomes a historic figure.

Whether it was President Neilson or Dean Comstock who invented the Warden neither of them could afterwards tell. They always discussed any plan or policy together so thoroughly and completely that they seldom remembered who had first proposed it. It had become evident to both of them that with the changing mores of the postwar world the duties of the Dean were too heavy for any one person to carry; a Dean who was to do useful thinking and planning on the educational side of the students' life could not at the same time oversee its domestic and social aspects. In 1922 the Dean's office was divided and Mrs. Laura Lord Scales of the class of 1901, Dean of Women at Carnegie Institute of Technology, was appointed Warden. The title excited, and still does, a good deal of disapproval and ridicule. To the average American it suggests a penitentiary but, as Neilson pointed out to the alumnae, it is the term commonly used for the office in the women's colleges of the English universities; it was already in use at Bryn Mawr; and none of the objectors had a better title to suggest.

The choice of Mrs. Scales to create the position was a singularly happy one. She had not only a powerful combination of charm and efficiency but a comprehension of the relation of her province to the academic side of the College, as fundamental but not superior to it, which made her an invaluable partner to the President and Dean. This Neilson recognized when, in 1931, he conferred on her an honorary L.H.D., speaking of her as the

> guardian of the physical and social welfare of our students, through whose wisdom, liberality, and understanding sympathy the life of the undergraduate becomes year by year broader, richer, and more and more wisely self-directed.

During the twenty-two years of his tenure Neilson added, in addition to the Warden, a considerable number of other new officers to the administrative staff. The teaching faculty sighed occasionally over the increasing population of College Hall but they recognized that one of the chief motives behind each appointment was the President's desire to lighten their administrative burdens. The other motive for increasing the administrative staff was Neilson's perpetual effort to adjust the College as neatly as possible to the individual student; he did not want her shoved into a mold but allowed to work in the way which would bring her the largest benefit.

His own most effective device for adapting the curriculum to the individual was probably the institution of Class Deans, introduced at Smith in the fall of 1918. The Class Deans were women professors who had demonstrated a personal as well as an academic interest in their students. Each of them was attached to a class in its freshman year and shepherded it through to graduation. During that time she was relieved of part of her regular teaching load and, when she had seen her class through its cycle, she returned to full-time teaching for at least two years before taking on the guidance of another class. The purpose of these regulations, Neilson said, was "to prevent a cleavage between the points of view of the teaching and the administrative staff." The four deans, with two other members of the faculty and Dean Comstock as presiding officer, formed the academic Administrative Board of the College.

The Class Dean had personal interviews with each of her four hundred odd students, making suggestions about their courses and learning all she could about their personalities. Some of them she met only occasionally, others again and again as problems arose during their four years. More often than not her students went to her spontaneously for sympathy and advice on matters within or without her jurisdiction.

The enthusiastic affection which each class came to feel for "their" Dean was an indication that in making his appointments the President understood the undergraduate tastes and needs. No less enthusiastic were the members of the faculty and the other administrative officials who came to rely on the Deans in every variety of academic, disciplinary, and personal problem.

The achievements of Neilson the administrator were visible a good many leagues beyond Smith College. One measure of this is the number of honorary degrees conferred upon him during his presidency. For a college to honor with a degree the head of a sister college is common practice, but the distinction, more often than not, is accorded to the institution rather than to the man. When a president is first appointed, before he has had time to prove himself, a neighboring institution often welcomes him with an LL.D. Neilson was so greeted in 1918 by Amherst and by Brown. More significant were the many occasions in later years when the academic world expressed its admiration for Neilson the scholar-administrator. Universities which had no connection at all with Smith, universities inclined as a rule to pay scant attention to the women's colleges, recorded their recognition of the way in which he was filling a difficult office. His collection of L.H.D. and Litt.D. hoods became so large that Mrs. Neilson confessed she groaned aloud when he brought home one more for her to take care of. Sometimes he would not even tell her beforehand why he was making a trip to another campus.

The citations which accompanied the degrees are interesting indications of the qualities which Neilson's fellow-administrators regarded with admiration, even with envy. All of them, apparently, thought it peculiarly difficult to be president of a woman's college. Harvard, still in 1935 intransigently anti-feminist, hailed Neilson as "a leader in a vital experiment in education—the trainer of the college woman of today." (This, Neilson was obliged to explain to his outraged alumnae, was intended as a compliment, implying that Smith is "a progressive institution always engaged in trying new things.") Yale, in 1927, put the case a little more gracefully:

> He had not been long in his new work before it was clear that a vital force was enlivening the whole College. The President was idolized by the students, and even beloved by the Faculty. He maintained the social integrity of the largest of our women's colleges; he introduced radical innovations in honors courses, the junior year in France, and other experiments.

Williams (1925), most effectively perhaps of all, summed up the whole matter:

> Profound thinker, whose keen wit is the polished tool of his idealism, brilliant scholar, educator who sees his aims with clearness and achieves them with originality, he brings the light and warmth of the humanities into all that he does as the skilled executive.

Foreign recognition included, in addition to degrees from McGill and Edinburgh, the Order of Alphonso XII, conferred 30 March 1930, in Madrid, where Neilson had gone in the interests of the International Institute for Girls in Spain and to make plans for Smith's junior year in that country, and, in 1935, the Cross of the Legion of Honor.

There were other institutions which expressed their admiration for Neilson's executive ability less openly than by the conferring of degrees yet even more emphatically: they suggested that he come to them as president. Most of these suggestions, by Neilson's choice, did not get beyond the stage of mutual discussion. The exception was the presidency of the Juilliard School of Music, which, at the suggestion of John Erskine, was offered to Neilson in 1926. The Juilliard trustees were quite aware that

Neilson was in no sense a musician but they had observed the flourishing, under his aegis, of the Smith department of music. Neilson gave this call serious consideration, but declined. On another occasion the rumor that he was going to leave Smith for a large state university swelled so loud that alumnae began to write in in alarm.

In all such negotiations Neilson made his point of view clear. Smith College, he said, is not a stepping-stone, and he did not think his work in Northampton was finished. The "larger" opportunities offered he declined with little regret. Much as he enjoyed administration he never regarded it as an end; it interested him only as a means to the increase of education, and education, he thought, could never really flourish in any institution committed to the pressures of intercollegiate football. "Smith," he used to say to other college presidents, "has never lost a football game."

14

The President and the Undergraduates

AFTER Neilson had been ten years in office as President of Smith his trustees persuaded him to take a sabbatical leave. Declining the year he compromised on one semester plus the summer and in June 1927 he and Mrs. Neilson sailed for Europe. When College opened in September the campus seemed "very dreary without him," according to the undergraduate reporter for the *Alumnae Quarterly*.

> It's queer how much he has to do with the color of the leaves, and whether or not the weather is nice. . . The freshmen must think this is a very commonplace kind of college—and it is. The point to us seems to have been lost.

This attitude towards President Neilson, and for twenty-two years it was practically universal among his students, was induced by his practice of talking to them, day after day, about goodness and truth. Those are topics which have been dealt with fairly frequently down the centuries by the educators of youth, but the Neilson discourses had a variant; it was a matter of vocabulary, a vocabulary used by a philologist with imagination. Neilson had a confident belief that his students were as much concerned with the great questions as he himself had been at twenty, yet he was acutely aware that they phrased their answers in a language very different from that of the nineteenth century; he took care, consequently, to speak to them in their own terms. This he admitted frankly in the baccalaureate address which, as President Emeritus, he returned to give to the class of 1940. He described to them a conference in which he had recently taken part. It was composed of "twelve men of high distinction [the group whose discussions produced *The City of Man*, see pp. 346-7] who had met to consider whether there was anything they could do regarding the situation in the world."

After a day of discussion, Neilson said, the twelve came to the conclusion that what they most needed to do was to arouse the youth of America to an awareness of the advantages of the system under which they live, of the democratic values which are largely ethical values. They turned to one of their number who was president of a large university [Robert M. Hutchins of Chicago] and asked him, from his knowledge of his students, what chance they had to create some awakening to these values. He told them, very little. From observation and talk with his students, he said, he had come to three conclusions about their attitude towards life: their main interest was in making a living; they were anxious to improve their social status; and they were greatly concerned with having a good time. Asked what principles underlay the thinking and action of these young men and women, he said they professed to believe that all principles were a matter of opinion; the only things they were sure were good were success and the freedom of the moment.

"I think," said Neilson flatly, "he was wrong. I do not believe that diagnosis. And I think he arrived at it by wrong methods.

If you get twelve bright young men together today and ask them by a show of hands which of them believes in God, not many hands will be held up. It is not smart to confess that you believe in God, in any sense of God. If you ask them again what are their fundamental ideals, they are likely to put up such a row of statements as I have quoted. It argues extreme naïveté and pedagogical inexperience in my colleague that he took them at their face value.

For I have asked you questions here, but not in that way. I have asked you, as I ask you this morning, whether you believe in fair play, whether you believe in sportsmanship, whether you believe in telling the truth to your friends, whether you believe in keeping your hands off other people's goods. And I know your answers. You all believe those things, and you all, for the most part, act upon them; and when you do not, you feel cheap. Nevertheless, that man had this on his side: not only did these young men tell him that, but they were only half aware themselves that it was not so; and they would be quite liable to take action on the assumption that it was so, and that these were the things that were really governing them.

It was this ability to show them how their own minds worked which endeared the President to his students, but it was an art he had to learn. It is difficult to make anyone who entered Smith after 1917 believe this, but during his first two semesters in office a large section of the undergraduate body regarded the new President with antagonism and distrust. They thought he was cynical; they thought he was unkind; they thought he was laughing at them. He did not use the phraseology they were accustomed to hear from the platform; he never spoke in oratorical platitudes; his tongue, as sharp often as it was rapid, frightened them; when he exposed some piece of public bombast they supposed he was ridiculing patriotism. Gradually he learned to temper his wit, and they began to sense the kindness and the wisdom that underlay it. Before long they were relying heavily upon that wisdom and kindness and taking delight in the wit.

Of course [as the undergraduate already quoted went on] it is a distinct paradox to say that we appreciate the President more now that he has gone away, but it is true. When he is here he keeps us so busy thinking about other things that we don't think about him at all—we just absorb him.

To keep two thousand young women so thoroughly interested required not only wisdom but extraordinary flexibility, for during the two decades when Neilson administered Smith College the changes between one undergraduate generation and the next were many and extreme. Probably the gap has never been wider than it was between the pre- and the post-World War I college girl.

President Seelye, meeting the first Smith College students in 1875, found that his chief task was to damp their too much zeal. They were earnest pioneers, afire with the opportunities and responsibilities that glowed before them. They had had difficulty in finding schools that could fit them for Smith's entrance requirements, which precisely paralleled those of contemporary masculine institutions. They had had, often, to convince a parent that going to college was a proper thing for "a daughter of mine" to do. They had had to step through the ridicule and disapproval of their friends. They were looked at askance by communities who thought that never again would they be desirable neighbors and citizens. After surmounting such barriers they had no intention of neglecting any of the privileges for which they had fought. President Seelye had to take care that they did not burn to excess the midnight oil, that they took enough exercise to keep them in good health, that they wasted a little time now and then in play.

President Burton's brief administration, 1910-17, occurred at the high point of the collegiate era, probably for the female college administrator the least taxing of all social periods. Going to college was still a little odd but the girl who undertook it needed now only self-confidence, not courage, and when she reached the campus she was delighted with what she found. She was interested in her studies, though it was fashionable to pretend that you were really not working very hard, and she never had the least desire to leave Northampton. All-girl dances took place happily week after week. Extracurricular activities were exciting and absorbing. To be a class officer, to edit the *Monthly,* to captain a class basketball team, to play the hero in *Candida* or *The Importance of Being Earnest* was to feel yourself a contributor to society as well as a "celeb." Interest in the world beyond the campus was so slight that almost the only embarrassing request President Burton's students made of him was permission to found a suffrage-discussion club—and that he denied.

When President Neilson arrived in the fall of 1917 this climate of progress, simplicity, and peace had been rudely dissipated by the German submarines. The undergraduates whom he addressed daily in John M. Greene Hall had had their security suddenly shattered and the proportions of their universe shaken awry. They were so serious about helping the war effort that disciplinary problems were few. They were happy to co-operate with Mr. Hoover by forgoing tearoom sundaes and accepting gamely small restrictions in the campus house diet. They asked permission to knit during classes as well as between them. They were eager to train as nurse's aids or as farmerettes to help the Connecticut Valley harvest its apples and onions and tobacco. They bought Liberty Bonds on shares with their friends when they could not afford them alone, and invented all sorts of ways to raise money for the Red Cross and the Smith College Relief Unit. They could easily have been induced to work and give beyond their means if Neilson had not taken care that appeals to their patriotism should be made by way of their minds and not their emotions. Most of the problems, then, with which their wartime guardians were presented were physical rather than social, but they were problems without precedent and often not a little trying to a new-fledged executive.

One of the worst was the coal shortage in the winter of 1917-18 which forced many institutions to close their doors for longer or shorter periods. It was only by shrewd thrift that Smith was kept continuously functioning.

> We are living from hand to mouth so far as coal is concerned [Neilson wrote in January] . . . we have closed the Students' Building, the Gymnasium, half of the Art Gallery and part of the Library, and some of the other buildings in the afternoon.

The next problem was posed by the eager patriots of the senior class who voted not to have any commencement at all—to the consternation of their parents, of the alumnae, and of the trustees, who had arranged to combine with commencement the inauguration of the new president. Neilson cut the tangle by pointing out to the seniors that their jurisdiction covered only the exercises on Ivy Day and that everyone would approve their desire to economize the time and expense of those ceremonies. The usual long week end was reduced to a Friday morning commencement preceded, on Thursday morning, by the inauguration. This was a very simple ceremony. No delegates were invited from other institutions. The only guests were representatives from the Alumnae Association and alumnae clubs, with one outsider, the President Emeritus of Harvard, who made the address.

Most difficult of all the war problems which the new President had to face was the influenza epidemic which swept the country in the fall of 1918, and became so serious in western Massachusetts that the College, in consultation with the State Board of Health, decided to suspend all exercises in the hope of reducing contagion. Students who wished to were permitted to go home; the others, about eleven hundred, were confined to their dormitories. One of the houses was converted into an infirmary where members of the faculty nursed the light cases. Those more serious went to the Dickinson Hospital, and there forty-two students, who had taken Red Cross nursing courses, offered their services as aids to the regular nurses. The College recorded one hundred fifty cases of influenza among which there were two deaths.

For the plan of the two weeks quarantine and its effective administration the President gave all credit to Dean Ada Comstock and the College Physician, Dr. Florence Gilman, but he shared in every section of the work, even to acting as a member of the itinerant troupe of faculty entertainers who toured the isolated dormitories.

For those students who did not take the infection the experience had its amusing aspects, assuming frequently, as the *Alumnae Quarterly* reporter put it, an Alice in Wonderland quality.

> To be at college and told not to go to classes was incredible. To have time to play and then to have toys and joys forbidden seemed unkind. . . The first thing Alice knew the faculty were trying to do things for her instead of trying to make her do things for them. They planned an entertainment circuit to go to the various houses on different afternoons and evenings: the President read, the music department played, the spoken English department elocuted, and the hygiene department taught folk dancing on the lawn.

A few weeks later a freshman diary of the period records:

> Great excitement. About 1:30 P.M. Beth MacDuffie came rushing into the house and said the War was over and for us to go to John M. Greene immediately. President Neilson talked. He was weak and pale and had to lean on the reading desk for support. At 3 P.M. we all paraded around the campus, sang and waved flags. In the evening a torch light procession, with fife and drum. We sang to President Neilson and he came out and said, "After all, Smith didn't

win the war." Then we laughed and cheered and sang, and he said, "I'm glad to see you're so pleased with yourselves!"

Neilson's words were more serious than they sounded. He was genuinely distressed by the undergraduate response which seemed to him hysteria rather than real joy. This was the occasion of the false armistice. The celebration of the true armistice Neilson himself described many years later as an illustration of the intensity of mass emotion. Speaking in chapel on 12 November 1932 he said:

> On the true armistice day the students, of course, paraded again, and of this second parade, I remember chiefly the noise. I remember, too, that the procession was coming down Elm Street in a highly excited condition, and I (being at that time nervous about the reputation of the College, and regarding it as a more delicate plant than I have since found it to be) came out of the gate at College Hall, hoping to head them off and keep them from going down Main Street among the shops. But before I knew what had happened I was seized by both arms and thrust into the middle of the procession. There was nothing I could do about this; but when we came to the corner of West Street I managed to swing them off to the right, and Main Street was saved!

Almost with the signing of the armistice the American college girl began to change. She tried all sorts of experiments with new manners and new morals, as her older sister was doing, and her mother. Why shouldn't a lady smoke, or drink, or bob her hair? Why must a girl be chaperoned? If women can vote why can't they—? Every past prohibition was challenged. College administrators found themselves suddenly obliged to take stands on issues which had hitherto not so much as raised their heads. And whatever stand they took was sure to be wrong from the point of view of parents and alumnae who were adapting themselves to the new world at a rate a little different from their daughters'. The situation was complicated by the fact that the campus was becoming less and less the center of undergraduate life. The automobile, no longer a rarity, was making it easy to spend week ends at home or at football games and proms, and the invasions from Dartmouth, Princeton, and Yale, which used to occur only on scheduled dates once or twice a year, now took place every Sunday. Extracurricular activities lost some of their importance and glamor. The "collegiate" attitude of the 1910's began to look a little old fashioned and funny; the world was wider now.

Some of the gestures of liberation did not need to be taken very seriously. There was, for instance, what an advertisement in the Smith College *Weekly* called "the battle of bobbed hair." This had an unfortunate fascination for the feature writers of the Boston papers who kept their constituency informed on the steady increase in Northampton of this dangerous trend. Without her crowning glory could woman continue to be worthy of her crown?

From this particular controversy Neilson managed to keep detached, though he confessed years later that he really found the new fashion a relief. His thrifty eye had been constantly grieved, in the long-haired days, by the appalling number of lost hairpins scattered along the campus walks. He was irked during the first years of his incumbency by some of the fads in dress which swept the campus annually–animal jewelry, plaid stockings, flopping galoshes, ear-muffs–but he learned to accept these irruptions philosophically, certain that their hour would be short. The disappearance of stockings worried him, he said, only to the extent of the damage it might do to the business of his good friend, the College's former Treasurer, George B. McCallum. The Charleston craze Neilson weathered by one simple prohibition: the Charleston may be danced only on the first floor. Ceilings in the older dormitories were not stout enough to stand the strain. To one fashion of the thirties he never became reconciled, the open caressing by young couples strolling about campus during a week end. When, at such seasons as Junior Prom, the town was particularly heavily invaded by the opposite sex, the President stayed in his own garden.

Troublesome out of proportion to their importance were the new practices which offended with their boldness the good citizens of Northampton. The College had from the beginning tried to show a respectful courtesy to the sensibilities of a New England community inclined to be conservative in its standards for the behavior of young ladies. The early field hockey players had conscientiously worn skirts over their bloomers when they walked up Elm Street to practice on Allen Field, and there had long been a recognized "hat line." The college girl was accustomed to going about bareheaded in all weathers long before Hollywood made the practice nationally fashionable, but at Smith it was agreed that she should put on a hat whenever she wanted to shop on Main Street "below Beckman's." This requirement, to the postwar undergraduate, came to seem a more and more unnecessary tenderness to elderly conservatism and the Student Government and its "hat cops" had increasing difficulty in enforcing the regulation. From time to time the President came to their aid with counsels of courtesy to one's elders but there were moments when he felt constrained to side with the students against the Northampton ladies. When some of them who lived near a college dormitory complained that the girls dressed and undressed without drawing their window shades, he suggested tartly that they might well pull their own shades down.

The hat impasse was solved in 1923 when an alert Student Council made a survey which convinced them that hatlessness was no longer an offence against New England standards. What the good citizens of Northampton did object to, it was found, was being pushed off their walks by girls marching four or five abreast and to being spattered with chocolate from Eskimo pies; so the "hat cops" were replaced by "politeness policemen."

Far more serious than these short steps towards woman's emancipation was the matter of smoking. Until 1925 all the women's colleges looked on smoking by young girls as a practice both unhealthy and indecent. Expulsion was a not uncommon penalty. Actually no girls were expelled from Smith for smoking, though it was sometimes reckoned in a cumulative burden of offence. The administration of the prohibition was in the hands of the Student Council and the President scrupulously left it there, although he saw that, since the issue was one of manners not morals, it would eventually disappear. In December 1925 he wrote to a parent who had expressed his approval of the College's stand against the practice, that the undergraduate attitude

> is, of course, largely determined by the way they have been brought up, and I cannot shut my eyes to the fact that more and more of them are coming from homes where they are familiar with women smoking, and where no objection to it is entertained. When girls re-

flecting this attitude come to be in the majority here, I doubt very much whether it will be possible for us to insist on the prohibition. It could be made effective only by an elaborate system of spying and detectives which would introduce into the situation an element which would be much more disastrous than smoking, and which in any case would be bound to fail.

The issue had, as a matter of fact, been raised already at an intercollegiate student government conference. Bryn Mawr was permitting smoking under certain restrictions and Vassar was about to follow suit. Smith debated the matter for four months—a very long time in undergraduate chronology—and most of the debate was deadly serious, though there were occasional flashes of humor, like the Rally Day stunt which pictured a house meeting ten years hence listening to a promulgation that during classes in the history of religion students may smoke only Egyptian Deities. Finally the Council presented the student body with a referendum and in April it was announced that smoking would be permitted in the living rooms of houses two-thirds of whose denizens approved the idea. Smoking in the students' own rooms was prohibited because of the danger of fire and students were requested not to smoke in the tearooms of Northampton. The College hailed its emancipation with a burst of flame and the blue haze of rumor spread wide. "Like all young things learning new habits," Neilson said to the alumnae, "they have smoked awkwardly, and sometimes disgustingly. . . I have been humiliated by that inexpertness." But he insisted that

If the administration trusts the Student Government Association to make decisions on these matters, it must be prepared to stand by whatever the Student Government does—its mistakes as well as its wisdom. . . The present situation must be frankly acknowledged to be the outcome of the principle of education on which we are proceeding, and we have no other apology to make.

The awkwardness of the young things continued for some time and the next fall there occurred, within a ten-day period, four incipient fires in campus houses. The President called the College together and spoke to them sternly. "Smoking," he began, "is a dirty, expensive, and unhygienic habit—to which I am devoted."

You do not, he told them, "smoke like ladies; you do not even smoke like gentlemen; you smoke like fools." This is perhaps as good an example as one can find of what the Smith undergraduate had in mind when she said that she "loved to be scolded by the President." But her delight in the unexpectedness of the presidential remarks never prevented her from taking them seriously. This time the Student Council, alarmed at what it had set going, suspended all indoor smoking until after Christmas. Then the College polled itself again and agreed that smoking should be done only in the crew house, the boat house, and such tearooms as cared to permit it. This proved for the time quite satisfactory to the majority of the students for whom cigarettes were still rather a banner of independence than an hourly necessity, and eventually provision for the addicts was made. The dormitories built in the thirties had smoking rooms in their basements and similar division of living quarters among the smokers and nonsmokers was arranged in all of the campus houses. The prohibition against smoking in bedrooms could not be relaxed and the President had from time to time to reiterate sharply why.

> There have been two cases this autumn [he announced at a chapel assembly in January 1933] of students who violated the rule against smoking in their rooms—that is, there were two who were caught. When I talked to the offenders, I found that they were unaware of the reason for that rule and of its seriousness. Upperclassmen, of course, know very well that that is the one rule concerning smoking that is not made by the Student Government, but is made by me. All the other rules about where else you may smoke and when are your own rules. But the rule about smoking upstairs is my rule, because I have the responsibility for the safety of the lives and property in the College.

Almost more disturbing to the alumnae than the sight of Smith undergraduates waving cigarettes was the young things' decision to abandon the immemorial tradition of the Ten O'Clock Rule. Promulgated when the College first opened to prevent the eager pioneers from too much late study, this regulation required each student to be, so the rubric ran, "in a horizontal position between the sheets," with her light out when the clock struck ten. Eventually "light cuts" were permitted for study but variations in their length and frequency were the only weakening of the regulation until the postwar undergraduates began to question it vigorously in the fall of 1921.

Neilson, when he first came to Northampton, had been skeptical about the rule's value but, watching it in operation, he became more and more convinced of its value and was as sorry as any member of President Seelye's alumnae when the students decided to give it up, substituting the requirement that each girl be in her own room and the house quiet at ten. By that time, however, as Neilson wrote to a protesting alumna, "the administration of the old rule had become so lax that if it were not to be the cause of demoralization through accustoming them to the breaking of rules, it would have been necessary, had the rule been maintained, to enforce it by administrative authority instead of through house organizations," and, as he had with the smoking regulations, he defended the Student Government's right to make mistakes. When he thought they were making mistakes, however, he told them so, and frequently in terms which they found more than a little disconcerting.

I am not prepared to say that the financial effect of the waste of electricity after ten o'clock is so great as to imperil the solvency of the College [he said in June 1923], but I should like to tell the classes which initiated that change and as seniors had the responsibility of it, the classes of 1922 and 1923, that that change which they made will absorb all the interest on the money which they contributed to the $4,000,000 Fund. Therefore, when you think with pride of your contribution to that Fund, you can remind yourselves that you put it into one of my pockets and took it out of the other, and that your total contribution to the College finances through this means has been to present your successors with the privilege of staying up late at night.

Though there were, of course, individual cases to be dealt with, drinking never became for Smith a serious problem. With the repeal of prohibition Neilson told the students that he saw no point in the imposing by the administration of any new legislation.

The fundamental rule which underlies all our rules and takes the place of many which we used to have, makes it incumbent on all of you to behave as you know members of this institution ought to behave both privately and in the public eye. No special rule will be necessary to justify the removal from the College of those who do not understand how to apply that rule, or who are not yet grown up enough to be trusted with the liberties we give our students.

More fundamental, actually, to the whole educational problem than any of the changes in female manners was the shift in the national attitude towards the college woman. The mother who had once been obliged to explain why she had let her daughter go to college now felt constrained to apologize for her girl who stayed at home. Going to college became suddenly, in the twenties, the thing to do and the women's colleges were flooded with applicants. This was not, Neilson thought, like the crowding of the men's colleges, a direct result of the war, for where, by 1925, the masculine enrollment had visibly slackened, pressure on the women's institutions remained as great as ever. He saw the situation as the culmination of a change in attitude which had been going on for half a century; the trail the pioneers had blazed had become a path and then a highway.

> Those who throng it are no longer exceptional spirits but merely the run of our brighter youth, and the needed qualities are merely good ability and some industry. . . During the last few years the remaining prejudices against the college woman, whether held by young men or old ladies, have been rapidly disappearing. (*The Nation*, 13 May 1925)

This victory for female education was very far from a blessing to the women's colleges. The run of the brighter youth who entered their gates came often without any clear idea of what they were looking for. Lecture rooms and laboratories they saw not as opportunities but as barriers to important pleasures. They employed their good ability chiefly in getting by, so that they might devote themselves more thoroughly to the pursuit of a good time. Neilson, who believed unshakeably that education is the key to the good life, could be humorous occasionally about this attitude but he found it increasingly hard to bear. In 1926 he regretfully compared the fifty-first year of the College with its first.

> At that time there gathered in the first assembly hall of the College for the last exercises of the year a handful of eager souls, brought

into this place because of their appetite for intellectual things. To-day we have here 2,000 students gathered—one must confess—largely in obedience to a social convention. One thinks with envy of the task of Mr. Seelye in feeding those hungry people, in contrast with ours of laboriously seeking to coax an appetite. . . Education is being defeated by its own success. Education is "the thing."

It was no simple task to adjust the College to this new atmosphere for Neilson declined the easy compromise. "We are determined," he told the undergraduates at the beginning of the next year, "that this shall be primarily an institution of learning." It would be very easy, he said, to turn the College into "a center of engaging social life with a few duties to give a kind of relish to a perpetual holiday. It isn't what we are here for."

To the solution of the problem, urged sometimes on the European analogy, educating only the brilliant few, Neilson never agreed.

One fundamental reason why we seek to educate so many is that we have not yet abandoned the democratic ideal. As a nation we still believe that culturally as well as politically and economically the road should be open to ability and industry. We know that our leaders have by no means always come from those born to wealth and privilege, and we believe that to reserve educational opportunity in general for a small class is to weaken the country and do injustice to the individual. ("Are American Colleges Wasteful?" *Scribner's*, June 1932)

It was this real care for democracy which motivated Neilson's first important action after he became President of Smith, an action unspectacular but fundamental: the building of new dormitories. Long before the days of Woodrow Wilson's quad plan and Harkness' gifts of "houses" and "colleges" to Harvard and Yale, Smith had worked out what she called, with New England modesty, the cottage system. Each cottage accommodated approximately sixty girls who lived and ate as a unit under the supervision of a "Lady in Charge" (later known as Head of House) and a resident member of the faculty. Sixty proved over the years to be the right number from both the financial and the social point of view. Financially the dormitories were paying investments; socially they mingled the four classes and made an entity large enough to be interesting but not confining. But in 1917 fewer than nine hundred of Smith's two thousand students lived in college dormitories. The others were accommodated in "off-campus houses," which had, of course, to be approved by the College and to agree to abide by its regulations but in which tone and discipline were far more difficult to achieve.

The freshmen, Neilson felt, suffered most from the situation. "The effects are evident in a distinctly lower average of scholarship and in a greater yielding to the modern temptation to be absorbed in social life outside the College." He put his finger also on another element in the situation which had not been hitherto so clearly seen. "We began this year," he said at the Last Chapel exercises in 1919, "with more than 2100 students with rooms for 850, and we call ourselves a resident college! It is manifestly an untruth."

At Neilson's suggestion the trustees began at once to buy up, as rapidly as they could afford them, the off-campus houses. In 1920 the property of the Capen School, including its dormitories, was willed to Smith. In that same year the almunae presented to the College a fund of four million dollars intended in part for the increase of faculty salaries, in part for new equipment. In 1922 three new dormitories, built from the fund, were opened and Smith was able to house 1400 of her students. In 1925 the alumnae gave the College a fiftieth anniversary present of six hundred thousand dollars for the erection of three more dormitories to complete what Neilson, thinking of Edinburgh, called the Great Quadrángle. (He pronounced it always, in the Edinburgh manner, with the accent on the second syllable.) This brought the number of on-campus students to 1725. In 1928 a completely unexpected legacy from Miss Mary Mandelle of Detroit, who had no connection of any kind with Smith, made possible the erection of two more dormitories, opened in 1930-1. By 1934 the President could report that "for the first time in more than fifty years, the College has been able to house on campus all its resident members." But that, he said, "does not close our efforts. Many of these houses are still unsatisfactory, and we now move on to an effort to convert certain of the wooden houses into dormitories of brick."

All the bedrooms in the new brick dormitories were singles. This was Neilson's idea, one on which he insisted in all the houses he built during his administration. He was genuinely disturbed by the perpetual gregariousness of the American girl, the "something akin to panic" which seized her at the prospect of even a brief solitude. Much as he himself loved talk and people he felt that many important and interesting experiences were to be had only by the individual alone. "To enjoy poetry, to listen to music, to get a real aesthetic experience from painting one must be able to withdraw from the crowd." And more than that:

In stillness grows personal dignity. The person who can afford to be alone with himself often and long acquires a quality of personal dignity which is dissipated and lost in any other kind of life. Self-possession, self-restraint, patience, the power of thinking things through and facing the facts of life—these are essentials for the acquisition of a philosophy and a religion.

That was part of a vespers sermon (October 1932) on the text, "Be still, and know that I am God."

You *will* not be alone [he said to his audience], and you will not let other people be alone. And you have not, as a matter of fact, nearly enough to say to make this continuous social intercourse worth while. The result is a constant babble about superficial things, trivial things—a wasting of time and energy; and, above all, the loss of the benefits of solitude.

Much of the blame for this silly gregariousness of the young rested, Neilson thought, on the parent, and especially the well-to-do parent who packed her children's hours so tight with engagements and activities that no corner remained for individual development. Invited, in the fall of 1934, to address the parents of the Brearley School in New York City, he charged them flatly with the offence, calling his remarks "Time Out!"

The older generation missed a lot and it is determined that its children shall miss nothing. Parents think they must harry children into an intolerable routine of activities vaguely imagined to be beneficial, that their lives must be filled to overflowing and then scheduled like a train.

The evil result is an appalling lack of curiosity and no capacity for solitude on the part of youth. In a measure, of course, the rapid changes and confusing interests of modern life are to blame. One might suppose that these changes and interests would be a powerful intellectual stimulus. But too often the constant impact on the mind of new and surprising things results in a blasé refusal to get excited about anything. The answers are given before the questions have arisen. The intellectual appetite is destroyed because the young are constantly fed before they are hungry.

An even more vigorous indictment of parental guilt was Neilson's disparagement of "Mother Love." The occasion was a banquet given (1937) by the New York Smith Club to celebrate the President's twentieth year in office. Six hundred guests had been expected; a thousand came; everyone wanted to shake the President's hand and the crowded rooms grew hot. The dinner began late and before the first course was over the trustees who were watching saw Neilson turn so sick and white that they got him quickly out of the room and called a doctor. It was a severe attack of his not infrequent stomach trouble, but he insisted, after a rest, on going back to the dais to make his speech. He talked for a time about the College, clearly and informatively but without his usual sparkle, then suddenly the color flooded back into his cheeks and the light returned to his eyes. His voice became gay and the relief from tension kindled his delight in teasing his friends.

Mother love [he said, looking at the thousand women around him] is the only element with which I have come in contact as a college president which makes me think less of human nature. Nine times out of ten, mother love is nothing but self love. Mother love is largely a matter of saving mother's face. Mothers don't want their daughters to fail in school, because it reflects on the mother and is socially awkward.

He added that Smith women as alumnae "presented no difficulties" but that as soon as they became parents they "became parents more than alumnae" and that while education progresses, "parents are static."

The alumnae-parents knew how to take this, the amusing exaggeration of the attack upon a fault of which they felt themselves all too guilty, but many newspaper readers next morning were appalled. The press associations had flashed the stricture across the country and letters began to pour into Northampton:

> My daughter will never go to Smith College—where the President throws mud at one of the most beautiful things in this world of ours—Mother Love.

> As the son of one of the finest mothers that a son ever had, I feel that I would be untrue to my love of her memory and the reverence that I bear to her if I did not raise my voice in protest.

Editorial writers were shocked; the President of the New York Parents League issued a statement; but the fan letters outweighed the others. Many of them came from grateful fellow-educators, some from magazine editors who wanted the President to enlarge his remarks into an article. Neilson had no desire to start a campaign for the abolition of parents, though his remarks had not been mere phrase-making; they were the distillation of scores of depressing encounters. As early as 1919 he had written to a friend:

> So far, my experience in this job tends to show that the most difficult class to handle in educational problems is that of the parents. Our college physician the other day said that the next job she was going to take would be in an orphan asylum. I think there are few administrators in educational institutions who would not sympathize with her.

Another element in the situation which the President often remarked was the curious parental lack of thrift:

> Why parents want students to cost them board at two places at once I do not know. Why they send them to us to be educated and at the same time invite them home for as many days a week as we shall allow, I do not know.

In line with the new freedom in other departments of life the faculty, in 1925, tried the experiment of leaving to the student herself the decision as to how many of her classes she ought to attend. The intention was to develop in the undergraduate a sense of responsibility and to put the faculty on their mettle, but it soon became apparent that the most fascinating lecturer could not compete with an easily accessible Broadway, and a not so distant Bermuda. Smith had no intention of ceasing to be a resident college, so the requirement was restated: the students might regulate, as before, their own class attendance but they were expected to be in residence in Northampton for sixteen of the seventeen weeks in each semester.

"Let it be clearly understood," Neilson wrote in his annual letter to the parents (1928), "that we regard it as a privilege to live in this community, not to be away from it as much as possible."

In 1921 Neilson and Dean Comstock had started the practice of sending in the fall a letter to the parents of each Smith student presenting the point of view from which the College was administered and asking their co-operation in meeting some of the special problems raised by the new era. In addition to weekend absences the letters discussed such matters as allowances—suggesting that they be kept in line with Smith's standard of simple living—and the new collegiate problem of the automobile. The administration finally ruled that no girl might bring a car to Northampton at any time during the college year. The exception to this prohibition—seniors in good standing during their last spring term—was Neilson's idea. He thought the Connecticut River Valley a very beautiful section of America and he wanted every Smith student to become familiar with it before she graduated.

For all the problems with which they presented him Neilson never, even in their most trying periods, really despaired of the younger generation. His faith in the perfectibility of human nature was solidly based and the worst of their excesses seemed to him the product of environment rather than inner depravity. When, in 1921, one of his own graduates, Dorothy Speare, wrote a novel of flaming youth which caused a good deal of shocked talk, he refused to be disturbed. *Dancers in the Dark,* he wrote to the editor of the *Delineator* in which the story ran serially,

seems to me a vivid picture of the life of young Americans of the well-to-do classes at the present moment. That the picture is in many respects a painful one is no fault of the author's, who has told her story and drawn her characters candidly yet without cynicism. It is not easy for the older generation to get at the precise facts of the new manners and customs and it is still less easy to interpret justly the spirit behind them. A document like that which has been produced by Miss Speare, which strives at truth rather than sensation —though some of the facts are sensational enough—is bound to be of value to those who are concerned with the moral and intellectual training of the rising generation.

And, in January 1930, discussing in the *Atlantic* "The Theory of Censorship," he said:

> It is my impression that most freshmen (of both sexes) come to college today already familiar to the point of losing interest with many of the facts and ideas which anxious parents are terror-stricken lest they acquire. And not only are they familiar with them, but they seem to have acquired a kind of immunity which leaves them quite as fresh and unspoiled as their ignorantly innocent parents were at their age.

Nineteen twenty-six and twenty-seven were the years, probably, when youth flamed highest. After that the fires burned more quietly, even before the depression damped them down. In 1928 Neilson, with that sensitiveness to group atmosphere which made him effective as a speaker, remarked a change. He had returned from six months in Europe and this, he supposed, sharpened his perception of the American scene. He reported his observations to the Alumnae Council in one of those casual phrases which made national headlines:

> What I saw in January in the College I seem to see as I go about the country. We have turned the corner and are now moving with our backs to the Jazz Age. We are reverting to Victorian formalism. Soon we shall be faced by undergraduates who will rebuke us, not for being old fogies, but for lack of dignity and proper ceremony. For example a freshman is said to have burst into Northrop House, asking who that man was with the little gray beard who twice bowed to her on the campus without being introduced!

The incipient decorum was accelerated by the depression, though the effect of that upon the College was not immediately felt. During the first year enrollment continued stable and, thanks to a surplus set aside in the lush days by provident trustees, 1931-2 ended without a deficit. But in the fall of 1932 Neilson reported to the alumnae that "the tornado has hit us." Withdrawals were many, applications decreased, and the College opened in September with eighty-two vacant places, a serious predicament for an institution accustomed to pay seven-eighths of its operating costs by fees from board and tuition. At the same time requests multiplied for scholarship aid. The administration determined that no student already embarked on a successful college career should have to cut it short for lack of money and, when the income from scholarship endowment had been exhausted, began to draw on the funds for current expenses. In 1934 Smith was giving, not proportionately but in actual dollars and cents, more scholarship aid than any educational institution in the East. At the same time Neilson was determined not, as so many institutions were doing, to reduce faculty salaries, and he never did. The alumnae rallied to the need, Scottish thrift operated more cannily than ever, and Smith in 1939 could still state that she had never had a deficit.

The undergraduate, sobered by troubles at home, aware as seldom before of the burden her education was imposing on her parents, was more inclined to take her college opportunities seriously, though she did not lose her youthful zest for life. The most impressive fact about the class of 1933, Neilson told them at Last Chapel, "has been that there has seemed to us who watched them, no diminution of gayety. . . They kept their nerve, they accepted the new circumstances, they played the game."

Bidding farewell in June to the class of 1935 Neilson said:

> Whatever truth there may be in the common impression that Americans are devoted to the accumulation of money, I do not believe that any country can show more cases of the loss of money and the necessity for a complete readjustment of economic and living standards being taken with greater gallantry than they were taken by the class represented in Smith College by 1935.

Two years later he congratulated the class of 1937 on the fact that their student Judicial Board, the criminal court of the College, "had an almost unexampled record in that no major cases came before it at all. It dealt with mild cases of discipline, but it had no tragedies to deal with."

Despite her increased seriousness, the undergraduate of the thirties did not leave the administration without problems. She was, for one thing, a great individualist, inclined to believe that anything approved by other people was probably wrong for her. And she wanted to direct her own education, to give the faculty advice on the curriculum and tell the administration what she thought about the faculty. She considered herself, too, to be a factor in national politics and international affairs. The greatest change that took place among the undergraduates in his time, Neilson thought, was the alteration in their attitude towards world affairs. It was an interest which he constantly encouraged though he sometimes took exception to the directions in which it shot off.

The young Republicans and Democrats, for instance, grew so excited over the Presidential election of 1936 (Roosevelt vs. Landon) that they actually came to blows. Since there was no other large auditorium in town, the College had lent John M. Greene Hall for a Republican rally on 13 October. When the Northampton parade, in which many Smith students marched, turned up the walk they found it lined on either side by student Democrats bearing banners and placards. These the Republican students tried to capture and in the ensuing scuffle banners were torn and one girl received a black eye. The United Press story spread across the country, growing as it spread, so that letters flooded in from alarmed alumnae asking details of a combat which was reported at times to have resulted in four hundred casualties.

Your conduct [Neilson told the students] is important not only to yourselves and to the intellectual life you are leading, but also to the whole cause of education for women. Every time you indulge in a display of bad taste you undermine some of the things this college was founded for and the things for which many people have made great sacrifices; you are disloyal to your sex and disloyal to your College. How did this come about? It came about, I think, because you were imitating the least admirable features of our political method in a presidential year.

With much of the pacifism which was so ardent a cause among college men and women in the mid-thirties Neilson was in active sympathy though he felt that the thinking behind the student Anti-War Weeks and Peace Strikes (a term he semantically deplored) was often illogical and superficial. "I do not think action by undergraduates is important," he said to them in 1938. "I do think that understanding by undergraduates is enormously important," and he tried to make them comprehend that the weakness of their efforts to create a public opinion on behalf of peace was their tendency to isolate the question. He warned them also against the inconsistency of those who called themselves pacifists yet were ready, on behalf of social justice, to contemplate a class war. He himself, though an ardent supporter of peace movements from the League of Nations on, was never able to accept the complete pacifist position, "because I could not trust myself in case of certain injuries—I believe in justice as well as peace." The whole matter stirred him deeply.

> In discussion such as you have been engaged in during this week [he said to the students in 1935] there is a tremendous temptation to be emotional, and I suppose you expect that I am going to tell you that you should not be emotional. I am *not* going to tell you this. The situation you are facing in the world at large, and the situation you may have to face at any time with regard to the imminence of war are situations that cannot be handled by people who have no feeling. It is very important that you should feel, and feel profoundly, about the issues you are discussing.

That some student pacifists could talk cheerfully about the coming social revolution, did not disturb Neilson. He saw the student radicals, as he saw the radicals on his faculty, as a stimulus useful to the community. Asked by an anxious group of alumnae how far he would permit the "leftist" students to go, he answered that they might invite anyone to speak at Smith College "who does not break the furniture."

Through these decades of rapid and violent change the Smith College student body preserved a unity of spirit so marked that it was commented on with delight by visiting alumnae and with envy by the administrators of other institutions. It was, as the undergraduates were well aware, President Neilson who indicated for them, day after day, the still point of the turning world.

The chief instrument by which he worked was the daily chapel service in John M. Greene Hall.

Eight-thirty morning chapel had begun with the beginnings of the College, a simple service, so carefully undenominational that almost anyone who cared to could find in it spiritual rest and refreshment. The choir and the congregation chanted antiphonally a psalm; the President read the Scripture and led the congregation in the Lord's Prayer. He spoke then for about ten minutes, and the service ended with a hymn. Any student who really found offence here to her religious beliefs was excused from attendance but those who tried to establish such a case were few for the assembly had other strongly attractive qualities. It was, for one thing, a place to meet your friends. "Chapel dates" were an almost universal practice, dates, more often than not, with people from other houses whom otherwise you might not see for days. And chapel was a kind of daily broadcast of college news; if you did not attend you were pretty certain to miss something interesting. Sometimes there were visiting speakers of distinction, sometimes the Dean or Warden or some member of the faculty led chapel, but most often, three or four times a week out of the six, it was the President.

In the prewar days attendance was on an honor basis, each student keeping her own record which she turned in periodically to the Registrar. Changing religious attitudes and the new freedom had made for increasing abuse of this somewhat indefinite system and, convinced that the spiritual life flourishes only in freedom, Neilson, in the spring of his first year of office, abolished compulsory chapel. Attendance dropped so sharply that the students, the majority of whom really liked the daily gathering, voted a new compulsion to be enforced by the Student Government. Everyone was expected to attend at least four times a week, and on the whole they did. Through the twenties, when most colleges were in active revolt against their compulsory chapel systems, Neilson could report that there was an average attendance of fifteen hundred at what he called Smith's "voluntary-compulsory chapel."

That the probability of the President's speaking was the chief factor which brought the students of two decades to John M.

Greene Hall was clear to everyone else if not to him. To his discussions, two or three times a week, of current events both faculty and undergraduates looked forward. He was, as a visiting alumna put it, so much better than the newspapers. Neilson was always very modest about his performance as a news commentator. He was not, he insisted, in any way an expert. He had no formal training in history, politics, or economics, yet, as so learned a critic as Professor Sidney Fay has testified, he practically never uttered an error in fact or judgment. His equipment for the task was his scholar's memory which could store the essential fact and summon it at will, and his peculiar power of swift analysis, his ability to strip off non-essentials and concentrate on the heart of the matter.

In the thirties the changing mores replaced voluntary-compulsory chapel with a required "assembly" on Wednesday morning, a voluntary assembly (student-conducted) on Friday, and a voluntary chapel service on the other three days. On Mondays Neilson spoke on current events, at the Wednesday assemblies usually on campus matters. These talks were sometimes serious, sometimes full of wit. They ranged wide, their topics neither classifiable nor predictable. Beneath them all was the exhortation to the pursuit of virtue and truth but that exhortation took an extraordinary variety of forms, many of them highly amusing. Whatever the event of the moment in the college community, pleasant or melancholy, important or trivial, the undergraduates were aware within twenty-four hours of the attitude of the administration. A particularly flagrant breach of rules would be put in its proper perspective. When, for instance, some undergraduates and their dates were apprehended swimming in the public reservoir the President concluded his censure:

> I want to make you understand distinctly from this day forth that neither the citizens of Northampton nor the members of this College care to have their drinking water flavored with Smith or Yale, Amherst, Harvard, or Williams.

When a full chapel had been required and not quite 100 per cent of the College had appeared, Neilson said next morning:

I was curious to find out something about those who were not here. I have a list of them according to houses. The most frequent explanation is that the absent were asleep—in more senses than one! . . . One student did not come because there was no penalty stated! Chapel was required, but there was no stated penalty for absence. This shows a mentality which the student ought to have emerged from before she left the primary school. This is the way little children reason. . . I have often spoken to you about your life here as an opportunity for growing up. The pace this young lady has to go in the next two years will be very giddy, if she is to catch up and become an adult.

On other disciplinary occasions Neilson made clear the necessity of "traffic rules" in this "co-operative commonwealth," and the necessity for rules "imposed upon us by the expectation of parents."

A large number of those going to college today need, in the opinion of their parents—probably a true opinion—a good deal of supervision. They would not be sent here unless a certain guardianship were exercised by the College. . . We are willing to assume reasonable observation and control for the sake of the peace of mind of your parents, and to aid in the transition that is taking place in many of your lives; but you will be more sympathetic towards the College if you realize that we undertake this with some reluctance and are on the side of your growing up.

The chapel talks were full of aids to the process of growing up. Some of these were pungent phrases which their hearers quoted for years.

The first step in scholarship is to learn to go for yourself to the authentic sources of information. A sophomore is not an authentic source of information.

It is better to pursue your studies than to be pursued by them.

You cannot steal a college education. You can steal a mark or a diploma.

The wrong road does not become the right road because it is crowded.

The creation of a self-respecting, self-conducting, self-directing individual is mainly what we are after.

For many of the earlier talks, though their substance went deep into minds and characters, only single phrases like these remain, but eventually the editor of the *Alumnae Quarterly* arranged to have a reporter not only at set affairs, like First and Last Chapel, but almost every day in the week, just in case. Many of these transcriptions are preserved in the *Quarterly*'s News from Northampton department. Some were published, at greater length, in a small collection issued in 1940 under the title *Intellectual Honesty*.

Intellectual honesty was discussed from the chapel platform in many different terms. Freedom was another frequent subject; so was the importance of making use of your opportunities.

Truth is the specific academic virtue, the special aim of learning.

I am impressed with the frequency with which the tragedy of dismissal seems to be brought about by mediocrity of aim, by students not shooting high enough. More girls, I think, fail because they thought it enough to get a "C," enough to get by, than for any other one reason. Aiming at that grade is despicable and dangerous. You ought not to be here unless you are ambitious of some kind of distinction. You have been chosen out of a large body of contemporaries in the country and given special opportunities. . . Distinction is your duty.

It is a shame that four years unlike anything else in your lives should in any degree, in any fraction, be wasted. I implore you to make your New Year's resolution one for a more critical and more intelligent scrutiny of your chances, and for a decision to make the most of things that you cannot get in the same way anywhere else. I close with the utterance of one of Shakespeare's most heroic characters before a great occasion:

> Oh, gentlemen, the time of life is short!
> To spend that shortness basely were too long.

The rigors of mid-year examinations—"that period of the most spontaneous work accomplished during the college year"—Neilson often lightened by teasing the undergraduates about their terror.

Any day during these last two weeks you could hear students announcing dramatically to anyone who cared to listen that they were sure they would be leaving college soon. I must admit I find this little drama amusing. I enjoy the spectacle of 2000 girls, mostly with their feet on the ground and understanding a good deal of their real place in the world, playing this little game with themselves and one another and apparently convincing themselves that anyone is humbugged by it.

Such comment Neilson took pains to follow with ironically appropriate hymns: "Through the night of dark and sorrow," or "Courage, brother, do not stumble," which the undergraduates sang with gusto. *The American Hymnal for Chapel Services,* compiled during Neilson's administration by a committee of the department of music on which he sat as literary adviser, contains probably as much good music and as many literate words as any collection of the kind.

To another seasonal state of mind, the September timidity of freshmen, the President was more compassionate. You have "a very subtle and delicate task" before you, he told a group of upperclass advisers.

A freshman, you know, is more or less like an unshelled crab: she takes impressions and experiences coweringly, she shivers and trembles at a touch. (That is, most freshmen do—some apparently have not yet cast their shells!)

Sometimes instead of a talk the President read: "When lilacs last in the dooryard bloom'd," perhaps, on 12 February; or it might be the Governor's Thanksgiving Proclamation, delivered with a cadence and timing which made ironic comment: "Sixty-seven per cent of the citizens have savings accounts. God bless the Commonwealth of Massachusetts!" One never knew where the lightning would strike next.

Neilson was one of those speakers who looks at his audience so that each individual has the impression that she is being directly addressed. Even though she had never talked with him each of his two thousand students felt that she knew the President personally. They all shared the state of mind of the freshman who, departing for Christmas vacation, left a package on the Neilsons' doorstep with a little note: "Dear President Neilson, Please take care of my goldfish." Hundreds of other students cherish today the recollection of some swift passing encounter: the sophomore, for instance, whose suitcase he carried up the hill from the station; the rainsoaked freshman whom he took under his umbrella and helped jump puddles on the way to the Library; the choir leader who, reaching chapel ahead of time one morning, was greeted with an amused reference to the early bird, and startled into profound self-analysis when, a few minutes later, the President put his head around the door of the robing-room to say, "But don't be the worm!" Hundreds of individuals Neilson remembered by name years after their graduation. A scholar's memory, if he cares to exercise it, is as effective as a politician's in recalling names and faces, and alumnae of all vintages were constantly delighted by Neilson's ability to recognize them and mention something significant about their particular accomplishments in college.

But to talk at length with the President, so "Philistia," a columnist in the undergraduate *Weekly,* once lamented, you had to be either very good or very bad. The Phi Beta Kappa students could invite President Neilson to the dinners given in their honor by their respective dormitories; Student Government officers could go to him for counsel; presidents of clubs of every kind might ask him for co-operation and advice, and, on the other hand, whenever a student was on the verge of expulsion the President had her in for a talk.

His contacts with the "very good" gave Neilson a high opinion of one of the elements in the undergraduate democracy: their skill in choosing their leaders. There were no politics about this, no campaigning, only a serious desire on the part of the citizenry to select the people most qualified and, on the part of the qualified, a readiness for public service. Even during the periods when it was fashionable to be indifferent to campus affairs, the President of Student Government and the Chairman of the Judicial Board were invariably admirable executives.

I have long ago given up being nervous about this annual morning [Neilson said when the announcement of new officers was made in 1932]. Year after year I watched with a good deal of apprehension, but my apprehensions were never justified, and now I always take it for granted that you know what you are doing. You have elaborated a method of selecting your leaders that seems almost infallible in bringing offices of responsibility and power to people fit for them.

The Student Government officers on their part felt that knowing the President was the highest perquisite of their jobs. It was easy they, and the other "very good," found to make appointments with him. His office door stood open much of the time and when one got inside he never seemed to be in a hurry but really to enjoy the chance of exchanging ideas. Only an acute consciousness of how busy he really was, from eight-thirty until midnight, kept the undergraduates from imposing too far on what appeared to be his genuine interest in everything that went on on campus. Certainly he would speak at the first meeting of the new Why Club; yes, he would be glad to read Christmas poetry in the Browsing Room, to address the Christian Association, preside at an intercollegiate debate, award the cup at the class choir contest. The evenings he had to himself were not many.

That the "very bad" also knew the President personally was quite true. Cases of academic discipline at Smith were handled by the Administrative Board of the faculty; cases of social discipline by the student Judicial Board (who were empowered to inflict minor penalties and to recommend expulsion) and by the Warden. With routine cases the President was not troubled but when the culprit or her parents appealed a sentence or when a penalty as drastic as expulsion was involved he concerned himself with the case. He was scrupulous not to exceed his constitutional authority. "The decisions with regard to these matters," he would write, "are in the hands of the Administrative Board and all I can do is to look into the facts and ask reconsideration if I see any elements which I think they have overlooked." Occasionally he went so far as to express regret that the Board had declined to alter a decision but never without adding an explanation of their reasons for declining. Everyone who worked with Neilson in an administrative or executive capacity proceeded under the assurance that he would back them in any honest and considered action. In his administrative correspondence are scores of letters of patient explanation: the Administrative Board in asking your daughter to withdraw from college is not imposing a penalty; they are giving you the wisest advice they can about the best employment of her time and her abilities; if she does not have the capacity for college work, we should be doing her no kindness to keep her here. And, again and again, this is followed by the statement, convincing because obviously sincere, that it is quite possible to lead a rich and useful life without a college diploma.

It is very important that Mary should be brought to understand that the kind of ability that makes for success in college is only one kind of ability, and the fact that the training we give here is not suitable for her does not mean that she has not abundant capacities in other directions. With her spirit I have no doubt about her finding a congenial line.

When Neilson undertook to review a case he went into it thoroughly, not only studying the record but talking with the student involved. Letter after letter begins: "When I talked with Martha I found—"

For students who had committed social misdemeanors Neilson was a strong believer in the second chance. He was not infrequently successful, when even a sympathetic Warden and Class Dean had failed, in extracting a complete confession which went to the root of an attitude of defiance or irresponsibility and such information he would take to the student Judicial Board, presenting an argument for clemency which they almost invariably accepted. Sometimes when he and the other administrative officials concerned had agreed that justice to the rest of the student body required a girl's removal, he gave her personal assistance in transferring to another college, writing to a fellow administrator a completely candid letter which seldom failed of response. The one fault he found it impossible to condone was dishonesty, but even to such offenders he lent assistance. Mrs. Neilson said that she always met the girls who got into serious trouble; they were invited to tea at the President's House, not to talk over their difficulties—that was done in the office in College Hall—but so that they might not feel themselves outcasts from society, might believe that even if they were being separated from the College they were not shut beyond the social pale.

Some of the "very good" among the students Mrs. Neilson knew, as well as the "very bad." Student string quartets often played at the President's House, excellently adapted for chamber music. A group of history or economics or English majors might be invited there after an evening lecture for informal discussion with the visiting speaker; and the Smith daughters of the Neilson's personal friends often came to lunch or tea. Their own daughters, too, personalities as individual as their parents, were Smith students.

The two Neilson girls approached their education in very different ways. Margaret, the elder, knew while she was still in her teens that what she wanted was to work on the land. Her parents, though surprised, were sympathetic. They let her interrupt her college course to spend a year in England on Lady Eve Balfour's experimental farm; they agreed that she might leave Smith, where she had done well as a Special Honors student, after her junior year, and take her degree at the Massachusetts State Agricultural College; then they helped her buy a farm of her own in West Stockbridge. In 1941 she married Peter Helburn, who shared her rural tastes, adding to them a skill in ornamental iron-working which caused Neilson to refer to him as "my blacksmith son-in-law." They have three children.

Caroline, the younger daughter, majored in mediaeval history and took her degree in 1938 summa cum laude. Her college course, she thought, was probably one of the most satisfactory anyone ever followed at Smith, for she talked all her elections over carefully with her father, who knew his faculty down to the youngest laboratory assistant and advised her so skilfully that she never had a dull instructor or an ill-taught course. Neither her teachers nor her classmates made her feel that she was in any way a marked individual and her father exerted no pressure of any kind on her to excel but she felt an impulsion always to work at the top of her bent. After college she worked with a documentary film company. In 1941 she married Harold Oram. They have two children. After a divorce in 1951 Mrs. Oram became a social worker in New York City.

For all his friendliness and informality no student regarded

Neilson with anything but profound respect. It is significant, perhaps, that he was never referred to as "Prexy." He was spoken of occasionally as King William, Our Highland Laddie, or, most often, Willy Nilly, but usually, even in the most casual undergraduate conversation, it was the President or President Neilson. There were, of course, attempts at taking him off, which he thought highly amusing and the students usually considered quite ineffective. It was easy enough to wear a gown as the President always did in chapel, and to suggest some of his physical attributes: the short stature (five feet, seven inches), the slight stoop (from carrying the bag of books to the Montrose school), the swift walk (but how to include its unconscious dignity?). The little pointed grey goatee was within the power of the make-up box but how to produce the glint in the eyes? How even to describe it? Of "twinkle," the word invariably applied, Neilson grew very weary, and most of the people who used it felt it was too trivial really to suggest the depth of the inner light.

Their affection, personal and collective, the undergraduates succeeded occasionally in making vocal. When Neilson returned from one of his flying visits to the juniors studying in Europe he found a crowded chapel where everyone rose to applaud his entrance and, after the service, lined the walk from the auditorium to College Hall so that they might applaud again. On one occasion, when he got in at ten-thirty in the evening, his arrival was noted from the windows of a neighboring campus house and the word spread through all the Quadrangle dormitories. Their doors had closed at ten but suddenly they all burst open and hundreds of girls in bathrobes surrounded the presidential mansion to serenade their returning hero.

From time to time an undergraduate spokesman in the *Quarterly* or *Weekly* would put the general sentiment into words: the President is the butter and jam on our daily bread; the President is always new and always right; or, describing the First Chapel of a college year:

> From the instant that the small and speedy toe of the presidential boot appeared around the door, a wave of smiles and quite audible purrs spread over our ordered ranks, and the year had begun.

The word which Neilson used most often in speaking of his relation with the students was co-operation, a word selected with his usual precision. He gave his students, as he gave his faculty, a sense that together they were making the College. It is significant too, perhaps, of his attitude that in speaking of the undergraduates he seldom said "girls." His daughters remember being reproved when they were small for talking about "the college girls." That is incorrect, they were told; they are students.

Of these students Neilson said in 1937 in reviewing his twenty years at Smith:

> They have been a very cooperative body of young persons who are convinced that we want to give them what they ought to have, and if they think of ways of getting it that we have not thought of they have an opportunity of presenting their proposals to us and getting an honest hearing. The matter of dealing merely with common honesty with the undergraduates is, in my opinion, all that is needed to insure a friendly relation between administration and undergraduate body today.

15

The President and the Alumnae

"In the long run I have no doubt that it is for the advantage of the College to have the alumnae alive, even if they are also kicking." Thus, to one of his masculine trustees, wrote President Neilson on 1 October 1919, when he had been in office just two years. He did not know, he went on, whether he had produced the present condition, but "I have certainly encouraged it."

When Neilson came to Northampton in 1917 the alumnae were so occupied with the support of their Relief Unit in France that they were not paying much attention to the progress of the College and the behavior of the undergraduates. When they did turn their eyes towards Smith they found the students earnest, patriotic, and hard working. But, on the signing of the armistice, with disconcerting suddenness, the picture changed. The postwar college girl was behaving in ways which her mother, her cousins, and her aunts found horrifying. Smith had not been like this in their day. Was this ferment, social, political, religious, the product of the times or the work of the new President? What manner of man was this William Allan Neilson?

Neilson was well aware that the alumnae were looking at him with suspicion.

Of course [he said later], they were courteous people, and they did not often make this suspicion evident when we were face to face.

But it crept out in correspondence and in reports I got. . . They doubted—naturally, since I was not a clergyman—whether I had any religion, and, if I had, whether what I had could be the right sort of religion. They had doubts about various elements in my character. That was the time, you will remember, when we expelled undergraduates for smoking; and the standards of conduct imposed upon the undergraduates by the College authorities were naturally expected to apply to the personnel of the staff itself.

Time and a closer knowledge of the College allayed most alumnae doubts. The kicks were fewer, though there were always enough of them to keep the Neilson wit well exercised; and the liveliness, encouraged by the President, increased. Neilson liked to remark to his colleagues in the men's colleges that *his* alumnae were neither a "pest" nor a "menace" but an asset. His complete freedom from the tangled web of intercollegiate athletics gave him a great advantage, he felt, in his relations with them.

The early contacts, to be sure, were, as he confided to an Alumnae Assembly at commencement twenty years later (1939), somewhat cold and solemn. It was the Smith College Relief Unit, "the heroic side of Smith College," which he learned to know first.

That group of young women seemed to me rather formidable; so that I began my relations with the alumnae with a certain sense of awe. This has gradually worn off. Other forms of nervousness have taken its place, and have worn off.

Before long, instead of troubling himself about what the alumnae were thinking of him, Neilson began to watch, he said, how *they* were behaving and how *they* fulfilled their obligations.

As soon as I got to the point where I was telling *you* what you ought to do instead of your telling me, the tension was released and our relations became quite different. For one thing I was getting older and the alumnae, from my point of view, were getting younger all the time. More and more of them had been students while I was here. The proportion who could pretend to take a maternal attitude towards me was less and less.

No alumna ever admitted to a maternal attitude towards the President, but they all rose as one to his concern that they fulfill their obligations. That was, in fact, the deep-set cornerstone of their affection for him: he took them seriously, both as women and as graduates of the College. The Neilson attitude towards women Ada Comstock defined when, as President of Radcliffe, she returned in June 1927 to speak at the annual Alumnae Assembly. She had been trying to think, she said, about his attitude towards women and had come to the conclusion that, "except for a slight flirtatiousness, he hasn't any."

> I have never seen the slightest reason to suppose that he thought the education of girls the least bit less important than the education of boys. He never discounts an idea because it is a woman's idea.

The Neilson attitude towards alumnae was that they were the "intelligent gentlewomen" President Seelye had desired to make them. He gave them, with candor and confidence, information about the whole state of the College, welcomed their advice as well as their dollars, and took it for granted that their ideals for the institution were as high as his own. It was to their admirable concern for the welfare of Smith that he attributed their early mood of suspicion.

In accepting the presidency Neilson, conscious of the fact that both his predecessors had been ordained Congregational ministers, had stipulated to the trustees that he, a layman, should not be expected to offer public extempore prayer. This, to the women who had attended the daily chapel services conducted by the Rev. Clark Seelye, was to strike a blow at the very foundations of Smith College. The heavenward petitions which President Seelye offered daily in his resonant, beautiful voice had summarized for the undergraduates of his day their highest youthful aspirations. As a member of the class of 1889 put it:

> Once more we bow our heads and hear his wise
> Wingéd, triumphant voice assail God's throne,
> Sweeping our childish prayers up with his own.

Neilson's practice was to read the Bible and then recite with the congregation the Lord's Prayer, and this at first seemed to the alumnae a cold substitute. But whenever one of them visited the campus and heard the new President's reading of the Scriptures her doubts began to fade. Here was a voice as rich, for all its different quality, as President Seelye's own, a care for what was read as deep as his, a familiarity with the Bible, even in its most obscure portions, which was definitely impressive. Dean Nicolson has recorded the amusement with which she watched visiting preachers at Sunday vespers make sure always that a bookmark was in place before their service began, while the secular President would stride to the lectern and turn the pages to any passage he wanted as rapidly and surely as he oriented himself in one of his own texts of Shakespeare. Neilson's students were convinced that he had the entire Bible cross-indexed, at least that is what they said when, in 1927, they presented him with a new chapel Bible. There seemed to be no occasion, ceremonious or casual, for which he could not find the appropriate scriptural passage. The parable of the Foolish Virgins, for instance, on the first day after Christmas vacation. Psalm 91 at the beginning of the examination period: "Thou shalt not be afraid . . . for the destruction that wasteth at noonday. A thousand shall fall at thy side, and ten thousand at thy right hand—." To the freshmen in the fall, as indicative of the opportunity before them: "I will give thee two thousand horses, if thou be able to set riders upon them." "Many daughters have done worthily but thou excellest them all," when he was obliged to announce Dean Comstock's resignation to accept the presidency of Radcliffe. Before long the alumnae were echoing a remark made by Professor Mary Augusta Jordan, after Neilson had conducted his first chapel service: *"Lire est orare."*

To other phases of the religious life of the College Neilson gave from the beginning serious attention. He felt, as he had when he founded the Religious Discussion Group at Harvard, that the needs of the orthodox student were receiving more attention, perhaps, than they required and the needs of the skeptics and free thinkers not enough. He discussed the situation in the summer of 1919 in a letter to Mrs. Ruth Bowles Baldwin, the alumna trustee in whom he felt the deepest confidence:

I have given a good deal of thought to the matter of the religious life of the College and am convinced that it is not wise or just to let it be taken for granted that orthodox preaching is all that can be offered by way of religious stimulus at a college whose basis, as defined by its founder, is Christian and not Calvinistic or anything sectarian.

During the Week of Prayer that year Raymond Calkins, pastor of the First Congregational Church in Cambridge, had been in residence, speaking each day and holding personal consultations in the campus houses and this had proved a satisfactory experience for the members of the Association for Christian Work.

We have, however [the letter to Mrs. Baldwin goes on], over one hundred Unitarians, nearly a hundred Jews, and, I presume, a large number nominally belonging to the orthodox churches but liberal or detached in their point of view. For them last year we had speakers like Mr. Ratcliffe, Mr. Holmes, Mr. S. A. Eliot, Mr. Odell, Mr. Cohoe of Providence, Kirsopp Lake, and, I suppose, myself . . . Personally I should be in favor of something that would be for the freer minds an equivalent of the Week of Prayer for the orthodox . . . those of us who are interested in the religion of the next generation cannot afford to let it be taken for granted that religion stands or falls with the old formulas.

As the alumnae came to realize, Neilson never took anything for granted in the religious life of the College but watched it with an always fresh interest, furnishing swiftly any assistance which seemed likely to vivify or enrich it in any way. In 1927 he appointed, at student request, a Director of Religious Work and Social Service. In 1935 he added to the college staff a full-time Chaplain. When a new Library wing was built he planned it to include a "Little Chapel" for services for which John M. Greene Hall seemed too large and cold. That this concern of his for the religious state of the College was, in its fundamentals, very similar to that of President Seelye was impressed upon the alumnae at the time of the death of the first President on 12 October 1924, in the seventh year of Neilson's presidency.

It had been Seelye's wish that his funeral be conducted as a college service in John M. Greene Hall, and the Seelye family asked Neilson to make the address. He could not, of course, refuse, but he faced the occasion as one of the most difficult of his life; he was expected to put into words the deep sentiment of thousands of women, many of whom thought that he could not comprehend it. So much was he troubled by the responsibility thrust upon him, that, for one of the few times in his life, he wrote his address out beforehand. His reading was so excellent that not six persons in his audience were aware of the unusual procedure, but those who listened and those who later read the printed words, saw, many of them for the first time, the deep similarities between these outwardly so different men.

Blessed is the man who has found his work: let him seek no other blessedness! To Mr. Seelye this modern beatitude applied with more than ordinary fitness. Fifty years ago he found his work, and thereafter he did not cease to rejoice in his blessedness. Believing heart and soul in the cause which he had made his own, he poured out in the service of that cause the full stream of energy that flowed from his supreme health of mind and body. From the whole-heartedness of his devotion there came that simplification of life and that calm of spirit which are the rewards of a complete surrender to a worthy ideal. Modern life is so varied, its calls upon our interest so manifold, that most of us allow our energies to be broken into a thousand fragments, so that our total accomplishment becomes negligible, unrecognizable as ours. The life of Mr. Seelye was first of all a notable proof of the wisdom of concentration, of the profitableness to the individual and to society of the choice of a great central purpose, a purpose giving spur to effort, proportion to the means employed, splendor to the end attained.

The dangers attaching to singleness of aim are narrowness and fanaticism, but from these President Seelye was freed, on one hand by the generosity of his nature, and on the other by the many-sidedness of his chosen task. He was convinced, yet tolerant; strong, yet tender; a seeker after righteousness, yet a lover of beauty. These personal characteristics in turn affected his conception of the institution he sought to create, and determined the type of character and intelligence into which he sought to mould the women who passed through the College under his influence. The type was liberally conceived, allowing infinite variety yet marking as fundamental and essential, integrity, intelligence, and breeding. Whatever restrictions these implied he was bound to insist upon; outside of these restrictions he delighted in the untrammeled manifestations of the joyous impulse of youth.

That the new President was seeking to cultivate in his students the very qualities which had seemed essential to President Seelye became continually more apparent to the alumnae body. They were impressed by this again when they saw his attitude towards the College's memorial to the "formidable" members of the Smith College Relief Unit. A replica of the wrought iron gates of the Château Robécourt at Grécourt in the Somme, the Unit's headquarters, was dedicated in the fall of 1924. The war memorial is one of the few not strictly utilitarian objects on the New England campus. There was hesitation, therefore, in some quarters about its erection but Neilson endowed it with immediate and continuous function; he presented it to successive generations of undergraduates as a conserver of tradition and an incentive to accomplishment. Sprung himself from a soil rich with memories, he knew the formative effect of history upon youth and took care that no student went through Smith College without some knowledge of the men and women who had built what she enjoyed.

Speaking to the students in later years Neilson often used the history of the Unit as a text:

> The Smith College Relief Unit [he said to the undergraduates in 1932] went to France in the autumn of 1917 and was given possession of certain ruined villages in the district of the Somme. Through the winter they worked with the peasantry of these villages, recivilizing the little children and giving people a means of livelihood and self-respect. The following spring the great German drive swept across that whole area and drove out all the villagers again. The Smith women evacuated the villages, helping old women pack their household goods, standing at crossroads and guiding the straggling remnants of the British fifth army, staying there till German shells were exploding around them, staying at risk of their lives. For some time after, while their field of operation remained in enemy hands, they worked in canteens and hospitals. When the tide of battle receded they returned to their villages and started once more to build them up. They did not evacuate them till 1922. . . When it was all over, they came back and melted into the life of this country. They did not organize themselves; they did not make any claim; the government did not insure them; they were paid no pension; they asked for no bonus. They did the thing for its own sake. Their activities

during those years will remain one of the most glorious and picturesque bits of the history of this College. I should like you to believe that this is the characteristic of those who have gone out from this College; that they have done the thing for its own sake; not for glory, not for reward, but because they knew it was well worth doing.

After his encounter with them as war workers, Neilson met his alumnae next in their most vigorous capacity, as collectors of resources for the College. The enormous increase in costs of all kinds during the 1920's brought very close to crisis an institution that had meticulously operated just within its means for nearly fifty years. The most serious element in the situation was the effect on the salaries of the faculty. "It is not," as Neilson put it, "necessary to give them the luxuries of life, but we must make peace of mind possible for them."

The need for larger faculty salaries was shared by all American institutions after the war. Smith had, in addition, a special problem which Neilson stated concisely in the spring of 1919: "We are endeavoring to carry on an institution for two thousand young women with an equipment calculated for one thousand." The Library, the auditorium, the building for biological sciences, and the chemistry building were adequate, he thought, for their purposes but "beyond that I can hardly go." The most important need of all seemed to him to be dormitories, an excellent investment, fortunately, for, as operated at Smith, they returned a 7 per cent profit which could be used for the increase of faculty salaries.

Confronted with the facts the Alumnae Association voted to raise for the College four million dollars, a courageous and an historic act; no sum approaching that magnitude had ever been thought of as a gift to a woman's college. As individuals the Smith alumnae had been generous but they had not before organized for an intensive campaign. When, in 1913 Smith raised the then staggering sum of one million dollars, President Burton, a consummate and joyous money-getter, had taken the initiative and done a large part of the work. "He seems almost to have taken delight," wrote Neilson with astonishment, "in invading a Wall Street office and emerging with a check or a pledge." Now, trustees and alumnae recognized, the College had grown up; a single executive could no longer be expected to perform all the administrative functions. If they wanted a scholar-president who would concern himself with the intellectual aspects of the institution, they must supply the physical means. The trustees had been perfectly aware of what they were doing when they appointed a man who made it a condition of acceptance that he would not raise money, and this agreement they scrupulously observed.

But the fact remained that Neilson was a master money raiser. He interpreted his own restriction very broadly and, though he seldom made a direct request for funds—he insisted that he was not a good beggar—he was always ready to state the needs of the College so lucidly and persuasively that even strangers were moved and alumnae felt spurred to Herculean efforts. The effect he produced was epitomized by the President of the Alumnae Association, Mrs. Dwight Morrow, when she presented him to a Smith audience at the opening of the Four Million Dollar campaign.

> I have observed [she said] that when a great ship is launched they always select a little woman to break a bottle of champagne over its bow. Today I am the little woman, and here [with a gesture towards President Neilson] is the bottle of champagne.

On the occasions when he did ask outright for cash Neilson did it with unblushing candor and a turn of phrase which made the appeal irresistible. When, for instance, at the Last Chapel exercises in 1933, the organ ciphered with a horrible discord, he remarked that it was asking piteously, in its dumb way, for the repairs which the College had not been able to afford.

In 1930 the College purchased for additional playing fields land which lay adjacent to the campus but on the opposite side of the little Mill River. Neilson said, during the first of the Commencement gatherings, that in order to reach that new field he wanted a bridge.

> We have plans for a bridge and I think it will be a very nice bridge. I have done what I shall continue to do until successful: urge upon friends of the College the uncommon opportunity for a very distinguished present to the College of something that will be beautiful, conspicuous, and constantly used.

A few days later, at the annual meeting of the Alumnae Association, when unexpected additions were being announced to the Alumnae Fund, Neilson rose to say that he was becoming a trifle nervous lest ten alumnae, in their enthusiasm, should offer him ten bridges. "But don't get bashful; I haven't one yet—and I could use two!" A bridge was presented by Mrs. Thomas Lamont of the class of 1893.

After the hurricane of 1938 had swept the campus Neilson suggested that some of the trees ought to be replaced and that "it is very seldom that one can obtain temporary immortality at so low a cost." Temporary immortality was quickly purchased by members of the faculty, staff, student body, and alumnae. Professor Paul Lieder made his gift a dogwood in honor of a well-known campus character, his German shepherd Eric.

Neilson also took frequent occasion, with cheerful gusto, to remind the alumnae that if each of them would write Smith College into her will the cumulative results would be, as the years went on, an important addition to income. The *Alumnae Quarterly* made a point of publishing news of legacies, following each announcement with a "suggested form of bequest."

This ability to state a need persuasively Neilson exercised again and again in the course of the Four Million Dollar campaign. Its opening gun was fired on 15 January 1920. During the fall an organization had been set up and strategy planned. The hope was to have the total amount in hand by June 1922. Asked whether this was a strategic moment for raising money—many of the men's colleges were already in the field—Smith women replied stoutly that any moment was strategic when the College needed funds and the alumnae believed in its future.

When the time arrived for presenting the College's case to the Foundations Neilson made the statements, verbal or written, with effect. The General Education Board made a grant of five hundred thousand dollars for faculty salaries; the Carnegie Corporation gave seventy-five thousand dollars. With individual potential donors the President talked from time to time but only after the ground had been broken by an alumna or a trustee and only when the possible benefactor had expressed a wish to discuss the matter with the President. Talks to Smith Clubs he gave whenever the Central Committee asked his help and, in the spring, he made a trip to the West Coast. In the course of that journey, between 20 March and 10 April, he spoke in Spokane, Seattle, Portland, San Francisco, Santa Barbara, Pasadena, Los Angeles, Salt Lake City, Denver, St. Louis, and Cleveland. He talked not only to Smith almunae about the College and the campaign but, in addition, to civic and commercial groups in each city on the Crisis in Education, and to the local colleges and universities on The Suppression of Talent in American Education. In speaking to the alumnae the President took care to remind them that they were working not only for Smith but for the whole cause of the women's colleges, which had subsisted hitherto on the crumbs from their brothers' tables.

So vigorously did the work of the Fund, begun in January, go on that by June more than three million dollars were in hand. The alumnae, gathered in Northampton for their class reunions, were fired to complete the total amount before Commencement was over.

> I have come this year [Neilson said at Last Chapel] to believe in impossible things. I had thought we were in for four years' steady grind before the Fund would be raised. But now the end is in sight. We want the rest of that money *now!* We want to know where it is coming from before the class of 1920 leaves town. It will be a much less painful operation to do it quick and have it over.

The alumnae took his advice. On Commencement Day they presented the College with four million dollars.

The men's colleges, whose fund raising was simultaneous with Smith's, were pleased when they could announce that 50 per cent of their alumni had subscribed. Smith's percentage was 85 and there was, consequently, no longer any question in the alumnae mind that they were working partners in the College. It never occurred to them to be silent partners. Neilson encouraged them to express their opinions, encouraged them even to kick when they saw real occasion; he objected only to strictures by critics who did not take the trouble to get at the facts and to "reformers" who improvised their own machinery instead of using that set up by the College. An alumna who wanted to effect a change could work through the *Quarterly,* through the officers of the Alumnae Association, who were in close touch with the administration, or through the alumnae trustees, whose number Neilson increased from three to four.

When expressed alumnae opinion took the form of complaint Neilson listened and replied patiently, with only an occasional turning of the tables.

> I want to criticize the alumnae [he said in the winter of 1921]. You criticize too soon. You pass judgment and circulate the results before you have found the facts. That is a common human weakness. . . Find out if you are right and why a thing is so, but do not join the large number of outsiders who are only too glad to disparage the College. And finally if you don't think our explanations meet your criticism, come here and tell us about it and thrash it out openly, but don't harbor secret grudges and don't believe mere rumor.

The militant DAR's and others of that stripe who, in the twenties, worried about Smith's radicalism Neilson took in his stride. Once only was he openly angry, when an alumna attempted to bring about the dismissal of a professor of sociology by circulating charges among alumnae clubs and the parents of students. The professor in question, Frank Hankins, had given to the members of a senior class studying the history of the institution of marriage a questionnaire composed by the students themselves, which made inquiry about their personal theories and practice in the matter of sex relations. The answers were, of course, anonymous and not intended for circulation beyond that particular classroom, but some of the students in that pre-Kinsey age were startled. One of them sent a copy of the questions home to her mother whose horror took the illogical form of sending the document to her local paper. A tempest blew up. In the twenties, to question the foundations of the home was not only sin but bolshevism. Neilson and Hankins agreed that the questionnaire should not be repeated, and that, from Neilson's point of view, was the end of the matter. Not so, from the point of view of a little group of alumnae who were determined that Hankins should be dismissed. The charges they circulated went, of course, beyond fact to rumor and plain misstatement; they reflected, quite unjustly, upon the College, and burdened Neilson for years with a disagreeable correspondence. In June 1926 he made a statement on the case to the Alumnae Association, urging them to make very clear to all their members the importance of using the regular means provided when they wished to effect any change in the organization or administration of the College. The Association immediately passed a unanimous vote of confidence in President Neilson. Such incidents were rare and all the agitating ladies ever succeeded in accomplishing was to waste the President's time.

No such high pressure campaign as the Four Million Dollar Fund was necessary again for many years but in 1925, the occasion of the fiftieth anniversary of Smith's founding, the alumnae decided to make a special birthday gift to their alma mater. Even enlightened businessmen in 1920 had supposed that the soaring postwar costs of building would eventually go down and the raisers of the Four Million Dollar Fund had talked cheerfully of fifteen new dormitories. The actual number was three, and, even with the purchase of off-campus houses and the legacy to the College of the dormitories of the Capen School, Smith was still far from being a resident college. Neilson, remembering, as he wrote to the President of the Alumnae Association, "what the alumnae have done, at what cost," had neither "the heart nor the assurance to make further appeals." But he felt bound to state the facts and the need stood clear. "We should like," said Mrs. Dwight Morrow, "to give our mother a pearl necklace for her birthday, but if what our mother needs is a cook stove, for heaven's sake let us give her the cook stove first." She accepted the chairmanship of a committee to collect six hundred thousand dollars for three dormitories to complete the Great Quadrangle.

The class organizations were the foundation of the work and by June 1925 the sum was raised. The presentation of alma mater's birthday gift was one of the gayer moments in an anniversary celebration conducted with proper academic dignity, even though, as Neilson phrased it, "the chief spectacle and the main entertainment was the family itself."

On this occasion, as at the time of President Seelye's funeral, the alumnae were struck by the completeness of Neilson's identification with their institution. He not only knew in rich detail the facts of its past but had assimilated them in the same way that he had assimilated himself to his adopted country. (No descendant of the founding fathers ever said "our country" with less self-consciousness than the Scotsman who had taken out his papers at the age of thirty-seven.) His historical address on the fifty years of Smith history was not only eloquent as summary but full of new illuminations. He was the first to suggest, for instance, that Smith should trace her ancestry to Mary Lyon, the founder of Mt. Holyoke. The wife of Sophia Smith's pastor and adviser, John M. Greene, was a graduate of Mt. Holyoke Seminary. Her enthusiasm for the educational advantages she enjoyed in that pioneer institution is, Neilson said, evident in her correspondence with her fiancé. "One is forced to infer that the training his wife had received must have been a powerful, perhaps the chief, factor in leading him to place opportunities for women's education among the greatest social needs of his time."

Neilson's address opened with the statement that "Smith College began in the conscience of a New England woman." Sophia Smith received her brother's legacy "not as providing means for luxury or display, but as laying upon her a burden of responsibility. She left it for the founding of a college for women because after much perplexity, deliberation, and advice, she had concluded that thus could she best fulfill a moral obligation.

"Smith College began in the mind of a New England minister. To John Morton Greene is due the idea whose realization after fifty years we celebrate today." After reading some passages from Miss Smith's will Neilson went on: "When one considers what would today be regarded as the somewhat narrow and puritanical type of culture in which the authors of these sentences were living, one cannot fail to be impressed by their wisdom, liberality, and far-sightedness. The general terms in which the purposes of women's education are defined are perfectly valid today. . .

"It is one thing to state an ideal and give a commission, it is another to carry them out. Laurenus Clark Seelye in 1873 undertook the presidency of the new College, land was bought and the first buildings erected, a prospectus was issued, and in 1875 the College was opened with fourteen students. The prospectus and the inaugural address laid down the main lines of educational policy on which the new College was to run, and again it is amazing to note how little these have to be modified to describe the College today." Then, tracing swiftly the accomplishments of Mr. Seelye, Mr. Burton, and the third administration, the Scotsman, who knew as well as Shakespeare the line between sentiment and sentimentality, made bold to speak of "the spirit of Smith College." "Mr. Seelye planted and Mr. Burton watered, and hundreds of teachers have cultivated the ground and in a thousand ways stimulated the growth. Two other important factors have counted." The trustees, "modest and self-effacing to a fault, but wise in counsel," and the students.

To them the opportunities were given, on them the influences played; and they took them and mingled with them their own youthful vitality, their gaiety, their zest, their enthusiasm, their illusions and disillusions, and created that mysterious but indubitable result —the spirit of Smith College. It is this spirit, one yet various, ever changing and ever being renewed, which we are assembled to celebrate today. . . And to this spirit, to the sustaining of it on the level of its best tradition, to the perpetuating of it on this campus and out in the world, and to the perfecting of it for the future and its needs we dedicate ourselves anew as we face the next fifty years.

The celebration was shared by a distinguished but carefully limited list of delegates, representing chiefly the women's colleges of the country and the men's colleges of New England. Greetings were presented from the State by the Honorable Wellington Wells, President of the Senate of Massachusetts; from the women's colleges by President Marion Park of Bryn Mawr; from the men's colleges by President G. D. Olds of Amherst; from the co-educational colleges by Dean William Hammond of Cornell. It was in the course of the more informal exercises of the Alumnae Assembly that Neilson made the first public statement of an impression that had been growing in his mind for some time: that the women's colleges, which had once looked up humbly to masculine academic attainments, were now setting collegiate standards themselves. He was quite serious in this belief though he expressed it with a humorous exaggeration. Referring to a passage in the will of Sophia Smith, he expressed the hope that some enlightened male will leave his fortune for the creation of an institution in which young men will have opportunities equal to those at present afforded in the best colleges for young women! The time has passed when colleges like this require to be stimulated to effort in order to equal the achievements of the colleges for young men; the time has come when Sophia Smith's ambition is ridiculously modest; when we have caught up and no longer can afford to set our pace to the strolling pace of our brothers.

The energies which had gone into the Four Million Dollar Fund and the Birthday Gift were then organized and channeled into a regular stream of giving, the Alumnae Fund, set going under the chairmanship of Mrs. Harriet Bliss Ford of the class of 1899. Neilson thought that the alumnae would do well if they raised in the first year twenty-five thousand dollars. In June 1928 they presented him with sixty thousand for the increase of faculty salaries. He was pleased, but cannily invested the money, using only the interest, for, as he told them when they expressed their disappointment, he was by no means sure that they could keep this pace up and he did not wish to increase a professor's salary one year and set it back the next. That his judgment was sound the alumnae ruefully admitted when, a few years later, they decided to erect an Alumnae House—a project Neilson approved—and agreed to devote for a few years the major share of the Alumnae Fund to that.

I am assured [Neilson said] that after three years you are going to change back to salary contributions. These three lean years will be covered by the hoardings of the three years when I did not believe you. They are the reward of lack of faith.

After that the giving flowed on smoothly; no more drives were necessary during Neilson's administration, and the College could count each year on a substantial addition to its income, the money earmarked for salaries or some other purpose which the trustees had approved. Each year new contributors were brought in, even during the depression. In 1933 eleven hundred regular givers increased their contributions.

The erection of the Alumnae House was a logical development in the relationship between the College and the Alumnae Association which had been growing closer year by year. Neilson had great admiration for the organizing ability of the Smith graduates though he was sometimes amused by it. The chapter on the alumnae in his History of Smith College begins: "The first alumnae came into existence in June, 1879, and, being Americans, two years later they organized." But he took full advantage of that national tendency. President Burton in his systematizing of the college machinery had centralized the Alumnae Association offices in College Hall, the general administration building. The Alumnae Secretary and the editor of the *Alumnae Quarterly* had offices just across the hall from the President and he constantly dropped in to exchange news and ideas.

Florence Snow of the class of 1904, Secretary of the Association, performed her duties with a combination of efficiency and charm which was admired not only by Smith alumnae but by the members of the American Alumni Council of which she became, in 1928, the first woman president. During all the years of her incumbency—she was the first secretary, appointed in 1907, and had to create the job—there is scarcely an issue of the *Alumnae Quarterly* in which some one is not extolling the ease, grace, and comfort with which an alumnae function has run off because it was directed by Florence Snow. As one class tribute put it: she "kept ten thousand women peaceful." That the tone of the alumnae attitude towards the College was set in large measure by her Neilson recognized. In 1925 he conferred upon her the honorary degree of Master of Arts.

The *Smith Alumnae Quarterly* also became famous in the national organization by reason of its comprehensive coverage of academic plans and policies. When editors from other institutions, who picked up what they could from printed reports, inquired how she did it, Edith Hill, of the class of 1903, liked to tell them that the gist of such or such an article was given her by President Neilson sitting on the edge of her desk, smoking his cigar and talking, freely and frankly, about his newest scheme or problem. He told her all the details, gave her the administrative point of view, and then left her to present it to her subscribers in her own way. He never took exception to what she wrote, and continually urged the alumnae to read the *Quarterly* if they really wanted to be informed about the College. And, because he insisted that everything of importance during the academic year had been thoroughly covered in the *Quarterly,* he declined to make his Annual Reports to the Trustees more than perfunctory summaries.

When, in 1936, the idea that the Association needed a building of their own was broached there was some opposition by alumnae who felt that it was perhaps too great a luxury; they might do better to turn over to the College all the money they could raise. They jumped to the conclusion that Neilson must agree with them and rumors about his "real" point of view flew so thick that at commencement time he mounted the platform, raised his right hand and stated in ringing tones:

> *I do believe in the Alumnae House.* I believe it will not only be a future convenience, but a necessity for your work and for the development of the Alumnae Association and for its relations with the College. We need it badly; we have begun to get it; we are going to get it; and it is time to drop all this hesitation, all scruples, all doubts, all differences of opinion, all these hole-and-corner conferences with me about my sincerity. That is my position; and anything that I can do to help you in the maturing of your plans for the Alumnae House I am going to do.

Two years later he accepted the deed of gift of the House, built on the campus, as a symbol of the continuity of the College. Some of the uses to which he saw it being put he described in picturesque detail.

> The returning alumna easily feels disconsolate when she comes back to the scene of exploits and experiences she had fondly thought immortal and finds of them all no trace or memory, not even a spot where she has a right to rest, not even a mirror to call her own. All this the Alumnae House is designed to correct.
>
> Here will be gathered the memorials of all the college generations. Here the officers of the Association will recognize, identify, direct, and console. Here the footsore will be refreshed. Here those chilled by the February blizzard will be warmed, the ravages of the heat of June will be repaired. Appointments will be kept, acquaintances will be renewed, plans laid, and all kinds of benefactions discussed and matured. The alumnae will be at home and happy.

Shortly after World War I, among alumni in all parts of the country, a desire began to stir for some contact with alma mater which should be intellectual rather than sentimental. Marching and singing at reunions, revisiting beloved campus landmarks was all very well but they left out the thing for which the former student was really most grateful, the impetus the College had given to his mind. Could not a college still do something in this kind for its aging sons and daughters? Experiments of various kinds began and in these Smith was a pioneer.

A scheme for faculty direction of alumni reading, originated by Amherst in 1924, was taken up by Smith and greeted with so much enthusiasm that the report on its inception had to be couched in carefully modest terms. It may be, Smith said politely, that the other colleges have prepared the ground for our project; at all events seventeen hundred former Smith students will this winter be continuing their connection with the College in a new way.

The scheme continued to flourish. A report published in 1938 offered the alumna her choice of sixty-five lists. Most popular that year was The Mediterranean, compiled for the Alumnae College in June. Next came Interior Decorating, while Child Psychology was reported in such continuous demand that a sequel had been prepared on The Growing Child.

Neilson was enthusiastic about the reading list experiment. He was genuinely concerned with the concept of adult education, both for "those who have not had in youth what are called 'advantages'" and for the college graduate, who was, he thought, in grave danger of becoming so concerned with success in a particular line that he (or she) found himself as a citizen unprepared to take his part in guiding the activities of the community, and incapable of a satisfying employment of his leisure time. It was with college graduates particularly in mind that Neilson undertook, for W. W. Norton in 1932, the editing of a book called *Roads to Knowledge* in which a dozen of the main fields of learning were discussed by scholars of repute. Each writer was asked to describe what seemed to him the main contents of the division of knowledge in which he was expert, to give his reasons for finding it of compelling interest, and to show how the study of that field might be best approached by the intelligent layman. The successful use of the volume, said the editor in his Preface, demands "a fair educational background, some curiosity, an active mind, and a willingness to apply it." The book fulfilled its purpose so well that an enlarged second edition was published in 1937.

Concurrently with the reading lists, Smith experimented with some Vocational Round Tables, gatherings of alumnae experts in special fields with members of the faculty, to discuss particular professional problems or to make suggestions to the College on the possibility of its offering useful training for their professions. Firmly opposed as he was to the vitiating of the liberal arts course with anything in the nature of vocational training, Neilson felt that the College might perhaps utilize its summer-idle plant for technical instruction which would save after-college time. He would gladly have tried some experiments of this kind if he had not found his faculty very fearful of any concession to the current trend towards vocationalism.

In 1928 another experiment was tried in the establishment of intellectual relations with alma mater. Smith held in October an Alumnae Week-end during which the graduates were invited to return to Northampton not to renew old memories with their classmates but to see the present College in action. They visited classes, attended chapel and vespers, inspected new buildings, dined in campus houses, enjoyed forums, concerts, plays, and sports, and listened to a report by the President on the present state of the College. The invitation was accepted by three hundred alumnae from the whole range of classes and from points as distant as California. They were so enthusiastic about the experience that the fall Week-end became a permanent institution.

By virtue of these small beginnings Smith evolved her highly successful contribution to the adult education movement; the Alumnae College, an idea which she did not originate but developed along quite original lines. Instead of attempting, as Neilson put it, "to intersperse among ivy chains, alumnae frolics and the like, serious lectures, with such disastrous consequences as might have been anticipated," Smith arranged to hold over those who had come to reunion and wanted something more and to welcome those who had shunned reunions altogether. The four-day "College" met directly after Commencement, the alumnae-students living in campus dormitories, using lecture rooms, library, and playing fields which had just been vacated by the undergraduates. The purposes of the College were two: to provide a stimulus and guide for reading and thought through the ensuing months, and to give the alumna opportunity to become acquainted, and reacquainted, with the Smith faculty, to see what manner of men and women they were and how they were now conducting a Smith education.

In the planning and conduct of the Alumnae College, in the first session in 1933 and in all the succeeding years of his administration, Neilson took an enthusiastic and active part. It was his suggestion that substituted for the usual series of unconnected lectures a central topic particularly pertinent to the moment: in 1933, Great Britain in the Twentieth Century; 1934, Germany since 1870; 1935, Modern France; 1936, The United States: Backgrounds of Contemporary Conditions; 1937, The Mediterranean; 1938, The Renaissance.

Alumnae response was enthusiastic beyond anything the organizers of the College had imagined. Enrollment figures for the first year are typical. The students, numbering 207, came from twenty-two states, one from London, one from Peiping. Forty-four of the fifty-five classes were represented. Both class representation and total enrollment increased as the years went on and many alumnae who came once returned again and again.

Neilson delivered a number of lectures in course: "Germany Today" (during one evening of that session Mrs. Neilson read German poetry); "Distinguishing Characteristics of American Education"; "As Shakespeare Says." Always he made the welcoming and concluding addresses, explaining to the students the plan of education on which they were entering and making certain that they took their opportunity seriously, not just as a pleasant four-day escape from the burdens of home. "If you come here and just take these lectures like eating candy, you are a fraud. You are entertained here for the purpose of receiving stimulus for your intellectual life in the next twelvemonth—see that you earn it."

Occasionally the President made comments to the alumnae-students as severe as those they had heard (and liked to hear) in their undergraduate days. In 1936, discussing the questionnaire they had been asked to fill with comment and suggestion, he deplored the evidence that in any group, however highly educated, only a small minority can read and understand a plain English sentence. The title of the course that year was The United States: Backgrounds of Contemporary Conditions.

A great many of you seemed to read that: Backgrounds *and* Contemporary Conditions, and you were disappointed hour after hour when the contemporary conditions continued to evade you. This was of malice aforethought on the part of your committee in charge of the program. . . I am an unrepentant member of this committee. I know that fifty per cent of you want to be told how to vote. It is not the function of the faculty of Smith College to save you thought.

But the President was in general delighted with the tone of the educational experiment and with its success. In addition to the effect it had on the personal thinking of its students, the College admirably fulfilled its function of enlightening the alumnae on the present condition of Smith. They were impressed by the development of the campus, by the music building, gymnasium, and dormitories they had helped to build, by the excellence of the college food served during their stay, by the quality of the pictures in the Tryon Gallery and of the music performed and commented on by members of the staff. Most of all they were impressed by the quality of the professors who lectured to them. As one "student" put it, other critical faculties might atrophy but appraising a lecturer is an accomplishment possessed by all American women. Here they found a type of speaker very different from those they had listened to at home on little gilt chairs. These speakers were concerned "not with pleasing but, astonishingly enough, with transmitting." Each man's technique is "developed in the dry air of learning, is incidental to a more important purpose, and is kept fluid by association with others whose medium is the same. The better the technique the more do students learn, is quite simply the formula."

As their affection for the President grew the alumnae, being after all feminine, insisted on giving it expression. As an indication that he was now an indivisible part of the College they insisted, after President Seelye's death, that Neilson take over a custom begun by the first President, which had grown to be a beloved commencement ceremony. The Ivy Day exercises began always with a procession of the reunion classes who filed before the President and then took their stand on either side of the long walk from the Students' Building to Seelye Hall, up which the senior ivy procession was to move. Just before the undergraduates advanced, the President, hat in hand, went "down the line," bowing right and left to his former students who pressed close to the ropes eager to catch his eye, sure, each one, as she had been from her freshman year, that his smile was directed particularly to her.

On the tenth anniversary of Neilson's presidency when the trustees were insisting on his taking a sabbatical leave, the alumnae presented him with a large and handsome suitcase, hastily asking him to look inside where he would find the price of a return ticket to Northampton.

In 1937—the twentieth anniversary gift having been raised two years in advance—they wanted to mark the occasion by a personal present and, learning from Mrs. Neilson that the President liked to have his own water supply beside him at the dinner table, presented him with a George IV silver pitcher. It was given to him at the Alumnae Assembly in a large ribbon-bound box and, as he mounted the platform to receive it, the entire audience rose and remained standing. Looking over his shoulder as he bent to untie the ribbons, Neilson asked, "Is this a mark of respect or curiosity?"

At such moments of sentiment he reverted instinctively to the Scottish. Responding to the address announcing the establishment of the Neilson Chair of Research [see p. 215] he began an eloquent and serious expression of gratitude with the remark that he had the distressing feeling of being present at his own funeral, "for in my own country at least, that is the only occasion on which people say things like that." To a former member of his faculty who had written a brief "profile" of him for the Merriam-Webster publication *Words,* he wrote:

The Merriam Company sent me your Profile, or rather my Profile by you. It seems to me somewhat incredible and I am afraid to meet you again lest the real truth should dawn on you. This does not prevent me from feeling grateful to you for your good will and for using your imagination so much to my advantage. I hope your conscience feels all right. A man at one of the learned meetings recently quoted a statement about Gladstone—that his conscience was not his guide but his accomplice.

But sometimes, after he had joked, Neilson could say what he really thought. On his tenth anniversary for instance (1927):

I want to thank the alumnae and the faculty and the trustees and . . . the undergraduates . . . on behalf of my family as well as myself, for the possibility of a life as interesting and as rich and surrounded by as much human warmth as anyone can hope to find on this earth.

16

The President and the Trustees

WHEN he took office at Smith Neilson had in his mind a definite conception of the ideal college trustee. The popular idea that a trustee's chief virtue is wealth, played little part in it. The fundamental trustee virtue, Neilson thought, is industry. A trustee should not simply lend the luster of his name; he should assume responsibility for the policies of the college and be prepared to expend time and energy in their execution.

His first care, then, was to prune, as tactfully as possible, the dead wood from the Smith Board. There was only a little: a few gentlemen of estimable character and wisdom but so occupied with other duties and responsibilities that they did not put their minds effectively upon the problems of Smith College. That the Board would function better without these part-time members was a conception rapidly grasped by the livelier, especially the feminine, trustees. Stirring faintly in academic circles after the war was the idea that, since professors are required to retire at sixty-eight, it is somewhat illogical for the governors of an institution to hold office till ninety, or beyond. Delicate methods of spreading this conception were being debated by various institutions when, in 1921, the Smith trustees simply, as one of them phrased it, "decapitated themselves," voting that a "permanent" term should thereafter equal ten years. No retiring trustee, it was arranged, could be immediately re-elected but, after a year's interval, anyone whom the Board thought indispensable might be recalled for a second ten-year term. Retirements were ordered so that one occurred each year, assuring the Board a perpetual influx of fresh thinking.

The industrious Smith trustee was expected to attend three meetings a year and to serve between times on at least one working committee. Neilson urged, therefore, that most of the members of the Board should live within easy traveling distance of Northampton, even at the cost of restricting somewhat the geographic representation of a thoroughly national college. He found that it also promoted efficiency to select as trustees, as often as possible, men who had Smith wives or daughters. Half the task of educating them about the College was then already done, and a spur to diligence was always in operation at home.

The second virtue Neilson wanted in his trustees was some kind of expert knowledge on which the College might profitably draw, and he took pains to see that when new elections were made the balance of talents was kept even. It was essential, of course, he thought, since the trustees are the guardians of the College's endowment, that a fair number of them be bankers or brokers, but investment is not the only matter on which a college needs expert advice. The Tryon Art Gallery at Smith, for instance, has a substantial endowment which makes possible each year the addition of important items to its collection. In making these purchases the Director of the Gallery and the President of the College would be glad to draw on expert wisdom. In 1921 the Smith Board elected to membership Professor Paul Sachs of the Fogg Museum at Harvard; on his retirement, they elected Frank Channing Smith, a trustee of the Worcester Art Museum, and then Philip Hofer of Harvard. When Neilson felt that the infirmary and the College's health service needed reorganization he urged the election of Dr. Kendal Emerson of New York. The Smith College School for Social Work benefited by the presence on the Board of psychiatrists and social workers. For the opinions of lawyers and clergymen there was always need, and Neilson thought it desirable to have among the trustees a representative of the secondary schools.

That some of this special knowledge might profitably be provided by women, Neilson was very ready to agree, the more so since he admitted that the women trustees usually worked harder than the men. During his regime the number of alumnae trustees—they served eight-year terms—was increased from three to four, and more women were appointed as "permanent" trustees, until, in 1930, he could say to the alumnae that the Board of Trustees of Smith College consists of "seven women and seven men—and the President. I have so long been regarded as a leading university woman that I am uncertain in which category I belong."

To employ a special alumna talent Neilson invented in 1932 the temporary post of "resident trustee." Mrs. Harriet Bliss Ford, '99, who had been active for many years in alumnae good works, was made Vice-President of the Board of Trustees and invited to take up residence in Northampton with a commission to familiarize herself thoroughly with the operation of the College so that she might be able to present its needs to potential donors. Since, during the depression years, potential donors were few, Mrs. Ford also traveled widely about the country, speaking to alumnae, meeting pre-college girls, and studying the impression Smith was making in regions far from Northampton.

To the suggestion, not infrequently made, that the faculty be represented on the Board of Trustees, Neilson was distinctly cool. "*I* represent the faculty," he said. The implication that when he became an administrator he ceased to think as a professor always hurt him. He did, however, suggest that the Dean of the College sit with the Board, though without a vote. The Smith faculty, on the whole, felt well disposed towards the Smith trustees, particularly after they had watched them, in a variety of trying situations, support the administration's defense of academic freedom. Most of the faculty, especially those who were graduates of the College and knew the alumnae trustees personally, felt free to offer comment and suggestion on college policies, though no definite machinery was set up for the purpose.

There was another quality, in addition to industry and special knowledge, which Neilson thought important in a trustee, though he did not hope to find it in every member of his Board. As a distinguished example of objective judgment he pointed to Ruth Bowles Baldwin of the class of 1887. Mrs. Baldwin served as a trustee for two ten-year terms. Her husband, William H. Baldwin, had served before her. Mrs. Baldwin, Neilson said, is

the wisest and altogether the most admirable woman whom I have ever known, and I have known a good many, especially since I came here. . . The most mild and gracious of persons in her personal bearing and relations, her allegiance to principle is absolute. I have never known her tempted to compromise; I have never known anyone who had such perfect power of feeling clearly the approval or the condemnation of the principle or the idea without any confusion with the persons standing for the principle or idea.

Two traditional practices of the Smith trustees seemed to Neilson excellent: the custom of having the President of the College sit as chairman of the Board, and the fixing of the number of trustees at fifteen. In a group of that size, he said, detailed discussion is possible. The huge boards, customary in so many universities, are necessary only when trustees take their functions lightly and are so often absent from meetings that it is difficult to get a quorum. A smaller number than fifteen—seven or eight was sometimes suggested—would not, Neilson felt, make it possible to staff the necessary working committees. When some educational radicals suggested the total abolition of the trustees so that the control of the College might be entirely in the hands of the faculty, he protested that the trustees were a real asset to the College, performing much labor which would otherwise devolve upon the faculty or the administrative staff. That this labor was performed without pay seemed to him another point in the trustees' favor.

Concerning the chairmanship of the Board, Neilson wrote in 1932 to President Stanley King of Amherst that it had always been the custom at Smith for the President of the College to be elected, annually, chairman of the Board of Trustees and he found it difficult to imagine that any other system would work as well.

The business of the Board meetings is always prepared by the President and I can't say that anybody else is in a position to do it. He also would have to present most of the questions since he knows the situations out of which they arise . . . The only advantage I can see of having the President of the Board someone else would be in the lessening of the President of the College's responsibility, and in getting some member of the Board to take more initiative than any member of the Board does with us. On the other hand, unless he lived here, I do not see how he could do much in that way . . . but Smith is the only college of its group where our practice prevails so I am forced to believe that the other method is quite workable.

One consequence of the absence of custodial figureheads from the Smith Board was a singular harmony in the trustees' discussions. Their meetings were full of questions and of curiosity but there were no factions, no close or bitter votes. As a matter of fact, their decisions were not arrived at by vote at all, only by discussions which finally resolved themselves into the sense of the meeting and were then formally phrased for the record. Neilson frequently did the phrasing. When it was quite clear what the group wanted, he would say, "Mrs. Emerson will move and Mrs. Morrow will second—" and then state their conclusion in perspicuous language. When any of their constituency remarked that such harmony suggested they were merely rubber stamps, the trustees protested hotly. They knew, they said, exactly what they were doing and why. It was only because Neilson presented his policies so lucidly and convincingly—"his magic power of exposition" they called it—that they were rarely inclined to take issue with him. Besides, as one of them put it, "after one of Mrs. Neilson's luncheons anybody would have voted 'yes' on anything."

The fourteen always lunched or dined at the President's House and all of them thought of the Neilsons as personal friends. Some of these connections extended themselves into family friendships, like that with the Dwight Morrows; the Neilsons visited them in Mexico, when Morrow was ambassador, and frequently in Maine, and the three Morrow daughters, all undergraduates during Neilson's tenure, were at home in the President's House.

On many of the committees of the Board Neilson sat either ex officio or by his own choice. The Committee on Dormitories he left to the care of the alumnae trustees but he was always an active member of the Committee on Buildings and Grounds. On the Committee on Honorary Degrees he thought himself something of a figurehead though he warmly encouraged the traditional Smith practice of granting comparatively few honorary degrees, giving most of them to women, and selecting those women as examples, each in her profession, of the qualities Smith was trying to develop in her students. There was an inclination, too, to prefer to the nationally conspicuous figure the woman who has done work of a kind which does not lend itself to publicity. The citations, which Neilson wrote and delivered himself, often stressed these points.

Mary Kirkbride . . . Assistant Director of the Division of Laboratories and Research of the New York State Department of Health, an able organizer, a tactful administrator, a fruitful investigator; brilliant example of that class of scientists whose achievements are recognized by their peers but who are content to work without notice from the larger public to whose health and safety they devote their lives.

Josephine Roche . . . President of the Rocky Mountain Fuel Company, a woman who has succeeded where many men have failed in an attempt best described in the words of the contract made between her and her union workers: "to establish industrial justice, to substitute reason for violence, confidence for misunderstanding, integrity and good faith for dishonest practices, and a union of effort for the chaos of the present economic warfare."

Eunice Hunton Carter, A.B., A.M., Smith College, of the class of 1921, Deputy Assistant District Attorney of New York County, whose distinguished record as an undergraduate has been followed by seventeen years of public service, in which her brilliant abilities have been devoted to the welfare of her city and have brought high credit to her college and her race.

Beatrix Cadwalader Jones Farrand . . . leading exponent in America of landscape architecture as a profession for women, who by her own creations and by the force of her example has added to the loveliness of the campuses of our universities . . . and has by her taste and imagination promoted the recognition of beauty as a necessary element in the American environment.

About his share in the work of the Finance Committee Neilson was modest. He spoke, and thought, of himself as an interested amateur among experts, but the experts frequently admired the wisdom of his judgments and the acumen of his suggestions. Reporting to the alumnae in 1935, for instance, George Stevens, a Hartford banker, member of the trustees' Investment Committee, announced the proposed construction of two new dormitories, and concluded:

President Neilson worked out the plan for financing the construction of the dormitories. It is a sound plan and far better than any that the rest of us had been able to think of. How great and how multiform is the debt we owe to that man!

The whole relationship between the administration and the trustees had a warmth which is not common in college governments. Neilson spoke with perfect candor when he said in his formal letter of resignation:

The twenty-two years I have spent here have been the most satisfying part of my life. The tasks which you have entrusted to me have given whatever capacities I possess the fullest scope. I am well aware of many things left undone and still more imperfectly done; but in spite of these my experience here has given me all and more than a man has a right to expect from life. The conditions that have made this possible have been created by you. No one could ask for a greater degree of cooperation, confidence, and generosity than you have given. I have never been conscious of a flaw in our relations, which have always been those of friends working together with a single eye for the welfare of the institution.

17

The President and the Campus

"I AM going to talk on some of the satisfactions of a college president," said Neilson to the Alumnae Council in the winter of 1930.

Bacon, in his essay on Gardens, speaks of the planting of a garden as being one of the purest of human pleasures. The purest of the experiences of the college president in the planting of the garden is the manipulation of the landscape around the college.

Neilson began his manipulation early for he saw almost at once that what the Smith College campus needed was the clearing away of obstructions that everyone had come to take for granted. With the excrescences out of the way, vistas opened which added to Smith's assets some well-composed views of Connecticut Valley hills and meadows. By the simple process, for instance, which he suggested in 1922, of removing from the banks of Paradise Pond the ruins of the old McCallum stocking factory, an ancient outgrown laundry, and a few frame buildings which could be set up elsewhere, Neilson presented to the students walking back and forth between classrooms and new dormitories a fine picture of Mt. Tom rising from green river meadows. The clearing of brush and the grading of slopes in various parts of the grounds encouraged further co-operation of art and nature and Smith began to take a new pleasure in her campus. Neilson's chief collaborator in this, and in all such good works, was Franklin King, for fifty years superintendent of Smith's grounds and buildings.

When Lilly Hall, the physics building, was under construction in 1886 President Seelye was struck by the qualities of one of the young carpenters who worked on it. He enlisted him in the permanent service of the College, one of the most fortunate, as Neilson put it, among the "thousand wise things that President Seelye did." By the time Neilson took office Franklin King was at the head of a body of one hundred and twenty-five skilled and devoted workers known affectionately to the community as "the King's Men." One of them, his son, the "Crown Prince," eventually succeeded him in office. The attitude of the King's Men, that they were not just employees but members of Smith College, was strengthened by Neilson who treated them as experts and as friends. They enjoyed his personal interest in them and their families and they recognized in him a fellow-craftsman who really knew when their work was good. There is a tale of a mason who, when he was coming down with influenza, declined to give up and go home because "nobody knows how these bricks should be laid except me and the President." Some of the workers even felt that the President taught them their jobs. Important among these was Samuel Bothwell, for many years a Campus Cop regarded with affection by eight hundred student bicyclists and even by the members of the faculty to whom he gave parking tickets. Bothwell maintained that he learned the proper way to assert authority by watching President Neilson. An engineer on the Boston and Main Railroad, Bothwell was laid off during the depression and went to Mr. King for any job he could get. He was disconcerted to find himself a campus traffic policeman. He did not like the idea, he said, of wearing a uniform and being cross to people. But his first day on duty near the chapel, he was greeted by President Neilson, and then began to watch the way the head of the institution talked to the men and women he met and how they responded. "I saw that you didn't have to be haughty; you could get people to do things by joking with them." One of the things Bothwell came to like best about his job was the opportunity it gave him for a daily exchange of banter with the President. They were both great cigar smokers and the President's envy of Bothwell's cigars, when he was forbidden to smoke because of his ulcer, was a favorite joke between them. How well Bothwell learned to enforce authority pleasantly one may gather from the note he used to leave in cars parked over time: "The management of the Smith College campus is regretfully obliged to call your attention to your violation of the posted rule against parking on the campus for more than thirty minutes."

Another friendship between the President and a campus guardian began on the evening in September 1917 when John Doleman, who had been night watchman since 1896, found a strange man inspecting the college buildings with a minute and curious interest. " 'Oo are ye now?" demanded John, who never departed from his cockney origins. "I thought," replied the stranger, "that I was the new President of the College." "Come on now, none o' that; 'oo are ye and what are ye doin' 'ere?" When the stranger congratulated him on knowing his business, John capitulated and decided that he liked the new President. Five years later, announcing John's death to the College, Neilson paid warm tribute to "one of the most familiar and beloved figures of our community":

> He has looked after the interests of the College with a zeal and skill which it is hard to exaggerate. He knew more people than anyone else in this College. He was known by more people. The kind of service that he performed is a kind of service that can never be bought and can never be paid for.

More than any other members of the staff, perhaps, the college gardeners received Neilson as a peer; he thoroughly understood their craft and liked to talk with them about it on his walks across the campus. When they learned that he was fond of the gold and white blossoms of the Cherokee rose they saw to it that some sprays of it were on his breakfast table on every morning of its brief period of bloom. Among trees, they discovered, he particularly liked the rowan (its American equivalent is the mountain ash), so some were planted for his pleasure. Neilson knew every tree on the campus and once, W. I. P. Campbell, the head gardener, related with admiration, won from him a bet of two cigars when he insisted that there was no tulip tree near Park House. A memorial to these various horticultural bonds flourishes on the Smith campus. One morning in May 1939, a month before Neilson was to retire, he found on his calendar an appointment with Campbell. This was a frequent occurrence and one he always enjoyed, nor was he surprised to be asked to step outside and give his opinion on a new tree, but he was completely taken aback to be met at the door of College Hall by a kilted piper playing "Hail to the Chief." The piper conducted him to the spot where, before the 1938 hurricane, a tall American elm had stood. There Campbell, born in Ayr and trained at the Edinburgh Botanical Garden, was joined by two other gardeners, natives respectively of Aberdeen and the Isle of Skye, and the three asked their countryman from Doune to plant a young Scotch elm they were presenting to the College in his honor. They took pleased note that he handled the spade they offered him as though he were planting a tree, not laying a cornerstone. The other members of the department of buildings and grounds presented the President with a farewell gift of a watch as "a token of their esteem and affection" for the man who, "as long as most of them have worked here, has been the head of the College and a friend and adviser of all."

Yet for all his love of growing things Neilson knew when not to be sentimental about them. The hurricane of 1938, which uprooted more than two hundred trees on the Smith campus, he called "one of those winds that blew somebody good."

> We have lost a great deal, but it is not all loss. We are here, as people generally are in this country, tree worshipers. We do not have courage to cut enough trees even to give the rest air and space, and to provide the views for which sometimes we have placed the houses where they stand. The wind came along, and the houses discover that once they looked over the range, and now they look over the range again.

The cutting and planting on the Smith campus had always been done under the supervision, when they could find time for it, of overburdened professors of botany. In 1934 Neilson succeeded in persuading the trustees to appoint a landscape architect, trained at the Cambridge School, who accomplished precisely the kind of order he had hoped for, though certain basic inconveniences of arrangement inevitably remained.

I suppose every executive [he wrote in 1926 to an inquiring dean] has played with the idea of how he would arrange a campus if he had the chance to begin all over again. My own ideal scheme is one of concentric circles or concentric squares. I should put in the center buildings used by everybody, administration building, library, chapel, auditorium say, these four forming a central quadrangle. Outside them the recitation rooms, and laboratories; outside of these the dormitories; and outside of that the athletic fields, gymnasium, and baths.

For the mountain ranges, the river meadows, the elms and maples, the tobacco and onion fields of the Connecticut Valley, Neilson developed a deep affection. The roots of attachment to place which he had had to pull up from Doune he set down again in Northampton. (His fondness for Cambridge was an attachment to people, not to locality.) He liked to show Smith College and its setting to visitors from across the Atlantic, urging them to come if possible in the autumn or the spring when the Valley was at its loveliest.

Because he loved the Connecticut Valley and because his romanticism included a belief in the beneficial power of natural beauty, Neilson insisted on continuing the College's traditional "Mountain Day" even when the automobile began to alter its character. Early in Smith's history it had become the custom to designate a day in October when classes should be suspended and the students set free to hike or bicycle through the flaming autumn Valley, to climb Mt. Tom and the Holyoke Range, to picnic in the woods or river meadows. Mountain Day was marked on the college calendar as definitely as Thanksgiving. But in the twenties the automobile and postwar mores began to turn it, for a major portion of the student body, into one more excuse for going to Boston or New York, for communing with night clubs rather than nature. When the faculty began to consider its deletion Neilson invented an ingenious device of salvage: Mountain Day no longer appeared on the College Bulletin; instead, on some golden October morning of the President's choosing—and no one was ever very successful at predicting what morning he would choose—the chapel bell rang long and loud at seven o'clock and the College, faculty and students alike, knew that classes were for that day suspended and everyone might take to the hills. In 1931 when the opening of the College was delayed two weeks by a polio epidemic and adjustments had to be made in the calendar which necessitated the canceling of Mountain Day, Neilson broke the news to the students gathered for the First Chapel assembly by stating blandly, "Mountain Day was yesterday," a turn of phrase which so amused them that they responded with laughter instead of groans.

The process of building fascinated Neilson almost as much as the care of the college grounds. His letters to architects and contractors when a new dormitory was going up are full of ingenious suggestions. He could analyze a construction problem and devise a way out with the same swift invention that cut administrative tangles in the committee room. And he could nearly always invent some way of saving money. He concerned himself not only with the total structure of a building but with the smallest details, as conscientiously as though he were making an Elizabethan text. When it was discovered, for instance, after the Neilsons had moved into the new President's House in the spring of 1921, that one of the gutters was sagging so that it overflowed constantly during a rain, Neilson wrote to the architect:

> If a layman may butt into the matter I should suggest that instead of attempting to raise the gutter where it has sagged, you extend the lip of copper, which protects the steps from overflow at present, further to the right and left. If in addition you can put larger goosenecks right and left, I think we shall have little trouble with the gutter overflowing. Mr. King agrees with me that this is worth trying before deciding that the pitch of the gutter itself must be altered.

When the music building, Sage Hall, was in progress he wrote the architects, Delano and Aldrich, in January 1924:

> My impression was that if we had the natural brass finish on the hardware, it would have to be kept polished, and in a building as

large as yours this amounts to a good deal of labor. Tarnished brass on inside doors looks very much neglected. I admit, of course, that nicely polished brass is handsomer than the finish we ordered, but the up-keep is too expensive for our type of institution. It may be that you can show us some brass that has oxidized, as you suggest, that will convince us that we are wrong. The brass with the mat finish which we have in most of our biuldings has never worn streaked.

Dean Gildersleeve of Barnard, when she visited Northampton a few years after Neilson's installation, remarked with amusement his pleasure and interest in these details of college housekeeping which she and some of the other feminine heads of women's colleges had supposed he would find irksome. He told her, she recalls, with gusto just how he had managed to heat some of his buildings at a lower cost.

In these matters of ingenuity and economy Neilson found in Franklin King a collaborator after his own heart. In the erection of new buildings and the upkeep of the old they worked together with mutual pleasure and respect. It was one of King's extraordinary accomplishments that the Treasurer's books at Smith College showed no depreciation. The early dormitories put up under his eye were so well built and were for decades so well maintained that in the 1930's they were worth a great deal more than when they were erected; insurance companies insisted on putting on them a replacement value higher than their original cost. When the last two dormitories which Neilson built were finished in 1936 the trustees, at his suggestion, named one of them Laura Scales, for the Warden, and the other Franklin King. A year later, when Franklin King died, Neilson made on his pride of craftsmanship a little homily for the undergraduates.

In the passage I read from the Apocrypha there is a sentence that states that the master workman giveth not instruction. I don't agree with that. The master workman always giveth instruction though he does not speak a word. And the instruction that Mr. King contributed to the education of this College was the instruction that comes from the capable and complete achievement of the craftsman. He was trained as a carpenter. The abhorrence of his life was shoddy workmanship. Poor material he could not endure. What he built himself he built solid and straight, of stuff that would last, and the reason why he left the whole mass of buildings that were entrusted to him better than he found them was that he would not put into them cheap, insufficient, impermanent material and would not have them erected in any but a workmanlike fashion.

In a life like yours, crowded with things to do, there is constantly a temptation to do them poorly, hurriedly, and in a transitory fashion so that the results do not last. And this is the instruction his craftsmanship and his life give you—the permanent value to the man himself, the permanent value to society, of honest building and the beauty that comes with it. He was a workman who did not need to be ashamed of his work.

The first piece of building which Neilson supervised on the Smith campus was the Mason Infirmary which had been planned before he arrived. The next was the new President's House which had been one of the conditions of his coming to Smith. In April 1919 he had written to Mrs. Baldwin:

Mrs. Neilson and I are very anxious that both committees should understand that we realize the change in building conditions since the house was promised and are accordingly entirely willing to release the trustees from any obligation they may feel to proceed with this now. Personally I feel that it would be better not to proceed than to cut down the plans to a point that would entail an inadequate building, since we are making plans not for the Neilson family but for all future Presidents.

But the trustees were agreed that the College had lacked too long a proper official residence, so the house was built and, in May 1920, the Neilsons moved into their new home.

The architect, Neilson's old friend John W. Ames of Boston, succeeded in producing a President's House which actually satisfied not only the many official groups constantly entertained there but the first family to live in it and the very different presidential families who followed. Ames selected the site, on the south bank of Paradise Pond, and set the house cleverly so that the view from the terrace, down a green avenue bordered with trees, composed pleasantly, with the pond and river in the foreground and Mt. Tom in the distance, slightly to the left. The front door, 8 Paradise Road, was just far enough from a campus walk so that students bicycling to class could be seen but not too distinctly heard. The College was so pleased with the originality, ingenuity, and thrift of the firm of Ames and Dodge, that they invited them to undertake the planning of the dormitories which Neilson felt so important to the social life of the College. The style decided upon, a modified Georgian, was dictated partly by its appropriateness in the New England scene, partly by economy—you get much less for your money when you build in collegiate Gothic. The architects were fired by the problem of constructing that rarity a Georgian quadrangle and the result was pleasant and eminently functional. The well-proportioned buildings are made with a good red brick, their only ornaments a few dormers, a necessary bell and clocktower, and some flights of steps imposed by the irregular terrain. In naming these buildings Neilson introduced an innovation. They were named not in honor of donors or even of trustees but for distinguished older members of the faculty and for alumnae of the kind Smith College liked to present to her undergraduates as models.

In addition to the dormitories Neilson had the pleasure of supervising the construction of an excellent gymnasium—the College had long since outgrown the one erected in 1891—and a fine building, Sage Hall, for the department of music. The gymnasium was designed by Ames and Dodge, the music building by Delano and Aldrich of New York, who also proved able to combine good construction with economy. The Tryon Art Gallery, a large addition to the Library (the architect was Karl Putnam, a member of the department of art), and an Alumnae House were also erected during Neilson's administration, and much remodeling and repair was done on the older buildings.

One useful by-product of these extensive operations was that the President, during the summer months, took a really adequate amount of exercise. Every afternoon, after tea, or sometimes after dinner in the long twilights, he made a careful inspection of the work that had gone on that day, studying it in the large and in detail. He understood precisely what was being done and the contractors said that if there was any careless bit of construction he was sure to discover it. These tours of inspection were for him not so much a duty as a pleasure; he could anticipate the effect the finished structure would have on the life of the College, and he took great pleasure in the sight of good craftsmanship. Most of what he saw was very good; only one thing about American workmen really troubled him—their extravagant wastefulness. Evening after evening Neilson came home his pockets stuffed with coils of wire or fine new nails which had been tossed away when a particular job was finished. His bureau was constantly littered with this salvage which he kept hoping it would be possible to put to some good use.

Neilson took as much interest in interior details as he did in matters of construction. A student Ivy Day orator in 1939, enumerating the ways in which the undergraduates thought of the President, concluded: "We see him down on one knee in some dormitory drawing room looking at the undersides of the chairs to see whether the upholstery is holding up as it should." The decorators, most of them alumnae, who planned the furnishings of the various dormitories were delighted as well as amused by his expert knowledge and by his concern with detail. He continually popped in and out of a new house when they were installing rugs and curtains; he appreciated their ideas about color; he was interested when they suggested trying photomurals or scenic wallpaper or using a fine painting to set the tone of a room; he made practical suggestions about having adjoining dining rooms that could be thrown together for large banquets or breaking up the arrangement of living room furniture so that "two peas won't occupy the whole plate"; and he gave them always a free hand, except for his insistence that beauty, which he thought important in undergraduate surroundings, should never involve pretence or show.

One reason for the stress Neilson placed on dormitory furnishing and decoration was the enjoyment he took in the beauty and order of his own home, where Mrs. Neilson's hand had managed a skilful blend of dignity, comfort, and individuality, so that the transition from official to family hospitality was effortless and inconspicuous. His wife's ability in these matters strengthened Neilson's conviction that it is the woman who controls American taste. That was one of his favorite arguments for the higher education of the sex.

Your American husbands [he told the New York alumnae in 1920] have taste and they are quite capable of exercising it, but they are too bored, too busy, too lazy, too stupid—pick out the adjective that fits your own case best—to take an interest in matters of taste that affect their lives and yours. . . The furnishing of the home, the choosing of its colors, the buying of pictures, the determination of the whole tone which in turn determines the children's judgments, as well as the man's aesthetic satisfaction, rests with the women. The American man cares very much about having his home beautiful. He does not realize what it depends upon; he does not realize how completely he is evading a great responsibility.

The front door of the President's House opens into a wide hall, two stories high, which forms the center of the house. Glass doors on the opposite side lead onto the terrace but, even in winter, the hall is large enough for the big receptions, for faculty, alumnae, parents, which are essential features in collegiate hospitality. On the right, at right angles to the hall, runs the living room, its paneling painted grey-green, a bay window, a fireplace, and a piano breaking it into pleasant smaller sections. It was always full of flowers arranged by Mrs. Neilson with a care for color and composition which made them as decorative as paintings. And she added a decorative note herself, as she received, charming in a white evening gown or in some subtle shade of blue.

On the other side of the great hall are a suite for official guests, the dining room, and the kitchen. It is not a state dining room. Official dinners seldom numbered more than eight or ten, for the Neilsons believed in general conversation. Mrs. Neilson was a connoisseur in talkers as she was in musicians and composed a dinner party as she would have organized an orchestra. She said sometimes that she wished she did not always have to invite a wife on the same night as her husband; even when she liked them both she often felt that their particular tones could be brought out better in different companies.

Mrs. Neilson believed, too, in food as a stimulus to talk and the presidential menus were unusual and delicious. The visiting dignitary, savoring them in comfortable content, seldom suspected what planning, labor, and inspired resolution of crises had been necessary to produce that exquisite European repast. The mill town of Northampton did not abound in trained domestic workers—presidential cooks had often to be imported from Boston, New York, or even the West Indies—but Mrs. Neilson, with her various governesses and assistants, usually French or German, managed miracles. One of her accomplishments was the training of a succession of little Polish girls, daughters of Connecticut Valley farmers, whom Neilson christened the Half-Pints.

The larger entertainments, teas, receptions, Washington's Birthday and Commencement luncheons, had the same tone of effortless perfection—even though the hostess was sometimes making sandwiches herself until the final moment. "My sandwich degree" she insisted on calling the honorary Doctor of Humane Letters which the trustees voted to confer upon her in 1939. She demurred at first when she was informed of their intention, convinced that degrees are intended only as rewards for academic accomplishment, but they succeeded in convincing her that the honor might properly be bestowed in recognition of a contribution to the general richness of academic life. "Presiding genius of the President's House" was the phrase her husband used in his citation, and genius was, as usual, the precise noun. Precise, too, was the adjective, not yet debased by advertisers, which students and alumnae invariably used in describing Mrs. Neilson—gracious. The class of 1937, for instance, dedicated its yearbook to "Elisabeth Muser Neilson whose presence on our campus adds to the dignity and graciousness of life at Smith College."

That same sense of American admiration for qualities just out of reach of a younger civilization colors nearly every reference to her. She carried with her, quite unintentionally, an aura of the regal, of a minor court, and this, intensified perhaps by her own shyness, made many of the faculty a little shy with her. She never extended her intimate circle very far. People usually thought of her as much less interested in the College than she really was, for she did not care for gossip and she was discreet. No one in Northampton ever knew how well acquainted she was with college affairs, how many of his problems her husband talked over with her in detail, on which ones her judgment, which she deprecated as non-academic but he valued for its intuitive wisdom, had thrown light. Though she by no means fitted their picture of the conventional college president's wife, the New England institution was grateful for the European touch she lent it. This was pleasantly augmented by a long visit paid by her parents, 1920 to 1922. Frau Muser, not in very good health, did not often leave the house, though the College came to look with pleasure at every concert for a glimpse of the charming little old lady with the lace cap. Herr Muser, on the other hand, rapidly became a campus favorite. He was interested in everything, went to classes, attended lectures, concerts, plays, and talked to everyone he met so delightfully that his return to Germany was as much regretted as the retirement of a favorite member of the faculty.

The second story of the President's House was as well planned as the first. Across the terrace end of the entrance hall ran a sort of gallery large enough to be used as an upstairs sitting room. To the right were the family bedrooms; to the left the President's study. This was a square room with windows looking towards the hills. The woodwork was painted white; bookshelves lined the four walls with, below, the kind of cupboards all scholars dream of for the storage of manuscripts and monographs. Over the fireplace hung a portrait of Professor Child. The desk stood in the middle of the room. There were one or two deep chairs and enough others to accommodate the Shakespeare seminar which met here on Thursday afternoons. Except for that, it was a place of retreat, for meditation and scholarship and writing. Interviews and committee meetings took place in the office in College Hall.

The Neilsons breakfasted usually at seven forty-five, and then the President spent a few moments in his study, looking at the newspaper and making his final preparations for morning chapel at eight-thirty. John M. Greene Hall, where all the large exercises of the College were held, was only a five minute walk, so that he always arrived before he had finished his cigar. One of the chapel organists recalls with amusement how he would put that cigar on an ashtray in the choir room, slip into his gown, and go onto the platform at precisely the indicated moment to conduct the service with invariable dignity, but how, as soon as the ceremony was over and he had followed the choir out, before he took off his gown, the cigar, still burning, was in his mouth again.

In his office, where he worked from nine till one, Neilson could smoke as much as he pleased and his incessant smoking seemed to agree with him, as did his practice of taking no exercise at all except the brisk little walks from home to office. The children lunched with their parents but Mr. and Mrs. Neilson had their coffee afterwards alone, for this was often the only moment in the day when they could talk without the presence of someone else. After that the President took a few minutes rest and went back to his office, theoretically till five but often till much later. He and Mrs. Neilson always had tea when he got home, even if they drank it just before dinner, and, when business permitted, teatime was an hour of leisure shared frequently with good friends like Leland Hall, the Fays and Welches.

Dinner was at six-thirty and when there were neither guests present nor lectures to be attended afterwards Neilson read aloud to the children for an hour before going up to his study for the evening's work, which might be college business, the planning of a speech, or the correcting of proof. For general reading of his own Neilson never had as much time as he wanted, though he managed a great deal of it whenever he made a journey by boat or train. Letters of thanks for a book say often that it looks "tempting" and that "I am watching for an opportunity to indulge myself."

By eleven-thirty the President was usually in bed, and he is probably one of the few executives of whom it can be said that he nearly always slept soundly and well. He had a capacity for leaving his worries—all except the very serious ones—on his desk in College Hall.

That is the outline of a normal presidential day, but the normal days were, of course, few. There was a perpetual flow of guests, of dinners, of evening meetings, and trips out of town. Neilson could accomplish rather more in twenty-four hours than most men, partly because his body moved so fast. Manual actions, like dressing or packing a suitcase, he performed at a speed which left even his family, after long custom, breathless. His wife was at first alarmed when, as they walked together in some strange city, he would suddenly vanish from her side. Finally she learned to look about for a tobacconist's sign and usually, before she had found it, her husband was coming out of the door of the shop with a fresh supply of cigars.

His mind worked with the same speed and with an exhilarating gayety. Anyone who talked with Neilson for ten minutes came away as buoyant as though he had been breathing mountain air. A member of the faculty, meeting a colleague on the campus, could tell from the way he walked that he had been having a conference with the President. And this perpetual sharing of vitality seemed to refresh, not exhaust him. The constant intercourse with people which many executives find wearing was to him a pleasure. His interest in people was practically inexhaustible. Mrs. Neilson once admitted to an inquiring reporter that, when they first came to Northampton, "I tried to protect him from so many visitors (I believe he is the most accessible college president in the world), but I soon learned that I did not help him in that way. For one thing, he knows best about whom he should see. For another, people do not tire him."

The presidential energy seemed so rich and inexhaustible that it was not until 1932 when an increasingly troublesome stomach condition was diagnosed as ulcer that most of his constituency realized that the President was ever subject to weakness or pain. The Scottish reticence, which regarded illness as a purely personal matter with which one did not trouble other people, had concealed from most of the college community the fact that the Scottish energy sometimes flagged. The same reticence prevented Neilson from complaining when, towards the end of his regime, he began to be increasingly troubled by deafness. When he found it difficult to catch all the questions and comments in a large company, he simply strained his quick eye and wit the more. He tried, in vain, a variety of remedies for the deafness but it did not occur to him to talk to his colleagues about it.

When the ulcer diagnosis had been made and a regimen prescribed, Neilson followed it scrupulously as he performed all duties. He drank his milk, subsisted on a far duller diet than he enjoyed, and, most difficult of all, ceased to smoke. The sight of the President without a cigar was so startling that everybody on campus began to worry about him but, though there were some serious periods of illness and enforced rest, the trouble improved and in a few years was well under control.

Far more of a drain upon him than his own ill health were the illnesses of his family, not the regulation colds and chicken pox—Mrs. Neilson coped effectively with those—but the rheumatic fever which struck both his elder children, Allan in the spring of 1925; Margaret, a year later. For many months they were confined to bed and both parents were subjected to a long strain of anxiety and wearying care. After the 1926 Commencement, when his college duties were a little lighter, Neilson sent his wife off to Germany to see her parents and "to get relief from the clinical thermometer," and took on himself the responsibility of supervising treatments and keeping two active minds entertained. In the course of the summer he read aloud to the children nearly all of Shakespeare's plays. "You have no idea how domestic I have become," runs a letter declining a week-end invitation, "making up the arrears of many years of negligence."

Margaret made an excellent recovery but Allan grew worse and worse. He understood quite well that he would never recover and faced the fact with extraordinary maturity and courage. On 1 December 1926 he died. The parents were so bowed with grief that they could scarcely afterwards bear to speak his name.

In Milton Academy hangs a commemorative tablet, the inscription written by Miss Comstock:

> Allan Neilson of the Class of 1928. 1909-1926. Not too young to hate meanness, to love beauty and honor and to end manfully.

18

The President as Scholar

THE crux of the scholar-president has never been solved. Scholarship requires not only time but consecutive time, and that it is difficult for an administrator to command. The Smith trustees acted with wisdom and generosity when they agreed to release their scholar-president from the burden of money raising. That gave him time to think about the problems of learning and teaching, but not time for the continuation of his own studies. Neilson had known, of course, when he made the decision to go to Northampton, that he could not teach as much or write as much as he had done in Cambridge but he thought that he would be able to command some hours a week at least for those two occupations which he loved. His study of Allegory, designed for the Types of Literature series he was editing for Houghton Mifflin, was three-fourths completed. He took the manuscript with him hopefully.

During the first two years of his presidency Neilson did not try to teach at all, devoting his entire attention to learning the details of his new and complex job. But in 1920 his former pupil Robert Withington, who was directing the sophomore Historical Survey of English Literature, asked him to give the weekly lectures in the course and he agreed. Having agreed, he kept conscientiously to the schedule, declining to let any but the most pressing administrative demands interfere. Withington used to call for him at his office about ten minutes before the Monday morning lecture hour and, while they walked the brief distance across the campus, Neilson would ask what the lecture that day was to be about. Then he fell silent for a few moments, arranging an outline in his mind, and stepped briskly onto the platform to speak to the big room full of students interestingly, informatively, often brilliantly. His younger colleagues, who taught the sections in the course, noted with admiration that every essential fact and date seemed to be immediately at his command, as though he had reviewed the subject the night before, that the emphases fell where one would wish to have them, and that the exposition was so lucid and provocative that the most somnolent sophomore could not choose but hear.

The next year Neilson taught, in addition to the survey, a graduate seminar in "Shakespeare: Special Problems," a course like that which generations of Harvard graduate students had thought exciting. The young women of Smith were no less enthusiastic, though Neilson found them inconveniently timid and less inclined than the men to be disputatious. On their side, the students made one complaint. They were planning, most of them, to be teachers and wanted to study the methods by which their teachers operated, but in a Neilson seminar so many things happened so fast that it was impossible to analyze the elements which made the hours exhilarating. All they could manage to discern was that the basis of the Neilson method seemed to be the posing of ingeniously stimulating questions. The seminar met on Thursday afternoons in the white paneled study in the President's House. At four o'clock Mrs. Neilson sent in tea, which Neilson insisted on pouring himself that there might be no dawdling over amenities. The time was always too short for the topics he wanted to cover.

In this teaching Neilson took great satisfaction, until, in 1926, he found that his students were asking him questions which he could not really answer: what did he think of this new theory, of that premise or discovery? He realized with a shock that, though he was aware of recent developments in Shakespearean scholarship, he had not had leisure to examine them in detail, to study and evaluate them as he would have done in Cambridge, and to formulate an opinion worth expressing. He was distressed by the idea that he was working behind rather than ahead of his students. It was not fair, he thought, to offer them a course ten years out of date. He asked his colleague, and appointee, Professor Esther Dunn, to take over the seminar. He dissociated himself at the same time from his lecturing in English 19. He kept his name hopefully on the roster of the English department in the catalogue and occasionally substituted for a colleague who was ill but that was all. The consequent loss to the profession was great. The students, his colleagues thought, would have benefited much from his instruction, even if it were not quite abreast of current scholarship, but that kind of incomplete performance Neilson's integrity did not permit him.

At about the same time he wrote to a younger scholar that, "My plans with regard to Allegory have been so long postponed by my change in profession that I do not think I have any rights in the field." A few years earlier, making the presidential address at the annual meeting of the Modern Language Association, he had concluded his remarks to the scholars before him with a plea to

> think of the branch of the profession to which I now belong less as arrogant autocrats than as harmless necessary drudges, whom you may use to rid you of thankless and vexatious tasks. So at least I seek to comfort myself as at long intervals I revisit the dusty shelves of my unused library, and open a volume here and there with a poignant sense of exile.

The by-products of scholarship—reviews, encyclopaedia articles, popular lectures—work that could be accomplished, in his phrase, by "simply skimming the top of your mind," Neilson the President managed very well. In the twenties he made his peace with the *Nation* and enjoyed reviewing for them books on Shakespeare and on Scottish literature and language which not many Americans were equipped to discuss. In the thirties Henry Canby pressed him into occasional service for his *Saturday Review of Literature*. Pronouncements on current problems in education Neilson was, of course, continually urged to make and this he did readily when he thought that he had anything substantial to say. He wrote on "Overcrowding in Women's Colleges" for the *Nation* (13 May 1925), "Should Women be Educated like Men?" for the *Forum* (February 1929), "Are American Colleges Wasteful?" for *Scribner's* (June 1932), "Education Can't be Better than the Teachers" for the *Survey Graphic* (October 1939). When he thought that he had nothing fresh to contribute to a discussion he declined to be drawn, and was quite frank about the reason.

The educational articles, probably because he had already treated the topics in speeches, have a greater ease of style than most of Neilson's writing. Without the immediate presence of an interlocutor his words seldom warmed into life. He found it difficult even to write letters. "I write only to my wife," he would say, and there is an illuminating confession in a note to Mrs. Roy Welch, to whom he occasionally paid what he called "the all but unprecedented compliment of a letter written with my own hand."

> After I got your letter I thought that I had all day Sunday to think about what I should write you—that is the only part of letter writing I really enjoy. When I take a pen, a panic to finish seizes me, and I cannot surrender myself to converse with anyone on paper as one gives one's self up luxuriously to the prospect of a long talk —or a long silence.

The same thing happened when he tried to write out a speech ahead of time. He knew always what ideas he wanted to convey and he liked to plot beforehand the order of his presentation. On the train on his way to a meeting, or in a brief interval before a dinner he would jot down an outline on the back of an envelope or a sheet of hotel stationery, but the living form that skeleton took would depend entirely on the nature of the audience he found before him, on their age, their intelligence, their response. He preferred, for that reason, a homogeneous audience. "You are not here," he would sometimes say to the parents and teachers at a school commencement. "You may overhear, if you like, but I am talking to the members of the senior class." To reporters and publicity directors who asked for advance copies of his addresses he was apologetic, but their requests seemed to him stupid; one does not talk to oneself; one communicates. When Neilson spoke on the platform the impact of his words was intensified by the quality of his voice, by the excellence of his diction—cosmopolitan, with some British cadences but no trace of Scots—by his sense of pause and timing, but even the stenographic transcripts of his speeches have a vividness which his pen generated only in occasional sentences.

The longest piece of writing Neilson did during the Smith presidency was the school *History of English Literature* (1921) which he and Ashley Thorndike had undertaken to prepare for Macmillan shortly before Neilson went to Northampton. In 1921 also Harcourt, Brace issued *Selections from Chaucer,* edited by Neilson and his colleague Howard Patch. When President Eliot died, in the summer of 1926, the selection from his speeches and writings which Neilson had made for Collier some years before, was hurried into print. From a brief essay he had written for the *Nation* (19 March 1924) on "President Eliot at Ninety," Neilson elaborated a prefatory Biographical Study which has the insights and the significant emphases of qualities which distinguish his character studies of retiring members of the Smith faculty.

These pieces of work, good in themselves, were, from the scholar's point of view, somewhat too brief and disconnected to be satisfying, but Neilson found, before he was halfway through his administrative term, a consecutive piece of scholarly labor in which he could take pride and which he could carry on without neglecting his administrative duties. This was made possible, in part, by a happy geographic accident. In 1924 Asa S. Baker, President of the Merriam Company in Springfield, asked him to assume the editorship of their second edition of Webster's New International Dictionary. The project immediately fired Neilson's imagination. His admiration for Webster's Dictionary was great: "There is probably no book that has been written in a hundred years that has done so much in this respect [education] for the country at large as his Dictionary." Here, in the editing of the new edition, was work for a philologist of the most important kind. Here was work for an administrator with a wide knowledge of the academic world; the recruiting of a staff of editors and consultants would present problems much like those of appointing a college faculty. The offices of the G. and C. Merriam Company were less than an hour from the Smith campus. He accepted the appointment as editor-in-chief and began his duties in the fall of 1924.

Editorship by college presidents was part of the Merriam-Webster tradition. The 1864 edition, known as Webster's Unabridged, was edited by Noah Porter, seven years before he became President of Yale. Porter also directed the 1890 revision with the assistance of President Ira Remsen of the Johns Hopkins. It was an honorable succession, indicative of the spirit that had informed the work since Noah Webster began it in 1828. That first edition of the American Dictionary of the English Language was financed by the profits from Webster's enormously successful American Spelling Book, which supported his family while he worked on the Dictionary, and, though the first edition of the Dictionary sold slowly, Webster proceeded with a revision which he published in 1840. After his death the unsold copies and the publishing rights were purchased by the G. and C. Merriam Company who revised the Dictionary and issued it, in 1847, in a single volume at six dollars. This sold so well that they were able to pay the Webster family a huge royalty and to move their offices to larger quarters in Springfield. Revised editions were issued in 1864, 1890, and 1909. "Webster's," said Albert Bushnell Hart, the Harvard historian, on the completion of Neilson's edition, "is one of the elements of America's civilization, a continuous work carried on from generation to generation."

When Neilson began his editorship he arranged to spend alternate Tuesday mornings in Springfield, going down by an early train and spending sometimes the morning, sometimes the whole day. He was very regular about this, missing a Tuesday only when college business required him to be away from Northampton. No member of the faculty, however urgent his business, thought of asking for an appointment on a Springfield Tuesday.

The first task which Neilson and Baker undertook was the selection of an editorial staff and of special consultants—they numbered 207—who would pass on definitions in their respective fields. As general editor they appointed with satisfaction Professor

Thomas Knott of the University of Iowa. This was, of course, a full-time position which required the resignation of his professorship, but Neilson persuaded him that he would find his scholarly competence and professional prestige increased by his association with the Dictionary.

Most of the discussion of appointments and other problems was carried on verbally but, since neither Baker nor Neilson liked doing business by telephone, some lively letters went back and forth between Northampton and Springfield.

NEILSON TO BAKER

26 August 1925

Logan Pearsall Smith is a member of a well-known and distinguished family of Philadelphia. His sisters are Mrs. Bernard Berenson and the first Mrs. Bertrand Russell. I think that President Thomas of Bryn Mawr is a cousin. I have thought of him as a somewhat elegant gentleman of leisure who would prefer to live in England and write little essays. I gather, however, that his book on words and idioms has a good deal of learning in it with some tendency to be arbitrary. I should think it very unlikely that he would be willing to work in harness even if he turned out to be properly equipped. So far as I know he has never held any academic or business position, and I suspect that he is too much of a kid-glove person for our purposes.

30 August 1926

Your definition of "tappit-hen" seems to me all that it is safe to say. I am not sure that anything more than "crested hen" is meant in the poem. I presume that your correspondent gives it a Freudian twist, but I don't think the dictionary is obliged to enter into the more precarious kind of literary interpretation.

Baker, Neilson, and Knott, with Paul Carhart, the managing editor, formed the editorial board which settled the Dictionary's policies, making hundreds of decisions ranging from the choice of editors to details of typography and punctuation. Their discussions were often heated. The other members of the staff listened with amusement to the sounds of conflict that seeped through the boardroom doors. A dictionary must be right and dictionary makers are not inclined to compromise, but the contenders emerged always on the best of terms. The various editors, when they took part in the Tuesday conferences, were impressed by Neilson's skill in presiding over the hot debates, by his ability to analyze a situation, reduce a question to its essentials, and bring the contending parties to an agreement. They were pleased, too, to find that he understood and was ready to make allowance for the demands of business, and they discovered with satisfaction that he wished to function not only as a supervising but as a working editor. He was not, they thought, a profoundly learned philologist, like Professor Harold Bender of Princeton who wrote the Dictionary's etymologies, but his knowledge was sound and his comments were wise and useful. He took special charge of a few minor divisions, such as Scottish words and British university terms. He made, too, many practical suggestions, for instance, the desirability of bringing the examples of word use up to date by replacing some of those in the 1909 edition with quotations from modern fiction. He increased the corps of readers for this kind of work by enlisting some interested students from Smith and Mt. Holyoke.

The publication of the Dictionary was celebrated on 25 June 1934 with a dinner at which Neilson presided as toastmaster, but the Merriam Company had no intention of letting his service end there. He collaborated with Knott in the editing of a Middle English Dictionary and supervised the editing of Webster's Dictionary of Synonyms (1942) and Webster's Biographical Dictionary (1943). In synonyms Neilson was even more interested than in definitions. He read every word of the copy for the synonym dictionary, often taking sheafs of it with him when he went on a train journey and returning it with detailed suggestions and annotations:

Candy: I don't know what currency *praline* (a chocolate) and *fondant* (a soft candy) have in English. The latter was familiar to me in Scotland sixty years ago. It was an amusing elegance in the speech of the lady in the "sweetie shop."

Ride and *drive:* Is it not the case that there is a difference between British and American usage in these words? *Ride* is much more used in America. I remember when a "buggy ride" or to "ride in a buggy" seemed odd to me (in Canada). In Britain we *took* a train or *went in* a train but never *rode*. Automobiles, of course, did not exist. It is an eight-hour *journey* from London to Edinburgh, but a twenty-hour *ride* from New York to Chicago.

While these various dictionaries were in progress, and after, the Merriam Company kept Neilson in collaboration on the preparations for Webster's New International Dictionary, Third Edition, which they projected at some time in the sixties. When a speaker at the 1934 celebration of the Second Edition had expressed his satisfaction in the knowledge that on the next morning the Merriam Company would "begin another collection for another dictionary," Baker had interrupted to say that his congratulations were just a little late—"We have already started that adventure." It was an adventure that Neilson highly enjoyed. While it did not return him to the world of scholarship, it kept his equipment from rusting altogether, making it possible for him to approximate, at least, the role he had hoped to create of scholar-president.

19

The President off the Campus

THE American college president has always been regarded by the community as a kind of general public servant whose opinion on any subject they are entitled to ask and on whose services they have the right to draw. Their point of view is that of the villagers of Doune who expected Neilson's schoolmaster father to do their surveying for them without charge. Part of the time the public-serving president spends outside his campus gates is distinctly beneficial to his college; part of it distracts him from his real job. His problem is to strike a balance.

Well expended, certainly, from the Smith College point of view, were the time and energy Neilson devoted to the service of the City of Northampton. The town and gown relationship never flared there, of course, into the kind of violent conflict sometimes engendered by men's colleges. Northampton was, on the whole, proud of Smith, though some anxious civic glances were cast as the College's tax-free property increased; the manners of two thousand lively young women did not always conform to conservative New England standards; the politics of the faculty were frequently disapproved; and, with notable exceptions, the academic community was inclined to live as a group apart. The Smith-Northampton relationship, therefore, was temperate rather than warm. When a new President of Smith arrived in 1917 the city was polite to him but non-committal. No New England community takes anyone to its heart without scrutiny and Neilson had several characteristics which aroused suspicion.

He was, to begin with, "foreign born" and his wife was German. Not long after his arrival he made a public address on the necessity of tolerance towards our enemies, crediting the Germans with more virtues than the average American was ready to do at that time. Where to place him politically the city could not tell, for he declined to enroll himself as either a Democrat or a Republican, but gossip had it that he had made some wittily disparaging remarks about Northampton's first citizen, Calvin Coolidge. Disturbing, too, was Neilson's refusal to ally himself with any of the local churches. The Protestant clergymen called on him in turn, urging the importance of "setting an example" of church-going to his undergraduates, but he insisted on keeping the religious independence he had maintained from boyhood.

Distrust wore off slowly. Many of the citizens of Northampton met Neilson personally and liked him. They learned that he responded with swift generosity to appeals for local good works of any kind or for cases of individual need. They heard him speak, on subjects other than Germany, and thought him sound. They watched the flourishing of Smith College under his guidance and felt that it reflected credit upon the city. But what eventually most endeared him to them—and the expressions of regret at his retirement carry as much affection as regard—was the daily evident fact that he thought of himself not simply as President of Smith College but as a citizen of Northampton, who was glad to serve the community in any way he could. When, in 1939, Neilson left the Connecticut Valley, he took with him a leather-bound volume of "personal letters," so the superscription ran, "from up and down the streets of a grateful city." The letters are typed on the letterheads of pharmacists, clothiers, florists, manufacturers, of doctors, dentists, bankers, lawyers, of the daily paper, the public schools, the post office, the offices of the local government, churches of all denominations. They express the writers' pleasure in associations with Neilson as a member of the Chamber of Commerce, of the Monday Club, of Rotary, as an adviser to the Hampshire Bookshop, as a trustee of the Clark School for the Deaf, of the community center known as the People's Institute, of the Academy of Music (during its plucky though unsuccessful struggle to establish a real municipal theater), of the play-reading committee of the Amateur Players. They recall his address when a new high school principal was installed, when the First Congregational Church celebrated its two hundred and seventy-fifth anniversary, his presidency of the Connecticut Valley Foreign Policy Association, his talks to the Woman's Club and to the churches. "Even if," one writer says, "we cannot see the farthest ripple, I know that everyone in town has through your influence gained in some degree a better appreciation of scholarship, of the beauty of English speech." And another:

> Being of a religion and heritage terribly hounded in many parts of the world my heart has felt for these unfortunates. I could not find words to express my horror, indignation, and sorrow. . . As long as I live I shall ever remember and cherish your words, your ideals, as expressed by you on the platform of the People's Institute at a rally of citizens to protest the actions of a Hitlerized Germany.

> It is certainly a most memorable feat [wrote Gerald Stanley Lee]—what you have done in the way of warming up this village by just being in it.

Beyond the confines of Northampton, Neilson engaged in many activities directly connected with education and so logical extensions of his administration of Smith. From 1920 to 1946, for instance, he was a trustee of the Carnegie Foundation for the Advancement of Education, serving on the executive committee from 1931 on. The Modern Language Association, in which he had been active during the years at Harvard, commanded his services on various committees and in 1924 elected him president, the highest office attainable by a literary scholar. On the College Entrance Examination Board Neilson sat at intervals from 1920 until the end of his life. Their "most provocative member," Claude Fuess calls him in his history of the Board's "First Fifty Years." "He would sit with chin held in his nervous fingers listening to debates with subdued and tolerant mirth in his restless enigmatical eyes." The subdued mirth was directed chiefly towards some of the Board's experiments in testing which seemed to Neilson to discount individuality and treat students as commodities which could be precisely weighed and measured. He was a persistent opponent, for instance, "with a devastating facility in argument and rebuttal," of the faction who thought that the writing of an essay in the English examination might be replaced by objective tests which would be easier to grade.

Meetings of the Phi Beta Kappa Society, of which he had been made a member while he was teaching at Harvard, Neilson attended always with great pleasure. He served two nine-year terms in the Senate, the governing body of the organization, and was one of the founders of *The American Scholar,* the magazine which the Society began to publish in 1932. Contributions being considered for publication were circulated among the editors who voted for or against and added comments. Neilson's opinions on the prose articles are definite and decisive but about the poetry his tone is often diffident. Most of it was in the modern idiom and this he found it difficult to enjoy. Indirection and ambiguity seemed to him deliberate blocks to communication. "I fear," he would write, "I am inclined to insist too much on poetry being articulate, for so much that you send me seems only half articulate." His daughter Caroline tried to explain to him why her generation preferred this kind of poetry to that of the nineteenth century and he listened patiently for his inability to move into the literary twentieth century troubled him greatly. He was not accustomed to find himself inflexible. In matters political, economic, social, his mind adjusted readily to new ideas, but with poetry his emotions were involved and he could not disentangle the roots set deep in romanticism.

In co-operation with Smith's sister colleges Neilson believed firmly. He set a high value on the Four College Conference—Mt. Holyoke, Smith, Vassar, Wellesley—initiated by his predecessor, Burton, for the discussion of mutual problems and procedures. At Neilson's suggestion Bryn Mawr was added to the group. Neilson played an important role, also, in what was generally known as the campaign of the Seven Colleges. In 1927 seven women's colleges—the five of the Conference joined by Barnard and Radcliffe—began a lively "agitation" (Neilson's word) designed not to raise any specific amount of money but to make the American public aware of the importance of giving as generously to women's education as to men's. One of the agitation's effective devices was a series of dinners at which the seven Presidents met with seven representatives of some large field such as the foundations, journalism, the law. Brief talks were given on these occasions by Neilson and President Park of Bryn Mawr. There were also dinners in such cities as New York, Philadelphia, Chicago, to which several hundred carefully selected guests were asked to listen to speeches by the seven Presidents.

Neilson took the same kind of interest in co-operation with the secondary schools, partly because he had been a schoolmaster himself, partly because he felt that the schools and colleges could strengthen each other's hands. He was so much concerned to direct college-trained women into schoolteaching that he played an active part in the organization and development of the Co-operative Bureau for Women Teachers, set up by the combined efforts of the schools and colleges. He had a firsthand acquaintance with many of the schools for he was in great demand as a speaker at commencements and other anniversaries. In self-defence, he accepted as a rule only invitations to speak at schools for girls.

Beyond the local and the academic circles the calls on Neilson's time were heavy and they increased with the years. So many American problems interested him that he found it difficult to say no, even when he knew that he was straining his energies too far. He would always take time to write a letter for a good cause and he put his signature to any pronouncement or petition in which he believed without counting the cost.

When he did not believe in the cause to which he was asked to lend his name, he declined to sign and made his reasons clear.

> I should be very glad to give publicity in the College to the proclamation about the Harding Memorial Week, and give facilities for enrolling members. On the other hand I should prefer not to have my name appear as a member of the committee as I think the names appearing prominently in this connection should be those who rank President Harding's services to the country higher than I do. [To Governor C. H. Cox of Massachusetts, 1923]

Neilson felt it incumbent on him, as an American citizen, to urge his elected representatives to particular courses of action. In the files of his correspondence are scores of brief but cogently reasoned letters to senators, representatives, governors, on some pending piece of legislation, such matters as the World Court, the pardoning of conscientious objectors, child labor, federal housing, the abolition of capital punishment, immigration quotas. Here, as in so many instances, Neilson departed from the standard pattern of the executive. He was not cautious in stating his approval of an unpopular measure; he did not think his time too valuable to be given away. Injustice always moved him to action, or at least to open expression. But in the casting of his vote he clung, with all his Scottish reticence, to the secret ballot. Politically he was, so he told the Smith undergraduates, one of those "broad-minded but despicable creatures called a mugwump." With his family and intimate friends, though, he was perfectly ready to discuss his politics. They knew that he voted for Cox, chiefly because of his support of the League of Nations, for Davis, La Follette, Al Smith, Norman Thomas (Neilson believed in state ownership of public utilities with room left for individual business initiative), for Roosevelt, and Truman. In talking to the undergraduates who, during the thirties, were inclined to become highly excited politically, Neilson liked to stress the importance of the Presidential office and the necessity, once an election is over, of treating with respect the man who has been chosen to fill it. On the occasion of Smith's fiftieth anniversary celebration he wrote to President Coolidge that the College would like to confer upon him an honorary degree of Doctor of Laws. (Since Coolidge was unable to attend the commencement exercises, Smith gracefully conferred a degree upon Mrs. Coolidge, an act which Neilson could perform with genuine pleasure.)

When he was asked not only for his moral support but for his time Neilson was more inclined to give it to organizations which were working a little ahead of popular thought and to causes which needed to be explained and interpreted to the public. His early support of such organizations as the Association for Adult Education and the Association for Mental Hygiene did much to make them the accepted organs of well-doing they seem today. The National Association for the Advancement of Colored People was another organization which placed a high value on his co-operation. He served for many years on its Board of Directors and Walter White, the Association's executive secretary, whose daughter graduated from Smith, thought the "situation" there better than in any other college in the country because racial equality was not discussed but simply taken for granted. Racial prejudice, Neilson was accustomed to say, was difficult for him to comprehend because he himself felt none towards men of any creed or race. Once, though, when an incredulous interlocutor pushed him hard, he admitted that he did have some instinctive misgivings about the Irish.

Whenever Neilson was appointed to a committee he seemed, inevitably, to become its chairman. Occasionally he volunteered for the office because he knew that he could clear up with dispatch business which had been dragging along for months; more often he was pressed into service by colleagues who had discovered his skill in bringing discordant factions to a working compromise. That art he learned, so he once told the Smith undergraduates, from Mazzini. Neilson had great admiration for the Italian patriot's attempt to teach his generation that the "rights of man" are not nearly so important as man's duties.

> Wherever you find [Neilson said in a chapel talk in October 1937] in any group of people a deadlock, a difficulty in getting common work done, you will find that it arises from the fact that each is concerned with his or her rights and not with his or her obligations. The moment the emphasis changes from rights to obligations the deadlock is broken, the clash is removed, and the thing becomes perfectly simple because the atmosphere is entirely changed. The application of that formula (if you can call it a formula) I have found to be one of the most useful in the actual conduct of life—in my own life, and in that of the people I have had to deal with, and in the understanding of difficult situations.

Probably the most misunderstood position Neilson occupied was his honorary presidency of the Institute for Cultural Relations with Russia. Though he had a fundamental distrust of the communist regime—he did not believe that a stable government could be founded upon revolutionary violence and had been particularly horrified by the brutal killing of the royal family—he thought it vital that Americans should understand the communist experiment and that a working relationship be established between the two great nations. The interchange of data among scholars in Russia and America seemed to him a useful procedure in which he might properly take the lead. He held office until 1934, when he withdrew because he felt that the Smith trustees had taken all the buffeting in his defence that he ought to ask of them. He himself, of course, was constantly subject to attacks in print and writing. On one occasion the opposition came close to physical violence.

That was in the spring of 1927 when Sacco and Vanzetti had been condemned to death for their alleged participation in a payroll robbery and a murder. There was a strong conviction, not only in Massachusetts but through the country, that the two Italians had been judged on their anarchist sympathies rather than on evidence. Many citizens of Massachusetts petitioned Governor Fuller to review the case and make certain that injustice had not been done. The Progressive Club of Northampton, whose most active members were Smith College professors, arranged a meeting for the drafting of a petition of this kind. They wanted to use Smith's large auditorium but Neilson thought the purpose of the meeting was so definitely partisan that it would not be proper to hold it on College property. He agreed, however, for he felt strongly on the subject, to act as chairman and the meeting was scheduled for the auditorium of the Northampton High School at eight o'clock on the evening of 19 April. The American Legion and many other Northampton citizens were aghast. Was the home town of Calvin Coolidge, President of the United States, to go on record as in sympathy with the reds of Union Square? Two hundred people were in line when the doors of the auditorium opened, twelve hundred crowded in, and scores were turned away.

This meeting [said Neilson in opening it] is of a very extraordinary nature. Citizens of Massachusetts have long been justly proud of their courts . . . but, the people of the whole country being in an extraordinary mood, things might happen which never happened before. . . You are here to hear a lawyer of standing who has studied the case in detail and to express what opinions you may have at the end of that discussion.

He introduced Professor James M. Landis of the Harvard Law School.

The audience was very quiet during Landis' long and lucid address. When he had finished Neilson called for a report by the committee on resolutions. He was interrupted by a former mayor of the town who began to question Landis' knowledge of the case. The meeting then became, according to the *Hampshire Gazette,* "intense and at times uproarious." Among the questions raised, the *Gazette* went on, were: Is President Neilson or Mayor Feiker a better authority on parliamentary law? and Is Harvard Law School better than Columbia Law School? "Six prominent Northampton lawyers spoke in defense of Judge Webster Thayer, of the Massachusetts Supreme Court, of Governor Fuller, of courts and juries in general, and of unrelated matters." Protests were made that the main speaker had been allowed an hour and a half while those speaking in rebuttal were confined to three minutes. The Smith students sometimes booed but more often laughed when they were arraigned as outsiders and biased upstarts. Had it not been for Neilson's coolness, said the *New York Times,* the fury of the townspeople would have transcended the bounds of orderliness. More than once there were cries of "Lynch him!" and Neilson's friends thought that the legionnaires in the front rows were about to make a physical assault, but he appeared to be oblivious of the danger and steadily kept the meeting to the point, recognizing speakers or firmly ruling them out of order. The town was determined that the undergraduates, who outnumbered the citizens in the hall, should not be allowed to vote. When Alderman Stimson demanded that Smith students be barred from the room some of them rose to protest but Neilson looked at them and shook his head. The undergraduates, he said, would be obliged to leave before the resolution could be put because they were required to be in their dormitories at ten. All the students present had "late permissions," such as they were accustomed to have for the theater, but, sensing that the Neilson wit was saving a tense situation, they rose and filed out of the hall. Their places were instantly taken by townspeople waiting outside and, after more acrimonious discussion, the resolution urging Governor Fuller to prevent a miscarriage of justice was put to a voice vote. Neilson ruled the vote inconclusive—Northampton citizens said next day that it was a clear four to one against the motion—and the meeting adjourned.

When they heard the report of this affair the Smith trustees, alarmed as much for Neilson's person as for his reputation, asked him to avoid in future active participation in such violently controversial causes. In all other respects they accorded him the same freedom of speech and action which he granted to his faculty. The more complex question of how much time a president may fruitfully spend away from his campus, they left to his own solution. He struggled with it daily but never succeeded in setting a balance which was thoroughly satisfactory. Even had his interests been less catholic, he could never have attained that singleness of purpose he had so much admired in President Seelye. The twentieth-century college cannot work out its destiny in academic seclusion as its ancestors did. National and international crises disturb the classroom; floodlights beat upon the campus; faculty and administrators are drawn inevitably into conflicts far outside the college gates. The biography of President Seelye is concerned, for the most part, with his valiant battle to prove that women may benefit from higher education. The scene is the Smith College campus, but, towards the close of the book, there is a chapter called "In the Arena," where the President steps to combat with forces outside the college. And those forces, in 1905, were—a demand by the City of Northampton that college property be taxed, and the decision of the trustees of the local Forbes Library to close its shelves to Smith students. In the decades of Seelye's administration progress and prosperity were certainties no American needed to question. The details of their operation might safely be left to President McKinley. Neilson held office in a very different era, when "in the arena" meant in the warring world.

20

President Emeritus

NEILSON'S last official act as President of Smith College was the conferring (12 June 1939) of an honorary degree upon his wife. Then, to the enthusiastic Commencement audience, suddenly fallen silent, he spoke quietly:

> Having now fulfilled the most delicate and embarrassing task the trustees ever laid upon me, I had better draw to an end. I do so with a heart full of envy for the younger man who will take my place, who will work with the most considerate of boards of trustees, who will inherit the comradeship of the faculty, the loyalty of the alumnae, and the irresistible responsiveness of the undergraduates. For the measure of that envy is the measure of my appreciation and gratitude for what you have given me. And so I take my leave.

Students, alumnae, faculty rose in a single motion and stood applauding as the Neilsons, side by side, walked down the central aisle of John M. Greene Hall and out of the gates of Smith College.

Neilson had intended to retire before he was seventy. He stayed on a little longer than he wanted to because the appointing of his successor proved so difficult a task. Whenever the trustees looked at a candidate they set him mentally beside William

Allan Neilson and of course his dimensions seemed wrong. We will not, they kept telling each other, try to find a "replica," but inevitably they did try. Finally Mrs. Dwight Morrow agreed to serve for a year as Acting-President and Neilson could be released. Mrs. Morrow described herself as "a patch of green between two administrations," but so signally successful was she as a vice-regent, that, had she been ten years younger, the Smith constituency might have overcome their stubborn prejudice against a woman president. As it was Neilson was primarily responsible for the selection of his successor, Professor Herbert John Davis of the department of English at Cornell. Davis, an Englishman trained at Oxford, had taught in Canada as well as in the United States. He was an eighteenth-century scholar, particularly distinguished for his work on Swift; the trustees were determined, as they had been when they appointed Neilson, that the president of Smith College must be a scholar. Whether a good scholar will make a good administrator is, Neilson assured them, merely a matter of luck. On the administrative side they must gamble, as they had gambled when they appointed him. The only point on which they ought to be certain beforehand was that the new president's ideas on learning and on freedom were sound. "There could have been no more eloquent and no more accurate statement of our purposes and ideals than we listened to this morning," Neilson said after Davis' inaugural.

That inaugural address (17 October 1940) began with the question, "What can the man do that cometh after the king?" and answered, with the answer of Solomon, "Even that which hath been already done." "When I took over from him," Davis wrote many years later, "I did it with the intention of trying to carry on his work; there was no break and no change of direction." Yet, satisfied that they agreed on fundamentals, Neilson left Davis an entirely free hand. He was, Davis thought, the ideal President Emeritus.

He never interfered, nor even allowed himself to appear worried or critical. He was always there when I wanted him, always ready to help if asked. We grew to be friends with endless things to talk of, and I would often meet him in New York or in Boston. Then later when he came to spend more of the winter in Northampton, I do not remember that ever for one moment I found his presence difficult, as it obviously might have been. I liked to feel that he was there, and I knew that he would give me support, and that his presence would keep in bounds the opposition and criticism that always attend a new regime. . . He never interfered or objected; he never exerted his influence, except to give me his help and encouragement both in public and in private.

The work which, four years after his retirement, took Neilson from time to time to Northampton was the final task the trustees had asked him to assume, the writing of a History of Smith College during his administration. Beginning in 1943 Neilson spent upon the History many months of devoted scholarly labor. He had almost completed it at the time of his death in 1946. This History of Smith College should have been written by someone else. Neilson's careful, lucid, accurate account of twenty-two exciting years in American education has neither life nor color, for Hamlet has been omitted from the play. A bodiless entity, called "Mr. Neilson," enters from time to time, when absolutely necessary, but he never speaks in the first person and there is no light in his eye. The proceedings of Smith College seem admirable, but dull. This anonymous quality of the History is not a gesture of false modesty; it is simply a particularly vivid demonstration of the Neilson mind, occupied so completely by the world around it that it could not focus on itself.

Before he undertook the writing of the History Neilson spent very little time in Northampton. Both he and Mrs. Neilson had grown fond of the town and would have been glad to stay there but Neilson felt that his permanent presence might be an inconvenience to his successor. He planned first of all to go abroad, sailing soon after Commencement and staying for several months, perhaps for most of the winter. When the outbreak of war made that impossible the Neilsons took an apartment in New York, in London Terrace on West 24th Street, but neither of them wanted to live long in the city. It was for that reason that Neilson declined the presidency of the Foreign Policy Association. After much searching they purchased in Brinton Hill, Salisbury, Connecticut, an eighteenth-century salt-box house, set on a hillside and commanding a fine view. They added a large wing which included a fireproof study, and Neilson, with his own hands, laid a slate terrace, set out a garden, and settled down to what he supposed would be a peaceful country life. He began, with pleasure, to work his garden, as he had always done in Cambridge, and started to read some of the books he had been setting aside reluctantly year after year. To the publishers—and there were many of them—who urged him to write his memoirs, he replied that this did not seem to him a project of much promise but perhaps he would think about it later. In reminiscence he seldom indulged—the future he found always more interesting than the past—but he thought back occasionally over his seventy years and sometimes said to his wife with quiet satisfaction, "I have had a good life."

One of the reasons for the selection of Brinton Hill had been its proximity to Margaret Neilson's farm in West Stockbridge but that she left when she married in 1941. Caroline Neilson also was married in 1941 and, when their husbands were in service, both daughters made frequent long visits to their parents. Neilson enjoyed their company and was amused when he found himself a grandfather, though the infant mind interested him just as little as it had in the Cambridge days. The eldest grandchild, Caroline Oram's son, carries on the William Allan name.

A good many of his educational activities Neilson continued after his retirement. He remained an active member of the College Entrance Examination Board, and in 1941 edited their Annual Handbook of college entrance requirements. He continued to serve on the executive committee of the trustees of the Carnegie Foundation for the Advancement of Teaching. He accepted many invitations to speak at schools and colleges. He was pleased when he was elected, in 1942, to the Harvard Board of Overseers, and did effective work as chairman of their Visiting Committee on the Department of English. President Conant, whose administration of Harvard he admired, consulted him often on academic problems.

Retirement did not decrease Neilson's interest in the undergraduate student. He continued his honorary chairmanship of the Open Road, an organization which planned European tours for college students, introducing them to their contemporaries in other lands. During the war it undertook to teach American students more about America. Neilson also served on the executive committee of the International Student Service because he believed it important to interest young people in international affairs. The cynical indifference to conditions in Europe affected by so many college students disturbed him deeply. Much of it was, he felt, the fault of the colleges themselves. Since World War I they had been teaching pacifism and suspicion of propaganda, so that their students "have been misled by false emphasis and incomplete information, and have drawn conclusions leading to a paralysing scepticism." He admired the members of the ISS who were trying to awaken their contemporaries to a sense of international responsibility. In the summer of 1941 he and Mrs. Neilson presided over the five-week session of the ISS Student Leadership Institute which met at the Roosevelt summer house on Campobello, New Brunswick.

His own scholarship the President Emeritus practiced with renewed vigor. In 1938, when he knew that his retirement was imminent, he had undertaken for Houghton Mifflin a complete revision of the text, introductions, and notes of his Cambridge Shakespeare. He enlisted the collaboration of his colleague Charles J. Hill of the department of English who undertook the bulk of the work on the tragedies, comedies, and poems, while Neilson concerned himself particularly with the history plays, though, as their Preface states: "The tasks of collation, annotation, and interpretation have been shared by the two editors of the present revision, and for whatever merits or shortcomings it may possess they are jointly responsible." The tone of this collaboration is indicated by a letter of Neilson's written 7 April 1941.

Dear Charles, I feel as if I had been carving you up these days, for I have been trying to cut the introductions to the Comedies down to the 1,800 words or so that can be got into two pages of the new type. It has meant the sacrificing of so much good stuff that I feel a criminal, yet I see no way out. Five and a quarter pages of typewriting seems all the law allows. My only comfort is that you may find, in your lectures and perhaps elsewhere, an outlet for many of the admirable critical remarks slaughtered by the exigencies of space.

The edition, which appeared in 1942, sold in the next ten years nearly fifty thousand copies.

All these activities Neilson had to a certain extent foreseen but he was surprised to find that the demands upon his time from national organizations, philanthropic and political, increased instead of diminishing. The burden of correspondence alone became almost intolerable for he wrote all his letters in longhand; it had not occurred to him to arrange for secretarial help. Some of the insistent demands he managed to decline but, as the situation in Europe grew darker, he felt constrained to lend what aid he could. The war affected him profoundly. With England, France, and Germany he had ties of personal affection which intensified his scholar's care for those great civilizations, but even more disturbing than his anxiety for the nations he loved was the shaking of his life-long "Gladstonian liberalism." The rising horror through the thirties struck at the roots of his belief in progress and the perfectability of man. Neilson's Smith colleagues noted a decline in his zest and gayety which had nothing to do with increasing age. Yet his faith in the future was not uprooted. Most of the work he did during the war was concerned with the planning of a better world after the carnage should cease.

As early as 1938, at the time of the dismemberment of Czechoslovakia, Neilson and a few of his colleagues—notably the distinguished exiles Hans Kohn and G. A. Borgese—began to discuss together the fundamental principles on which it might some day be possible to build a new world. It seemed to them that no lastingly effective political action could be taken unless the statesmen and other leaders of the nations had clearly in mind the basic principles on which civilization must stand. It was the scholars' task, they thought, to assist in the analysis and enunciation of these principles. In the spring of 1940 they arranged a three-day meeting at Atlantic City where, under Neilson's chairmanship, thirteen scholars and men of letters discussed intensively the problem of war and peace, a redefinition of democracy, and the part to be played by education, religion, and economic reform. A subcommittee, with Neilson as chairman, drew up a statement embodying the ideas and purposes on which the conference had agreed. The other members of the subcommittee were

Herbert Agar, W. Y. Elliott, Lewis Mumford, and G. A. Borgese, who gave the statement literary form. Under seventeen signatures this was published (1940) by the Viking Press as *The City of Man,* a Declaration on World Democracy.

The foundations on which the City of Man rests are freedom and justice, the elements which had always seemed to Neilson essential to the good society. Though the phraseology of the pronouncement is not his, one hears, again and again, the echo of his thinking.

> And, first of all, we reaffirm that the meaning and goal of human life, individual and collective, are progress and growth in intellect and action, and that peace, universal peace, is the prerequisite of progress and growth.
>
> The City of Man must be much more than a League of Nations. . . It must be the Nation of Man embodied in the Universal State, the State of States. . . And the pluralistic system of the American Commonwealth, although prevented so far from reaching a complete expression . . . had shown in its best age that the combination of local autonomy with unitary authority is . . . feasible on a continental scale, and therefore ultimately on a world-wide one.

Such an ideal union was, Neilson believed, perfectly practicable. It was to help shape the form in which it might go into action that he agreed to work with the Commission to Study the Organization of Peace, accepting, in 1940, the chairmanship of its executive committee. The hundred members of the Commission met monthly in New York at the old Murray Hill Hotel. The meetings were always held on Sunday and they lasted through the day. The text of a proposed publication was circulated beforehand for critical analysis by the members and the discussion both of ideas and phrasing was long and often heated. Professor James T. Shotwell, chairman of the Commission, who presided, came to count heavily on Neilson's "unyielding moral purpose which refused to compromise on essentials while recognizing the validity of different lines of approach towards a common goal." He credited Neilson, too, again and again, with the lucidity of a report's final phrasing. He was amused by Neilson's attacks on the international lawyers and other experts when their technical jargon became heavy. "What did you say?" Neilson would ask and when the speaker repeated his remarks, supposing that Neilson had failed to catch them, he would repeat, "What did you say?" until the expert saw the point and tried to express his ideas in simple English. Many of the Commission's proposals, particularly those concerned with the provisions for human rights, were written into the Charter of the United Nations.

Again, in his work with the Reconstruction Service Committee, the American Scholar put his special knowledge and equipment at the service of the nation, helping to form the policy of UNRRA (United Nations Relief and Rehabilitation Agency) and the ERA (Economic Reconstruction Agency). The Reconstruction Service Committee, organized in April 1942 by Harold Weston, had thirty-six members. President Mary Woolley of Mt. Holyoke served as chairman; Neilson as vice-chairman. During its year of existence the Committee worked without publicity because the Roosevelt administration felt that the attention of the public must still be fixed exclusively on winning the military war, but the State Department was glad to have the Committee working on problems to come, listened attentively to its proposals, and adopted many of them: on the training of military governors, on reconstruction, on relief. Governor Lehman, as head of the Office of Federal Relief and Reconstruction Operations, made use of the Committee's wisdom. In 1943, when it was felt that the services of an unofficial group were no longer needed, the Reconstruction Service Committee dissolved itself and set up, at Government request, Food for Freedom, an educational organization which worked to convince the public that "hunger as well as the enemy must be driven out," and that the essence of the "declaration of Interdependence" is that "peace depends on sharing." Neilson persuaded Mrs. Dwight Morrow to accept the chairmanship of Food for Freedom while he served as chairman of the Board of Directors.

While he worked thus towards the future Neilson felt impelled also to promote justice and freedom by some action which would produce immediate and concrete results. For the plight of the refugee intellectuals he felt particular concern. He had appointed as many as he could to the Smith College faculty and he tirelessly wrote letters and talked with his administrative friends in the endeavor to find posts for others. He was troubled by the reluctance of many institutions to appoint foreigners and particularly by the excuse, frequently advanced, that there was still unemployment among American teachers.

> We have often [he wrote, 1938, to a fellow administrator] to give jobs to natives who aren't good enough, and I thought all college presidents agreed that God didn't make enough good teachers. Consequently I am in favor of giving a good man from abroad a chance, even if it means that some of our native drudges have got to go back to life insurance.

With the Emergency Rescue Committee and the National Refugee Service Neilson worked both publicly and privately. Again and again he lent money from his personal funds or signed the affadavit guaranteeing financial support which made it possible for a German writer or teacher to gain entrance to the United States.

From his concern for the refugees, his belief that the American indifference to their plight came from "lack of imagination and sheer ignorance," grew a book which, in co-operation with his daughter Caroline, Neilson edited for Macmillan in 1941. *We Escaped* contains "Twelve Personal Narratives of the Flight to America," a few written by the refugees themselves, most of them taken down from their lips and translated by Caroline Neilson.

> They are bald, factual narratives [the Introduction runs], the force of which is derived from the events and experiences themselves. And their authors are only a dozen out of thousands who have undergone similar sufferings or who have not yet been able to escape from the tyranny and cruelty of their oppressors.
>
> What is America going to do about it?

In 1941 also a proposal was made to Neilson from the opposite side of the world. The Australian government invited him to make a good-will speaking tour. He and Mrs. Neilson were preparing to sail early in the new year when the project was cut short by the bombs at Pearl Harbor.

While he labored by these various means against the European tyranny Neilson set himself to a piece of work for freedom and justice at home. In July 1943, immediately after the hideous race riots in Detroit in which thirty-four people were killed, Neilson sent letters to a long list of leaders of American thought and action proposing that they join in signing a statement calling upon Government officials at all levels for wise measures to prevent a repetition of the Detroit horrors. The statement was issued to the press over signatures of many distinguished men who came to be known as the "Committee of 100" of the National Association for the Advancement of Colored People. Scores of public officials wrote Neilson pledging their co-operation and thousands of private citizens sent letters asking, What can *I* do? He replied at once: contribute to the Legal Defense Fund of the NAACP so that adequate legal assistance may be provided for the more than one thousand two hundred Negroes who were arrested by the Detroit police while defending themselves during the rioting. The sum of twenty-nine thousand dollars was swiftly subscribed. The Committee of 100 then took upon itself the financing of all the legal work of the NAACP and, during the three years of Neilson's presidency, was able to number among its accomplishments the arguing of cases before the Supreme Court which resulted in such far-reaching decisions as that in the Texas "white primary" case and the Irene Morgan case which forbade segregation in inter-state transportation.

Even had he felt less keenly about the misery he was trying to assuage, the weight of the tasks he had set for himself was heavy for a man past seventy. It is not surprising that Neilson developed a heart condition which caused him frequent weakness and pain. To his physician's admonition that he must move more slowly, especially when climbing stairs or walking up hill, he paid comparatively little heed; following a regimen when you are ill is one thing, he thought; taking precautions lest you become ill is quite another. He continued to move at his accustomed speed and it was this probably which precipitated the attack of coronary thrombosis which caused his death.

So that he might finish the final chapters of his History of Smith College he and Mrs. Neilson planned to spend several months that winter near the College. They stayed at the Hotel Northampton from which Neilson walked each morning to the Library where he had an office. The fatal heart attack occurred on 10 February. Neilson was taken at once to the College Infirmary where he died on the evening of Wednesday, 13 February 1946.

The funeral service was held in John M. Greene Hall at eleven o'clock on Saturday morning, 16 February. Like President Seelye's funeral it was a college chapel service. The choir of a hundred undergraduates sang the seven-fold Amen after the Lord's Prayer and led the congregation in Old Hundredth, the "Smith College hymn." Some of these students had seen Neilson about the campus or had heard him speak; to all of them he was a lively legend, for President Davis had taken care that they should know how far the shape of their College and its spirit were of Neilson's creation. To the other men and women who filled the hall Neilson's death was as much a personal as an institutional loss. There were his faculty, his staff, his trustees, representatives of the many national organizations he had served, and, in addition, a large group of his alumnae, for the Alumnae Council was meeting that week in Northampton. A trustee of the College, the Reverend Henry Pitt Van Dusen, President of Union Theological Seminary, delivered the invocation and prayer. President Davis read Psalm 90, "The work of our hands establish thou it," and the third chapter of the Book of the Wisdom of Solomon, "The souls of the righteous are in the hand of God," passages which Neilson had often read from that platform. As a closing prayer, the Reverend A. Burns Chalmers, Religious Director of the College, read from Arnold's *Rugby Chapel:*

> Languor is not in your heart,
> Weakness is not in your word,
> Weariness not on your brow.
> Ye alight in our van; at your voice,
> Panic, despair, flee away.

Honorary pallbearers were Robert Bradford, Lieutenant-Governor of Massachusetts, Walter White, Secretary of the National Association for the Advancement of Colored People, and three former and three present members of the Smith College Board of Trustees: Harold E. Hoskins, John Hanes, Thomas S. Lamont; Philip Hofer, George Stevens, Franklin C. Parker, Jr. The bearers of the coffin were King's Men, those who had been longest in the employ of the College. During the service the College Hall bell tolled slowly, one stroke each minute, to mark the seventy-seven years of the life of William Allan Neilson.

His temporal reversion nourishes the significant soil of Smith College. On a quiet slope in the botanical garden rests a New England granite boulder. A broom plant leans over it, golden in the spring; a little clump of heather grows on either side. The inscription is simply: William Allan Neilson, 1869-1946. Standing beside that stone one looks, on the left hand, to the Neilson Library; on the right, across the waters of little Paradise, to the hills—and thinks on the virtue and the praise.

APPENDIX

Books which Neilson read while a student at the University of Edinburgh. The list is reproduced as he set it down in his commonplace book (see pp. 37-9), the occasional inconsistencies and inaccuracies uncorrected.

Xmas 1888	"Story of an African Farm"	Olive Schreiner
April 1889	"Robert Elsmere"	Mrs. Humphrey Ward
	"Compromise"	John Morley
	"Meditations"	Marcus Aurelius
May 1889	"Two Chiefs of Dunboy"	J. A. Froude
	"Paul of Tarsus"	Author of Rabbi Jeshua
June 1889	"St. Bernards"	"Aesculapius Scalpel"
	"Obiter Dicta"—2nd Series	Augustine Birrell
	"The World of Cant"	Anonymous
	"King John," "Henry IV" and "V," "Richard II"	Shakespeare
	"Makers of Venice"	Mrs. Oliphant
	Tennyson's "Balin and Balan," "Rizpah," etc.	
July 1889	"The Religion of Humanity"	A. J. Balfour
	"Poems and Ballads"—3rd Series	Swinburne
	Selections from DeQuincey	
	Early Letters of Jane Welsh Carlyle	Ritchie
	"Transformation"	Nathaniel Hawthorne
	Parts of Hallam (Const. Hist.), Green's "Making of England," Green's "Short History"—Kemble, Langmeade, and other Historical books	
	Browning—finished Vol. V	
	"Episodes in a Life of Adventure"	Laurence Oliphant
Aug. 1889	"Diana of the Crossways"	Geo. Meredith
	"Saul" etc.	Robert Browning
	Some Essays on Browning	Nettleship
	"Jane Eyre"	Charlotte Brontë

	"Ivan Ilyitch"—Stories from	by Count Leo Tolstoi
	"An Evening of Society"	Henrik Ibsen
	"Autocrat of the Breakfast Table"	O. W. Holmes (part)
Sept. 1889	"Harvest"	John Strange Winter
	"Pretty Sister of José"	Mrs. F. H. Burnett
	"The Hansa Towns"	Helen Zimmern
Oct. 1889	"Shakespere—His Mind and Art"	Ed. Dowden (1st part)
	"All's Well That Ends Well"	
	"The Blue Veil"	Du Boisgobey
	"Underwoods"	R. L. Stevenson
Nov. 1889	Rhubaiyat of Omar Khayyam	McCarthy (part)
	"Times and Days"	Anonymous
	(Occasionally Tennyson, Browning, Mazzini, Whitman, Ballads)	
Dec. 1889	Allan Ramsay—Poems—(Gentle Shepherd in Aug.) Life, J. L. Robertson	
	The Book of Job—with Article by J. A. Froude	
Jan. 1890	"Shaving of Shagpat" and "Farina"	George Meredith
Feb. 1890	"A Memory of Edward Thring"	Skrine
	"Education" by Herbert Spencer	
April 1890	Poems by Keats (also in September)	
	"Demeter and other Poems"	Lord Tennyson
May 1890	"Theism and Science" etc.	Principal Fairbairn
	"The Last Days of Pompeii"	by Lord Lytton
	Memoir of Mazzini	by Madame E. A. Venturi
	"Thoughts on Democracy" and "Duties of Man"	by Mazzini
	"Silas Marner"	George Eliot (2nd time)
	"Old Friends"	Andrew Lang
	"Essays and Addresses"	Bernard Bosanquet
June 1890	"Piccadilly"	Laurence Oliphant
	"Kreutzer Sonata"	Tolstoi
	"Adventures of Harry Richmond"	Geo. Meredith
	"The Blithedale Romance"	Nath. Hawthorne
	Republic of Plato	Jowett, and Martineau
	"Keats" (English Men of Letters)	by Sidney Colvin
July 1890	Dr. Heidenhoff's Process	Ed. Bellamy
	Aristotle's Ethics with Grant's Essays	
	Caird's "Spinoza"	
	George Eliot's "Middlemarch"	

Aug. 1890	"The Ordeal of Richard Feverel"	Geo. Meredith
	"Sandra Belloni"	Geo. Meredith
	"Practicable Socialism"	Rev. S. A. Barnett and Mrs. B.
	"The Red Flag"	Hon. Roden Noël
Sept. 1890	Vol. I of "Types of Ethical Theory"	Martineau
	"Meditations"	Descartes
Oct. 1890	Fabian Essays in Socialism	
	"True History of Joshua Davidson"	E. Lynn-Linton
	"Father Damien"	R. L Stevenson
	"Cardinal Newman"	"John Oldcastle"
	"The New Republic"	W. H. Mallock
	"Wee Willie Winkie"	Rudyard Kipling
	"Black and White"	Do.
	"Under the Deodars"	Do.
	"Spinoza"	F. Pollock
	Essays on Berkeley and Descartes	T. H. Huxley
Nov. 1890	"Plain Tales from the Hills"	Rudyard Kipling
	"Vittoria"	George Meredith
	"Swift" E.M.L. [English Men of Letters]	Leslie Stephen
	Do. Eng. Humorists	Thackeray
Dec. 1890	"The Phantom Rickshaw"	Rudyard Kipling
	"The Record of Badalia Herodsfoot"	Do.
	"Congreve's "Way of the World"	
	Plato's Protagoras, Theaetetus, Republic, etc.	
Jan. 1891	"Hume"–E.M.L. Series	T. H. Huxley
	Memoir of John Keats	Lord Houghton
Feb. 1891	"Essays in Little"	Andrew Lang
	"Ballads"	R. L. Stevenson
	Kant's "Critique of Pure Reason"	in J. H. Stirling's Text Book
	Hume's "Inquiry concerning Human Understanding"	
	(Miscellaneous Philosophy)	
	"The King's Tragedy" etc.	D. G. Rossetti
May 1891	"The Egoist"	Geo. Meredith
	"Jonathan and his Continent"	Max O'Rell
	"The Art of Literature"	Schopenhaur
	"Greek Life and Thought"	Mahaffy (part)
	"The Earthly Paradise"	Wm. Morris (part)
	"Elementary Politics"	T. Raleigh
June 1891	"Tonar"	J. L. Nicolson

July 1891	"All Sorts and Conditions of Men"	Walter Besant
	—	Lewis F. Day
	"An Actor's Wife"	George Moore
	"Notes on American Schools"	J. G. Fitch
Aug. 1891	"General Sketch of Eur. History"	E. A. Freeman
	"English Prose"	J. Earle
	"Master of Ballantrae"	R. L. Stevenson
	History of Canada	Greswell
	Geography of Canada	—
	"Bride of Lammermoor	Sir W. Scott
	Philology	J. Peile
	Introduction to New Testament	M. Dods
Sept. 1891	"Schiller"	Carlyle
	"The Newcomes"	Thackeray
Dec. 1891	"The Little Minister"	J. M. Barrie
	Sir W. Scott's Journal	
	"Studies in Literature"	Morley
	Lowell's Essay on Chaucer	
	"Chaucer" E.M.L.	A. W. Ward
	"Scott" E.M.L.	R. H. Hutton
Jan. 1892	"Waverly"	
	"Chris"	W. E. Norris
	"The Fine Arts"	G. Baldwin Brown
	Kipling's "Soldiers Three" etc.	

INDEX

Under "Neilson, W. A." are listed only the personal facts of his career. Other topics will be found throughout the Index under such headings as "books," "Harvard," "health," "opinions." Entries such as "campus," "department of music," "faculty," etc. refer to Smith College.

P

R

S